JOURNAL FOR THE STUDY OF THE OLD TESTAMENT
SUPPLEMENT SERIES
343

Sheffield Academic Press

J. Maxwell Miller

The Land that I Will Show You

Essays on the History and Archaeology of the Ancient Near East in Honour of J. Maxwell Miller

**edited by
J. Andrew Dearman and
M. Patrick Graham**

Journal for the Study of the Old Testament
Supplement Series 343

Copyright © 2001 Sheffield Academic Press

Published by
Sheffield Academic Press Ltd
Mansion House
19 Kingfield Road
Sheffield S11 9AS
England

www.SheffieldAcademicPress.com

Typeset by Sheffield Academic Press
and
Printed on acid-free paper in Great Britain
by MPG Books Ltd
Bodmin, Cornwall

British Library Cataloguing-in-Publication Data

A catalogue record for this book is available
from the British Library

ISBN 1 84127 257 4

CONTENTS

PREFACE

It is with sincere appreciation, respect, and friendship that this collection of 17 articles is presented to J. Maxwell Miller by his colleagues and former students on the occasion of his 65th birthday. The topics covered in the essays reflect the wide range of Miller's own interests—from the reconstruction of the history of the ancient Near East to the archaeological exploration of that land to text-critical and grammatical matters related to the study of texts that were composed there. The contributors are not drawn from a single school of thought and are not united methodologically. Rather, the body is international in composition, represents diverse perspectives on the study of the ancient Near East, and so illustrate the breadth of Miller's own interests, critical engagement and international connections.

The papers have been arranged alphabetically by author under four general rubrics. First, there is a biographical sketch on the volume's honoree, along with a select bibliography of his publications. Next, there is 'History', which comprises articles dealing with the historiography encountered in Chronicles (Ben Zvi) and the Deuteronomistic History (Sasson and McKenzie), a comparative study of the historiographies of Qohelet and Nagarjuna of India (Buss), examinations of matters related to Israel's internal (Edelman and Irvine) and external (Knauf and Kuan) political and military conflicts, and finally two studies of chronological problems (Hayes, and Hooker and Hayes). The third section is entitled 'Archaeology and Geography' and consists of four articles. The first two are archaeological studies that deal with the question of Edom's continuation into the Neo-Babylonian and Persian periods (Bienkowski) and the influence of Assyria on the culture of Ammon in the Iron Age (Daviau). The third paper distinguishes the potential of (secular) archaeology for writing a history of Israel from that of biblical archaeology to do the same (Davies), and the final contribution engages historical geography to address the matter of Israel's exodus route (Van Seters). Two papers constitute the section on 'Manuscripts and

Epigraphy'. The first takes up the matter of textual reconstruction in the study of the Qumran Scrolls (Callaway), and the second is a study of syntactical aspects of the Mesha‘ inscription and their parallels in pre-exilic biblical Hebrew prose.

It is the editors' hope that these articles will make a modest contribution to the study of ancient Near Eastern history, archaeology and texts. To the extent that this is achieved, the texts will honor one who has been a creative scholar, a conscientious and talented teacher, and a faithful friend.

Finally, the editors would like to express appreciation to Professors David J.A. Clines and Philip R. Davies of Sheffield Academic Press for their support of this project and their decision to include it in the JSOT Supplements Series. The creativity and vigor of this press under their talented leadership has placed all students of Scripture in their debt.

M. Patrick Graham
J. Andrew Dearman

ABBREVIATIONS

AASF	Annales Academiae Scientarum Fennicae
AASOR	Annual of the American Schools of Oriental Research
AB	Anchor Bible
ABD	D.N. Freedman (ed.), *The Anchor Bible Dictionary* (6 vols.; New York: Doubleday, 1992)
ABS	Archaeology and Biblical Studies
ACOR	American Center of Oriental Research
ADAJ	*Annual of the Department of Antiquities of Jordan*
ADPV	Abhandlungen des Deutschen Palästinavereins
AfO	*Archiv für Orientforschung*
AJBA	*Australian Journal of Biblical Archaeology*
AnBib	Analecta biblica
ANET	J.B. Pritchard (ed.), *Ancient Near Eastern Texts Relating to the Old Testament* (Princeton: Princeton University Press, 3rd edn, 1969)
AnOr	Analecta orientalia
AOAT	Alter Orient und Altes Testament
ARAB	D.D. Luckenbill, *Ancient Records of Assyria and Babylonia* (2 vols.; Chicago: University of Chicago Press, 1926–27)
AsJT	*Asia Journal of Theology*
ASOR	American Schools of Oriental Research
ASORAR	ASOR Archaeological Reports
AThD	Acta theologica danica
AusBR	*Australian Biblical Review*
BA	*Biblical Archaeologist*
BAMA	British Academy Monographs in Archaeology
BARev	*Biblical Archaeology Review*
BASOR	*Bulletin of the American Schools of Oriental Research*
BAT	Botschaft des Alten Testaments
BEATAJ	Beiträge zur Erforschung des Alten Testaments und des antiken Judentums
BethM	*Beth Mikra*
BETL	Bibliotheca ephemeridum theologicarum lovaniensium
BHS	*Biblia hebraica stuttgartensia*
Bib	*Biblica*
BibInt	Biblical Interpretation Series

BibInt	*Biblical Interpretation: A Journal of Contemporary Approaches*
BibRes	*Biblical Research*
BibSem	Biblical Seminar
BN	*Biblische Notizen*
BO	*Bibliotheca orientalis*
BR	*Bible Review*
BTB	*Biblical Theology Bulletin*
BWANT	Beiträge zur Wissenschaft vom Alten und Neuen Testament
BZAW	Beihefte zur *ZAW*
CBC	Cambridge Bible Commentary
CBQ	*Catholic Biblical Quarterly*
CBQMS	*Catholic Biblical Quarterly*, Monograph Series
CBSC	Cambridge Bible for Schools and Colleges
CH	*Church History*
CJA	Christianity and Judaism in Antiquity
ConBOT	Coniectanea biblica, Old Testament
DJD	Discoveries in the Judaean Desert
ErFor	Erträge der Forschung
ErIsr	Eretz Israel
FAT	Forschungen zum Alten Testament
FOTL	The Forms of the Old Testament Literature
frg(s)	fragment(s)
FRLANT	Forschungen zur Religion und Literatur des Alten und Neuen Testaments
GAT	Grundrisse zum Alten Testament
GBSOT	Guides to Biblical Scholarship: Old Testament Series
HALAT	L. Koehler *et al.* (eds.), *Hebräisches und aramäisches Lexikon zum Alten Testament* (5 vols.; Leiden: E.J. Brill, 1967–95)
HAT	Handbuch zum Alten Testament
HBT	*Horizons in Biblical* Theology
HSAO	Heidelberger Studien zum alten Orient
HSM	Harvard Semitic Monographs
HSS	Harvard Semitic Studies
HTR	*Harvard Theological Review*
HUCA	*Hebrew Union College Annual*
ICC	International Critical Commentary
IDB	G.A. Buttrick (ed.), *The Interpreter's Dictionary of the Bible* (4 vols.; Nashville: Abingdon Press, 1962)
IDBSup	*IDB*, Supplementary Volume
IEJ	*Israel Exploration Journal*
ILB	Indiana Literary Biblical Series
Int	*Interpretation*
JANESCU	*Journal of the Ancient Near Eastern Society of Columbia University*

JAOS	*Journal of the American Oriental Society*
JBL	*Journal of Biblical Literature*
JEA	*Journal of Egyptian Archaeology*
JETS	*Journal of the Evangelical Theological Society*
JNES	*Journal of Near Eastern Studies*
JNSL	*Journal of Northwest Semitic Languages*
JSJSup	Journal for the Study of Judaism, Supplements
JSOT	*Journal for the Study of the Old Testament*
JSOTSup	*Journal for the Study of the Old Testament*, Supplement Series
JSPSup	*Journal for the Study of the Pseudepigrapha*, Supplement Series
JSS	*Journal of Semitic Studies*
KAH	L. Messerschmidt and O. Schroeder, *Keilschrifttexte aus Assur historischen Inhalts* (2 vols.; Ausgrabungen der Deutschen Orient Gesellschaft in Assur. E. Inschriften, 16; Osnabrück: O. Zeller, repr., 1970)
KHAT	Kurzer Hand-Kommentar zum Alten Testament
KJV	King James Version
KTU²	M. Dietrich, O. Loretz and J. Sanmartín, *The Cuneiform Alphabetic Texts from Ugarit, Ras Ibn Hani and Other Places: KTU* (Münster: Ugarit-Verlag, 2nd edn, 1995)
LXX	Septuagint
MAVA	Materialien zur allgemeinen und vergleichenden Archäologie
MT	Masoretic Text
NCB	New Century Bible
NGTT	*Nederduitse Gereformeerde Teologiese Tydskrif*
NIDOTE	W. VanGemeren (eds.), *New International Dictionary of Old Testament Theology and Exegesis* (5 vols.; Grand Rapids: Zondervan, 1997).
NRSV	New Revised Standard Version
NSKAT	Neuer Stuttgarter Kommentar, Altes Testament
OBO	Orbis biblicus et orientalis
OLA	Orientalia lovaniensia analecta
OLP	Orientalia lovaniensia periodica
Or	*Orientalia*
OTL	Old Testament Library
PEQ	*Palestine Exploration Quarterly*
PJ	*Palästina-jahrbuch*
PRS	*Perspectives in Religious Studies*
PTMS	Pittsburgh Theological Monograph Series
Qad	*Qadmoniot*
RB	*Revue biblique*
REB	Revised English Bible
RSB	Resources for Biblical Studies
SAAS	State Archives of Assyria Studies

SAM	Sheffield Archaeological Monographs
SAOC	Studies in Ancient Oriental Civilization
SBL	Society of Biblical Literature
SBLDS	SBL Dissertation Series
SBLMS	SBL Monograph Series
SBT	Studies in Biblical Theology
SBTS	Sources for Biblical and Theological Study
SEÅ	*Svensk exegetisk årsbok*
SHCANE	Studies in the History and Culture of the Ancient Near East
SJOT	*Scandinavian Journal of the Old Testament*
SOTSMS	Society for Old Testament Study Monograph Series
SSEA	Society for the Study of Egyptian Antiquities
STDJ	Studies on the Texts of the Desert of Judah
StudPh	Studia Phoenicia
TA	*Tel Aviv*
TAUMS	Tel Aviv University, Monograph Series of the Sonia and Marco Nadler Institute of Archaeology
TCS	Texts from Cuneiform Sources
TDOT	G.J. Botterweck and H. Ringgren (eds.), *Theological Dictionary of the Old Testament* (10 vols.; Grand Rapids: Eerdmans, rev. edn, 1977–)
TLOT	E. Jenni and C. Westermann (eds.), *Theological Lexicon of the Old Testament* (3 vols.; Peabody, MA: Hendrickson, 1997)
TTod	*Theology Today*
UF	*Ugarit-Forschungen*
VT	*Vetus Testamentum*
VTSup	*Vetus Testamentum*, Supplements
WBC	Word Biblical Commentary
WMANT	Wissenschaftliche Monographien zum Alten und Neuen Testament
YNER	Yale Near Eastern Researches
ZAW	*Zeitschrift für die alttestamentliche Wissenschaft*
ZDPV	*Zeitschrift des deutschen Palästina-Vereins*

LIST OF CONTRIBUTORS

Ehud Ben Zvi, University of Alberta, Edmonton, Canada

Piotr Bienkowski, Liverpool Museum, Liverpool, England

Martin J. Buss, Emory University, Atlanta, GA, USA

Phillip R. Callaway, Austin School, Dunwoody, GA, USA

P.M. Michèle Daviau, Wilfrid Laurier University, Waterloo, Canada

Philip R. Davies, University of Sheffield, Sheffield, England

J. Andrew Dearman, Austin Presbyterian Theological Seminary, Austin, TX, USA and Visiting Professor, Dept of Old Testament, University of Stellenbosch, South Africa

Diana Edelman, University of Sheffield, Sheffield, England

M. Patrick Graham, Emory University, Atlanta, GA, USA

John H. Hayes, Emory University, Atlanta, GA, USA

Paul K. Hooker, Presbytery of St Augustine, Presbyterian Church (USA), Jacksonville, FL, USA

Stuart A. Irvine, Louisiana State University, Baton Rouge, LA, USA

Ernst Axel Knauf, Faculty of Theology, University of Bern, Bern, Switzerland

Jeffrey K. Kuan, Pacific School of Religion/Graduate Theological Union, Berkeley, CA, USA

Steven L. McKenzie, Rhodes College, Memphis, TN, USA

Anson F. Rainey, Tel Aviv University, Tel Aviv, Israel

Jack M. Sasson, Vanderbilt University, Nashville, TN, USA

John Van Seters, Wilfred Laurier University, Waterloo, Canada

Part I

J. MAXWELL MILLER

J. MAXWELL MILLER, SCHOLAR AND TEACHER: A SKETCH

J. Andrew Dearman

1. *Family and Career*

James Maxwell Miller was born in Kosciusko, Mississippi, on 20 September 1937. Max, as he is known to a wide circle of friends, is the older of two sons born to James Hoyt and Nora Cagle Miller. His father was a bookkeeper.[1] The Miller family has its roots in Ulster (Northern Ireland), and its American wing is descended from David Miller, a Scotch-Irish immigrant who settled in North Carolina.

Max was educated in the state-funded schools of Kosciusko, a small town in rural Mississippi, and his family were members in good standing of the Methodist Church there. So after completing high school, it seemed a natural step for him to enroll in Millsaps College, a Methodist liberal arts institution located in Jackson. He compiled a fine academic record as a history major, played on the college football team (as center and guard), and graduated with an AB degree in 1959. While a student at the college he was elected both 'Mr Millsaps' and president of the student senate. In 1984 his Alma Mater awarded him an honorary doctorate.

Max was one of the first persons enrolled in the (then) newly formed doctoral program in religious studies at Emory University in Atlanta. Emory University had an undergraduate department of religion and also a seminary/divinity school supported by the Methodist Church, namely Candler School of Theology.[2] The faculties of both the seminary and the religion department combined to form the graduate faculty in religious

---

1. James H. Miller died on 30 May 1967.

2. On the history of Candler School of Theology and its relationship to Emory University, see B.M. Bowen, *The Candler School of Theology—Sixty Years of Service* (Atlanta: Candler School of Theology, Emory University, 1974). In the preface to the volume, Bowen gratefully acknowledges the editorial assistance of John H. Hayes in bringing the manuscript to completion.

studies. Max chose Hebrew Bible (or Old Testament as it was then called) as his field of specialization. That part of the newly developed program commenced with the 1959 fall term, and he was the first person to graduate with a PhD from Emory in Old Testament studies (1964).

In the American system, it is somewhat unusual to move directly from the bachelor's degree to a doctoral program in the field of religion, but Max's strong performance as an undergraduate student convinced the admissions committee that he was capable of making the transition.

There were four scholars in the field of Hebrew Bible at Emory who taught him: Boone M. Bowen, Frederick C. Prussner, Martin J. Buss and Immanuel Ben-Dor. Each brought different sub-specialties and distinctive academic pedigree to his teaching. Bowen, himself a graduate of Candler, joined its faculty in 1931. He had earned his PhD at Yale University and retired after 36 years of distinguished service. Prussner, the son of German-speaking missionaries, was a graduate of the Divinity School of the University of Chicago and wrote his thesis on method in Old Testament Theology.[3] He joined the Candler faculty in 1953. Buss came to Emory University in 1959 to teach in the Department of Religion, having written a thesis at Yale University on the book of Hosea.[4] Ben-Dor was European born and trained (PhD from the University of Rome) and worked 18 years on the staff of the Palestinian Department of Antiquities (1936–54). He also served briefly on the faculties of the Oriental Institute of the University of Chicago and the Divinity School of Harvard University before his appointment to the Candler faculty in 1958. He retired from Candler in 1969 and died that same year.[5]

In the summer of 1960, Max took an extended trip that would prove influential in the shaping of his career. He headed first to Europe in hopes of attending lectures at German universities and also of broadening

---

3.   After his death, the first part of Prussner's dissertation was edited and supplemented by John H. Hayes, a colleague at Candler, and published as *Old Testament Theology: Its History and Development* (Atlanta: John Knox Press, 1985). Prussner died in 1978.

4.   The revised form of this thesis was published as *The Prophetic Word of Hosea: A Morphological Study* (BZAW, 111; Berlin: A. Töpelmann, 1969).

5.   Concerning Ben-Dor, Bowen writes, 'The fact that he was Jewish made his appointment a notable innovation at Candler' (*The Candler School of Theology*, p. 101).

his general education. One of his goals was to hear Gerhard von Rad lecture at Heidelberg. When Max arrived in Heidelberg, he learned to his chagrin that von Rad was in the United States! Nevertheless, he stayed in Heidelberg for several weeks. On this occasion he met Dr Manfred Hoffman, a Methodist pastor, who soon came to the Candler faculty as professor of church history.

Max eventually left Heidelberg to 'hitchhike' to the Middle East. He shared a ride with a Turkish man who was on his way to Istanbul, and then he continued south through Syria, Palestine and Egypt, visiting historical sites and museums throughout the region. Since Max had little money for the trip, his itinerary was sometimes determined by the availability of inexpensive campsites or the generous offer of a roof or porch where he might spend a night. On his return trip through Europe, he fell ill and was hospitalized for six weeks in Vienna, but he made it back to the States by Christmas. Max's keen interest in history was further stimulated by these months of travel. In coming years he would return both to Europe and the Middle East for research purposes, and his appreciation for the history and cultures of the Middle East would also draw him time and again to the region.

While at Emory, Max met Ms Alice Julene King and they were married 11 August 1962. He and Julene have two sons, David Weldon and Charles Dushan. David, a physician, was born in Atlanta on 21 July 1963, and Charles, an officer in the US Coast Guard, was born in Birmingham, Alabama, on 29 September 1966.[6]

As might be expected, Max's dissertation subject was an examination of a historically oriented topic: the Omride dynasty in ancient Israel. The thesis was supervised by Bowen and completed in 1964: 'The Omride Dynasty in the Light of Recent Literary and Archaeological Research'. The title reveals the author's strong interests in what is commonly known as the historical–critical method, and more particularly, his methodological commitments to literary or source analysis and to archaeological research as twin underpinnings of historical reconstruction. Although the thesis itself was not published, its substance can be found in several scholarly articles published soon after its completion (see below).

While a doctoral candidate at Emory, Max began his teaching career.

---

6. Both sons married in 1992. David married Debra Vaughan. They have one son, Daniel Vaughan. Charles married Julianne King. They have three daughters, Savannah Gentry, Emma Marin and Molly Anne.

In 1962–63, he was an instructor in Old Testament studies at the Inter-denominational Theological Center in Atlanta. In the following year he served as an assistant in the teaching of Hebrew at Candler School of Theology, and in 1964, the year of his graduation from Emory, Max and Julene moved to Birmingham, where he would serve for three years as an assistant professor of Old Testament studies at Birmingham-Southern College.

In 1967, Professor Bowen retired from the Candler faculty and Max was chosen to succeed him. He and Julene moved back to Atlanta, where he began 32 years of teaching at Candler and in the Graduate Division of Religion at Emory University. The skills and intellectual gifts Max displayed while a student at Emory were such that the faculty was pleased to call back one of its own. He rose through the ranks of professorial appointment, being awarded tenure in 1971 and promoted to full professor in 1978. In 1983, Max's teaching load was reduced by half when he began his decade-long tenure as director of the Graduate Division of Religion at Emory. This administrative post was followed by his return to teaching for several years, during which he directed the Master of Theological Studies program at Candler, and his subsequent retirement from Emory in 1999.

His three teaching colleagues in the field of Hebrew Bible during his first years at Emory were F. Prussner, M. Buss and I. Ben-Dor. As noted above, all of them had been his teachers. In 1970, Gene M. Tucker was called to the Candler faculty after brief teaching stints at the University of Southern California and Duke University. He had completed his doctoral work at Yale University in 1963, specializing in form-critical analysis of biblical and ancient Near Eastern texts.[7] In 1972, John H. Hayes also came to Candler after several years on the faculty of Trinity University in San Antonio, Texas. For four years, Hayes was employed as a visiting professor, but in 1977, his position on the faculty was regularized. His doctoral work was completed at Princeton Theological Seminary in 1964.[8]

---

7.   Tucker retired from Emory in 1995. Two volumes of essays were published in his honor: J.L. Mays *et al.*, *Old Testament Interpretation, Past, Present, and Future: Essays in Honor of Gene M. Tucker* (Nashville: Abingdon Press, 1995); and S.B. Reid, *Prophets and Paradigms: Essays in Honor of Gene M. Tucker* (JSOTSup, 229; Sheffield: Sheffield Academic Press, 1996). For a brief bio-graphical overview of Tucker, see the sketch by Reid on pp. 9-10.

8.   His unpublished dissertation is entitled, 'The Oracles Against the Nations in

Although Max developed solid working relationships across the faculty—as is evident by his selection as Director of the Graduate Division of Religion—his collegial manner resulted in particularly close professional relationships with Tucker and Hayes. These three were relatively close in age, their research interests intersected at various points, and each proved to be remarkably productive as a scholar and teacher. Miller and Tucker co-authored a commentary on the book of Joshua, published in 1974.[9] Friends of the two scholars are occasionally tempted to engage in source and redaction analyses of the text to guess at the authorship of sections in the book. It is a safe bet, however, that at least the two sections of the commentary devoted to geography and place names are Max's work. In 1977, Miller and Hayes edited a volume on historical reconstruction and the interpretation of the Hebrew Bible.[10] This widely cited volume was followed in 1986 by a second collaborative work, *A History of Ancient Israel and Judah*.[11]

Inevitably the three scholars had differences of opinion with respect to research conclusions and faculty politics, but their common professional enthusiasm served as a stimulus to keep conversations and projects on track. Their combined talents also proved to be quite a draw for doctoral candidates seeking a productive location for graduate work in Hebrew Bible. After Prussner died in 1978, the strong research interests of the trio (and of Martin Buss) were supplemented by the addition of Carol Newsom to the Candler faculty. She completed her dissertation at Harvard University[12] and has amply demonstrated her

the Old Testament: Their Usage and Theological Importance'. A volume of essays by his former students was presented in tribute to Hayes in 1993: M.P. Graham, W.P. Brown and J.K. Kuan, *History and Interpretation: Essays in Honour of John H. Hayes* (JSOTSup, 173; Sheffield: Sheffield Academic Press, 1993).

9.   J.M. Miller and G.M. Tucker, *The Book of Joshua* (CBC; Cambridge: Cambridge University Press, 1974). Max's second book, *The Old Testament and the Historian* (GBSOT; Philadelphia: Fortress Press, 1976), was published in the Guides to Biblical Scholarship series. Tucker was an editor of the series.

10.   J.H. Hayes and J.M. Miller, *Israelite and Judaean History* (OTL; Philadelphia: Westminster Press; London: SCM Press, 1977).

11.   The volume was also published by Westminster Press and SCM Press. The preface contains details of the respective contributions of the two authors. Max was primarily responsible for the first nine chapters and John for chapters 10–12. Chapters 13–14 were solely the work of Hayes. The two authors are currently at work on a revised edition.

12.   C.R. Newsom, *Songs of the Sabbath Sacrifice: A Critical Edition* (HSS, 27; Atlanta: Scholars Press, 1985).

scholarship through her subsequent publications and editorial activities.

Twice during his career Max was the recipient of funds from the Alexander von Humboldt Stiftung, which provided opportunities for living in Germany and carrying out a research project at one of the country's universities. During parts of the years 1974/75 and 1981/82, the Miller family lived in Germany, while Max worked in the Biblisch-archäologisches Institut at Tübingen University. Other prestigious research grants came to Max in the course of his teaching career at Emory as well.[13]

As their two children matured, Julene Miller entered the business world in Atlanta. She is the founder and current president of Academy International Travel Service. In addition to the usual travel services offered to the public, Julene's company has developed relationships with several academic institutions and assists them in planning travel seminars to Europe and the Middle East for their students. In recent years her company has also served the American Schools of Oriental Research by assisting its members with travel arrangements to and from ASOR's annual meeting. Through her company she and Max have had the pleasure of introducing many—including both students and vacationers—to travel and study in the Middle East.

Max and Julene remain busy in Atlanta. She continues her work at the travel agency, and Max serves as an archaeologist on the staff of the Fernbank Museum of Natural History.[14] His brother John, a businessman, and their mother, Nora Miller Hamaker, live in Atlanta as well.

2. *Research, Writing and Professional Societies*

The fruit of Max's doctoral dissertation was published in a series of articles. The first to see print contained the proposal that the battles with

---

13. Among his grants are the following: National Foundation of the Arts and Humanities (summer, 1966), Emory University (summers, 1967, 1969, 1972, 1978, 1979, 1982), Woodruff Research Support Grant (with John Hayes, 1980), Association of Theological Schools (1981/82), and National Endowment for the Humanities (1987/88).

14. While a professor at Emory, Max played an important role in the university museum's effort to exhibit its Syro-Palestinian, Mesopotamian and Egyptian holdings. Many of the museum's early holdings had been acquired by the Reverend W.A. Shelton, the first professor of Hebrew and Old Testament at Candler. In 1920, Shelton participated in an American expedition to the Middle East led by Professor James H. Breasted of the University of Chicago.

the Arameans attributed to King Ahab of the Omride dynasty (1 Kings 20 and 22) could more plausibly be dated to the Jehu dynasty, perhaps during the reign of Jehu himself or that of his son Jehoahaz.[15] His conclusions were based on a literary (i.e. source and redaction) analysis of the relevant portions of 1–2 Kings and have implications for reconstructing the history of Ahab's reign, the chronology of Israel's monarchy, and the sequence and activities of Aramean kings in Damascus, among other things. Three articles that followed developed some of these implications.[16]

As part of his study of the Omride dynasty, Max had evaluated the pertinent elements in the record of the excavations at ancient sites such as Samaria, Megiddo and Hazor. He recognized early on that excavation results played a major role in historical reconstruction and also that he needed additional training in excavation method.[17] So, during his early years as a professor he spent several summers working on excavation projects. In the summer of 1966, he worked on the excavation of Tel Zeror, a site located in the Sharon Plain. The following summer he worked at Tel Arad in the Negev. In the summer of 1969 he worked at two sites, Et-Tell (often equated with Ai of the biblical narrative) in the central hill country and at Tel Sheva in the Negev. In 1972 he served on the staff of the excavation at Buseirah in southern Jordan. It is important to note the range of experience gathered during these summers. The expedition at T. Zeror was organized by the Japanese Society for Near Eastern Research. Those at T. Arad and T. Sheva were organized by Israeli scholars under the direction of Y. Aharoni. Et-Tell was directed by Professor Joseph Callaway[18] of Southern Baptist Theological Semi-

15. 'The Elisha Cycle and the Accounts of the Omride Wars', *JBL* 85 (1966), pp. 441-54.

16. See the following articles in the bibliographical appendix: 1967a, 1967b, 1968a. One should also compare Max's *The Old Testament and the Historian*, pp. 21-39, and *A History of Ancient Israel and Judah*, pp. 250-307.

17. It is worth noting in this context that his teacher and (later) colleague, I. Ben-Dor, had extensive experience in archaeological fieldwork. His first excavation was at Beth Shan in 1927. He also worked in Egypt (Meydum), Italy (Minturnae), Mesopotamia (Tepe Jawra) and Transjordan (Jerash, Petra), as well as at other sites in Palestine (Samaria, Beitin, Tell al Ajjul, Jericho and Arad). Max and Ben-Dor worked together at Arad in 1967.

18. Callaway began his excavation career by working with G.E. Wright at Shechem (1960). He also spent a sabbatical year during postgraduate study at the Institute of Archaeology, University of London, under the direction of Mortimer

nary in Louisville, Kentucky. The work at Buseirah was directed by Ms Crystal Bennett of the British School of Archaeology. Max gained firsthand experience working with international teams of scholars who employed various methods in their excavation procedures.

For all of his intellectual curiosity, Max was not overly interested in the science of excavation or more broadly the refinement of archaeological technique. Obviously he recognized the importance of these matters, but he was more interested in the employment of the data gathered as part of the tasks of historical geography and historical reconstruction. His own training at Emory, broadly speaking, followed the approach of W.F. Albright to biblical and Near Eastern sources—both Bowen and Ben-Dor stood essentially in that intellectual tradition and interpretive approach, even if neither had taken a degree at Johns Hopkins. Max enthusiastically embraced the opportunities that living and working in the region offered.[19] His interests in the crafts of historical reconstruction and site identification would continue in his research and publications throughout his teaching career.

The mid-1970s saw the publication of three books under his name. The first was the volume on Joshua that he wrote with Tucker. The second was the introductory guide entitled *The Old Testament and the Historian*.[20] In this work one sees a teacher at work, patiently bringing a reader along through basic questions of historical analysis and reconstruction as part of the task of biblical interpretation. The third was the scholarly volume *Israelite and Judaean History* that he edited with Hayes.[21] This last volume has earned a significant place in the history of biblical scholarship, especially on the American scene, for the scope of its concerns and in the manner of methodological questions addressed. The list of 14 contributors to the volume is international and ecumenical. With the hindsight of nearly 25 years, one can see scholarship

Wheeler and Kathleen Kenyon. Max and Joe Callaway developed not only a professional relationship, but a solid friendship as well. Along with two of Callaway's students, J.F. Drinkard and G.L. Mattingly, Max edited a Festschrift in Callaway's honor: *Benchmarks in Time and Culture: An Introduction to the History and Methodology of Syro-Palestinian Archaeology* (ABS, 1; Atlanta: Scholars Press, 1988).

19. In the summers of 1993–94, Max returned to excavation work, serving on the expedition to Qarqur (Syria), directed by Dr Rudolph Dornemann. On Max's survey work in central Jordan, see below.

20. Philadelphia: Fortress Press; London: SPCK, 1976.

21. Philadephia: Westminster Press; London: SCM Press, 1977.

emerging in various ways out of an Albrightian interpretive model that had dominated at least the American scene and been influential also in international circles.

Miller's written contribution to this third volume was a thorough treatment of the exodus and conquest period(s). His methodological approach is as important to note as the conclusions drawn. He begins with the affirmation that the relevant biblical accounts are 'composite, based on various ancient traditions which represent various literary genres and which have undergone changes during the process of transmission from ancient times' (p. 213). He examines the biblical texts, taking source-critical and traditio-historical matters into account before looking at the relevant Egyptian and archaeological data respectively. Similarly, his examination of the archaeological data takes into account the complexities and inevitably subjective elements in seeking historical information about early Israel from the data. Quests for harmonization between texts and archaeological data, and also premature efforts at synthesis, are resisted. If his suggestions for historical reconstruction can be described succinctly, they are more in the line of Alt, Noth and Weippert, but without dependence on the nomadic or outsider identity of earliest Israel or a tribal confederation based on the model of Greek amphictyonies. Notably, he shows how difficult it is to defend a thirteenth-century BCE conquest model on the basis of the archaeological evidence, and he does not resist the conclusion that earliest Israel was culturally Canaanite (i.e. indigenous), although he opposes Mendenhall's thesis that the early Israelite community arose as an internal revolt against Canaanite urban overlords.[22]

Several narratives about pre-monarchic Israel are set in the central hill country of Palestine. While engaged in the excavation at Et-Tell, Max took the opportunity to explore the geography of the broader region. His preferred method of exploration (in addition, of course, to careful analysis of the written sources!) was walking. He was and remains a vigorous walker. On foot, he traversed thoroughly the hills and narrow valleys between Et-Tell and Jerusalem during the summer

---

22. See also his methodological observations in 1977a and his later treatment in *A History of Ancient Israel and Judah*, pp. 54-79. The concluding paragraph in this last named source begins, 'We decline any attempt to reconstruct the history of the earliest Israelites therefore, and begin our treatment with a description of the circumstances that appear to have existed among the tribes in Palestine on the eve of the establishment of the monarchy' (p. 79).

of 1969, and he brought that experience to bear on the relevant biblical texts and scholarship associated with them. Two studies subsequently emerged that took up the topic of site identification and historical reconstruction (1974b, 1975). In the first study Max takes up the question of the location and identity of Jebus (e.g. Josh. 15.8; 18.16; 2 Sam. 17.17). His analysis extends through the tribal border lists of Judah and Benjamin as well as the efforts of interpreters to identify the modern wadi systems near Jerusalem with the names of their ancient counterparts. He concludes that in the early Iron Age Jebus was a settlement directly north of Jerusalem, at or near modern Sha'fat. Moreover, he sees no reason to doubt that Jebusites influenced or even at times controlled Jerusalem; he simply proposes that it is a case of mistaken identity to equate Jebus with Jerusalem. In the second study Max takes up the question of Geba/Gibeah of Benjamin, and more specifically, whether two sites or one are indicated in the biblical texts, and whether the prominent hill of Tell el-Fûl north of Jerusalem preserves the ruins of Saul's capital. In an influential study W.F. Albright had claimed in 1924, after a season of excavation at Tell el-Fûl, that 'no topographical point in Palestine is more certainly fixed than the identity of Tell el-Fûl with Gibeah of Benjamin and Saul'.[23] After a thorough study of both the pertinent biblical texts and commentators (classical and contemporary), Max comes to the conclusion that only one site qualifies as the Geba or Gibeah of Saul and that its ruins are located at modern Jeba.[24]

Both of these studies show an analytical mind at work, questioning assumptions and patiently working through the combination of literary-critical analysis and historical geography.[25] John Hayes, Max's colleague, was heard to remark facetiously that no theory was safe when Max was walking around the Holy Land. Max's study on Saul (1974d) also owes its inspiration, in part, to his peripatetic explorations.

In the 1986 volume co-authored with John Hayes, *A History of*

---

23. *Excavations and Results at Tell el-Fûl (Gibeah of Saul)* (AASOR, 4; New Haven: American Schools of Oriental Research, 1924), p. 43.

24. Patrick M. Arnold, a student of Max's, took up these matters in his doctoral thesis, which was subsequently published as *Gibeah: The Search for a Biblical City* (JSOTSup, 79; Sheffield: JSOT Press, 1990). Recently, Max returned to his studies of Benjaminite sites (1999).

25. For his methodological comments with respect to site identification, one should consult his 1983a study. For his thoughts about the work and legacy of Albright, see his presentation (and response to E.F. Campbell) in 1979c.

Ancient Israel and Judah, Max brought together the various lines of his inquiries noted above, along with a number of other proposals of historical reconstruction. He was primarily responsible for chs. 1–9, which treat the beginnings of the people of Israel through the Jehu dynasty. The volume is intended for students as well as scholars, and it continues with a characteristic of Max's writings, namely a beginning point with the biblical text as it now exists. One sees this feature in his chapter in *Israelite and Judaean History* and in *The Old Testament and the Historian*. He begins with the narrative 'storyline', steps back from it, and notes the tensions and difficulties that a straightforward reading encounters. When it is made clear that certain choices must be made with respect to reconstruction, he proceeds first with literary-critical proposals and then with suggested historical reconstructions. It may seem simplistic to call attention to this point of beginning with the text as it stands—after all, the volume is intended for use by students—but it does stand out characteristically in several of Max's writings when compared with other scholars. There is, furthermore, something fundamental at stake for Max in this approach, and it concerns the steps of crafting historical reconstruction. In his opinion scholars too often offer historical proposals and then choose from among literary and textual-critical options those that are most congenial to the proposal, while giving the impression that what they offer is congruent with the claims of the biblical text.

It is interesting to compare the co-authored history with John Bright's well-known volume *A History of Israel*, which has exerted a wide influence in English-speaking circles and continues to sell well after 40 years.[26] The two books are published by the same press, Westminster/ John Knox, a company which has contracted to publish yet a third history of Israel/Judah by V.P. Long, T. Longman and I. Provan. Whether intended or not, the press will offer histories that span a range between 'maximalist' and 'minimalist' approaches to the subject (to use terms currently in vogue). When compared to either Bright or the forthcoming volume by Long, Longman and Provan, the volume by Miller and Hayes is more congenial to the 'minimalist' approach. Nevertheless,

26. The first edition was published by Westminster Press (Philadelphia) in 1959. The author carried out two revisions (1972, 1981). Bright died in 1995. A fourth and posthumous edition, with a new introduction and appendix by W.P. Brown, was published in 2000. Brown was a student in Emory's PhD program in Hebrew Bible.

neither Miller nor Hayes would align themselves with those currently associated with the minimalist camp (e.g. T.L. Thompson, P.R. Davies, N.P. Lemche, K.W. Whitelam). They make it clear in the foreword to the volume that they expect that their work will be unsatisfactory for some who think the authors too skeptical and for others who think them too gullible (p. 19).

In 1987, the *Journal for the Study of the Old Testament* devoted most of an issue to matters related to Old Testament history. The issue was prompted in large part by the publication of the 1986 Miller–Hayes volume and by useful discussions on the volume held in November 1986 at the annual meeting of the Society of Biblical Literature. In the introduction to the issue Philip Davies[27] helpfully described the Miller–Hayes volume as an example of the genre of 'biblical history', because the authors give priority to the biblical text in formulating their reconstructions. Davies went on to ask if the Miller–Hayes volume is essentially the 'end of the road' for such a genre—and answered his question in the affirmative—since in his assessment the way forward was with the social sciences (sociology, anthropology, archaeology) having methodological priority. Max would concur essentially with Davies's judgment about the genre of the co-authored volume, but not with the relegation of the biblical text in the manner proposed by Davies. This matter separates him from the work of the minimalists, even when he concurs with some of their conclusions.

While he is often perceived as 'anti-Albrightian', Max shares with Albright and his followers an approach that gives priority to the biblical text in reconstructing biblical history, even if, on occasion, he differs considerably in the conclusions drawn about the text.[28] In several respects his approach (though not some of his conclusions) resembles more the approach of Albright and Bright than that of the scholars now assigned to the so-called minimalist camp.

In the mid-1970s, James A. Sauer, then director of the American

---

27. 'The History of Ancient Israel and Judah', *JSOT* 39 (1987), pp. 3-4.

28. See J.H. Hayes, 'On Reconstructing Israelite History', *JSOT* 39 (1987), pp. 5-9 and J.M. Miller, 'In Defense of Writing a History of Israel', *JSOT* 39 (1987), pp. 53-57. Both are responses to the articles contributed to *JSOT* 39 that offer evaluations of the Miller–Hayes volume. See also Max's 'Is it Possible to Write a History of Israel without Relying on the Hebrew Bible?', in D.V. Edelman (ed.), *The Fabric of History: Text, Artifact and Israel's Past* (JSOTSup, 127; Sheffield: Sheffield Academic Press, 1991), pp. 93-102.

Center of Oriental Research in Amman, Jordan, delivered a guest lecture on the Emory campus. In response to a question about future work in Jordan, Sauer replied that there was a serious need for basic archaeological survey work to be done. He noted that Nelson Glueck's surveys in Transjordan were 40 years old and virtually the only source available on several matters for scholars to consult. Sauer's reply caught Max's interest, and he began a conversation with Sauer (whose knowledge of the ceramic history of Jordanian cultures was unrivaled) about the possibility of conducting an archaeological survey project in Jordan. One thing led to another with the result that the Central Moab Survey, a project organized and directed by Max, was carried out on the Kerak plateau east of the Dead Sea during the years 1978–82.[29]

Max had already developed quite an interest in the region and history of ancient Moab prior to beginning the survey. As part of his dissertation he had investigated the Omride link to Moab as narrated in 2 Kings 3, along with the well-known Iron Age inscription of the Moabite king Mesha and its reference to Omri and his son/sons (lines 4–9). Indeed, before the organization of the Central Moab Survey, he had published a study of the Moabite king's inscription (1974c), where he had proposed on the basis of form-critical parallels that the inscription was best understood as a memorial stela, a retrospective of King Mesha's reign as a whole, rather than a chronologically organized narrative of the king's military and building exploits. He was quite aware also, as he worked through the issues surrounding Israel's origins and settlement in the land, that several scholars had used Glueck's survey results to date the emergence of Israel and Moab as nation-states.

In the annals of scholarship, Max's name will be forever linked with the explorers and scholars A. Musil, R.E. Brünnow, A. Domaszewski, W.F. Albright, N. Glueck and G.L. Harding, each of whom made foundational contributions to the investigation of central Transjordan in antiquity. The teams of the Central Moab Survey attempted to build on the work of these and other pioneers as they sought to identify the archaeological sites on the Kerak plateau and to collect surface pottery

---

29. A major contributor to the project was Jack M. Pinkerton, a businessman and student at Candler. He wrote his master's thesis under Max's direction, based on the results of the first survey season. As is evident from the publications listed in the appendix, Max published several articles related both to the survey work and to Moab. For survey results, related articles, details of participants on survey teams etc., see Miller 1991.

sherds from them. One will see immediately the influence of the Central Moab Survey in subsequent treatments of Transjordan in antiquity.[30]

For those who want to evaluate the accomplishments of the Central Moab Survey, it is important to take into account not only the results of previous explorations in the region, but also Max's listing of the survey's goals[31] and particularly his cautions in using statistics of surface sherd collections (1991: 19-20). Recent soundings in the region and subsequent rechecking of the survey's materials confirms the tentative and preliminary nature of trying to date a site on the basis of ceramic sherds collected through surface surveys.[32] At the conclusion of the survey's work, and after proposing several qualifications to the conclusions drawn by Glueck for the history of the region, Max remarked more than once on his increased admiration for Glueck and what he had accomplished under difficult circumstances.

During his years as a professor Max served in several capacities as a member of academic societies and institutions. As a member of the Society of Biblical Literature, he was active in both regional and national affairs. He served as Vice-President and President (1969–71) of SBL's Southeastern Region. At the national level, he was a member of the steering committee for the History of Israel Section (1975–88), serving as its chair for many of those years, and thereby helping make that section a prominent feature of the annual SBL meeting. Also, he

---

30. A good example would be B. MacDonald, *'East of the Jordan': Territories and Sites of the Hebrew Scriptures* (ASOR Books, 6; Boston: American Schools of Oriental Research, 2000), pp. 157-83. His treatment of the regions of southern Ammon and Moab is heavily indebted to the work of the Central Moab Survey and related work produced by team members. MacDonald visited with the Central Moab Survey Project in 1979 as part of his own preparation to begin archaeological survey work in the Wadi al Hasa and regions immediately to the south of the Hasa. See further B. MacDonald *et al.*, *The Wadi el Hasa Archaeological Survey, 1979–1983, West-Central Jordan* (Waterloo: Wilfred Laurier University Press, 1988), and *idem*, *The Southern Ghors and Northeast Arabah Archaeological Survey* (SAM, 5; Sheffield: J.R. Collis, 1992).

31. 'The primary goal of the survey was to develop an accumulative and comprehensive gazeteer of the archaeological sites of the [Kerak] plateau' (1991: 18).

32. Cf. P. Bienkowski *et al.*, 'Soundings at Ash-Shorabat and Khirbat Dubab in the Wadi Hasa: The Stratigraphy', *Levant* 29 (1997), pp. 41-70; *idem*, 'Soundings at Ash-Shorabat and Khirbat Dubab in the Wadi Hasa: The Pottery', *Levant* 31 (1999), pp. 149-72.

served terms on the editorial boards of the society's dissertation series (1980–83) and its *Journal of Biblical Literature* (1985–88).

Max was just as involved in the various activities of the American Schools of Oriental Research. He served more than one term on ASOR's board of trustees and one term as president of its Southeastern Region. He has had multiple roles in the governance of overseas institutes affiliated with ASOR. He served a term on the executive committee of the Albright Institute of Archaeological Research in Jerusalem and a year as president of the institute (1994–95). He also had a term as a member of the trustees of the American Center of Oriental Research in Amman.

His contributions to learned societies were not limited to the North American societies named above; he has been a member of the Palestine Exploration Fund and the Deutscher Verein zur Erforschung Palästinas. Over the years he has developed personal friendships and professional relationships with members of both distinguished societies.

3. *Teacher*

As a person Max is straightforward, energetic and a self-starter. The pursuit of research matters and the presentation of issues in the history of biblical interpretation or of historical reconstruction provide much personal satisfaction to him. These characteristics also marked his teaching style at Emory. He added high expectations to this mixture, both for himself and his students. He simply assumed—so it seemed to students—that since he enjoyed the subject matter and was willing to work hard at its mastery, all class participants would do the same. Some students, of course, followed his lead, but others could be intimidated by him. He insisted, for example, that all students in the doctoral program in Hebrew Bible should have some training in history, archaeology[33] and site identification, whether their dissertation subject required it or not. Many a student in the program will recall Max's large-scale map of Syria–Palestine that he kept in the Bowen Seminar Room and his use of it in evaluating them!

It should be kept in mind that in the American system even doctoral

---

33. His commitments to the subject matters of archaeology and historical analysis are clearly reflected in his effort (toward the end of his teaching career) to preserve his extensive slide collection through digitization and in placing the collection in the library for public usage.

candidates are required to enroll in seminars in which they receive a letter grade. Only the registrar knows for sure, but the student rumor mill held that Max was a tough evaluator. Students did receive, however, something far more important than a seminar grade: a teacher who was willing to fan the flame of their interests and who offered concrete suggestions and assistance as they worked to master the subject matter. His straightforward manner dwelt almost exclusively on the subject, and he cared relatively little about formality in the classroom or the maintenance of professorial prerogatives. Students were allowed to address him by his first name, and they were certainly encouraged to ask whatever questions they wanted. If, by chance, Max did not know the answer to a question, he would simply admit it and say that he hoped to have a more informed reply at a later time. He also appreciated candor from students, preferring a spirited exchange from those who had prepared adequately to the acquiescence of the timid.

Students were also the fortunate recipients of personal interest taken in their welfare by both Max and Julene. They opened their home to host public functions and departmental parties. They even assisted students with mundane but very important matters such as finding an apartment to rent near the Emory campus.

Over the years Max also developed into an 'extra-mural' teacher through his many travel seminars held in Mediterranean and Middle Eastern countries. These have been a gift not only to Emory students and those of other institutions (e.g. Columbia Theological Seminary), but also to members of the traveling public.[34] In these endeavors he has worked closely with his wife Julene, whose professional expertise and business contacts abroad helped ensure a positive experience for participants. These travel seminars have offered two advantages to participants. First, Max provides reading materials in preparation for the seminar,[35] and when 'on-site' he provides informed commentary. Museums are

34. An Atlanta businessman, H.G. Pattillo, who observed firsthand some of the work of the Central Moab Survey in 1979, subsequently underwrote the costs of several travel seminars to the Middle East for students from various theological institutions.

35. Max eventually wrote *Introducing the Holy Land: A Guidebook for First-Time Visitors* (Macon, GA: Mercer University Press; London: SCM Press, 1982), intended for visitors to the Holy Land. A friend and professional colleague of his, Professor J.P.J. Olivier of Stellenbosch University, translated the work into Afrikaans in 1987. In 1988, Max was a guest lecturer at the University of Stellenbosch.

significant parts of the itinerary. Second, the itinerary is typically fuller in geographical and cultural senses than the usual packaged tour elected by Americans, which at times give the unfortunate impression that Israel and Egypt are the only Middle Eastern countries worth visiting. Max and Julene have organized trips that also include thorough itineraries in Turkey, Syria and Jordan. Indeed, in spite of tense official relations between Iran and the US, they have organized travel in Iran as well. Although the travel seminars are a part of Julene's business, both she and Max continue in their preparation, because they take pride in the educational benefit to participants.

In his retirement from Emory, Max is keeping his teaching 'edge' through travel seminars and the arrangement of exhibits at the Fernbank Museum of Natural History in Atlanta. Not long after he joined the staff of the museum, it sponsored a large exhibit of Egyptian artifacts entitled, 'Life and Death under the Pharaohs: Egyptian Art from the National Museum of Antiquities in Leiden, The Netherlands'. In 2002, the museum plans an equally impressive exhibit from Syria.

If Max (and also Julene) remains busy with various projects in the aftermath of his retirement from Emory, it comes as no surprise to his friends. May he and Julene find continued joy in their many activities and in their life together.

Appendix: Select Bibliography of J. Maxwell Miller

Dissertation

1964   'The Omride Dynasty in the Light of Recent Literary and Archaeological Research' (PhD dissertation, Emory University).

Books

1974   *Joshua,* co-authored with G.M. Tucker (CBC; Cambridge: Cambridge University Press).

1976   *The Old Testament and the Historian* (GBSOT; Philadelphia: Fortress Press; London: SPCK).

1977   *Israelite and Judaean History*, co-edited with John Hayes (OTL; Philadephia: Westminster Press; London: SCM Press).

1982   *Introducing the Holy Land: A Guidebook for First-Time Visitors* (Macon, GA: Mercer University Press; London: SCM Press). Translated by J.P.J. Olivier as *Die Heilige Land* (Rooderproort, SA: Cum-Boeke, 1987).

1986   *A History of Ancient Israel and Judah*, co-authored with J.H. Hayes (Philadelphia: Westminster Press; London: SCM Press).

1988   *Benchmarks in Time and Culture: An Introduction to the History and Methodology of Syro-Palestinian Archaeology*, co-edited with J.F. Drinkard and G.L. Mattingly (ABS, 1; Atlanta: Scholars Press).

1991   *Archaeological Survey of the Kerak Plateau*, editor (ASORAR, 1; Atlanta: Scholars Press).

Articles and Chapters

1966   'The Elisha Cycle and the Accounts of the Omride Wars', *JBL* 85: 441-54.

1967a   'Another Look at the Chronology of the Early Divided Monarchy', *JBL* 86: 276-88.

1967b   'The Fall of the House of Ahab', *VT* 17: 307-24.

1968a   'The Rest of the Acts of Jehoahaz', *ZAW* 80: 337-42.

1968b   'So Tibni Died', *VT* 18: 392-94.

1969   'Geshur and Aram', *JNES* 28: 60-61.

1970   'The Korahites of Southern Judah', *CBQ* 32: 58-68.

1972   'In the "Image" and "Likeness" of God', *JBL* 91: 289-304.

1974a   'The Descendants of Cain: Notes on Genesis 4', *ZAW* 86: 164-74.

1974b   'Jebus and Jerusalem: A Case of Mistaken Identity', *ZDPV* 90: 115-27.

1974c   'The Moabite Stone as a Memorial Stela', *PEQ* 106: 9-18.

1974d   'Saul's Rise to Power: Some Observations Concerning 1 Samuel 9.1–10.16; 10.26–11.15 and 13.2–14.46', *CBQ* 36: 157-74.

1975   'Geba/Gibeah of Benjamin', *VT* 25: 145-66.

1977a   'Archaeology and the Israelite Conquest of Canaan: Some Methodological Observations', *PEQ* 109: 87-93.

1977b   'The Israelite Occupation of Canaan', in Hayes and Miller (eds.), *Israelite and Judaean History* (OTL; Philadelphia: Westminster Press; London: SCM Press): 213-84.

1977c   'Joshua, Book of', *IDBSup* (Nashville: Abingdon Press): 493-96.

1977d   'The Patriarchs and Extra-Biblical Sources: A Response', *JSOT* 2 (1977): 62-66.

1979a   'Archaeological Survey of Central Moab: 1978', *BASOR* 234: 43-52.

1979b   'Archaeological Survey South of Wadi Mujib: Glueck's Sites Revisited', *ADAJ* 23: 79-92.

1979c   'W.F. Albright and Historical Reconstruction', *BA* 42: 37-47.

1980   'Reports: Moab Survey, 1979', *PEQ* 112: 69.

1981   'Renewed Interest in Ancient Moab', *PRS* 8: 219-29.

1982a   'Approaches to the Bible through History and Archaeology: Biblical History as a Discipline', *BA* 45: 211-16.

1982b   'Recent Archaeological Developments Relevant to Ancient Moab', in A. Hadidi (ed.), *Studies in the History and Archaeology of Jordan*, I (Amman: Department of Antiquities): 169-73.

1983a   'The Ben Hadad of the Melqart Stele', *PEQ* 115: 95-101.

1983b   'Site Identification: A Problem Area in Contemporary Biblical Scholarship', *ZDPV* 99: 119-29.

1985a   'Chronology (Old Testament History)', in P.J. Achtemeier (ed.), *Harper's Bible Dictionary* (San Francisco: Harper & Row): 181-83.

1985b   'Israelite History', in D.A. Knight and G.M. Tucker (eds.), *The Hebrew Bible and its Modern Interpreters* (The Bible and its Modern Interpreters; Philadelphia/Chico, CA: Fortress Press/Scholars Press): 1-30.

1987a   'Biblical Maps: How Reliable Are They?' *BR* 3/4: 32-41.

1987b   'The Emergence of Iron Age Kingdoms in Syria–Palestine', 'Mapping Biblical Narratives', 'The Kingdom of Saul', 'David's Consolidation of the Kingdom', 'Israel and Moab', in *Time-Life Biblical Atlas* (London: Times Books): 70-75, 78-81, 100-101.

1987c   'In Defense of Writing a History of Israel', *JSOT* 39: 53-57.

1987d   'Old Testament History and Archaeology', *BA* 50: 55-63.

1987e   'Palestinian Archaeology: Some Definitions and Antecedents', in Miller *et al.*, *Benchmarks in Time and Culture: An Introduction to the History and Methodology of Syro-Palestinian Archaeology* (ABS, 1: Atlanta: Scholars Press): 3-15.

1987f   'Rehoboam's Cities of Defense', in L.G. Perdue, L.E. Toombs and G.L. Johnson (eds.), *Archaeology and Biblical Interpretation: Essays in Memory of D. Glen Rose* (Atlanta: John Knox Press): 273-86.

1989a   'Moab and the Moabites', in J.A. Dearman (ed.), *Studies in the Mesha Inscription and Moab* (ABS, 2; Atlanta: Scholars Press): 1-40.

1989b   'New Directions in the Study of Israelite History', *NGTT* 30: 152-68.

1989c   'Recent Archaeological Exploration in the el-Kerak Plateau', *JNSL* 15: 143-53.

1990a   'Six Khirbet el-Medeinehs in the Region East of the Dead Sea', *BASOR* 276: 25-28.

1990b   'Archaeology (Old Testament)', in R.J. Coggins and J.L. Houlden (eds.), *A Dictionary of Biblical Interpretation* (Philadelphia: Trinity Press International; London: SCM Press): 51-56.

1990c   'David', 'Gibeah', 'Saul', in Watson Mills (ed.), *Mercer Dictionary of the Bible* (Macon, GA: Mercer University Press): 198-99, 329, 798-99.

1990d   'The Israelite Journey Through (Around) Moab and Moabite Toponymy', *JBL* 108: 577-95.

1990e   'Moab During Iron I', in N. Na'aman and I. Finkelstein (eds.), *From Nomadism to Monarchy: Archaeological and Historical Aspects of Early Israel* (Festschrift Moshe Kochavi; Jerusalem: Israel Exploration Society): 242-56.

1991a   'Is It Possible to Write a History of Israel without Relying on the Hebrew Bible?', in D.V. Edelman (ed.), *The Fabric of History: Text, Artifact and Israel's Past* (JSOTSup, 127; Sheffield: Sheffield Academic Press): 93-102.

1991b   'Solomon: International Potentate or Local King?', *PEQ* 123: 28-31.

1991c   'Ammonites', 'Edom', 'Moab and the Moabite Stone', 'Transjordan', in T.C. Butler (ed.), *Holman Bible Dictionary* (Nashville: Holman Bible Publishers): 44-45, 395-97, 982-83, 1362-63.

1992a   'Early Monarchy in Moab?', in P. Bienkowski (ed.), *Early Edom and Moab: The Beginning of the Iron Age in Southern Jordan* (SAM, 7; Sheffield: J.R. Collis): 77-92.

1992b   'Moab', *ABD,* IV: 882-93.

1992c   'Reflections on the Study of Israelite History', in J.H. Charlesworth and W.P. Weaver (eds.), *What Has Archaeology to Do with Faith?* (Faith and Scholarship Colloquies; Philadelphia: Trinity Press): 60-74.

1993a   'Israel, History of' and 'Judah', in B.M. Metzger and M.D. Coogan (eds.), *The Oxford Companion to the Bible* (Oxford: Oxford University Press): 329-32, 388-91.

1993b	'Reading the Bible Historically: The Historian's Approach', in S.R. Haynes and S.L. McKenzie (eds.), *To Each its Own Meaning: An Introduction to Biblical Criticisms and their Application* (Philadelphia: Westminster/John Knox Press): 11-28.
1994	'Introduction to the History of Ancient Israel', in L.E. Keck (ed.), *The New Interpreter's Bible* (Nashville: Abingdon Press): 244-71.
1995a	'The Ancient Near East and Archaeology', in J.L. Mays, D.L. Peterson and K.H. Richards (eds.), *Old Testament Interpretation: Past, Present and Future* (Nashville: Abingdon Press): 245-60.
1995b	'Explorations in Ancient Moab', *Qad* 28: 77-82.
1997a	'Ancient Moab: Still Largely Unknown', *BA* 60: 194-204.
1997b	'Archaeology and the Bible', in *International Biblical Commentary* (Collegeville, MN: Liturgical Press; Spanish edn, Verbo Divino Estelle; French edn, Editione du Cerf Paris): 203-11.
1997c	'Moab', in E.M. Meyers (ed.), *The Oxford Encyclopedia of Archaeology in the Near East*, IV (5 vols.; Oxford: Oxford University Press): 38-39.
1997d	'Separating the Solomon of History from the Solomon of Legend', in L.K. Handy (ed.), *The Age of Solomon: Scholarship at the Turn of the Millennium* (SHCANE, 11; Leiden: E.J. Brill): 1-24; in the same volume, 'Response to A. Millard': 55-56.
1999	'Notes on Benjaminite Place Names', *JNSL* 25: 61-73.
2000a	'Burckhardt-Robinson Features in Nineteenth-Century Maps of the Kerak Plateau', in L.E. Stager, J.A. Greene, and M.D. Coogan (eds.), *The Archaeology of Jordan and Beyond: Essays in Honor of James A. Sauer* (Harvard Semitic Museum Publications; Studies in the Archaeology and History of the Levant, 1; Winona Lake, IN: Eisenbrauns, 2000): 351-66.
2000b	'Jerusalem', in D.N. Freedman (ed.), *Eerdmans Dictionary of the Bible* (Grand Rapids: Eerdmans): 693-98.

Select Book Reviews

Ahlström, G.W., *The History of Ancient Palestine from the Palaeolithic Period to Alexander's Conquest. Int* 49 (1995), pp. 80-84.

Bimson, J.J., *Redating the Exodus and Conquest. JBL* 99 (1980), pp. 133-35.

Bright, J., *A History of Israel* (3rd edn). *BTB* 12 (1982), pp. 59-60.

Kenyon, K.M., *Royal Cities of the Old Testament. JBL* 92 (1973), pp. 447-48.

Malamat, A. (ed.), *The Age of the Monarchies: Political History* and *The Age of the Monarchies: Culture and Society*, IV/1-2. *BA* 45 (1982), p. 190.

Mann, T.W., *Divine Presence and Guidance in Israelite Traditions: The Typology of Exaltation. TTod* 35 (1979), pp. 516-17.

Mazar, B., *The Early Biblical Period: Historical Essays. CBQ* 51 (1989), pp. 177-78.

Pitard, W.T., *Ancient Damascus: A Historical Study of the Syrian City-State from Earliest Times until its Fall to the Assyrians in 732 B.C.E. JBL* 107 (1988), pp. 733-34.

Sanders, J.A. (ed.), *Near Eastern Archaeology in the Twentieth Century: Essays in Honor of Nelson Glueck. JBL* 90 (1971), pp. 231-32.

Schulte, H., *Die Entstehung der Geschichtsschreibung im alten Israel. Int* 28 (1974), pp. 233-34.

Thompson, T.L., *Early History of the Israelite People: From the Written and Archaeological Sources. JBL* 113 (1994), pp. 509-10.

Part II

HISTORY

SHIFTING THE GAZE: HISTORIOGRAPHIC CONSTRAINTS
IN CHRONICLES AND THEIR IMPLICATIONS*

Ehud Ben Zvi

1. *Introduction*

Much has been written about the ability of historians to shape constructions of the past according to their own worldviews, theologies or
ideologies, and on the influence of social location on historiography. In
fact, there is abundant proof that the ancient historians responsible for
such books as Kings and Chronicles could mould their accounts to serve
particular theological, ideological, literary and rhetorical purposes.[1] To
be sure, the same holds true for most histories. Such a situation is to be
expected, since theological/ideological (hereafter, theological) frames
and considerations influence the *significance* ascribed to events in the
past.[2] Moreover, the articulation of the significance of an historical
event requires that the event be set within a comprehensive historical
narrative[3] that most often includes the historical causes and effects of
the event, and at times, even alternative paths that were open to but not
chosen by the historical agents. In other words, events as understood

---

*   It is with great pleasure and humility that I dedicate to Max Miller this paper
on ancient history and historiography, two topics that are close to his heart. May it
serve as a small token of my gratitude for all the support he provided my family and
me during my period of graduate study at Emory and for his friendship since.
    1.   On historiographic and literary considerations that influenced the writing of
Chronicles, see I. Kalimi, ‏ספר דברי הימים. כתיבה היסטורית ואמצעים‎
‏ספרותיים‎ (Biblical Encyclopaedia Library, 18; Jerusalem: Mosad Bialik, 2000).
    2.   These types of issue have been discussed, in one way or another, numerous
times in articles in *History and Theory*. See, for instance, L. Hölscher, 'The New
Annalistic: A Sketch of A Theory of History', *History and Theory* 36 (1997),
pp. 317-35; R. Martin, 'Progress in Historical Studies', *History and Theory* 38
(1998), pp. 14-39.
    3.   'Narrative' is here understood in a broad sense.

and construed within a larger narrative (or meta-narrative), rather than the events per se, are the bearers of social and theological significance in accounts of the past. Significantly, the (implied) author of Chronicles (hereafter, 'the Chronicler')[4] was mainly interested in communicating the social and theological significance of Israel's history (or that portion of it covered in Chronicles; on this matter, see below).

The Chronicler constructed and communicated meaning through the creation of a historical narrative that included numerous accounts of past events, shaped so as to convey a particular significance. The Chronicler used sources, imitated them[5] and substantially deviated from them, as it is abundantly attested. In fact, today almost every serious commentary on Chronicles addresses at length these deviations and explains related literary and theological issues. There is still much to be learned from this research perspective.

Recently, however, I became more interested in 'lack of deviation', or, in other words, on which 'historiographic facts' the Chronicler accepted or had to accept as givens. Which facts[6] could the Chronicler *not* deny, even if they were theologically or rhetorically problematic from the viewpoint of Chronicles? And why these facts, but not others? In more general terms, I became more interested in the question of limits of historiographic malleability in ancient Israel. I am convinced that an examination of these limits is likely to shed much light on the social context and the related discursive constraints within which the writing of Israelite history occurred in the Persian period, when Chronicles was written.[7] Moreover, this type of study contributes substantially to our knowledge of the 'facts' about Israel's past that were shared by the community at the time, or at least among its literati. This understanding permits a clearer view of their world of knowledge.[8]

4. Who likely resembled the actual author(s) of Chronicles on this matter.

5. J. Van Seters, 'Creative Imitation in the Hebrew Bible', 2000 presidential address, Canadian Society of Biblical Studies.

6. To be sure, by 'fact' here and hereafter in this paper I do *not* mean something that actually happened, but something that was thought to have happened (e.g. the first of humankind was Adam).

7. They may be conducive to a better understanding of similar processes at different times, e.g. Josephus's times.

8. It goes without saying that the fact that we know the main sources of Chronicles makes this analysis feasible. Josephus's works serve as the other excellent case study that may be used, but it belongs to another time period. Notwithstanding Auld's claims to the contrary, this work assumes that Chronicles was

Thus, in a recent article, I built on the observation that chronological data in Kings—related to regnal length and the age at the ascension to the throne—is maintained in Chronicles, even when it is difficult in itself, and I dealt with what follows from this observation of the constructions of time advanced in Chronicles, as well as about the Chronicler's use of sources.[9] In addition, in August 2000, I presented a paper entitled 'Malleability and its Limits: Sennacherib's Campaign Against Judah as a Case Study', before the European Seminar for Historical Methodology.[10] In this paper I addressed the issue of malleability and its limits in different ancient histories—including Chronicles—from the perspective of a particular case-study.

The present contribution continues my exploration of these issues but differs from the earlier works by focusing on the book of Chronicles as a whole. To be sure, a fully comprehensive, case-by-case study of malleability and its limits in Chronicles would exceed the limits of this paper. Therefore, the present study will concentrate on a set of diverse and paradigmatic cases, and then on the implications that arise from this set.

It is worth stressing at this point that due to the goal of this study, the approach to the selected texts should bear the imprint of kind of reverse critical gaze, that is, the main focus must be on the historical data taken from the Chronicler's sources that has not undergone a substantial change in Chronicles. This is the opposite of what we often do when we study Chronicles. Further, since this essay deals with the construction(s) of the past advanced by Chronicles, what has to be studied is the extant

---

based on and largely imitated the texts included in the so-called Deuteronomistic History. The Chronicler was also knowledgeable of such sources as Pentateuchal traditions or texts, the text of some Psalms and most likely some prophetic books. Auld's position is expressed in A.G. Auld, *Kings without Privilege: David and Moses in the Story of the Bible's Kings* (Edinburgh: T. & T. Clark, 1994); *idem*, 'What Was the Main Source of the Books of Chronicles?', in M.P. Graham and S.L. McKenzie (eds.), *The Chronicler as Author: Studies in Text and Texture* (JSOTSup, 263; Sheffield: Sheffield Academic Press, 1999), pp. 91-99; *idem*, 'What if the Chronicler Did Use the Deuteronomistic History?', in J.C. Exum (ed.), *Virtual History and the Bible* (Leiden: E.J. Brill, 2000), pp. 137-50.

9. See 'About Time: Observations about the Construction of Time in the Book of Chronicles', *HBT* 22 (2000), pp. 17-31. An oral version of the paper was presented at the 1999 meeting of the Society of Biblical Literature in Boston.

10. The paper will be published along with the other presentations in the near future in L.L. Grabbe (ed.), *'Shut up Like a Bird in a Cage': The Invasion of Sennacherib in 701 BCE* (Sheffield: Sheffield Academic Press, forthcoming).

book, that is, a narrative that reports and shapes an image of past events. In fact, there is no real choice in that matter. The intended rereaders[11] were not asked to take more seriously or view as more authoritative the non-parallel than the parallel accounts, and certainly not to dismiss the latter. The (hi)story told in the Chronicles not only encompasses both types of account but also interweaves them into a single narrative and by so doing it denies their separate existence. The 'voice' of the implied author resonates in both types of account equally. So if the implied author is referred to as 'the Chronicler', as is the case here, also the Chronicler's voice carries both types of account equally. In sum, studies of the historical narrative stated in Chronicles, the world it construes, and its reception by the intended and primary rereadership must deal with the entire text, without making differences between parallel and non-parallel texts—which are in fact scholarly constructions.

If the type of research envisaged here is to be successful, the selection of case-studies must be made carefully. It is imperative that the focus be on issues that were central to the discourse of the period, rather than on some assorted marginalia that covers minor points of agreement between the books of Chronicles and its sources. Not much is at stake in marginal details, and therefore reverberations or direct citations from sources may be explained in terms of the simple practicalities of composing a text on the basis of written sources.[12]

Taking these considerations into account, the following cases were selected for this paper: (a) basic genealogies and the sense of identity they create, (b) the kings of Judah and the construction of the monarchic past in terms of regnal periods by Davidic kings, (c) the existence and leadership of northern Israel, (d) major events in Judahite[13] monarchic history (such as conquest of Jerusalem, the building of the temple, the division of the kingdom, Jerusalem's salvation in Sennacherib's times and its destruction in Zedekiah's), and (e) the motifs of exodus and exile.

11. It should be noted that the readership of the book is most likely and most often a rereadership, since the book was read *and* reread. So it is more precise to refer to rereadership than to readership. All further references will be to rereadership.

12. Biblical authors were not constrained by 'copyright' nor did they have to mention the actual written sources they used. To copy them when there was nothing of substance at stake was not only simpler, but also probably conveyed an aura of authority to the writing.

13. Or following Chronicles' theology, 'Israel's monarchic history'. On the concept of 'Israel', see below.

2. Shifting the Gaze: Some Observations on Selected Issues

2.1 Some Observations about Genealogies

Genealogies occupy the first nine chapters of Chronicles. They construct a world within which Israel—with whom the rereaders of the book identify—finds its place, indeed a central place.[14] Later, they organize Israel according to tribes, families and, above all, leading families of national and even cosmic importance, due to the role of Jerusalem and its temple in the 'cosmic' sphere (e.g. the Davidids, the priests).[15]

To be sure, the genealogical sequences in Chronicles are not presented for their own sake, but for their ability to convey and shape a particular ideology (or theology). One may notice, for instance, the powerful rhetoric of a presentation in which the entire human genealogy quickly narrows to the line that leads to Israel, for a moment rests on those most closely related to Israel, that is his only brother Esau (1 Chron. 1.35-54) and then to Israel itself. While only one chapter is allocated to all the nations outside Israel, eight chapters deal with Israel. Such a theological construction of the world map reflects and shapes a conception about the centrality of Israel.[16] It also affects the way in which the genealogies are treated. For instance, it creates a strong incentive to 'streamline' through omission in 1 Chron. 1.1-26.[17] At other points, however, the Chronicler may add or rearrange information in such a manner that subtly communicates a particular theological position. A typical example is Chronicles' opposition to the view expressed in Ezra–Nehemiah regarding marriage with non-Israelites and 'ethnic purity'.[18]

14. See M. Oeming, *Das wahre Israel: Die 'genealogische Vorhalle' 1 Chronik 1–9* (BWANT, 128; Stuttgart: W. Kohlhammer, 1990).

15. Cf. Ben Zvi, 'About Time'.

16. It goes without saying that this kind of self-conception was most common in the ancient world (cf. the understandings of Assyria, Egypt and Babylon of their places in the 'universe'). Needless to say, similar viewpoints have been attested in numerous polities throughout history, including modern days.

17. All the names in 1 Chron. 1 are derived from Genesis. On these lists, see esp. W. Johnstone, *1 and 2 Chronicles. I. 1 Chronicles 1–2 Chronicles 9: Israel's Place among the Nations* (JSOTSup, 253; Sheffield: Sheffield Academic Press, 1997), pp. 24-36.

18. See S. Japhet, *The Ideology of the Book of Chronicles and its Place in Biblical Thought* (BEATAJ, 9; Bern: Peter Lang, 2nd edn, 1997), pp. 346-51; cf. G.N. Knoppers, ' "Great among his Brothers", But Who is He? Social Complexity and Ethnic Diversity in the Genealogy of Judah', *Journal of Hebrew Scripture* 3/6

In all these cases, it is evident that the narrative in which particular genealogical data are mentioned strongly contributes to the ability of the data to communicate desired significance to the rereadership of the book. Thus, the significance of the data and, at points, the data itself seem malleable. Indeed there are numerous differences between the genealogical lists in 1 Chronicles 1–9 and those in its sources.[19]

But it is also worth emphasizing that at all the crucial points for Israel's identity and for the construction of its place in the world, the Chronicler follows tradition. Thus, Adam, Seth, Noah, Abraham, Isaac, Jacob and others all appear at their expected places. In fact, Chronicles communicates the same basic construction of identity in terms of general humanity (see the main signposts, i.e. Adam, Seth, Noah) and of Israel and its neighbors that is developed in the patriarchal narratives. Even the concept of ten generations between Adam and Noah and between Shem and Abraham is maintained. Similarly, Saul remains a Benjaminite, and all the kings of Judah are Davidids, to mention only two obvious examples. The question is why one does *not* find in Chronicles that Jacob or Israel[20] is Abraham's son, or that humanity did *not* begin with Adam;[21] or for that matter that Ishmael, rather than Esau, is Israel's brother?

The most likely answer to this question is that such claims would have contradicted some known 'facts' (hereafter, facts) agreed upon by the community within which the book was composed and first read and reread (i.e. 'consumed' as theological, cultural artifact). Yet there were facts and facts. Not all facts were equal. If one assumes, as it is most likely, that this community's world of knowledge included the book of

---

(2000), and esp. §6.11 and 7.1 (available at www.purl.org/jhs and archived [and available] at the National Library of Canada), and see *idem*, 'Intermarriage, Social Complexity and Ethnic Diversity in the Genealogy of Judah', *JBL* 120 (2001), pp. 15-30.

19. See A. Bendavid, *Parallels in the Bible* (Jerusalem: Carta, 1972), pp. 14-30. Minor differences appear even within Chronicles itself (cf. 1 Chron. 8.29-38 and 1 Chron. 9.35-44).

20. Chronicles (MT) prefers the name 'Israel' over 'Jacob' in the genealogical section (see 1 Chron. 1.34; 2.1), in which the concept of 'the children of Israel' is reflected, communicated and set in the background of all humanity (but see 1 Chron. 16.13, too).

21. The Chronicler could and did omit Eve but could not begin a world history without mentioning Adam or claim that someone other than Adam was the first man. Gender counted.

Genesis, other pentateuchal books and those included in the collection of books usually called the Deuteronomistic History, then it is clear that the Chronicler could and did omit, and even contradict, some of the facts mentioned there. It seems, therefore, that a distinction was drawn between 'core facts' that cannot be challenged and all other facts, within the community within which Chronicles was composed and read. Sure, genealogical changes or shifts were possible within the community's discourse, but outside the core. The central genealogical elements that bear the main narrative of Israel about itself stood already beyond the limits of historical malleability.

In fact, it is because Chronicles shares so much with the accepted genealogical story of Israel about itself, that it is able to persuade at least some of its rereadership to accept or entertain the changes advanced in the text. The Chronicler may subtly attempt to reduce the status of a given fact by omitting or contradicting it, or may advance a particular theological agenda, such as opposition to social and theological streams that come to the forefront in Ezra–Nehemiah (see above). All in all it seems that Chronicles' ability to persuade the rereadership to consider change required the Chronicler not to alter or contradict any of the central pillars of the main genealogical (meta)narrative that provided a sense of self identification to Israel.[22] One may go even further and ask how likely it is for such a society of Israel (Jerusalem centered, Achaemenid period Yehud) to raise a successful historian who would even wish to deny these accepted facts?

2.2 *Some Observations on the Kings of Judah*

Chronicles imitates the regnal accounts in Kings, but as it is well known, it also deviates from them on numerous occasions and for several reasons. It is worth emphasizing, however, that Chronicles does not propose a different list of kings of Judah. Chronicles reports the same kings and in the same sequence as Samuel and Kings.[23] This is

---

22. Other implications will be discussed in §3.

23. Sometimes the names by which the kings are designated are different. For instance, Kings tends to use the name 'Azariah', but Chronicles refers to the same king as 'Uzziah'. Still, the Chronicler learned from Kings that this king could be referred to by two names (Azariah and Uzziah; see 2 Kgs 15.30, 32, 34); the name may be different, but the persona is the same. In fact, Kings' use of the name 'Azariah' seems to have influenced the composition of the report about him in Chronicles (see 2 Chron. 26.7, 15 and the general tenor of the passage). The

particularly noteworthy, since this does not hold true for positions of authority and legitimacy other than kings in monarchic Judah. For instance, the list of prophets mentioned in Chronicles includes many who do not appear elsewhere, and at least some are likely to be created in and shaped by the book of Chronicles. In addition, not only does the book of Chronicles include high priests who were not mentioned in Kings and Samuel, but it also presents a list of high priests that communicates a sense of temporal expansions and contractions according to theological and rhetorical concerns.[24] The Chronicler and the intended (and primary) rereaders of Chronicles could imagine, communicate and accept a past of Israel populated by characters (including a priestly elite) unknown from other sources, but there were limits to such freedom. The composition of the regnal list itself was not an open issue. It seems that within the discourse of the period any construction of the past had to include the same list of Judahite kings advanced in the book of Kings.[25] There was room for historiographic innovation, but there were limits to that innovation too.

Moreover, the book of Chronicles is completely consistent only rarely,[26] but it is so in relation to the composition of the list of kings

---

preference for the name Uzziah may be related to the presence in Chronicles of another character, the prophet Azariah who confronts Uzziah/Azariah. On these matters see, I.L. Seeligmann, 'ניצני מדרש בספר דברי הימים', *Tarbiz* 49 (1979), pp. 14-32 (15-16); H.G.M. Williamson, *1 and 2 Chronicles* (NCB; Grand Rapids: Eerdmans, 1982), pp. 333-34. Slight shifts in the form of the name, such as יחזקיהו instead of חזקיה, or the more theologically satisfying אביה instead of אבים—though see S. Japhet, *I and II Chronicles* (OTL; Louisville, KY: Westminster/John Knox, 1993), pp. 683-84—are of no relevance for the issue at stake here, since the referent of the name, no matter how the name is written, is clearly the same king.

24. Four generations are allocated to the time of Solomon, four to the time between Solomonic Azariah and the reform of Josiah (i.e. well over 300 years in Chronicles' main timeline), and four to the approximately 50 years in that timeline that spans from Josiah (including his entire reign) to the destruction of Jerusalem. On this matter see Ben Zvi, 'About Time'. (The question of whether these connoted expansions and contractions of time are the result of redactional activity is irrelevant for the purpose of the present discussion, since the primary and intended rereaders of Chronicles in its present form were not asked to read it in such a way that would discard portions of it as 'secondary'. They accessed a list, and this list of high priests connoted a clear construction of time.)

25. The same holds true for Josephus, for instance.

26. From the viewpoint of the primary (re)readers of Chronicles (and from that of the implied author of the book, i.e. the Chronicler), this lack of 'consistency' is

and also regarding the length of the regnal periods (and the age of the king at accession). Chronicles does not deviate from the (MT) Kings on those issues,[27] no matter how much it deviates and even contradicts the report in Kings about a particular monarch, and no matter the theological difficulties that maintaining the length of regnal periods may involve.[28] Elsewhere I have developed the idea that inflexibility in this matter is deeply associated with a particular construction of sequential time in Chronicles and with the (implicit or explicit) notion of the king as a marker of social and cosmic time. The latter, of course, reflects and communicates a very high status for the Davidic king.[29]

Since the Chronicler was able to change much from the received sources in relation to other aspects of the regnal accounts, it seems that from the perspective of the Chronicler there were some 'core facts' agreed upon by the community and expressed in the book of Kings about regnal accounts that were beyond malleability. Other facts about them were malleable.

2.3 *Some Observations on the Northern Kingdom*

The division of the kingdom was one of the main events in the narrative of Israel's monarchic past in Yehud and among the literati elite within which Chronicles was composed. According to their story about themselves, the consequences of such a critical event were never erased. Hope for change was left to a distant, utopian future.

As is well known, Chronicles never grants legitimacy to the northern kingdom. This attitude also affects the way in which it construes the historical background of the split of the united monarchy—which is somewhat different from the one advanced in Kings. Still, it is important to stress that Chronicles neither denies the division of David and Solomon's kingdom nor locates it in a different chronological period than does Kings. According to Chronicles, it happened just after the death of Solomon and at the beginning of the reign of Rehoboam. Surely Chronicles shapes the details of the event to convey a particular

not an incidental matter that is best ignored, but an important theological marker. It provides a sense of theological proportion to the book. See my 'A Sense of Proportion: An Aspect of the Theology of the Chronicler', *SJOT* 9 (1995), pp. 37-51.

27. Contrast with LXX Kings or Josephus.

28. On all these issues, see Ben Zvi, 'About Time'.

29. See Ben Zvi, 'About Time'.

meaning,[30] but the basic 'data' associated with the event, such as the matter at stake (i.e. the division of the kingdom), the main characters involved, and the temporal reference, do not seem to be changeable.

Chronicles refers to the northern kingdom as Israel—as was the case in the discourse of the period. To be sure, this way of naming the northern kingdom leads to a situation in which two contemporaneous polities were referred to as 'Israel'. The use of the term for pointing to the northern kingdom in opposition to or as separate from Judah is found in numerous cases in Chronicles (e.g. 2 Chron. 13.12, 15-18; 16.1-4; 17.4; ch. 18 *passim*; 20.35; 21.6), but the term 'Israel' is also used in the book to refer to Judah, the only theologically legitimate polity of Israel during the post-Solomonic monarchic period from the viewpoint of Chronicles (see 2 Chron. 12.5; 17.1; 20.29, 34; 21.2). In fact, the double meaning of Israel (i.e. as referring to two different polities) comes to the forefront in passages in which the two meanings appear in close textual proximity (see 2 Chron. 20.29, 34, 35; 21.2, 6). This situation, of course, calls attention to the question of which polity ought to be considered Israel, which is important in Chronicles' theology and reconstruction of the monarchic period. In addition, in Chronicles—as in the general discourse of the period—the term 'Israel' points to the theological concept of Israel as YHWH's people and as a people with a particular past and commandments to follow.[31] In sum, the term 'Israel' *also* in Chronicles creates an ongoing ambiguity or better potential or actual polyvalence that helps to construct the identity of the intended rereadership, which is also Israel.[32] Chronicles does not

30. See G.N. Knoppers, 'Rehoboam in Chronicles: Villain or Victim?', *JBL* 109 (1990), pp. 423-40.

31. See, for instance, the construction of the past that begins with the genealogies, the references to Moses and the divine commandments associated with him (see 2 Chron. 5.10; 8.13; 23.18; 24.6, 9; 25.4; 30.16; 33.8; 34.14; 35.6, 12), Saul, David, Solomon and the Jerusalem temple, as well the one to its precursor, the tent of meeting that Moses made in the wilderness (see 2 Chron. 1.3), and Davidic instructions concerning the way in which the 'work' of the temple is supposed to be carried out.

32. The use of the term Israel with multiple meanings in Chronicles and the way it expresses a certain theology and develops identity through its tensions is similar to the one present in Mic. 1. See E. Ben Zvi, *Micah* (FOTL, 21b; Grand Rapids: Eerdmans, 2000), pp. 30-31. To be sure, there are constraints on the level of freedom assigned to this polisemy. At times, the potential for theologically unacceptable formulations, which may derive particularly from the use of the term Israel for

deviate from the discourse of its time in this regard.[33] In fact, this potential polyvalence is a theological, literary and meta-narrative necessity at some points in the Chronicler's narrative (see discussion on 1 Chron. 1.9 below).

To be sure, Chronicles removes anything that might suggest that the northern kingdom as a polity was comparable to Judah in theological (or ideological) terms. Chronicles does not recognize the northern kings as legitimate kings of Israel, or their polity as YHWH's kingdom and house (contrast 2 Chron. 17.14). The removal of the reports about the northern kings in Chronicles—which in Kings suggest that the two kingdoms are at least potentially comparable—and the lack of explicit temporal synchronisms between the Judahite and Israelite kings (except in 2 Chron. 13.1) indicate that the kingdoms of Judah and Israel are not similar from YHWH's perspective—and should not be from that of the Chronicler or subsequent rereaders. In all this, Chronicles clearly deviates from the source being imitated, namely Kings.

Still it is important to emphasize that Chronicles explicitly recognized the kings of (northern) Israel as kings (see, for instance, 2 Chron. 16.1, 3; 18.3). Moreover, although not all the kings of Israel are cited,[34] those who are mentioned in the narrative appear at their proper times, as the latter are reported in the book of Kings. So Jeroboam is contemporary with Rehoboam and Abijah, Asa with Baasha, Ahab and

the northern kingdom, led to the presence of some unequivocal sign in the text that serves to mark the referent as the northern kingdom *only*. This may be achieved by presenting a contrast between Judah and Israel (e.g. 2 Chron. 13) or by the addition of fool-proof disambiguating clauses (e.g. 2 Chron. 25.7).

33. On this aspect of the discourse of postmonarchic Israel, see E. Ben Zvi, 'Inclusion in and Exclusion from Israel as Conveyed by the Use of the Term "Israel" in Post-Monarchic Biblical Texts', in S.W. Holloway and L.K. Handy (eds.), *The Pitcher is Broken: Memorial Essays for Gösta W. Ahlström* (JSOTSup, 190; Sheffield: JSOT Press, 1995), pp. 95-149.

34. And why should they? According to the theological organization of the book, the regnal accounts in Chronicles deal with the kings of Judah. The kings of Israel are to be mentioned when it is necessary for the narrative, that is only when they interacted with Judah. It is important to stress that this policy of omission does not imply at all a denial of their existence. It simply communicates a negative stance concerning the place they should take in the historical memory of the community within which and for which Chronicles was composed, and concerning their significance in the larger historical scheme of (theological) Israel. Moreover, these omissions result from the decision to report only the regnal accounts of Judah, so as to avoid any suggestion of comparability between the two polities.

Ahaziah with Jehoshaphat, Jehoram and Jehu with Ahaziahu,[35] Jehoash with Amaziahu, and Pekah with Ahaz. Further, notwithstanding the numerous differences in detail and the significance of the accounts for the message of Chronicles, the *basic* outline of the political interactions between the kings of Judah and Israel are consistent with the world described in Kings.[36]

Moreover, although Chronicles does not reproduce the regnal accounts about the kings of Israel that appear in the book of Kings, their presence is felt in Chronicles. To illustrate, the account of Rehoboam's building activities served as (theologically proper) response to the report about Jeroboam's building activities in 1 Kgs 12.25[37] and implies an authorship and rereadership of Chronicles that is aware of the latter. Significantly, although Chronicles does not mention Jeroboam's building activities, it also does not deny the veracity of the account in Kings either. Instead it deals with the resulting theological dissonance by advancing a report about the far larger building activities of Rehoboam, the legitimate king. Similarly, the exile of northern tribes in Tiglath-pileser III is not mentioned in a place parallel to that in Kings, nor could it have been within the literary and theological frame governing the organization of Chronicles. But such exile is certainly part and parcel of the historical awareness of the Chronicler and of the rereadership of Chronicles, as 1 Chron. 5.25-26 demonstrates. This historical awareness reflects the acceptance of a set of facts about the past agreed upon by the community within which the authorship and rereadership of Chronicles emerged.

In sum, the Chronicler could and did change details, omit references to some known facts about the northern kingdom, and certainly shape the significance of those mentioned in Chronicles. At the same time there was a set of core facts about the northern kingdom that was agreed upon within the community/ies in which and for which Chronicles was

35. Ahaziahu is called 'Azariah' in 2 Chron. 22.6 and 'Ahaziahu' in the rest of the chapter. Both names refer to the same individual, as the context unequivocally requires.

36. For instance, Pekah attacked Ahaz, and there was war between Rehoboam and Jeroboam or Asa and Baasha, but peace and alliance between Ahab and Jehoshaphat.

37. See E. Ben Zvi, 'The Chronicler as a Historian: Building Texts', in M.P. Graham, K.G. Hoglund and S.L. McKenzie (eds.), *The Chronicler as a Historian* (JSOTSup, 238; Sheffield: Sheffield Academic Press, 1997), pp. 132-49 (142-43) and the bibliography cited there.

written. Not only does Chronicles not contradict these agreed-upon facts, but also, at times, it clearly assumes them.

2.4 *Some Observations on Major Events in Judahite Monarchic History*
Undoubtedly an important component of the memory of the monarchic past was the conquest of Jerusalem. Although the details of the conquest in Chronicles are different from those in 2 Samuel,[38] the *basic* outline is similar. In both cases, David marched against the Jebusite city, overcame its resistence, and then rebuilt or repaired it after his conquest. The stronghold of the city is named 'the city of David', and David's name became greater and greater, for YHWH the Lord of Hosts was with him. Whereas there was some flexibility with the details of the story, the basic outline reflects what seems to be a set of facts agreed upon by the community, which were not malleable.[39]

Another major event in the memory of Israel as construed in Yehud was the construction of the (first) temple. Although Chronicles does much to lionize the figure of David and construe him the true founder of the temple,[40] it clearly maintains that Solomon was the actual builder. In addition, Hiram/Huram remains an important secondary character in the story. Further, the description of the dedication of the temple and the report about Solomon's prayer point again at a corpus of facts agreed upon in Yehud. To be sure there is abundant evidence that minor changes in the recounting of the events associated with the building of the temple were allowed—any comparison between the texts immediately shows them—but just as compelling is the evidence that there was a set of core facts from which deviance was impossible.[41]

38. Compare 2 Sam. 5.6-10 with 1 Chron. 11.4-9.
39. Cf. Josephus, *Ant*. 7.61-65.
40. Cf. W. Riley, *King and Cultus in Chronicles: Worship and the Reinterpretation of History* (JSOTSup, 160; Sheffield: JSOT Press, 1993). Temples in antiquity were established by royal orders. The second temple was established by the orders of a Persian king, but the legitimization of the temple mainly in terms of Persian kings was theologically difficult. The legitimization of the second temple and its worship was dependent on its being a continuation of the first. There is the wholly expected emphasis on the Mosaic basis for the first (and second) temple and its worship, but Chronicles construes a past in which the Davidic king par excellence, David, organized its worship in detail. The result is that David, rather than a Persian king, becomes the actual founder of the temple—first and second—at the symbolic and theological level. See E. Ben Zvi, 'What Is New in Yehud', forthcoming in a volume edited by Bob Becking and Rainer Albertz on 'Yahwism after the Exile'.
41. Cf. Josephus, *Ant*. 8.61-129.

The same can be said of many other events in Judah's history. For instance, there is much variation between the Chronicler's account of Sennacherib's confrontation with Hezekiah and the one reported in the book of Kings.[42] The significance of the story is substantially different.[43] However, the core facts are shared: there was an Assyrian campaign, the main characters remain the same, and the result of the campaign is identical. Significantly, the same can be said about the main outline of the report of another crucial event: the destruction of Jerusalem in Zedekiah's reign.

These examples can be multiplied. Whereas the Chronicler could shape the stories of the past of monarchic Judah to a point and construe the significance of events in new ways, the Chronicler did not—and could not—deviate from the basic narrative outline and the basic set of core facts that appeared in the books Samuel and Kings. Although, it is important to notice that Chronicles shows theologically motivated omissions, emendations, additions, explanations and the like, it is as important to notice and emphasize that a set of core facts and outlines seemed to stand beyond malleability also here.

2.5 *Some Observations on 'Missing' Periods in the Israelite Story of their Own Past, on Exodus, Exile and 'Empty Land'*

S. Japhet wrote, 'Chronicles presents a different view of history: the dimensions of the Babylonian conquest and exile are reduced considerably, the people's settlement in the land is portrayed as an uninterrupted continuum, and, in the same way, the constitutive force of the exodus from Egypt is eliminated. Chronicles simply omits the entire historical context—slavery, exodus, and conquest.'[44] These words had an important impact in the study of Chronicles. From the perspective of the endeavor taken up in this paper, several relevant questions may be raised. Were the intended and primary rereaders of Chronicles supposed to construe their past as one characterized by an uninterrupted settlement in the land? And if so, had Sinai—which is, outside the land—no role to play in such a historical reconstruction? Turning to less theologically charged issues, but still significant for the construction of

---

42. Or in Isaiah, for that matter.

43. See E. Ben Zvi, 'Malleability and its Limits: Sennacherib's Campaign Against Judah' in Grabbe (ed.), *'Shut up Like a Bird in a Cage'*.

44. Japhet, *Ideology*, p. 386.

the past of the rereadership, does it follow from the fact that the *main* narrative about the story of the people in the land begins with the death of Saul and the rise of David that the intended and primary rereaders were supposed to construe their past without Joshua, the conqueror of the land, or for that matter without Samuel, since the story of his leadership as reported in 1 Samuel is not included in Chronicles?

Several items are worth considering as one begins to assess these questions. There is only one reference to Joshua the son of Non in Chronicles (1 Chron. 7.27), but one must keep in mind that there is also only one in the text that Chronicles imitates the most, namely Samuel–Kings (1 Kgs 16.34). The reference to Joshua in 1 Chron. 7.27 is at the conclusion of the genealogy of Ephraim. It suggests the presence of a teleological perspective or awareness in this genealogy. Further, S. Japhet correctly observed 'the pedigree of Joshua the son of Non resembles that of David in I Chron. 2.10-15, except that the formula is "X, Y his son", rather than "X begot Y"'.[45] This being so, it is unlikely that the community of rereaders of Chronicles construed (a) the Chronicler as one who was unaware of Joshua's role in Israelite history,[46] and (b) a history in which Joshua had no role. In fact, it is very unlikely that the intended and primary rereaders thought that they were asked by the Chronicler to construe a picture of its past that did not include Joshua. The reason for the absence of a direct reference to Joshua's exploits in Chronicles must, therefore, be found elsewhere. It would suffice at this point to state that this paper will maintain that this absence has do with the thematic structure of Chronicles.

Similarly, the story of Samuel's leadership in 1 Samuel is also absent in Chronicles. There is no parallel to that story, just as there is no parallel to Joshua's narrative. Does it mean that the Chronicler was construed as being unaware of Samuel or that the rereadership of Chronicles was supposed to be persuaded that there was not such a character or that he was essentially irrelevant? The answer to both questions is unequivocal and negative. To begin with, Samuel is mentioned in 1 Chron. 6.28, 33. Here the genealogy of Samuel is attached to that of Kohath. The addition results in a genealogy that is much longer than those of Gershom and Merari. As mentioned above, genealogical time expands

---

45. Since 'Chronicler' here stands for the implied author (or communicator) of the book, it is construed by the readership.

46. Japhet, *I and II Chronicles*, p. 183.

for important periods in Chronicles and contracts for the less significant (see §2.2). In any case, the genealogy provides the required Levitical pedigree for Samuel, and it is based on the texts 1 Sam. 1.1 and 1 Sam. 8.2.[47] Samuel, the seer, is also mentioned in 1 Chron. 9.22, along with David, as those who established the gatekeepers in their offices. Samuel appears as the prophetic (primary) recipient of YHWH's word regarding David's anointing (see 1 Chron. 11.3), which is a major event from the Chronicler's perspective. Samuel is mentioned also in relation to Saul, Abner and Joab in 1 Chron 26.28. In 2 Chron. 35.18 he is characterized not only as a prophet but also as a leader of Israel. Finally there is a reference to Samuel also in 1 Chron. 29.29, which characterizes him as a seer and writer and sets him in the time of David.

The case of Samuel illustrates the need for caution in reaching conclusions from the non-appearance of a story where one would expect it to be, if the Chronicler had been under full obligation to follow the so-called Deuteronomistic History in all its main narratives. The non-appearance of a narrative may be due to many different factors. The study of the understanding(s) of the text within the milieu of its primary and intended rereadership demands consideration of its world of knowledge, discourse and the expectations that the text assumes from its intended rereaders.

It is worth stressing the role that *one's* implied expectations may play in discerning the significance of lack of reference to a character or to his or her story. The case of Samuel in the book of Kings is helpful in this regard. Samuel is not explicitly mentioned anywhere in the books of Kings. To the best of my knowledge, no one concluded from this simple observation that the rereaders of Kings were supposed to be persuaded by the book that there was no Samuel, or that if there was such a character he played no substantial role in the history of Israel. No one, to the best of my knowledge, suggested that such was the intention of the author of Kings. The reason for the absence of these proposals is clear: there was no expectation of the presence of explicit references to Samuel in Kings. Although the name or memory of Samuel could have been mentioned in Kings, this was not necessary. The absence of references to him is explained—if noticed at all—in terms of the thematic structure of 1 Kings. There was no necessity to mention him to advance the book's narrative and theological claims. It

---

47. On these matters, see S. Japhet, *I and II Chronicles*, pp. 153-54.

is assumed that the primary rereadership did not require the explicit mention of Samuel, and that both the author of Kings and the rereadership were already well aware of him.

In sum, the absence of references to a figure or event in the world of knowledge of a community does not necessarily mean denial or even a desire to downgrade such a figure or event. If this holds true for the absence of references, then how much more so for the lower profile that some persons or events assume in the narrative.

With these considerations in mind, we may turn to the theologically charged term 'Sinai'. The word does not appear in Chronicles, but a keen observer would recognize that it rarely appears outside the Pentateuch (Judg. 5.5; Neh. 9.13 and Ps. 68.9, 18). Also there is only one reference to Horeb in Chronicles (2 Chron. 5.10), but again the term 'Horeb' seldom appears outside the Pentateuch.[48] Yet where it occurs in Chronicles is most instructive. It contains an explicit reference to the two tables that Moses placed in the ark at Horeb, when YHWH made a covenant with the children of Israel on their way out of Egypt. It is self-evident that such a text assumes a rereadership familiar with Moses, and whose reconstruction of history includes the covenant at Horeb and the exodus from Egypt. In fact, the text not only utilizes such knowledge for rhetorical purposes—the legitimization of the ark and of Solomon's activities—but also reaffirms it. The narrator's reference to these matters in 2 Chron. 5.10 is further supported by the text of the quotation from YHWH's promise that the Chronicler places in Solomon's mouth.[49] It contains the phrase 'since the day I brought my people out of the land of Egypt' (2 Chron. 6.5), a text that evokes the exodus narrative, along with its main human character (i.e. Moses) and the associated theophanies. References to the exodus also appear in 1 Chron. 17.21 and 2 Chron. 7.22 (and cf. 1 Chron. 17.15).

References to Moses are not rare at all in Chronicles,[50] despite the fact that there is no account of the exodus or of the Sinai/Horeb event in the place that one would assume it to be had the Chronicler been

48. 1 Kgs 5.9; 19.8; Mal. 3.22; Ps. 106.19. Most of the references to Horeb in the Pentateuch are, of course, in Deuteronomy.

49. Solomon is certainly characterized here as a reliable figure.

50. Alternatively, E.M. Dörrfuss has argued that these references to Moses are typically the product of later redactional activity. *Mose in den Chronikbüchern: Garant theokratischer Zukunftserwartung* (BZAW, 219; Berlin: W. de Gruyter, 1994).

obliged or desired to follow the main story line of the Primary History in all its main subnarratives. Moses is mentioned in 1 Chron. 6.34; 15.15; 21.29; 22.13; 23.15; 26.24; 2 Chron. 1.3; 5.10; 8.13; 23.18; 24.6, 9; 25.4; 30.16; 33.8; 34.14; 35.6, 12. He is explicitly associated with the exodus and the Horeb covenant (2 Chron. 5.10), Israel's stay in the wilderness (במדבר; 1 Chron. 21.29; 2 Chron. 24.9), the 'Tent of Meeting' (אהל מועד; 2 Chron. 1.3), the tabernacle (1 Chron. 21.29), Aaron and implicitly with Israel's worship in the wilderness (1 Chron. 6.34), the cultic regulations for the three main festivals (2 Chron. 8.13) and, of course, with Torah or the Book of Torah or the word of YHWH in his hand (2 Chron. 23.18; 25.4; 30.16; 33.8; 34.14; 35.6, 12). There is nothing surprising about these references. Moses, and all the themes associated with him, had a prominent place in the world of knowledge and discourse of the society within which and for which Chronicles was composed. Moreover, Chronicles assumes and interprets many of the instructions and laws in the Pentateuch, especially those regarding the cult.[51] In fact, at times Chronicles attempts to harmonize them.[52] In any event, such a process of interpretation and harmonization assumes the authority of the texts that are interpreted and harmonized. But if Pentateuchal texts (and particularly Exodus–Deuteronomy) are important for the theology of Chronicles—as indeed they are[53]—then how can one expect the Chronicler or the literati for whom Chronicles was primarily written[54] to be dismissive (or ignorant) of the main claims of these texts about Moses, the exodus, Sinai/Horeb, the covenant or the stay in the wilderness?

Within this social, theological and historical context it is certain that the Chronicler was construed by the intended and primary rereadership of the book as an historian who was aware of core facts associated with

51. See, for instance, the following statement by H.G.M. Williamson: 'it should be noted that, despite appearances, there is no superseding of the Mosaic regulations. The Chronicler repeatedly affirms, either by explicit reference or allusion, that as far as was practicable the worship of the temple was ordered in conformity with the stipulations of the Pentateuch', *1 and 2 Chronicles*, p. 30.

52. See, for instance, M. Fishbane, *Biblical Interpretation in Ancient Israel* (Oxford: Clarendon Press, 1988), pp. 135-38.

53. It is worth noting that the Pentateuchal books are more authoritative than Kings or Samuel in Chronicles. On these matters see I.L. Seeligmann, 'ניצני מדרש בספר דברי הימים'.

54. After all, it is a written text whose reading and rereading requires a high level of literacy.

these events in the Pentateuch and in much of biblical literature, in which allusions to them are abundant. In this regard, the Chronicler was not imagined as different from the rereadership at all.[55]

Turning to the question of 'the exile'. It is obviously true that the book conveys a clear sense that the exile is temporally limited (see 2 Chron. 36.21) and that this limitation reflects and reaffirms Israel's authoritative literature (as interpreted by Chronicles).[56] It is also true that the book looks beyond the exile and that it even begins to construe time in a new manner for an Israel (Yehud) not ruled by Jewish kings (see below). Yet it does not follow from any of these considerations that the exile is negated—nor for that matter is the constitutive myth of the community in Yehud, namely the one about exilic Israel returning to an empty land to rebuild the temple when Persia ruled.

The (Babylonian) exile is explicitly mentioned in 1 Chron. 9.1 and 2 Chron. 36.11-20, and at the expected time and during the expected reign. The exile of Judah was not only total in Chronicles (see 2 Chron. 36.20) but *had to be* total, since according to Chronicles the land *had* to be desolate for 70 years to fulfill its sabbaths (following the Chronicler's understanding and harmonization of Lev. 26.34-35, 43 and Jer. 25.11-21; 29.10).[57] If the land was desolate and uninhabited, then any community settling in the land after Zedekiah must come from outside the land. The text makes clear that such a community emerged from the Judeans exiled to Babylonia (2 Chron. 36.20-23). Such an understand-

55. In blunt terms, claims that David brought the children of Israel out of Egypt, that the covenant of Horeb took place in Solomon's days, that associate YHWH's Torah with Hezekiah rather than Moses, that there was no exodus or that Israel should not care much whether there was an exodus or a Sinai event—as construed by postmonarchic communities—would have been unthinkable within that society of literati.

56. Cf. 2 Chron. 36.21-22 with Lev. 26.34-35, 43 and Jer. 25.11-12; 29.10. As I have discussed elsewhere, the language of 2 Chron. 26.21 recalls and makes explicit the story of the exile and the promise of hope that are implicit in Lev. 26.14-45. As such, it associates the text with a sense of fulfillment and legitimacy. The 70 years are explicitly related to Jeremiah (see 2 Chron. 36.21-22; cf. Jer. 25.11-12; 29.10). One of the results of this activity is a legitimization of the prophetic text that is carried out by the explicit reference to its fulfillment. In addition, the fact that it closely links the prophetic text to the Leviticus text serves to create a sense of harmony and coherence among sources that are authoritative for the Chronicler and the community within which and for which Chronicles was composed. On these matters see Ben Zvi, 'About Time' and the bibliography cited there.

57. See preceding note.

ing is consistent with numerous postmonarchic texts and has important implications concerning the concept of Israel.[58]

As mentioned above (§2.3) at times, the potential polyvalence of the term Israel turned into a theological, literary and meta-narrative necessity. The best example of this case in Chronicles is directly relevant to the issue of exile. 1 Chronicles 9.1 states first that 'all Israel was enrolled by genealogies'. Obviously, the Chronicler could not have used 'Judah' to refer to all the tribes and groups whose genealogies precede the verse in the book. Although the signifier remains 'Israel' and so textual cohesion is maintained, the signified (i.e. the referent of Israel) changes in the next clause in the same verse, for it reads 'all Israel was enrolled by genealogies and these were written in the Book of the Kings of Israel'. The same book is mentioned in 2 Chron. 20.34 and 2 Chron. 33.18. Since the kings mentioned are the kings of Judah, and since one of them (Manasseh) reigned after the destruction of the northern kingdom, it is clear that the referent of the word 'Israel' in these verses is not the northern, but rather the southern kingdom, viz., Judah. Moreover, even without the other references to the book, it is extremely unlikely that the Chronicler would have claimed that the best (only?) source for the genealogies of all Israel is the book that reports the deeds of the kings of the northern kingdom. It is much more likely that kings mentioned in 1 Chron. 9.1 are the kings of Judah, and that since their kingdom is the only legitimate polity of Israel, it was called 'Israel' (cf. 2 Chron. 12.5; 17.1; 20.29, 34; 21.2). Textual cohesion and meta-narrative cohesion are maintained by a subtle shift from 'Israel' as the whole of the tribes to 'Israel' as a theologically viewed kingdom, namely, Judah in practical terms. This subtle shift is necessary to maintain the textual and theological cohesion of the entire verse, which as a whole reads, 'all Israel was enrolled by genealogies and these were written in the Book of the Kings of Israel. But Judah [i.e. the "Israel" whose kings were noted in the previous clause] was taken into exile because of their unfaithfulness.' Significantly, the text then moves to a description of new community of Israel formed by the returning exiles (1 Chron. 9.2-38) in Judah (=Yehud).[59]

58. I have discussed some of these matters in Ben Zvi, 'Inclusion in and Exclusion from Israel'.

59. Whether 1 Chron. 9.2-17 is based on Neh. 11.3-19 or vice versa, the textual relation between the two clearly shows an ancient understanding of the text in

Whereas there are historiographic and theological reasons that probably required that Chronicles end with the reference to Cyrus's words
about the rebuilding of the temple in Jerusalem, they do not necessarily
apply to the genealogies. Here, the Chronicler could complete the
presentation of Israel by pointing to the new, postmonarchic, Persian-
period community or commonwealth of Israel (1 Chron. 9) centered on
Jerusalem and its temple.[60]

Further, Chronicles not only looks beyond the exile, but it also considers the exile a turning point: it is at this point of destruction and exile
that sequential time—so consistently construed in regnal terms—ceases.
Significantly, it is replaced in the book with a construction of time in
terms of a textual centeredness, with an emphasis on the coherence,
consistency and legitimacy of the authoritative texts on the one hand
and astronomic or cosmic data on the other.[61]

In sum, it is not only that Chronicles does not deny the exile, but also
that the motif of the exile and much of its mythical and theological roles
in the discourse of Persian-period Yehud are still present in Chronicles,
even if they are not salient in the narrative.[62]

Chronicles as referring to the postmonarchic community. The reference to the exile
of Judah in 1 Chron. 9.1 makes such a referent far more likely than any possible
alternative (cf. already Radak; see Miqraot Gedolot, note on 1 Chron. 9.1, 'And
Judah was carried away into exile to Babylon for their unfaithfulness'). Of course,
if the reference to Judah's exile is removed from the text, or if its value is down-
graded on the claim that it is secondary, then a different text is created. The same
holds true for emendations to the phrase 'the Book of the Kings of Israel'. One may
contrast this approach with that advanced in Japhet, *I and II Chronicles*, pp. 206-
208. The references to Benjamin, or Ephraim and Manasseh (1 Chron. 9.3-9) do not
necessarily point to a return of people other than those exiled from monarchic
Judah (cf. Neh. 11.3-19). See also E. Ben Zvi, *A Historical–Critical Study of the
Book of Obadiah* (BZAW, 242; Berlin: W. de Gruyter, 1996), pp. 197-229. It bears
noting that Chronicles indicates the presence of people from tribes other than Judah
in Jerusalem or Judah in monarchic times (see 2 Chron. 11.13-17; 35.18).

60. Generations of Davidids also continue well beyond the time of the
Babylonian exile in 1 Chron. 3.

61. See Ben Zvi, 'About Time'.

62. On the importance of the concept of exile for the Chronicler, see J.E. Dyck,
The Theocratic Ideology of the Chronicler (BibInt, 33; Leiden: E.J. Brill, 1998).

3. *Conclusions*

3.1 *On the Reason for 'Missing' Accounts or for Slight References to Them*

As mentioned above the exile and return were not highlighted in Chronicles. Similarly, anyone who reads Chronicles against the background of the Primary History immediately recognizes that there are no parallels in Chronicles to many important stories (e.g. the exodus, Sinai) and descriptions of entire periods (e.g. Judges, Samuel) in the Primary History. It has been shown again and again that these supposed 'lacks' should not be construed as evidence for a denial or for an implied request to dismiss or devaluate the periods that are not mentioned, nor their main figures. In fact, these precise figures (e.g. Moses) may be found to hold a central position in Chronicles' theology.

The Chronicler's choice not to describe these events or periods—nor even to refer to them in significant ways[63]—is better explained in terms of the Chronicler's design for the book. Chronicles sets Israel among the nations and structures in genealogical lines, and moves quickly and directly to the (hi)story of the legitimate kingdom of Israel (i.e. the 'united kingdom' of David and Solomon and then Judah). Just as it includes a glimpse of the period leading to the establishment of this kingdom, it contains a glance at the period that follows the fall of monarchic Judah and looks in particular towards the establishment of the new commonwealth in Yehud. The focus on this monarchic polity is consistent with the fundamental importance given to Jerusalem and particularly to the temple (and the legitimization of the second temple in terms of the first), which are central theological themes in Chronicles.[64]

---

63. It goes without saying that there is no need to expect manifold references to an event, when the main account of such an event is not included in Chronicles, because of the reasons mentioned below. On the other hand, there is no need to assume that the Chronicler would systematically erase all references to such an event in the sources that were available for and imitated in the writing of Chronicles. Of course, if there is no expectation of full or consistent mention, there is no 'absence' too. Contrast this approach with that advanced in Japhet, *Ideology*, pp. 380-84, esp. pp. 382-83.

64. As an aside, one may mention the case of an opposite topical selection, namely Pseudo-Philo.

3.2 *On Core Facts Accepted by the Community about its Past and their Implications*

This paper has pointed again and again at a set of 'core facts' about Israel's past that were agreed upon by the literate elite of Yehud. The Chronicler did not challenge these core facts. Nor is it likely that the author(s) of Chronicles could have done so, even had they wished, which is itself an unlikely proposition. It is implausible that ancient Yehudite historians would have simply decided to deny the core facts 'agreed to by all' in their society, particularly those that provided the basis for the main narrative that provides a sense of self-definition and identity to their community. Even if such individuals were to be found, then it would have been extremely unlikely that the community of literati would have accepted such an innovation. The production of a history of Israel—the construction of the people's past—is a social phenomenon. Its writing and later reading and rereading did not take place in a vacuum, but in a social landscape in which discursive and theological expectations (as well as a particular world of knowledge) existed. Although the proposition of alternative facts was certainly a possibility within this milieu, as Chronicles clearly demonstrates, some core elements of the history of Israel agreed upon by the Yehudite elite were not subject to revision.

Finally, the report of facts per se is not necessarily the domain of history writing. History writing, also in antiquity, involved explaining the facts mentioned. The Chronicler offered an explanation of the accepted core facts, on the basis of a particular and quite balanced theology and on historiographic and literary considerations.[65] To be sure, these explanations may develop a power of their own, and their logic sometimes questions aspects of received narratives. Thus, historical explanations begin a process of 'improving' the construction of the past by adding what was likely to have happened and omitting what was unlikely to have happened. Core, agreed facts, however, are unlikely to be subject to such a process since people were sure that they had happened.

---

65. On the aspect of balance in the Chronicler's thought, see my article, 'A Sense of Proportion'. On historiographic and literary considerations, see Kalimi, ספר דברי הימים.

A Projection for Israelite Historiography: With a Comparison Between Qohelet and Nagarjuna

Martin J. Buss

Max Miller has distinguished himself in Israelite historiography (including geography) by giving attention to both literary and archaeological investigations. He was, of course, not the first one to do so, nor was he working alone. Yet his strength lay in interweaving both kinds of consideration.

This scholarly approach fulfilled projections made early in the twentieth century. At that time, archaeological excavations were unearthing data that were relevant for understanding Israelite history. Some rather quick generalizations were made (such as by the 'pan-Babylonian' school). That was understandable and perhaps fruitful for stimulating scholarship. Later work has refined and greatly expanded our knowledge of ancient Near Eastern culture. Not only texts, but also physical artifacts—walls of cities and houses, pottery, animal bones and many other items—have been unearthed and have added greatly to an understanding of the history and culture of the people who lived near the Jordan River.

Much more can still be done in examining evidence that has been discovered in the ancient Near East. Yet investigations in this area have reached a certain maturity, and it is unlikely that analyses that have been made by Miller and others (including John Hayes, who has been a co-author with him) will be overturned altogether.

In a certain way, this situation is comparable to the condition of biblical scholarship at the end of the nineteenth century. At that time, Wellhausen had presented a reconstruction of the history of the literature of the Hebrew Bible that became widely accepted. This reconstruction has not been changed greatly during the twentieth century. It is true, during the first half of the twentieth century, there were moves to assign earlier dates for some of the material (especially, for J).

Subsequently, however, this trend was largely reversed, and dates later than those set forth by Wellhausen have become widely accepted, although some notable scholars date some items earlier than Wellhausen had done. Even if one accepts the largest divergences that have been proposed for the history of Israelite literature, the distance traveled during the twentieth century in regard to this topic is considerably smaller than that traveled during the nineteenth. Twentieth-century discoveries, however, greatly expanded a recognition of the background and history of Israelite society and culture, as distinct from the history of literature. It is in this respect that Miller has made his primary contribution—specifically, by giving attention to archaeology without neglecting the historical criticism of biblical literature that had been established earlier. In my opinion, this line is now also reaching a certain maturity.

The pattern of intellectual development that I am describing can be observed repeatedly in the history of scholarship. Careful investigation of a phenomenon leads to reasonably stable conclusions that are not completely overturned by later study, although they may be modified or expanded. Then, after a certain maturity has been reached in a particular endeavor, a modification or expansion of previous conclusions comes as a result of the introduction of new vistas. These come in the form of data that have not been considered previously (perhaps since they are newly discovered) or in the form of new questions.

It is true, the pattern just outlined is stated in somewhat vague terms, so that it is not very useful for predicting the future. The point at which a given line of endeavor reaches 'a certain maturity' may be clear only in retrospect, when further efforts along the same line appear to have increasingly less effect. For instance, my judgment that this point has been reached in the study of Israelite history in the light of archaeological discoveries may be in error. Nevertheless, an awareness that a cumulative pattern operates has practical implications.

One implication is that scholarly endeavor may indeed achieve what it supposedly seeks to achieve, namely to reach some sort of truth. If it were true that scholarly paradigms follow one another in a noncumulative way, scholarship would make only short-term intellectual contributions. Of course, it can be argued that an absence of long-range contributions is not a problem, for scholarship may still provide insights that are temporarily useful. However, if any conclusions that are reached do not hold in the long run, one can wonder whether it makes sense to say that they are even approximately valid. Perhaps they are simply illusions that accommodate prejudices. Some recent theories of the history of science indeed approximate such a sceptical outlook. However, there have been strong arguments countering this sceptical position.[1] Since I am discussing this issue elsewhere, I will not do so here in a comprehensive way, but only furnish some examples drawn from biblical scholarship.

The most important 'critical' (nontraditional) points regarding the history of the Hebrew Bible—a post-Mosaic date for the Pentateuch and a Maccabean one for Daniel—were made already by early thinkers critical of Christianity. Nineteenth-century scholarship accepted these points and elaborated on them. For a long time, Jewish and Christian biblical scholars engaged in linguistic and formal analyses, which are also still largely valid. The fact that ideological, including socio-political, factors played major roles in all of these endeavors[2] does not mean that no 'truth' was reached. Rather, it reveals the perspectival character of all investigations: only partial truth is ever attained.

This perspective has a significant theological aspect. If it is the case that human beings can attain insights that may be passed on to future generations, then human intellectual activity is not in vain. Biblical religion exhibits a strong element of receptivity toward the divine—a receptivity that can ground an openness to all beings—but human activity, including reflection, is also encouraged in the Bible, most notably in the third division of the Jewish canon. Other religious traditions, too, allow for activity along with passivity. Human beings, in such views, are not simply involved in futile endeavors (although Qohelet is sometimes read that way).

It is true that scholarship appears rather frequently to be conducted in such a way that its only aim seems to be that of scoring points in a competition and of obtaining 'credit' for the writer. A scholarly finding, then, would have no more intrinsic value than a football has apart from its place in a competitive game. Yet, there is a possibility that scholarship can in some way enhance human life. I must admit uncertainty in

---

1. E.g. P. Thagard, *Conceptual Revolutions* (Princeton, NJ: Princeton University Press, 1992). Even Thomas Kuhn, who is often thought to have championed a noncumulative view of science did not, in fact, do so, nor did Foucault in his later years.

2. M.J. Buss, *Biblical Form Criticism in its Context* (JSOTSup, 274; Sheffield: Sheffield Academic Press, 1999).

regard to this possibility, but it seems to me that most of human good involves the cooperation of faith and intelligence.

In any case, there is reason to think that scholarly insights are quite regularly carried beyond their own time as an intellectual contribution to future generations, whether or not they enhance human life in other ways. There is nothing inevitable about such a carry-over, but it does happen repeatedly, so that the potential effect of human activity reaches beyond its own local time. Even when a contribution is forgotten for decades or centuries, later scholars can often retrieve it, as is happening now in relation to medieval Jewish exegesis. Of course, if (or, rather, when) humanity ceases to exist, all this information will in some sense be lost, unless it can be transferred to a successor species. Nevertheless, the possibility (not inevitability!) of a continuing contribution can furnish encouragement to scholars and may also set before them an ethical challenge.

Continuity of scholarship not only furnishes encouragement but also has another important implication: there is no need to repeat the same endeavor indefinitely. Once a given path has reached a saturation or near-saturation point, it is best not to limit oneself to that endeavor, for what has been done already can regularly stand well enough so that it does not have to be redone. This needs to be said, for sometimes it seems easiest simply to go on in a way that is already established. Yet, unless there are new materials to which the procedure can be applied, the problem arises, how one will do better than the one who has worked on this issue earlier. Of course, opening a new path involves a great deal of uncertainty. The first steps on this path will probably require major correction. But is that necessarily a problem?

In regard to the history of Israel, new vistas can be opened by expanding the framework within which one works. During the nineteenth century, the focus was primarily on the testimony furnished by the biblical text. During the twentieth, account was taken of data discovered by archaeologists in the Near East. It is time to move geographically beyond that area. To some extent, African phenomena and Greek traditions have already been drawn into the sphere of consideration. Yet, much more can be done in relation to these, and the written cultures of India and China call for attention far beyond what they have already received.

Of course, distant traditions are not likely to have had a direct influence on ancient Israel.[3] However, a valid question is: What place did the Israelite complex have in the history of humanity? This question is not only interesting intellectually, but it is also important in terms of present social and political concerns, for just as Israel had to face international issues after the exile in a way that it had not needed to do earlier, global issues are now inevitable (not necessarily good, but unavoidable). In fact, a number of non-Western scholars have already presented comparative analyses involving the Hebrew Bible. I have been told that they welcome cooperation and do not wish to be segregated. Certainly, biblical scholars in general should take account of what is being said in this sphere; for that reason alone, they should have a basic knowledge of the history of religions.

In particular, a macrohistorical issue appears in the well-known phenomenon that Israel's 'great' eighth- and seventh-century prophets appeared during a time that approximates the rise of mysticism in India. So far, possible reasons for this phenomenon have been only weakly explored. Were there parallel social conditions that brought about a radical dissatisfaction? Or was dissatisfaction due to the kind of reflection that can be nourished by a literate culture? Is there perhaps some truth in both of these considerations, as well as perhaps in others? Such questions seem to be important for an understanding of history, insofar as understanding is possible. Considerations of this kind are what make a history different from a chronicle.[4]

In addition to assessing the place of Israel in the history of humanity, comparison can shed light on phenomena that might otherwise seem strange. For instance, a major feature of Israelite society was the fact that king and prophet played joint roles at the top, with the king occupying the chief political/military post and the prophet having the chief religious/moral authority. That this was not a purely fortuitous arrangement—such as one based on an arbitrary divine action—can be

---

3. 'Ancient Israel' existed historically in some form, although certain images of it may not be quite correct.

4. Major world-historical observations have already been made by A. Kuenen (*National Religions and Universal Religions* [Hibbert Lectures, 1882; New York: Charles Scribner's Sons, 1882]), W.F. Albright (*From the Stone Age to Christianity: Monotheism and the Historical Process* [Baltimore: The Johns Hopkins University Press, 1940]), and R.K. Gnuse (*No Other Gods: Emergent Monotheism in Israel* [JSOTSup, 241; Sheffield: Sheffield Academic Press, 1997]), but not by many others with a speciality in Hebrew Bible.

seen from the fact that in India the prince and the brahman represented a similar duality. Of course, it is worth noting that the correspondence is not precise.

I will discuss in a little detail only one item: a parallelism between Qohelet and Nagarjuna. As biblical scholars know, Qohelet is often dated about 200 BCE. As many biblical scholars unfortunately do not know, Nagarjuna wrote about 200 CE and is widely thought to have marked a transition to the Mahayana form of Buddhism. The difference in time is not negligible, yet also not huge within the sweep of human history. Qohelet's key word was *hebel*, translated 'vanity' in the KJV. Nagarjuna's key word *sunyata* has commonly been translated 'emptiness'. Both translations are somewhat too negative. 'Vanity' calls forth the idea of sheer nothingness or futility, as does 'emptiness'. However, *hebel* means literally 'mist', something ephemeral. The word can indeed refer to something that is 'in vain', but Qohelet envisions and even celebrates limited pleasures.[5] Nagarjuna's somewhat comparable position was that all objects lack 'substantial' reality, in the double sense that they cannot stand on their own[6] and that they are not lasting. He advocated a 'middle path' between nothingness and solid reality.[7]

The similarity of Qohelet's and Nagarjuna's positions potentially points to several conclusions. First, a sense of relativity, with a degree of scepticism about recognizable order, is old and widespread (in fact, it has appeared elsewhere in the ancient Near East, in Greece, in China and in oral cultures).[8] Second, this sense may have been especially pronounced near the beginning of our time reckoning, although this possible conclusion must be stated cautiously in view of the perennial

5. See, e.g., M.V. Fox, *A Time to Tear down and a Time to Build up: A Rereading of Ecclesiastes* (Grand Rapids: Eerdmans, 1999) for data and previous positions. His interpretation of *hebel* as meaning 'absurdity', however, is probably somewhat one-sided.

6. In Aristotelian and subsequent philosophy, 'substance' means something that can stand on its own. Thus this word can be used as an English translation for *svabhava* ('inherent existence' [D.F. Burton, *Emptiness Appraised: A Critical Study of Nagarjuna's Philosophy* (Richmond, Surrey: Curzon Press, 1999), p. 2]), which, according to Nagarjuna, beings do not have.

7. See, e.g., Burton (*Emptiness Appraised*) for data and previous positions. His interpretation of 'emptiness' as 'mental construction' seems to be less than adequate and leads him to charge Nagarjuna with inconsistency.

8. Cf. P. Radin, *Primitive Man as Philosopher* (New York: D. Appleton, 1927), pp. 375-84.

character of such an outlook. Third, more-or-less mild scepticism of this sort may be current especially among intellectuals, that is, among persons who spend much of their time in thought. Finally, there were specific historical connections between the cultures to which Qohelet and Nagarjuna were indebted. This fourth conclusion has to some extent been pursued by particularist historians, but the mere fact of a historical connection tells us very little about the meaning of the two positions.[9] The other conclusions, insofar as they are valid, are trans-historical in character and have implications also for the present. For instance, in today's culture, intellectuals—or, at least, academics—are those most inclined toward scepticism.

One can ask whether an awareness of Nagarjuna's position can aid an understanding of Qohelet (or vice versa). In dealing with this issue, one has to resist a temptation to read one work too much in terms of the other, for two reasons: (1) individual traditions and thinkers do differ in important ways, and (2) the precise nature of the positions in question is subject to considerable debate. (For both positions, I have presented what seems to me to be a reasonably adequate interpretation, but if I am wrong for one of them, a positive comparison between the two may become questionable.)

Nevertheless, some interesting explorations are possible. For that purpose, one must consider Nagarjuna's position somewhat carefully. Nagarjuna arrived at a conclusion that became a central theme of Mahayana Buddhism. He argued that since all beings are 'empty' or insubstantial (conditioned and relative), they are in a sense equivalent to nirvana, the mystical no-thing. Nirvana, then, is not to be sought out-side of the realm of *samsara* (that is, ordinary existence), but *in samsara* by recognizing its insubstantiality. Thus a basic Mahayana formula is: samsara = nirvana. This quasi-equation of the two bears a resemblance to the Christian doctrine that salvation is available in the present. In fact, a striking macrohistorical phenomenon is that the

9. That Qohelet was in part indebted to the form of Buddhism that preceded him was argued by E.J. Dillon in 1895 (*The Sceptics of the Old Testament: Job, Koheleth, Agur* [London: Isbister, 1895], pp. 122, 129). In fact, there is reason to think that Hellenistic scepticism received an impact from Buddhism; thus Buddhism may have had an indirect influence on Qohelet. S. Lorgunpai ('The Books of Ecclesiastes and Thai Buddhism', *AsJT* 8 [1994], pp. 155-62) compared Qohelet with Thai Buddhism (which is thought to be in line with the older type of Buddhism), without considering a possible historical connection between them.

theme of a present transcendence of existence (joined with a certain acceptance of existence) has been prominent in two world religions for the past two millennia.[10] (Do they express a deep alienation that is only overcome paradoxically?)

In comparing Qohelet with Nagarjuna, one can observe both an important difference and an important similarity. A difference lies in the fact that Qohelet, unlike Nagarjuna, did *not* find a mystical presence or absence in the day-to-day world (perhaps Qohelet reflected an alienation that was less severe so that it did not need to be overcome—after all, God plays a role in creating, giving and so forth in the book). A similarity between them, however, lies in the fact that Qohelet found enjoyment in the fleeting and, in many ways, unjust world. One of the major puzzles of the book of Qoheleth has been how to relate its affirmative to its sceptical statements. It is not my intention to solve this problem here, but Nagarjuna's writing shows that a joining of the two sides was not unique. Does that say something to us, too, especially to those of us who are intellectuals in some sense?

The example I have discussed belongs not so much to political as to social and cultural history. In fact, 'cultural' history has recently been a major focus within the discipline of history and is worth being pursued by biblical studies. It thus represents an open area for Israelite historiography, one that perhaps cannot be carried out well without attention to comparative issues.

In short, major opportunities lie ahead for the study of Israelite history. Although studies focusing on the ancient Near East should not cease, it would be good if they are complemented by a wider vision. Miller's careful examination of Israelite history, then, will not simply be overthrown but extended.

---

10. There is even a possibility that some Christian stimulation contributed to Nagarjuna's view, but even if there should have been a connection between these two religious traditions, one cannot rightly explain huge international movements on the basis of a minor, more or less accidental, contact. Some more intrinsic shift (a growing social alienation?) appears to be at work.

DID SAULIDE–DAVIDIC RIVALRY RESURFACE
IN EARLY PERSIAN YEHUD?*

Diana Edelman

Since my first meeting with Max was at the 1986 SBL Meeting to discuss my then recently completed dissertation dealing with the rise of the Israelite state under Saul, it seems only fitting to revisit an aspect of the Saul narrative in this piece dedicated to him as a colleague, mentor, and friend. Our mutual interest in Saul over the years has been a common bond between us, and I have valued our many conversations that have moved on to cover many aspects of history, archaeology, and texts in the past 16 years. Thank you, Max, for treating a young, budding scholar as an equal and serving as a role model for a historian in an era when history had entered its 'dark age' in biblical studies.

Introductory Considerations

The present form of the books of Samuel provides divine justification for the replacement of the Saulide dynasty by the Davidic dynasty and grants an eternal covenant to the Davidic line. The sanctity of the Lord's anointed is a strong theme in the materials as well. Neither Saul nor David is idealized or totally vilified; both are depicted as flawed human beings with both achievements and failures, and in the end YHWH's rejection of Saul seems to lack cogent grounds, especially in light of his allowing David's dynasty to continue after the king's many episodes of bad judgment. To a modern reader at least, the narrative raises questions of divine fairness, highlighting the unpredictability of the divine nature and accenting divine whim. It leaves the final impression that no

*   This article expands upon ideas presented in a paper entitled, 'Why Is Saul Not YHWH's Chosen?', which I presented at the 2000 annual SBL meeting in Nashville. I wish to thank the British Academy for awarding me an Overseas Conference Grant to help defray the meeting expenses.

king can rule adequately; all will inevitably make mistakes that will have certain adverse effects on the nation. The question asked by the men of Beth Shemesh in 1 Sam. 7.19 ('Who is able to stand before YHWH, this holy God?') reverberates strongly as a key issue, suggesting, perhaps, that the elimination of kingship in favor of YHWH's direct rule over his people is the inevitable solution to a situation being addressed by either the author of 1 Samuel or a subsequent editor.

The range of themes and issues noted above seem to reflect at least two different socio-historical situations: one in which the question of whether a Saulide or Davidide should be head of the nation, where tensions were running high enough that the message that YHWH's anointed was sacrosanct was deemed necessary to head off assassination; and one in which this issue becomes irrelevant, and the elimination of a human king from leading the nation is being endorsed. In this article I will focus on identifying the likely social situations that gave rise to each of the two central ideologies visible in 1 and 2 Samuel.

The original author of 1 and 2 Samuel had an audience in mind for the composition, as did subsequent editors and redactors of the work. Since only the educated elite of society would have been able to read and write, and since the narrative is in written form, its primary target audience would have been the aristocracy and court in whatever period it was written. This is also true of subsequent audiences for the editors and redactors. It is possible that we need to consider a wider, original intended audience or subsequent audience that included illiterate members of the society as well, if the text were written for formal reading aloud. We cannot know, however, whether this was a regular practice or not, or even whether certain texts eventually were popularized in ancient times and given a wider actual audience than the one originally intended by the author. The situation envisioned in Nehemiah 8–9 of the public reading of the Law of Moses may have been an exception rather than the rule; it is purported to be the official means of promulgating the legal code for the inhabitants of Yehud. Whether the narrative in 1 Samuel 8–1 Kings 3 would ever have been read to common people in the context of a religious occasion (as the readings of the Exodus account at Passover or the book of Esther at Purim) is equally unclear.

Eventually, when this narrative became part of a larger body of writings deemed canonical for various religious communities, it came to be read on an annual cycle to people in the context of worship, thus broadening its actual audience. At this point, however, the context of the narrative had also changed from its original composition—addressed to a narrow, elite audience for the purpose of legitimizing claims of the Davidic monarchy to rule rather than the Saulide monarchy—to a broad audience for the purpose of depicting the relationship of a deity named YHWH to a particular group of people over time as a basis for asserting the god's worthiness of loyalty and worship.

Saulide–Davidic Rivalry, the Eternal Davidic Covenant, and the Sanctity of YHWH's Anointed

Since 1 Samuel does not stand alone but is an integral part of the larger Deuteronomistic History, the ramifications of the proposed social settings that produced the two outlined ideologies will need to be considered separately.

Some preliminary observations should be made as we consider a likely social setting for the themes (noted above) that justify the Davidic takeover of the Saulide throne, confirm the Davidic right to rule through an eternal covenant initiated by YHWH, and stress the sacrosanctity of YHWH's anointed. First, any setting should explain why the rivalry is between the Davidic and the Saulide dynasties, and not, for example, the Omrides or the line of the last Israelite king, Hoshea. If, for example, the purpose is to lay the groundwork to legitimate Davidic rule in the territories that were formerly part of the nation of Israel but that had become the Assyrian province of Samerina, why would a story about YHWH replacing the first northern dynasty with the Davidides help strengthen that case? It would seem to be more logical to demonstrate how the Davidides were made divine successors to the last (rather than the first) dynasty in such a case. In addition, the implied audience would seem to need to include members of Judah (or its successor, the Persian province of Yehud) and members with Israelite or Benjaminite roots (Israelite, since Saul was the first king of Israel; and Benjaminite, more specifically because Saul was a Benjaminite). There seems little point otherwise in spending so much space justifying the Davidic replacement of the Saulides.

The eternal dynastic covenant initiated by YHWH in 2 Samuel 7 reinforces the message that the Saulides have been divinely rejected in favor of the Davidides but goes beyond it to emphasize that the replacement period is eternal. Even if individual future Davidic kings act disobediently, YHWH promises that they will be chastised, but not rejected as was Saul (vv. 14-16). The covenantal theme seems designed to counter an argument that YHWH inserted David into the Saulide line as a temporary interloper but did not intend his descendants to rule after him in place of Saul's descendants. Thus, it seems to imply that some group in the community is asserting the right of Saulides to rule over against Davidides.

The stress on the sacrosanctity of the king or king-elect[1] as YHWH's anointed implies that there is conflict within the community at the time of writing that could easily end in royal assassination. When combined with the first two themes, the conflict can be seen to be over whether a Saulide or Davidide should be king or king-elect.

Two social settings are plausible for explaining the three related themes and their implications as described above: (1) the tenth century BCE, in the immediate aftermath of either Saul or Eshbaal's death, and (2) the last third of the sixth century BCE, soon after the appearance of either Sheshbazzar or Zerubbabel and Yeshua to claim leadership of the Persian province of Yehud. In the first instance, tensions would have run high in certain circles in Israel when David replaced the Saulide dynasty on the throne. Assassination of David would have been a looming possibility, especially in the wake of Eshbaal's assassination. The eternal Davidic dynasty would have been a logical ideological strategy to gain acceptance of David and his line in the North.

The problem with a tenth-century setting is that the narrative in its current form has several historical inaccuracies that are apparent to modern scholars.[2] It seems unlikely that the narrative would have been effective on its intended target audience if it contained lies that were

---

1. Since both Saul and David are depicted as YHWH's anointed ones simultaneously in the narrative in 1 Sam., it seems wise to extend the concept of anointed one to include a king-elect, as David was, as well as the king, which is the usual sense associated with anointing. I suspect that the practice of anointing the high priest was a late, secondary phenomenon that developed after the demise of kingship, when the office of high priest evolved and took over the former role of royalty as temporal head of the nation in addition to serving in a new post, that of head of the religion.

2. For details of four, see D.V. Edelman, 'The Deuteronomist's Story of King Saul: Narrative Art or Editorial Product?', in C. Brekelmans and J. Lust (eds.), *Pentateuchal and Deuteronomistic Studies: Papers Read at the XIIIth IOSOT Congress, Leuven 1989* (BETL, 94; Leuven: Peeters; Leuven University Press, 1990), pp. 218-19.

readily discernible by members of the ancient audience. The target audience would seem to have been primarily the elite of the former Saulide court, who needed to be persuaded that David was the legitimate heir to the Saulide throne, but secondarily also the elite of Judah, who would be expected to uphold the Davidic claim of legitimacy. Since the target audience was most likely the elite of both courts, it is probable that they were well informed about the political machinations of their days through gossip and rumor. So, for example, to claim that Eshbaal was 40 years old when he became king (2 Sam. 2.10), when the genealogies indicate he was Saul's youngest son (1 Chron. 8.33; 9.39) and the eldest son, Jonathan, was probably only in his twenties when he died, having fathered a single infant son (2 Sam. 4.4; 9.1-4), would dupe no one at either court. Eshbaal's survival at the battle of Gilboa was due to his failure to be old enough to fight alongside his older brothers, making him a minor, perhaps a young teen, at his accession to the throne.

A date in the last third of the sixth century BCE, after the return of members of the *golah* community to Yehud and the appointment of a Persian-approved leader from the *golah*, provides another cogent setting in which Davidic–Saulide rivalry could have surfaced anew. Those living in the villages that did not go into exile in 586 BCE, located primarily in the territory of Benjamin, were included within the borders of the Persian province of Yehud and would likely have favored the appointment of a descendant of the Saulide throne to be the new governor and puppet king of Yehud. Saul was of Benjaminite origin, so interest in the re-establishment of his dynasty in particular (as opposed to a Davidide) would have been strong. Since they were descendants of the court elite of Jerusalem who went into exile in 598 and 586 BCE, members of the *golah* community, on the other hand, would have favored the re-establishment of a Davidic descendant to power.[3]

---

3. My proposed two factions correspond in some ways with Morton Smith's 'local' and 'YHWH alone' parties in Yehud, but his are defined primarily on the basis of religious beliefs, whereas mine are in terms of regional allegiance and loyalty to a particular royal line. He argues that some of the locals would have joined the YHWH-alone party, because they were not syncretists, and that not all who returned from Babylon would have had YHWH-alone leanings, including some of the priests. My groupings imply that local loyalty would have taken precedence over religious beliefs so that those returning would have felt they had little in common with those who had not experienced exile, regardless of their views about the exclusivity of YHWH as the only god in heaven (M. Smith,

Three scenarios are possible. The first two would have taken place after the arrival of Sheshbazzar as a government appointee. His royal ancestry is not transparent in the texts, where no patronymic is given at all. As S. Japhet has argued, however, the books of Ezra–Nehemiah, which contain all references to Sheshbazzar, seem to have deliberately downplayed the Davidic connections of early Persian appointees in order to discourage any attempts to use them or their descendants as centers of rebellion against the Persian empire in bids to re-establish a Davidide on the throne of an independent kingdom of Judah.[4] Thus, although it is possible to conclude from the lack of patronymic that Sheshbazzar was not of Judahite ancestry, let alone Davidic lineage,[5] it is equally possible that he was, in fact, of royal blood.

Were Sheshbazzar of Davidic ancestry, his appointment by the Persian court would have led to dissatisfaction among the Benjaminite sector, who felt that a Saulide descendant had as legitimate a claim to leadership as a Davidic descendant, if not more so. In the wake of their official protests to the Persian court, the *golah* leadership would have composed the sections of 1 and 2 Samuel that (1) justify the Davidic succession to the throne in place of the Saulide dynasty, (2) argue that the Davidides have a divinely guaranteed eternal covenant to rule, and (3) stress that the king or king-elect is sacrosanct. Their target audience would have been the elite of Yehud, belonging to both factions, but primarily, the Persian court. The narrative would have functioned as a justification to the new Persian overlords that asserted the historical primacy of the Davidic house over the Saulide house, thus maintaining Sheshbazzar in power. The Benjaminites may or may not have submitted a separate written appeal to the Persian authorities, but as the losers in the contest, whatever they may have produced has not survived.

Palestinian Parties and Politics that Shaped the Old Testament [Lectures on the History of Religions, NS, 9; New York: Columbia University Press, 1971], pp. 99-125).

4. S. Japhet, 'Sheshbazzar and Zerubbabel: Against the Background of the Historical and Religious Tendencies of Ezra–Nehemiah', *ZAW* 94 (1982), pp. 66-98.

5. So, e.g., P.R. Ackroyd, *Exile and Restoration: A Study of Hebrew Thought of the Sixth Century B.C.* (OTL; London: SCM Press, 1968), p. 143; H.G.M. Williamson, *Ezra, Nehemiah* (WBC, 16; Waco, TX: Word Books, 1985), pp. 17-19; G.W. Ahlström, *The History of Ancient Palestine from the Palaeolithic Period to Alexander's Conquest* (JSOTSup, 146; Sheffield: JSOT Press, 1993), pp. 837-39.

Were Sheshbazzar of non-Judahite ancestry, dissatisfaction within both the newly arrived *golah* community and the established Benjaminite community over the appointment of someone without royal pedigree to be in charge may well have led to conflict.[6] Both sides could have petitioned the Persian authorities to remove Sheshbazzar in favor of a descendant of royal blood, but then each side could have demanded that their royal line be appointed in his stead, setting forth arguments to support their candidate. The portions of 1 and 2 Samuel that justify the Davidic succession to the throne in place of the Saulide dynasty, argue that the Davidides have a divinely guaranteed eternal covenant to rule, and stress that the king or king-elect is sacrosanct, would reflect the views of the leaders of the *golah* community. Their target audience would have been the elite of Yehud, belonging to both factions, but primarily the Persian court. The narrative would have functioned as a justification to the new Persian overlords for the historical primacy of the Davidic house over the Saulide house. Since the *golah* community gained political ascendancy in the province, their version has been preserved; whether the Benjaminite opposition also wrote a version of the past to justify their claims to Saulide legitimacy is not known.

The third scenario would have taken place after the arrival of Zerubbabel to serve as governor of Yehud. As with Sheshbazzar, his Davidic ancestry is not transparent in the books of Ezra–Nehemiah nor in Haggai or Zechariah, where he is simply given the patronymic 'son of Shealtiel', with no explicit Davidic connections. However, 1 Chron. 3.19 names Shealtiel as the son of Jeconiah, but then proceeds to make Zerubbabel the son of Pedaiah, Shealtiel's brother, rather than Shealtiel

---

6.   Cyrus appears to have continued the Babylonian policy of administration in territories that had belonged to Babylon (J.L. Berquist, *Judaism in Persia's Shadow: A Social and Historical Approach* [Minneapolis: Fortress Press, 1995], p. 24). Since the Babylonians had initially made a member of the royal line governor in 586 BCE, the use of members of the native dynasty as provincial officials should have been an acceptable practice. A review of Yehud's brief provincial history under Zedekiah and Gedaliah would have demonstrated the wisdom in appointing a member of the Davidic house as governor to discourage assassination. Whether Yehud had subsequent Babylonian governors after Gedaliah or was simply placed under the jurisdiction of the governor of Samerina is not known. For the strong assertion that the Persians continued the earlier policy of keeping defeated kings on the throne as governors, see P. Sacchi, *The History of the Second Temple Period* (JSOTSup, 285; Sheffield: Sheffield Academic Press, 2000), pp. 51-75.

himself. Nevertheless, it assigns him Davidic ancestry in either case, even if one considers the Zerubbabel, son of Pedaiah, to be a different person. In addition, Hag. 2.20-23 states that YHWH Sebaot was soon going to make Zerubbabel, his chosen one and servant, as his signet ring after overthrowing the strength of the nations and destroying their armies. Jeremiah 22.24 describes Jeconiah as the signet ring on YHWH's right hand, demonstrating the use of this expression for a member of the Davidic royal line. Thus, it is highly probable that Zerubbabel was of Davidic ancestry.

Zerubbabel's appointment by the Persian court would have led to dissatisfaction among the Benjaminite sector, who felt that a Saulide descendant had as legitimate a claim to leadership as a Davidic descendant, if not more so.[7] In the wake of their official protests to the Persian court, the *golah* leadership would have composed the sections of 1 and 2 Samuel that justify the Davidic succession to the throne in place of the Saulide dynasty, argue that the Davidides have a divinely guaranteed eternal covenant to rule, and stress that the king or king-elect is sacrosanct. Their target audience would have been the elite of Yehud, belonging to both factions, but primarily, the Persian court. The narrative would have functioned as a justification to the new Persian overlords for the historical primacy of the Davidic house over the Saulide house, in order to maintain Zerubbabel in power. The Benjaminites may or may not have submitted a separate written appeal to the Persian authorities, but as the losers in the contest, whatever they may have produced has not survived.[8]

An interrelated issue that would have been raised in any of the three scenarios would have been the site that was to become the new provincial capital and house the rebuilt sanctuary of YHWH.[9] Since

---

7.   This scenario would require Sheshbazzar not to have been of Davidic ancestry, so that the issue would not have been raised at his appointment, and it would also point to the recent arrival of a significant *golah* community with Zerubbabel and Joshua that supported the former's right to govern.

8.   My understanding of the intended audience, regardless of which of the three social settings is adopted, is a revision of my comments about intended audience in my earlier book, *King Saul in the Historiography of Judah* (JSOTSup, 121; Sheffield: Sheffield Academic Press, 1991), p. 21. There I include the wider Judahite citizenry in the original audience alongside the court elite. I now suspect that there was a widening of the intended and actual audiences over time in the post-exilic period, as the history was edited and used in new ways.

9.   While it appears that Cyrus planned to use sanctuaries rebuilt at royal

religion went hand in hand with government, it would have been likely that an administrative center, even in a backwater area such as Yehud, would have included a temple dedicated to the native deity. Mizpah may have continued to serve as the seat of provincial government under Cyrus, had it remained the seat of Babylonian control after Gedaliah's murder. If so, a new seat would not have been needed but may have been lobbied for in anticipation of the appointment of a member of one of the two royal houses as governor. In each case, the argument would have been to return to the historical seat of power.

It is possible, however, that after Gedaliah's murder, the remaining intact villages in Judah were annexed to the province of Samerina. In this case, the appointment of a provincial governor for Yehud would have required the selection of a site to serve as the new provincial seat. The *golah* community's push for a Davidide to be in charge of Yehud would simultaneously have advocated Jerusalem as the site of the rebuilt temple of YHWH and the site of the local Persian seat of power and administration. The Benjaminite push to place a descendant of Saul in charge of Yehud, however, may well have included a bid to make Saul's old capital, the site of the first sanctuary of YHWH during the monarchy, and the predecessor to Jerusalem, to become the local Persian seat of power and administration. While the Deuteronomistic historian has gone to some lengths to conceal the identity of this site, various factors point to Gibeon as Saul's capital and the home of the first national sanctuary.[10]

Corroborating evidence to support the proposed date in the late sixth century BCE for the resurgence of Saulide–Davidic rivalry is meagre but arguably present in two sets of post-exilic texts: the Gibeonite genealogies in 1 Chronicles and Zech. 12.10-14. 1 Chronicles 8.29-40 and 9.35-44 shows that some group maintained interest in the genealogy

expense as bases of local Persian administration in strategic or central cities that had been part of the former Babylonian empire, he does not seem to have extended this policy routinely to outlying or backwater areas of the former empire such as Yehud. For details, see P.R. Bedford, *Temple Restoration in Early Achaemenid Judah* (JSJSup, 65; Leiden: E.J. Brill, 2001), pp. 132-57. Darius continued Cyrus' policy in the early years of his reign but then reorganized the consolidated holdings of the empire into new administrative units headed by loyal Persian appointees (Berquist, *Judaism*, p. 54).

10. E.g. J. Blenkinsopp, 'Did Saul Make Gibeon his Capital?', *VT* 24 (1974), pp. 1-7.

of the Saulide house down to the post-exilic community, and both genealogies link the Saulides to the town of Gibeon. The first occurrence in ch. 8 presents the Saulides as descendants of Benjamin before the exile, while the same genealogy recurs in ch. 9 as a bridge between the account of the resettlement of Jerusalem in the Persian era (9.1-35), when some Saulides moved from Gibeon into Jerusalem, and the severely abridged Saul–David narrative. The genealogy indicates that interest in the royal house of Saul was kept alive within Benjamin in particular and that there was a close link between the Saulide house and the site of Gibeon.

A careful examination of the two genealogies in Chronicles indicates that the Saulide family tree has been grafted secondarily onto the Gibeonite list. The appearance of a certain Ner in both lists allowed the Chronicler to accomplish his task with relative ease. In 1 Sam. 9.1, Ner is listed as Saul's uncle, the father of Abner. Elsewhere in tradition, Ner is consistently named as Abner's father (1 Sam. 14.50, 51; 26.5, 14; 2 Sam. 2.8, 12; 3.25, 28, 37; 1 Kgs 2.5, 32; 1 Chron. 26.28), and so his status as Saul's uncle (and not his grandfather, as in 1 Chron. 8.33 and 9.39) seems historically correct. By fictitiously making Ner Kish's 'father' instead of his brother, and by eliminating the names of Saul's genuine ancestors that were available in 1 Sam. 9.1, the Chronicler was able to graft the Saulide genealogy onto that of Gibeon by implying that Jeiel's son, Ner, was the same person as Saul's uncle. From the wider context in 1 Chronicles 1–10, it can be seen that Jeiel was the 're-founder'[11] of Gibeon in the post-exilic period.[12] His 'son' Ner could not possibly have been identical with Saul's uncle.

---

11. Jeiel's status in Gibeon is difficult to assess. He may be (1) an individual or a clan, and (2) he/they may represent members of the *golah* community who have taken up residence in Gibeon among an existing local population (or may simply represent the main authority in Gibeon, a settlement that continued to be occupied after 586 BCE by those who were not exiled). In the latter case, Jeiel's presentation as the 'refounder' would be a deliberate fiction intended to imply that the community of Gibeon was started anew after the return of the *golah* community. This, then, would represent a compromise position, in which non-*golah* inhabitants were being accepted by the *golah* authorities by creating a fiction that they had returned, rather than simply stating that Israel in the post-exilic community included local and *golah* members.

12. Jeiel's status as the post-exilic refounder of Gibeon has also been acknowledged by W. Rudolph, *Chronikbücher* (HAT, 21; Tübingen: J.C.B. Mohr [Paul Siebeck], 1955), p. 81.

The Gibeonite–Saulide genealogy in 1 Chron. 9.35-44 currently serves as a bridge between the introductory section detailing Israel's ancestry and roots (1 Chron. 1.1–9.45) and the narrative section that explains how the tribes were exiled and subsequently restored to their homeland. The introduction is an extremely abbreviated summary of the ensuing narrative section. After depicting Israel's place among the nations and elaborating its tribal genealogies from the pre-exilic period, it mentions the exile (1 Chron. 9.1) and then immediately moves on to the restoration (1 Chron. 9.2), focusing specifically on the re-establishment of Jerusalem (1 Chron. 9.3-44). 1 Chronicles 10.1 begins the narrative account that explains how and why the exile occurred, beginning with Saul's death at the hand of the Philistines for his unfaithfulness to YHWH (1 Chron. 10.13-14).

The other Gibeonite unit appears as a secondary detail in the section that deals with the post-exilic settlement of Jerusalem. In 1 Chron. 9.7-9, the names of Benjaminite family leaders who resettled in Jerusalem are given. Jeiel and his clansmen are introduced as relatives of those Benjaminites who resettled in Jerusalem (v. 38), who were dwelling opposite their relatives in Gibeon.[13] While describing the re-founding of Gibeon, the main focus is still on Jerusalem. The report of the Saulide genealogy then begins to shift the time-frame and focus to Gibeon. One learns that the town of Gibeon in the earlier monarchic period, indeed, at the very founding of the monarchic era, was the home of the first royal family. The main function of 1 Chronicles 9, then, is to set the scene for the unfolding of the subsequent story that will involve interaction between these two neighboring settlements with royal connections. Jerusalem is clearly depicted as the central focus of the post-exilic community, hinting that Gibeon's early pre-eminence will become eclipsed by Jerusalem during the course of the monarchic period until it is finally replaced during the postexilic rebirth of the nation. At this time, former Gibeonite clans and families will choose to dwell in Davidic Jerusalem instead of their old Saulide home of Gibeon, signalling their acknowledgement of YHWH's chosen family and home.

---

13. By understanding the larger ideological setting, it becomes clear that the context in 1 Chron. 9 is the one that generated the formation of the combined Gibeonite–Saulide genealogy, rather than the one in 1 Chron. 8. The latter occurrence is a secondary use to supply details for the Benjaminite genealogy. The absence of Ner from the list of Jeiel's sons in 1 Chron. 8.32 can be seen as an accidental loss in light of the name's pivotal function.

The Chronicler's linking of the royal Saulide genealogy with the city of Gibeon appears to have been motivated primarily by his perception that Gibeon had served as the official religious sanctuary of Israel under the Saulides and David. References to Gibeon in the introductory section of the Chronistic History, especially 1 Chronicles 1–2, focus on its role as the legitimate predecessor to Jerusalem in the monarchic period, where Solomon went to receive the divine command to build a new temple in a new location (2 Chron. 1). By contrast, the Deuteronomistic historian seems to have deliberately avoided making references to Gibeon in the Saulide era in a context that would reveal its function as Saul's capital and has removed the dream incubation from any immediate context that would have made it clear that Gibeon had functioned as the national sanctuary under Saul and David (1 Kgs 4–5).

The excavations at Gibeon el-Jib provide material remains that point to the association of Saulide-related clans with Gibeon. Among the hundreds of wine jars dated to the Iron II period[14] are some with the personal or clan name of Nera' inscribed on the handles.[15] The final *aleph* suggests that this is an Aramaicized form of the name Ner/Neriah/Neryo. As already noted, Ner figures prominently in tradition as Saul's uncle and appears to have served as the point of overlap between a list of Gibeonite clans and the Saulide genealogy. This is probably not simply coincidence; there are a number of hints scattered throughout the Hebrew Bible that Saul's home town was Gibeon, even though the Deuteronomistic History has worked hard to disguise this fact.[16] Thus,

14. J.B. Pritchard, *Winery, Defenses, and Soundings at Gibeon* (Museum Monographs; Philadelphia: University Museum, University of Pennsylvania, 1964), esp. pp. 12-17.

15. J.B. Pritchard, *Gibeon Where the Sun Stood Still: The Discovery of the Biblical City* (Princeton, NJ: Princeton University Press, 1962), p. 47. In addition, other handles bear the name or term 'gedor', which also appears as a Gibeonite clan in 1 Chron. 8.29 and 9.35 but is not part of the appended Saulide genealogy (Pritchard, *Gibeon Where the Sun Stood Still*, pp. 41, 49). The connection between the Saulide Ner and the Nera' on the jar handles has been noted in previous discussion by A. Dempsky ('The Genealogy of Gibeon [1 Chronicles 9:35-44]: Biblical and Epigraphic Considerations', *BASOR* 202 [1971], pp. 16-23). Dempsky has a different dating scheme for the genealogy but still draws the connection, noting the suggested epigraphic dating of the handles to the sixth century BCE, which supports my reconstruction, not his.

16. For some details of this phenomenon, see P.J. Kearney, 'The Role of the Gibeonites in the Deuteronomic History', *CBQ* 35 (1973), pp. 1-19; J. Blenkinsopp,

the Ner in 1 Chron. 9.36 may represent (1) a clan named after and descended from Saul's ancestor, (2) Saul's direct ancestor, who simply
bore the name of his clan, or (3) the name of a clan that was
fictionalized in subsequent tradition as an individual, that is, Saul's
relative.

Since there is no break in the pottery tradition in the central Cisjor-
danian highlands as a result of the exile, particularly in communities
that were not destroyed in 586 BCE, it is not possible at this time to state
definitively whether the wineries excavated at Gibeon went out of use c.
586 BCE or continued into the early Persian period. It is only c. 500
BCE, with the arrival of a number of Greek imports, that what is
typically designated 'Persian pottery' can be dated confidently, even
though the so-called Persian era had been underway for about half a
century.

We cannot be certain whether Gibeon was destroyed in 586 BCE and
remained unoccupied until the alleged return of exiles or remained
occupied through the end of the Babylonian rule and into the early
Persian period. Since the published reports do not mention any
evidence of widespread destruction at the end of the Iron II,[17] I am
suggesting that the latter situation prevailed. The lack of destruction
evidence, however, must be considered carefully in light of the claim
that the later Roman settlement had cleared earlier debris and building
remains down to bedrock before beginning construction.[18] In addition,
the majority of the excavated area was not residential but covered the
great pool and the wineries, none of which would have contained the
kind of destruction debris that is readily visible in building remains, so

*Gibeon and Israel: The Role of Gibeon and the Gibeonites in the Political and
Religious History of Early Israel* (SOTSMS, 2; Cambridge: Cambridge University
Press, 1972); D.V. Edelman, 'The Rise of the Israelite State under Saul' (PhD
dissertation, University of Chicago, 1986), pp. 211-42.

17. Pritchard, *Gibeon Where the Sun Stood Still*, p. 161. 'No evidence has
appeared thus far for a general destruction by fire within either the Iron I or the Iron
II.' As C.E. Carter has noted, however, the reports are inconsistent about the
destruction date of the site's wall, for example, and are unreliable in general about
distinguishing the Neo-Babylonian period at the end of Iron II from the early
Persian and Persian periods in ceramic readings, so the status of the site is difficult
to assess (*The Emergence of Yehud in the Persian Period: A Social and
Demographic Study* [JSOTSup, 294; Sheffield: Sheffield Academic Press, 1999],
pp. 119-22).

18. Carter, *Emergence of Yehud*, p. 81.

the lack of clear evidence for late sixth century BCE destruction in the limited areas of excavation cannot be taken as proof that no destruction took place.[19] Since small portions of a residential area were excavated, and did not reveal destruction debris, it is plausible to suggest that the site was not destroyed in 586 BCE by the Babylonians but remained occupied through the late sixth century and into the fifth century BCE.[20]

The report in Jer. 41.12 that the forces of Johanan confronted Ishmael, murderer of the Babylonian-installed governor of Judah, and his group of captives at 'the great waters that are in Gibeon' does not require the site to have been occupied in the years immediately after 586 BCE; the waters, whether referring to the reservoir dug within the town walls or to the spring outside the walls, would have been a local landmark on their own.

Similarly, the inclusion of people from Gibeon in the list of returnees in Neh. 7.25 need not require that the site lay abandoned until the return. On the one hand, some returnees could have settled in the pre-existing town, mixing with those who had not experienced exile; on the other hand, the list may reflect an attempt to incorporate non-exiles into the exilic community at a point after the major conflicts between the locals and the *golah* community in Yehud were resolved.

The second potential source of evidence is Zech. 12.10-14, which provides an intriguing link between the Saul–David complex and the early post-exilic community, depending on how one dates this passage. In an oracle concerning Israel, the house of David, and the families of Jerusalem, each by itself will mourn over the death of the peoples round

19. Another area of four squares on the summit of the site, excavated in 1959, turned out to be disturbed from Turkish gun emplacement in 1917; el-Jib had been the bastion of Turkish resistance in the war in 1917, and as such, had been not only disturbed by military trenching on site, but also had been disturbed by heavy shelling by the British from Nebi Samwil across the valley. In this case, traces of destruction could easily have been modern rather than ancient, but the area was abandoned after only one week, once the reason for the mixture of strata was explained, and the results were not published (Pritchard, *Gibeon Where the Sun Stood Still*, pp. 87-88).

20. O. Lipschits argues that the wine decanters with name inscriptions, many of which were found in the fill from the great pool, are definitely Babylonian in date, reflecting exilic occupation at the site ('The History of the Benjamin Region under Babylonian Rule', *TA* 26 [1999], pp. 155-90 [174-75]). I prefer a late monarchic date.

about whom they have killed. Verses 12 and 13 name specifically among these families: the family of the house of David, that of the house of Nathan, that of the house of Levi, and the family of the Shimeites. This is an odd, but revealing list. Mention of a house of Nathan brings to mind the prophet Nathan in the David story, and the singling out of the family of Shimei is also noteworthy since in 2 Sam. 16.5-14, a Shimei ben Gera of the family of the house of Saul appears and curses David for usurping the throne of Saul. I find this overlap with characters named in the Saul–David story to go beyond coincidence and suspect that the mention of namesakes of Nathan and Shimei in the Saul–David complex is done deliberately as a way to address issues being raised in the time that Zechariah is prophesying. The inclusion of Shimei seems to indicate a resurgence of Saulide–Davidic rivalry.

The date of Zech. 12.10-14 is widely disputed, since the text belongs to what is called Deutero-Zechariah. It is not necessarily to be dated to the time of the rebuilding of the temple (as is Zech. 1–8) but could date from shortly thereafter.[21] Thus, the curious overlap noted above cannot provide firm corroboration for Saulide–Davidic rivalry in Yehud in the last half of the sixth century BCE, but raises interesting possibilities, nonetheless.[22]

The Kingship of YHWH and the Elimination of a Human King

Another important theme found particularly in 1 Samuel is YHWH's direct kingship over Israel and the inadequacy of human kingship. This

21. For a survey of opinions that argue for dates ranging from Josiah to the Greek period, see R.L. Smith, *Micah–Malachi* (WBC, 32; Waco, TX: Word Books, 1984), pp. 169-73. Those who argue for a date in the early post-exilic period include, e.g., J. Wellhausen, *Die kleinen Propheten* (Berlin: W. de Gruyter, 4th edn, 1963), pp. 196-200; B. Otzen, *Studien über Deuterosacharja* (AThD, 6; Copenhagen: Prostant Apud Munksgaard, 1964), pp. 173-84, esp. pp. 183-84; Smith, *Palestinian Parties*, pp. 116, 249 n. 73; Sacchi, *History of the Second Temple Period*, pp. 65-66.

22. Following Wellhausen, M. Smith has suggested that Zech. 12.2-10 reflects the same historical circumstance as the next pericope (which include my pericope 12.10-14) and sees it as referring obliquely to the murder of Zerubbabel by other members of the Davidic family, who decided to ally themselves with the locals/syncretists to eliminate a relative whose messianic pretensions could bring ruin, whether successful or unsuccessful (*Palestinian Parties*, p. 116). Sacchi agrees (*History of the Second Temple Period*, pp. 66-67).

idea is expressed directly in the account of the people's request for a king in 1 Samuel 8: YHWH announces that the people have not rejected Samuel but Him from being king over them (v. 7), and then subsequently, in 1 Sam. 12.16-25, YHWH confirms Samuel's statements that the people have done evil in asking for a human king to replace Him, their true king, by sending rain at the wheat harvest. These direct assertions of divine kingship as the correct form of political leadership of the nation in place of human kingship tend to be corroborated or reinforced by the portrayals of Saul and David as flawed humans, whose faulty judgments lead to national suffering: in Saul's case to constant Philistine attacks; and in David's to civil war and constant attacks by surrounding nations.

In addition, the final-form narrative of the intertwined careers of Saul and David raises the issue of divine fairness or impartiality, with YHWH rejecting the house of Saul for less serious infractions than those committed by David and yet entering into an eternal covenant with the Davidic house. The narrative as a whole can be seen to indict YHWH as a reliable, just king, emphasizing his unpredictable, whimsical nature, while at the same time advocating His right to be sole king of Israel.

The two interrelated themes of the kingship of YHWH in place of human kingship and divine unpredictability imply a social setting in which human kingship is no longer a viable option, on the one hand, and one in which YHWH has not lived up to national expectations, showing himself to be undependable or fickle, on the other. A date after the bitter experience of the exile would account well for the latter ideology, and one after 586 BCE and the loss of status as an independent nation headed by a Davidide king is likely for the other. Combining both suggested dates, a more specific social setting can be proposed: a date in the latter part of the reign of Darius, after the death of Zerubbabel, when the Persian administration decided to appoint loyal Persians to serve as governors in various provinces in place of puppet kings descended from former royal houses. Once the latter policy was put in place, leaders of the two main factions in Yehud may have effected a rapprochement, the issue of a Saulide vs Davidide leader having become moot and Jerusalem having become the site of the capital, with its temple rebuilt.

To secure acceptance of the new Persian policy, the few explicit passages advocating the kingship of YHWH over Israel and the evil nature of the nation's request for a human king 'as all the other nations' would have been added to 1 Samuel to emphasize the lack of need for a human king in Yehud, even a Davidic descendant.[23] At the same time, the message would be sent to the elite of Yehud that in spite of claims by the Persian king to be head of his empire and temporal ruler of Yehud, YHWH was the true king of the province and so was owed obedience ahead of the human overlord. Failure to obey could trigger the unpredictable divine ruler to punish the community severely, as demonstrated by the events of 598 and 586 BCE. The message about YHWH's status as true king of the province suggests strongly that the editors responsible for these additions belonged either to priestly circles, whose power would be increased by the assertion of divine rule, the need for obedience to YHWH's revealed law, and the need for guidance from the priesthood to know the law of YHWH, or to levitical circles, whose power or prestige would have been enhanced as teachers of the revealed law.[24]

Larger Ramifications

The arguments put forward in the preceding sections bear directly or indirectly on several other tangential issues. I will briefly address three.

The argument that the early post-exilic setting was a logical time for a resurgence of Saulide–Davidic rivalry between the Benjaminite and *golah* factions within the province of Yehud does not require the initial composition of the books of Samuel at this time; it is possible that a much more abbreviated account of the reign of both kings was part of a late monarchic document, the so-called Deuteronomic History. Any final decision about the date of the first written forms of 1 and 2 Samuel

---

23. It is possible that some of the stories about David under the curse were added at this time to highlight his flawed nature, while passages that made Saul a more sympathetic character were added as well, to emphasize the inconsistency of the divine decision to continue to reject the Saulide line and uphold an eternal covenant with the Davidic line, in spite of good and bad behavior from both men.

24. This role is explicitly associated with the Levites in 2 Chron. 17.7-9; whether it is a phenomenon that developed only in the post-exilic community can be debated, since this role is not specifically assigned to the Levites in the Deuteronomistic History. In addition, the date of the introduction of the practice in a post-exilic setting needs to be clarified, since it is possible that it developed under Greek rule rather than under Persian rule, for example, thus explaining its absence from the Deuteronomistic History.

must be made taking into consideration arguments for the dating of the larger narrative complex extending from Deuteronomy to 2 Kings.

The date of the establishment of the northern boundary between Judah/Yehud and Samerina, which includes not only traditional Benjaminite clans but also southern Ephraimite clans from Bethel and Gilgal, for example, has a direct impact on understanding plausible socio-historical settings for the themes involving Saulide–Davidic rivalry, the eternal Davidic covenant, and the sanctity of the king or king-elect. It has long been noted that the northern boundary of the Persian province did not correspond to the boundary that separated Judah and Israel when they existed as independent political entities. It also has been noted that the tribal list for Benjamin in Josh. 18.11-28 includes within it 12 settlements that would have belonged to the kingdom of Israel prior to 721 BCE (vv. 21-24). The big question, then, is *when* the change occurred that included some of southern Ephraim within Benjamin, and by extension, the state of Judah or the province of Yehud.

One suggestion is that the boundary shift took place under Josiah, who took advantage of the failing strength of the Assyrian empire to push the northern border of Judah northward into Mt Ephraim. The mention in 2 Kgs 23.15-20 of Josiah's destruction of the altar at Bethel and also his desecration of 'all the shrines and high places that were in the cities of Samaria' is cited as evidence to support this proposed dating.[25] This suggestion presumes that the border did not change substantially in 721 BCE when the heartland of the kingdom of Israel became the Assyrian province of Samerina. A date after 721 BCE for the incorporation of the 12 villages in the list in Josh. 18.21-24 is indicated by the inclusion of the settlements of Kefar-Ammoni (literally, 'the village of the Ammonites') and Avvim, a site named after one of the foreign groups introduced by the Assyrians (2 Kgs 17.31). Both groups would have been settled in place of the exiled Israelites.

If this dating of the incorporation of southern Mt Ephraim into Judah is correct, then it would be possible to argue that the themes justifying

25. So, e.g., A. Alt, 'Judas Gaue unter Josia', *PJ* 21 (1925), pp. 100-16; N. Na'aman, *Borders and Districts in Biblical Historiography: Seven Studies in Biblical Geographic Lists* (Jerusalem Biblical Studies, 4; Jerusalem: Simor, 1986), p. 229. Contrast, e.g., Z. Kallai, who dates the list segment to conquests in Mt Ephraim by Abijah, which continued through the reign of Jehoshaphat, hence to one of these two kings (*Historical Geography of the Bible: The Tribal Territories of Israel* [Leiden: E.J. Brill; Jerusalem: Magnes Press, 1986], p. 337).

Davidic ascendancy over the Saulide royal line, the divine granting of an eternal Davidic covenant, and making the king or king-elect sacrosanct could have been produced during Josiah's reign. This would have been part of an attempt to persuade members of the southern court—as well as the elite within the newly conquered territory—that YHWH had intended the Davidic house to rule forever over Josiah's territory *and* over Samerina and those other lands that had once been part of the kingdom of Israel. As such, the framing of the books of 1 and 2 Samuel would have had a twofold aim: (1) to convince opposition at the court that the time was right to move even further into Samerina and take over the entire central hill country and more, as the Assyrian empire was crumbling; and (2) to gain the support of newly added population groups by appealing to a long-established divine plan that historically had included the people living in the central hill country, Galilee and parts of Gilead, which had called for Davidic rule over them after the failure of the Saulide line. The emphasis on royal sacrosanctity would have been designed as extra insurance, as the loyalty of the newly incorporated groups would not have been guaranteed. In addition, it could have been designed to head off any potential assassination attempts within Judah by the pro-Assyrian opposition.

The reason for the emphasis specifically on the Saulide–Davidic rivalry is not explained well by this dating. Since many (if not most) of the population groups within Samerina were not descended from former Israelites but were newcomers resettled by the Assyrians, there would have been little reason to highlight the divine rejection of the first Israelite royal house in favor of the Davidides. Perhaps, however, it was simply a matter of expanding on history; Saul had been the first king of Israel and David the third (after Saul's son Eshbaal), and it was important for the intended southern audience even more so than for the intended northern audience to justify the Davidic claim to the northern throne as part of a divine plan for the future.

The resurgence of the Egyptian empire in Cisjordan under Psammetichus I and Necho during the reign of Josiah, also in response to the crumbling of Assyrian power in the region, would not have prevented the writing of the Deuteronomic History, but it certainly prevented Judah from gaining control over Samerina, if this were, in fact, the intention of Josiah.

Alternatively, it is possible that the northern border between Judah and Samerina was first changed either by the Babylonians, or by the

Persians, resulting in the assignment of the 12 towns in Josh. 18.21-24
to Benjamin rather than Ephraim. After the assassination of Gedaliah
(the Babylonian-appointed governor of Judah in 586 BCE, who ruled
only two months) the fate of the newly incorporated territory of Judah
under the Babylonian central authority is not known. Either a new
governor was appointed, or the territory was annexed to Samerina and
ruled by that province's local governor. In the latter case, the traditional
boundary between Samerina and Judah would have disappeared, paving
the way for a different border to be established 50 to 75 years later by
the Persians, when they made Judah a separate subprovince, removing
it once again from the jurisdiction of Samerina. It is possible that the
description in Josh. 18.21-24 reflects the situation in the Persian era[26]
rather than the Josianic era and that the story of Josiah's move against
Bethel and all the shrines of Samaria (2 Kgs 15.20) was created to
justify the eventual boundary in the Persian period by having it exist
already at the end of the monarchy. The mention of the desecration of
shrines throughout Samaria may be a later expansion to glorify this
king even further or, if original, wishful thinking about a future
expansion that never happened.

The final set of tangential issues that may be related to the proposed
resurgence of Saulide–Davidic rivalry in the early Persian period
involves the negative attitude toward Gibeon in the Deuteronomistic
History, the portrayal of the Gibeonites as foreigners, and the filling in
of the great pool at the site of Gibeon/el-Jib. P. Kearney has pointed out
the strong, anti-Gibeonite bias that pervades the Deuteronomistic History, including a conscious attempt to avoid mention of Gibeon altogether or to vilify the people or towns in references that were allowed to
stand.[27] He was unable to suggest a reason for this tendency, however.
The proposed rivalry between the non-*golah* community centered in
Benjamin—including the traditional villages of the Gibeonites—
Gibeon, Chephirah, Beeroth, and Kiriath-jearim (Ezra 2.20, 25; Neh.
7.25, 29)—and the returning *golah* community centered in Yehud
provides a plausible background for the negative portrayal of Gibeon
(the rival seat for the provincial capital) in particular, as well as for the
negative attitude toward the Gibeonite 'federation'. These four towns

26. Of the 12 villages named, three appear specifically in the lists detailing the
settlements of Persian Yehud: Jericho (Ezra 2.34; Neh. 3.2; 7.36), Bethel (Ezra
2.28; Neh. 7.32; 12.31) and Geba (Ezra 2.26; Neh. 7.30; 12.31).

27. Kearney, 'Role of the Gibeonites', pp. 1-19.

may well have been the center of resistance to the *golah* community's attempt to control the new Persian province. Their depiction as non-Israelites could stem from the limitation of the term 'Israel' to members of the *golah,* with the story of their eventual incorporation into Israel and the traditional tribe of Benjamin reflecting the eventual resolution of conflict and integration of the two population groups. The tradition in Joshua 9–10 in which they are made hewers of wood and drawers of water for the temple of Elohim and for the altar might also be an exaggerated retrojection of the status of the priesthood of Gibeon that lost out to Jerusalem in the early Persian struggle.

A date and motivation for the filling in of the great pool at Gibeon can also be tentatively proposed in connection with the situation in Yehud in the second half of the sixth century BCE. Since the town apparently was not destroyed in 598 or 586 BCE but remained a center of habitation through the exilic period and into the early post-exilic period, the filling in of the pool has to have been a conscious act by a group in power locally. It is not likely that the inhabitants would have done it themselves and eliminated ready access to water from within the settlement. It makes more sense to suspect that an outside power decided to fill in the pool to prevent the inhabitants from having access to the water from inside their city—but why might this have been a threat? If Gibeon were the center of a resistance movement that wanted a Saulide puppet king restored to the throne in Gibeon (which would then become the new provincial capital of Yehud), the leaders of the *golah* could easily have decided to avert a possible coup or revolt by preventing the town from becoming a refuge to the opposition that could withstand armed attack with its own internal access to water and standing walls.[28]

Among the pottery in the fill that was excavated from the pool was a jar with the name *mṣṣh* written on a handle.[29] The date and significance of these handles is debated, but distribution is limited to the territory of Benjamin in its expanded state (Josh. 18.21-28) and is thought to be either exilic or early post-exilic, but more likely exilic, when Mizpah

28. In light of the problems of dating at the site, it is possible that the destruction of the town walls should be dated to the same time as the filling in of the pool, and for the same reason.

29. J.B. Pritchard, *Hebrew Inscriptions and Stamps from Gibeon* (Museum Monographs; Philadelphia: University Museum, University of Pennsylvania, 1959), p. 27.

served as the provincial capital.[30] The majority of handles has been
found at Tell en-Nasbeh. Thus, the reason I have proposed (above) for
the filling in of the pool is consistent with the current archaeological
evidence.[31]

Conclusion

In seeking to discern the most plausible socio-historical context(s) for
the use of five dominant themes in the Saul–David stories as vehicles of
effective communication to a elite target audience, the following
proposals have been made.

The three, interrelated themes, which (1) justify the Davidic takeover
of the Saulide throne, (2) confirm the Davidic right to rule through an
eternal covenant initiated by YHWH, and (3) stress the sacrosanctity of
YHWH's anointed, presume the situation of a community divided over
whether a Saulide or Davidide should be in charge, with the threat of
assassination looming large. I have suggested that Saulide–Davidic
rivalry resurfaced in the early Persian province of Yehud sometime
between the affirmation of the *golah* party to leadership after 538 BCE
and the rebuilding of the temple in Jerusalem in 515 BCE. Tension
developed between the non-*golah* community in Benjamin and the
golah group over (1) whether the descendants of the Saulide or Davidide
royal houses should be appointed governor and (2) where the temple
should be rebuilt—in Gibeon or Jerusalem. The Saulide genealogies in
1 Chron. 8.29-40 and 9.35-44 provide indirect corroboration for this
tension, and Zech. 12.10-14 may also reflect these tensions.

The themes of the kingship of YHWH over Israel in place of human

30. So J.R. Zorn, J. Yellin and J.L. Hayes, 'The *m(w)ṣh* Stamp Impressions and
the Neo-Babylonian Period', *IEJ* 44 (1994), pp. 161-83. For different options about
the date and purpose of the jars, see, e.g., Carter, *Emergence of Yehud*, pp. 131-32,
260-66. Since the two handles from Jericho may represent a secondary use of the
jars in the early Persian period, we should be cautious in concluding from their
location in one of the 12 villages that were formerly part of Ephraim that the
boundary between Samerina and Yehud was already in place under the Babylonian
administration.

31. Lipschits has noted that two private seal impressions that were found deep
in the fill are local imitations of widespread Achaemenid motifs and so suggest that
the pool did not fill in gradually on its own, over time, as Pritchard had proposed,
but must have been deliberately filled in at some unspecified point in the Persian
period ('History of Benjamin', p. 176).

kingship and the unpredictability of the deity presume a time when (1) there was no longer a monarchy and (2) the justifications for the exile are being questioned. The most likely setting would be sometime after 515 BCE, when the earlier conflicts between the non-*golah* and *golah* factions had been resolved and a single community in Yehud for dealing with its Persian overlords had been created.

Finally, three ramifications of the proposed conflict in the early Persian province have been discussed: (1) the fact of Persian settings for the four themes does not indicate that the entire complex of Saul–David stories was first composed at this time; (2) uncertainty over the date at which the northern boundary of the province was established and its relation to the Benjaminite village list in Josh. 18.21-14 does not allow us to know if the Persian provincial boundaries were different from the Neo-Babylonian ones or not; and (3) the anti-Gibeonite bias in the Deuteronomistic History, the composition of Joshua 9–10, and the filling in of the great pool in Gibeon as well as the destruction its town walls all are explainable if Gibeon, Chephirah, Beeroth, and Kiriath-jearim were the center of Benjaminite resistance to the *golah* party.

The Beginning of the Regnal Year in Israel and Judah

John H. Hayes

Attempts to determine the chronology of Israelite and Judean kings encounter enormous problems and difficulties.[1] Debate has occurred, for example, over when the calendar year and thus the regnal year began: whether in the spring or fall; whether both kingdoms began the year at the same time or at different times; and whether the same systems were employed in both kingdoms throughout their history. The fact that the Hebrew Bible contains no statements about a new year's day or when a new year began has greatly contributed to uncertainty.

Practically all scholars have assumed that the new or regnal year began on the first of a month, whether this month was in the spring or autumn. Opinions vary between 1 Nisan and 1 Tishri,[2] although Auerbach proposed 1 Marheshvan.[3] Also assumed is the view that the Mesopotamian data, that is evidence from Neo-Assyrian and Neo-Babylonian sources, reflect a regnal-year reckoning that began on 1 Nisan.

Some statements in the Babylonian Chronicles are relevant to this issue and suggest that the new regnal year did not begin on the first day

---

1. See, most recently, the works of M. Cogan ('Chronology, Hebrew Bible', *ABD* [1992], I, pp. 1002-11), J. Hughes (*Secrets of the Times: Myth and History of Biblical Chronology* [JSOTSup, 66; Sheffield: JSOT Press, 1990]), G. Galil (*The Chronology of the Kings of Israel and Judah* [SHCANE, 9; Leiden: E.J. Brill, 1996]), and J. Finegan (*Handbook of Biblical Chronology: Principles of Time Reckoning in the Ancient World and Problems of Chronology in the Bible* [Peabody, MA: Hendrickson, rev. edn, 1998]).

2. D.J.A. Clines provides full bibliographical references on those advocating various positions on the issues of the autumn versus spring reckoning; see his 'Regnal Year Reckoning in the Last Years of the Kingdom of Judah', *AJBA* 2 (1972), pp. 9-34; and 'The Evidence for an Autumnal New Year in Pre-Exilic Israel Reconsidered', *JBL* 93 (1974), pp. 22-40.

3. E. Auerbach, 'Der Wechsel des Jahres-Anfangs in Juda im Lichte der neugefundenen babylonischen Chronik', *VT* 9 (1959), pp. 113-21.

of the month Nisan. Chronicles 2–5 report on the reign of the Babylonian king Nabopolassar (625–605 BCE) and the early years of his son
and successor Nebuchadrezzar II (604–562 BCE).[4] The texts report that,
after the Babylonian army had inflicted a defeat on Assyrian forces on
12 Tishri, Nabopolassar ascended the Babylonian throne on 26
Marheshvan. The chronicles proceed to report on the events of his 21-
year rule.[5] In the chronicles, the account of each year's activities is
clearly demarcated not only by an introductory phrase, 'the X year of
Nabopolassar', but also by a horizontal line drawn across the tablet,
thus dividing the material into yearly sections.

The first section of Chronicle 5, for Nabopolassar's 21st year, reports
Nebuchadrezzar II's defeat of the Egyptians at Carchemish, the death of
Nabopolassar on 8 Ab, and the ascension to the throne in Babylon by
Nebuchadrezzar II on 1 Elul. A horizontal line then marks off the
accession year of the new king, and then the text reports on the new
king's return to the west and his subsequent journey home with booty.
The last line of this section reports, 'In the month Nisan he [Nebucha-
drezzar II] took the hand of Bel and the son of Bel (and) celebrated the
Akitu festival.' This statement is followed by a horizontal line and then
a report on 'the first year of Nebuchadrezzar (II)'.

Two conclusions may be drawn from this evidence. First, Nebuchadrezzar II's accession year (*resh sharruti*), which began on 8 Ab, extended through the celebration of the Akitu festival in Nisan. Second,
his first regnal year did not begin on 1 Nisan but only at the completion
of the Akitu festival. Although the details of the festival are uncertain,
the celebrations seem to have covered the first 11 or 12 days of Nisan.[6]
This means that Nebuchadrezzar II's first regnal year would not have
begun until 11 or 12 Nisan. This fact has already been recognized by
Wiseman. In the latter's edition of the Babylonian Chronicles, he wrote:

4. A.K. Grayson, *Assyrian and Babylonian Chronicles* (Texts from Cuneiform
Sources, 5; Locust Valley, NY: J.J. Augustin, 1975; repr. Winona Lake, IN: Eisen-
brauns, 2000), pp. 87-102. These chronicles were first published in D.J. Wiseman,
Chronicles of Chaldean Kings (626–556 B.C.) in the British Museum (London:
British Museum, 1956).

5. Due to damage to the tablets, the narration for years four to nine for
Nabopolassar are missing at the end of Chronicle 2.

6. On the festival, see J. Klein, 'Akitu', *ABD*, I, pp. 138-40, and M.E. Cohen,
The Cultic Calendars of the Ancient Near East (Bethesda, MD: CDL Press, 1993),
pp. 400-53.

> The Chronicle treats the events following the day that Nebuchadrezzar 'sat on the royal throne at Babylon' until the celebration of the New Year Festival eight months later as a distinct period—'the accession year'—marked off from the events leading up to the accession and from those of the first full calendar year of his reign. This is particularly significant because the celebration of the New Year Festival (*issinnu akitu*) in the month Nisan is included as the culminating event of Nebuchadrezzar's accession year rather than as the first public occasion of the following year. It would seem that the first official regnal year commenced only after the point in the celebrations where the king 'took the hands of Marduk and Nabu' to lead them in the procession to the *akitu*-temple.[7]

In a note to line 14 of this tablet (B.M. 21946), however, Wiseman seems to imply that beginning Nebuchadrezzar II's first regnal year after the Akitu festival was somewhat unusual: 'It appears that Nisan could not be included in the first year of the reign, because Nebuchadrezzar was not formally king until the festival made him so.'[8] There is no reason to make such an assumption since the text had previously noted that he had ascended the throne on 1 Elul and had returned to Babylon from the west in the month Shebat, two months prior to the festival. The logical deduction to be drawn from the text is that the normal beginning of the regnal year was at the culmination or completion of the festival, that is, almost at the middle of Nisan, the first month of the year.

If the new regnal year in Mesopotamia began after the major Akitu festival in Nisan, might the regnal year in Israel and Judah not have begun until after a major festival? According to 1 Kgs 12.32-33, Jeroboam I established a feast that fell on the 15th of the eighth month in Bethel, at which time he offered burnt offerings on the altar.[9] This festival is said to have been analogous to the one observed in Judah, presumably being held a month later in the north than in the south. This 15th day of the month was no doubt 'the day of the king' (Hos. 7.5).

In 1 Kgs 12.32-33, the name of the festival is not given, but here as elsewhere, references to 'the festival' imply the fall festival. If the new regnal year did not commence until the completion of the fall festival,

---

7. Wiseman, *Chronicles*, p. 27.
8. Wiseman, *Chronicles*, p. 85.
9. On this festival, see S. Talmon, 'Divergences in Calendar-Reckoning in Ephraim and Judah', *VT* 8 (1958), pp. 48-74 (reprinted in 'The Cult and Calendar Reform of Jeroboam I', in his *King, Cult and Calendar in Ancient Israel: Collected Studies* [Jerusalem: Magnes Press, 1986], pp. 113-39 [see esp. pp. 118-23]).

then it becomes clear why Exod. 23.16 and 34.22 refer to the time of this festival as 'the going out of the year' (בצאת השנה)[10] and 'the turn of the year' (תקופת השנה). Also, it explains why the fall festival is listed last in the festival calendar, even though the new year began in the fall. Clines has argued that the listing of the fall festival last in the festival calendar indicates that the year probably began in the spring; otherwise—if the year began on the first of a fall month—the fall festival would have been the first in the new year and thus listed first.[11] If the above arguments are correct, then Clines's conclusions will not hold.

---

10. For interpreting this phrase as a reference to the end of the year, see E. Kutsch, ' "...am Ende des Jahres": Zur Datierung des israelitischen Herbstfestes in Ex 23, 16', *ZAW* 83 (1971), pp. 15-21; as a reference to the beginning of the year, see H.L. Ginsberg, *The Israelian Heritage of Judaism* (Texts and Studies of the Jewish Theological Seminary of America, 24; New York: Jewish Theological Seminary of America, 1982), pp. 49-50.

11. Clines, 'The Evidence for an Autumnal New Year'.

THE YEAR OF JOSIAH'S DEATH: 609 OR 610 BCE?

Paul K. Hooker and John H. Hayes

In his work on biblical chronology, Jeremy Hughes writes, 'Josiah's death...is securely dated to the summer of 609 BC.'[1] Hughes certainly speaks for the majority of biblical scholarship on this matter; indeed, the datum of a 609 BCE death-date for Josiah is virtually unchallenged in recent literature.[2] Nonetheless, there seems to be sufficient warrant for reassessing the assignment of the date of Josiah's death to 609 BCE, especially when one examines the evidence from Egyptian as well as biblical and Babylonian sources. It is the purpose of this article to suggest that, in fact, Josiah's death should be assigned to 610 BCE.

The events surrounding the passage of the Judean throne from Josiah to Jehoiakim are intimately connected with the protracted struggle between Babylonian and Assyrian forces for control of the city of Harran in the final days of the Assyrian Empire. The principal source of information concerning that struggle is Babylonian Chronicle 3 (B.M. 21901).[3]

---

1.   J. Hughes, *Secrets of the Times: Myth and History in Biblical Chronology* (JSOTSup, 66; Sheffield: JSOT Press, 1990), p. 225.

2.   Writing shortly after the publication of D.J. Wiseman, *Chronicles of Chaldean Kings (626–556 B.C.) in the British Museum* (London: British Museum, 1956), H. Tadmor claimed, 'the new chronicle B.M. 22047...settles finally the date for the fall of Josiah in Megiddo...sometime in Sivan/Tammuz 609' ('Chronology of the Last Kings of Judah', *JNES* 15 [1956], pp. 226-30 [228]). Few scholars have differed with Tadmor's conclusion. Writing prior to the publication of the Wiseman chronicle, M.B. Rowton ('Jeremiah and the Death of Josiah', *JNES* 10 [1951], pp. 128-30) argued for 608 BCE, and J.E. Reade ('Mesopotamian Guidelines for Biblical Chronology', *Syro-Mesopotamian Studies* 4/1 [1981], pp. 1-9) has provided more recent support for the same date. The date of 610 BCE is proposed by the current authors in our *A New Chronology for the Kings of Israel and Judah* (Atlanta: John Knox Press, 1988), pp. 88-90.

3.   The chronicle can be found in two primary English editions: Wiseman, *Chronicles*, pp. 55-56; and A.K. Grayson, *Assyrian and Babylonian Chronicles*

For the 16th year of Nabopolassar (Nisan 610–Nisan 609 BCE) the chronicle reports:

58. The sixteenth year: in the month Iyyar (April/May) the king of Akkad mustered his army and marched to Assyria. From [the month…] until the month Marchesvan (October/November)

59. he marched about victoriously in Assyria. In the month Marchesvan the Umman-manda, [who] had come [to hel]p the king of Akkad,

60-62. put their armies together and marched to Harran [against Ashur-uball]it (II) who had ascended the throne in Assyria. Fear of the enemy overcame Ashur-ubballit (II) and the army of Eg[ypt which] had come [to help him] and they aban[doned] the city […] they crossed.

63. The king of Akkad reached Harran and […] he captured the city.

64. He carried off the vast booty of the city and the temple. In the month Adar (February/March) the king of Akkad left their […]

65. He went home. The Umman-manda, who had come to help the king of Akkad, withdrew.[4]

Two things are worthy of note for the year. First, military action in and around Harran took place between Iyyar [April/May] 610 and Adar [February/March] 609 BCE. Second, during that period, the Egyptian army (presumably under the command of the pharaoh) was present at Harran.

The chronicle goes on to report the following events for the 17th year of Nabopolassar (Nisan 609–Nisan 608 BCE):

66. <The seventeenth year>: In the month Tammuz (June/July) Ashur-ubballit (II), king of Assyria, the large army of Egypt […]

67. crossed the river (Euphrates) and marched against Harran to conquer (it) […] they [capture]d (it).

68. They defeated the garrison which the king of Akkad had sta-

(Texts from Cuneiform Sources, 5; Locust Valley, NY: J.J. Augustin, 1975; repr., Winona Lake, IN: Eisenbrauns, 2000), pp. 90-96.

4. Chronicle 3, ll. 58-65. Translation from Grayson, *Assyrian and Babylonian Chronicles*, pp. 95-96.

tioned inside. When they defeated (it) they encamped against Harran.

69. Until the month Elul (August/September) they did battle against the city but achieved nothing. (However) they did not withdraw.[5]

70. The king of Akkad went to help his army and … […] he went up to Izalla and

71. the numerous cities in the mountains … […] he set fire to their […]

72-73. At that time the army of […] [ma]rched as far as the district of Urartu. In the land … […] they plundered their […]

74. The garrison which the king of […had stationed in it set] out.

75. They went up to […] The king of Akkad went home.[6]

Despite the broken condition of this entry for the 17th year, it is possible to ascertain that the Assyro-Egyptian counterattack against Harran occupied the summer months of 609 (June through September) but apparently did not succeed in regaining control of the city. It should be noted that this counterattack began only a few months after the Assyro-Egyptian withdrawal in February/March 609, and that during this interim the Assyro-Egyptian forces were located somewhere west of the Euphrates.

Biblical evidence pertinent to this period fits rather well into the picture provided by Chronicle 3, the Babylonian source. 2 Kings 23.29-35 reports that Pharaoh Neco II had Josiah killed at Megiddo while on his way 'up to the king of Assyria to the river Euphrates'. In addition, the text states that Jehoahaz (II) was subsequently placed on the throne by the Judeans and ruled for three months before being deposed by Neco II and imprisoned in Riblah, which is located south of Hamath. Riblah, although located at some distance from Harran, is west of the Euphrates and may have been the staging area for the Assyro-Egyptian counterattack in 609 BCE. The final biblical datum is that Neco II placed Jehoiakim on the Judean throne and, returning to Egypt, carried Jehoahaz with him as a captive.

Primary evidence from Egyptian sources relevant to the issue

5. For a different reconstruction of these lines, see N. Na'aman, 'The Kingdom of Judah under Josiah', *TA* 18 (1991), pp. 3-71 (53 n. 67).

6. Chronicle 3, ll. 66-75. Translation from Grayson, *Assyrian and Babylonian Chronicles*, p. 96.

concerns only the date of accession of Neco II, since no known Egyptian text refers to any northern campaign through Syria–Palestine by Neco II. An unpublished donation stele indicates that Psammetichus I, Neco II's predecessor, began the 55th year of his reign early in 610 BCE.[7] His 55th year would have begun on 23 January 610 BCE.[8] The earliest unequivocally attested date in the reign of Neco II is 31 August 610 BCE, based on the stele inscriptions of Bentehhor (Louvre A 83).[9] Neco II could thus have succeeded to the Egyptian throne no earlier than 23 January and no later than 31 August 610 BCE.

Recently, in a study of the demotic papyrus P. Berlin 13588, M. Smith has succeeded in fixing more precisely the death of Psammetichus I and thus the accession of Neco II.[10] The papyrus contains an account of a young priest from Daphnae, who reports on events in which he participated that centered around the embalming of a Pharaoh Psammetichus. Smith is able to demonstrate that the pharaoh was Psammetichus I. In the narrative, reference is made to the fact that an eclipse of the moon occurred at sunset during the time of the pharaoh's embalming. Such a lunar eclipse was visible at Daphnae on 22 March 610 BCE. Thus, by late March 610 BCE, Neco II would have replaced his father as ruler of Egypt. Since the Egyptian army was present at Harran only after this date, it is clear that only Neco II could have been pharaoh during the Assyro-Egyptian defense of Harran.

Unfortunately, none of the preceding texts allows one conclusively to determine the death-date of Josiah. Since Egyptian forces were present at Harran in both 610 and 609 BCE, and Neco II would have been on the Egyptian throne during either expedition, a confrontation between Neco II and Josiah at Megiddo in either 610 or 609 BCE could satisfy the inscriptional and biblical evidence. We must turn then to secondary factors to see which of the two alternatives better fits the situation visible within that evidence.

7. D. Meeks, 'Les donations aux temples dans l'Égypte du I millénaire avant J.-C.', in E. Lipiński (ed.), *State and Temple Economy in the Ancient Near East: Proceedings of the International Conference* (OLA, 5–6; Leuven: Departement Oriëntalistiek, 1979), II, p. 675 (number 26.1.55).

8. M. Smith, 'Did Psammetichus I Die Abroad?', *OLP* 22 (1991), pp. 101-109 (105).

9. O. Perdu, 'Prologue à un corpus des stèles royales del a XXVI dynastie', *Bulletin de la sociéte francaise d'egyptologie* 105 (1986), pp. 24-26. See also Smith, 'Did Psammetichus I Die Abroad?', p. 105.

10. Smith, 'Did Psammetichus I Die Abroad?', p. 105.

The first of these factors is the history of cooperation between Egyptian and Assyrian forces as the latter faced the growing threat of Nabopolassar.[11] As early as 616 BCE, Egyptian forces are found in support of Assyrians against Nabopolassar at the town of Gablini in the Tigris–Euphrates valley.[12] A cooperative relationship probably existed between Psammetichus I and Sin-shar-ishkun of Assyria. It is altogether reasonable to assume that, following first the succession of Ashur-uballit II to the Assyrian throne in 612 BCE and then the succession of Neco II to the Egyptian throne in 610 BCE, the two would have taken the earliest available opportunity to renew the relationship that existed between their predecessors. That opportunity would have presented itself in 610 BCE as the Assyrians sought to maintain control of Harran.

Psammetichus I may have been headed for a meeting with Ashur-uballit II when he met his death. The above-mentioned account of the young priest concerning the embalming of Psammetichus I makes it clear that the king died outside the land of Egypt. This could be taken to indicate that Psammetichus I had begun a journey toward Harran when he died. If so, it would be reasonable to assume that Neco II, upon succeeding to his father's throne, undertook to join forces with the Assyrians as soon as possible, in pursuit of his father's policy at the time of his death.

The second factor is timing. Only a few months elapsed between Nabopolassar's attack on Harran, the city's capture and despoliation, and the king's return to Babylon in Adar (February/March), 609 BCE, and the Egypto-Assyrian counterattack in Tammuz (June/July), 609 BCE. This was hardly enough time for the Egyptian army to have packed up and left Harran, traveled all the way to Egypt, refitted, and returned to Harran, stopping in the meantime at Megiddo to dispose of Josiah. In addition, such a move must be regarded as strategically foolhardy, since it would have left the Assyrians alone and vulnerable to a subsequent Babylonian assault. If Josiah were killed by Neco II on the latter's way north to Harran in the early spring of 609 BCE, it would mean that Neco II had not wintered with his army in the north, but had

11. The authors have argued elsewhere that Assyrian kings from Sargon II through Ashur-uballit II regarded the princes of the Nile Delta as allies, albeit not as equals. For a discussion of this thesis, see P.K. Hooker, 'The Kingdom of Hezekiah: Judah in the Geo-political Context of the Late Eighth Century BCE' (PhD dissertation, Emory University, 1993).

12. Chronicle 3, l. 10.

traveled to Egypt and back without it and would thus have encountered Josiah without benefit of his full military force. From the point of view of both timing and strategy, therefore, the late summer or early autumn of 610 BCE would appear the more likely date for the fatal encounter between Josiah and Neco II.

The third factor is the reference in 2 Kgs 23.33 to the imprisonment of Jehoahaz II in Riblah. The fact that Jehoahaz II was brought from Jerusalem to Riblah—rather than to the Egyptian city of Sais—indicates clearly that at the time Neco II was in the district of Hamath, west of the Euphrates. According to Chronicle 3, Egyptian and Assyrian forces were quartered west of the Euphrates during the late winter and early spring of 609 BCE,[13] and the hostilities occurred around Harran during the three months of Tammuz, Ab and Elul 609 BCE. From 2 Kgs 23.31 comes the datum that Jehoahaz held the throne for three months, after which he was taken to Riblah. A death-date in the early spring of 609 BCE for Josiah, in Sivan or early Tammuz, would have brought Jehoahaz II to the throne only shortly before the beginning of the Assyro-Egyptian counterassault at Harran. The reign of Jehoahaz II would thus have fallen during the period that Neco II was at Harran, i.e. Tammuz–Elul, 609 BCE, and the removal of Jehoahaz II would have coincided with the retreat of the Egyptians from Harran and their return to Egypt. There was therefore no reason for Neco II to have commanded that Jehoahaz II be brought north to Riblah, since Neco II himself would have been moving south toward Egypt at that time. If, on the other hand, Josiah were killed in the late summer or early autumn of 610 BCE, while Neco II was en route to Harran for the first battle, there would have been ample time for the 'people of the land' to place Jehoahaz II on the Judean throne, and for Jehoahaz II to have reigned there without Egypt's permission for three months before being deposed and brought to Riblah.

While none of these factors is conclusive in and of itself, when taken together they do weigh heavily in favor of late summer or early autumn 610 BCE as the date of Josiah's death. Under the assumption that Josiah did, in fact, meet his death at Megiddo in 610 BCE, the following recon-struction of events seems likely:

13. Chronicle 3, ll. 61-62 makes it clear that the Egypto-Assyrian retreat from Harran in Adar 609 BCE took the joint force west of the river. Similarly, ll. 66-67 indicate that the Egypto-Assyrian counterattack in Tammuz 609 BCE began when they 'crossed the river'.

(1)　　After his accession in March 610 BCE, Neco II carried out plans—possibly already begun by his father—to aid the new Assyrian king Ashur-uballit II at Harran.

(2)　　Marching north through Palestine, Neco II had Josiah killed at Megiddo for reasons unknown.[14] Since the Egyptians were present at Harran by Marheshvan (October/November) 610 BCE, the death of Josiah must have occurred no later than this. Under the assumption that Neco II was in some haste to arrive at Harran, it is reasonable to assume that the death occurred only shortly before this time, perhaps in Elul (August/September) or Tishri (September/October).

(3)　　The Egyptian army moved north to establish a command center or staging area west of the Euphrates, presumably at Riblah in Hamath. The Judeans, meanwhile, retrieved the body of their slain king and returned it to Jerusalem, whereupon they proclaimed Jehoahaz II his successor without the consent of Neco II.

(4)　　From Marheshvan (October/November) 610 BCE until Adar (Febuary/March) 609 BCE, Neco II and the Egyptian army joined Ashur-uballit II and the Assyrian army to engage the Babylonians at Harran. The Egypto-Assyrian force was defeated and withdrew west of the Euphrates.

(5)　　After retreating from Harran, Neco II had Jehoahaz II brought from Jerusalem, deposed and then imprisoned in Riblah. Jehoahaz II had reigned for only three months (2 Kgs 23.31). In addition, a fine was imposed upon Judah for its unilateral elevation of Jehoahaz II to the throne.

(6)　　Between Adar (Febuary/March) and Tammuz (June/July) 609 BCE, the Assyrian and Egyptian armies were reinforced and refitted for the counterassault on Harran.

---

14. Scholarly discussion of the nature and circumstances of Josiah's death has been underway for years and need not be repeated here. It will suffice to say that considerable doubt has been cast on the reliability of the account of the battle between Neco II and Josiah in 2 Chron. 35.20-36. See S.B. Frost, 'The Death of Josiah: A Conspiracy of Silence', *JBL* 87 (1968), pp. 369-82; A. Malamat, 'Josiah's Bid for Armageddon: The Historical Background of Josiah's Encounter with Necho at Megiddo', *JANESCU* 5 (1973), pp. 267-78; H.G.M. Williamson, 'The Death of Josiah and the Continuing Development of the Deuteronomistic History', *VT* 32 (1982), pp. 242-48; and Na'aman, 'The Kingdom of Judah under Josiah', pp. 51-55.

(7)   From Tammuz until Elul (August/September) 609 BCE, Egyptian and Assyrian forces besieged Harran, but without success.

(8)   Neco II returned from Harran to Egypt sometime after Elul 609 BCE, passing through Judah. While there, he placed Jehoiakim on the Judean throne (2 Kgs 23.34).[15] Jehoahaz II was taken captive to Egypt, where he died.[16]

15. There is no reason to assume that the enthronement of Jehoiakim followed immediately when Neco II deposed Jehoahaz II and imprisoned him in Riblah. In fact, the biblical text (2 Kgs 23.34) associates the latter event with Jehoahaz II's removal to Egypt. D.J.A. Clines ('Regnal Year Reckoning in the Last Years of the Kingdom of Judah', *AJBA* 1/5 [1972], pp. 9-34) dates the death of Josiah to 8 June 609 BCE and the accession of Jehoiakim to 8 September 609 BCE. This assumes an efficiency of both travel and communication that could hardly have existed in antiquity.

16. Jehoahaz II is credited with a three-month reign as opposed to a reign measured in years. This implies that he did not remain on the throne long enough to celebrate the New Year's festival in Nisan (March/April) 609 BCE. The elevation of Jehoiakim to the Judean throne, on the other hand, did not occur until after Elul 609 BCE. Thus, no king was on the throne at the time of the New Year Festival in Nisan 609 BCE, and as we have argued elsewhere, the year went unattributed in the Judean monarchical chronology. The latter months of 609 and the early months of 608 BCE constituted the accession year of Jehoiakim, and Nisan 608–Nisan 607 was his first regnal year. A Nisan to Nisan year had been adopted in Judah under Josiah. See Hayes and Hooker, *New Chronology*, pp. 86-90.

THE RISE OF THE HOUSE OF JEHU

Stuart A. Irvine

2 Kings 9–10 describes the revolt of Jehu in Israel during the late 840s
BCE. The story notes that, on the eve of the revolt, Jehoram of Israel
and Ahaziah of Judah were fighting Hazael of Syria at Ramoth-gilead.
When the Syrians wounded Jehoram, he returned to Jezreel to recu-
perate and Ahaziah came to visit him (9.14-16; cf. 8.28-29). Meanwhile, one of the 'sons of the prophets', commissioned by the great
prophet Elisha, went to Ramoth-gilead and privately anointed as king
the Israelite commander Jehu (9.1-10). The whole army subsequently
acclaimed him (9.11-13). Jehu rode to Jezreel where he killed Jehoram,
Ahaziah and the queen-mother Jezebel (9.16-37). He then executed the
rest of the Omride family in Jezreel and Samaria, as well as the princes
of Judah (10.1-17). Finally, in Samaria Jehu killed all the prophets,
priests and worshippers of Baal, and destroyed the temple of Baal
(10.18-27).

Scholars disagree on the date and reliability of this account.
According to H. Donner, 'the reported facts and consequences, on the
whole, merit trust, even if one must concede that the author, in wording
the account, did not spurn the artistic devices of dramatic presentation
and allowed himself to be led by strong interests'. 2 Kings 9–10 is 'an
excellent and roughly contemporary historical source, and at the same
time one of the most brilliant pieces of Hebrew literary art'.[1]

---

1. 'Die mitgeteilten Tatbestände und Abläufe verdienen in der Hauptsache
Vertrauen, auch wenn einzuräumen ist, dass der Verfasser stilisiert hat, die
Kunstmittel dramatischer Darstellung nicht verschmähte und sich von handfesten
Interessen leiten liess…eine ausgezeichnete und wohl auch ungefähr zeitgenössische
Geschichtsquelle, zugleich eines der glänzendsten Stücke hebräischer Erzählkunst'
(H. Donner, *Geschichte des Volkes Israel und seiner Nachbarn in Grundzügen* [GAT,
4; Göttingen: Vandenhoeck & Ruprecht, 1987], p. 275). For earlier proponents
of this view, see A. Jepsen, *Nabi: Soziologische Studien zur alttestamentlichen*

In contrast, G.W. Ahlström views the narrative as pro-Jehu propaganda, not history, and he assigns it to a time long after the revolt.[2] The account, he contends, misrepresents the revolt in three main ways. First, on the eve of the revolt Israel was at war with Assyria, not Syria. Secondly, Jehu was not a religious zealot in the cause of pure Yahwism, but rather a pragmatic, pro-Assyrian commander who saw that continued warfare with Assyria would prove disastrous for Israel. Thirdly, the primary purpose of the revolt was to appease Shalmaneser III, the king of Assyria, not to avenge or correct the social and cultic sins of the Omride dynasty. By exterminating the 'House of Ahab' and immediately paying tribute to Shalmaneser III, Jehu reversed the anti-Assyrian policy of Israel during the previous decade and thereby saved the nation from further harm at the hands of the Assyrian king.[3]

J.M. Miller and J.H. Hayes also regard 2 Kings 9–10 as late propaganda.[4] They date it specifically to the last years of Jeroboam II (785–745 BCE), when many Israelites—including the prophet Hosea—opposed the Jehu dynasty and denounced the bloodshed with which it had begun (see Hos. 1.4-5).[5] The Kings account appears as an attempt to counter this opposition by justifying Jehu's massacre as the will of Yahweh. However, Miller and Hayes also observe that, despite its pro-

Literatur und Religionsgeschichte (Munich: C.H. Beck, 1934), p. 73; J.A. Montgomery and H.S. Gehman, *A Critical and Exegetical Commentary on the Books of Kings* (ICC, 10; Edinburgh: T. & T. Clark, 1951), p. 399; and O.H. Steck, *Überlieferung und Zeitgeschichte in den Elia-Erzählungen* (WMANT, 26; Neukirchen–Vluyn: Neukirchener Verlag, 1968), p. 32 n. 2.

2. G.W. Ahlström, *The History of Ancient Palestine from the Palaeolithic Period to Alexander's Conquest* (JSOTSup, 146; Sheffield: JSOT Press, 1993), pp. 589-96. Ahlström does not date the story precisely, but he apparently thinks of the years that followed Jehu's reign (p. 594 n. 1). The biblical writer, he suggests, was unfamiliar with the history of the earlier period when Jehu first rose to power.

3. For a similar view of 2 Kgs 9–10 and the history behind it, see M.C. Astour, '841 B.C.: The First Assyrian Invasion of Israel', *JAOS* 91 (1971), pp. 383-89. The interpretation depends upon dating Jehu's revolt precisely to 841 BCE, the same year that, according to Assyrian texts, Shalmaneser III defeated Hazael's forces at Mt Senir, besieged Damascus, destroyed towns in the Hauran region, marched to the coast at Mt Ba'al-ra'si, and there received Jehu's tribute (see *ANET*, pp. 280-81).

4. J.M. Miller and J.H. Hayes, *A History of Ancient Israel and Judah* (Philadelphia: Westminster Press, 1986), pp. 255, 284-87, 309.

5. Cf. J.M. Miller, 'The Fall of the House of Ahab', *VT* 17 (1967), pp. 307-24 (309, 322).

Jehu bias, the narrative 'does not wince from describing the bloody deeds'. This candor is taken as a sign of the account's reliability, and Miller and Hayes thus depend on the story for the essential details of Jehu's revolt.[6]

If 2 Kings 9–10 is propaganda from the reign of Jeroboam II, as Miller and Hayes plausibly suggest, it is worthwhile to examine more closely the biased claims of the account and to explore further their rhetorical force in the context of Jeroboam's troubles c. 750 BCE. The results of this study, in turn, will provide a basis for explaining the discrepancy between the Kings narrative and a recently discovered stela at Tel Dan. As will be seen, there is good reason to question the historical reliability of the biblical account for even the essentials of Jehu's revolt.

The Pro-Jehu Bias of 2 Kings 9–10

2 Kings 9–10 casts Jehu in a favorable light. Editorial additions may enhance the positive picture here (e.g. 9.7-10a), but even apart from these, the account glorifies Jehu as an agent of divine punishment.[7] The text justifies his coup with the following explicit and implicit claims. The great prophet Elisha supported and even instigated the revolt (9.1-3). Jehu's 'zeal for Yahweh' motivated his actions (10.16). The revolt carried out Yahweh's revenge on the Omrides for their social and religious sins (9.22, 26; 10.18), and it was supported by other strict

---

6.   Cf. J.H. Hayes and P.K. Hooker, *A New Chronology for the Kings of Israel and Judah and its Implications for Biblical History and Literature* (Atlanta: John Knox Press, 1988), pp. 41-43.

7.   Scholars disagree widely on the extent of redaction in 9.1–10.27. See M. Noth, *The Deuteronomistic History* (JSOTSup, 15; Sheffield: JSOT Press, 1981), p. 72; M. Cogan and H. Tadmor, *II Kings* (AB, 11; Garden City, NY: Doubleday, 1988), pp. 117-18; H.-C. Schmitt, *Elisa: Traditionsgeschichtliche Untersuchungen zur vorklassischen nordisraelitischen Prophetie* (Gütersloh: Gütersloher Verlagshaus, 1972), pp. 19-27; and S. Timm, *Die Dynastie Omri: Quellen und Untersuchungen zur Geschichte Israels im 9. Jahrhundert vor Christus* (FRLANT, 124; Göttingen: Vandenhoeck & Ruprecht, 1982), pp. 136-42. According to L.M. Barré, the original narrative in 2 Kgs 9–10 depicted Jehu negatively (*The Rhetoric of Political Persuasion: The Narrative Artistry and Political Intentions of 2 Kings 9–11* [CBQMS, 20; Washington, DC: Catholic Biblical Association of America, 1988], pp. 42-55, 97-98). The arguments for this interpretation are not convincing, and few scholars have followed it.

Yahwists such as Jehonadab the Rechabite (10.15). It resulted in the destruction of the apostate cult of Baal in Israel (10.23-27), and it restored order or 'peace' (שלום) in Israel (see 9.18-19, 22).[8]

The bias of the narrative goes even further. Several observations indicate the writer's concern to paint the figure of Jehu in prophetic colors.

1. The prophetic 'madman' (המשגע, 9.11) anoints Jehu as king, and subsequently Jehu drives to Jezreel 'with madness' (בשגעון, v. 20). The verbal parallelism hints at a comparison of the two figures, as though Jehu too was impelled by a prophetic spirit.[9]

2. After killing Jehoram, Jehu addresses his officer, Bidkar, and quotes a divine speech (9.25b-26a):

> Remember when you and I were riding side by side behind Ahab his father, Yahweh raised this oracle against him: 'Surely I saw yesterday the blood of Naboth and his sons, says Yahweh, and I will repay you on this plot of ground, says Yahweh.[10]

As it now stands, the text presents the divine speech as a threat against Ahab years earlier. However, if v. 25b is a secondary insertion, as J.M. Miller proposes, the oracle may have been directed originally against Jehoram at the time of Jehu's revolt.[11] In any case, the important observation here is that v. 26a is one of the few instances in the story of an oracle that is not attributed to Elisha or Elijah. Jehu, of course, may be quoting one of the prophets without saying so explicitly. A more straightforward interpretation, however, would suggest that Jehu is speaking here in his own voice as a proclaimer of Yahweh's word.[12]

---

8. On שלום as a leitmotif in the story, see S.M. Olyan, 'Hăšālôm: Some Literary Considerations of 2 Kings 9', *CBQ* 46 (1984), pp. 652-68 (660-68). In its present form the narrative also asserts that Jehu's actions fulfilled the prophetic word of Elijah (see 9.36aβ; 10.10b, 17b). This claim, however, may derive from late editors, who sought to expand on an implicit connection they saw between Jehu and Elijah in the original story (see below).

9. See Olyan, 'Hăšālôm', p. 663.

10. Unless otherwise noted, translations of the biblical text and of the Tel Dan inscription are the author's.

11. Miller, 'The Fall of the House of Ahab', pp. 308, 314-17.

12. Cf. Timm, *Die Dynastie Omri*, pp. 139-41. He regards the whole of vv. 25b-26 as an addition. However, the verb ושלמתי ('repay') in v. 26 plays on the leitmotif of שלום in 9.18-22, thus tying the verse to the original story. Only the concluding phrase, כדבר יהוה ('according to the word of YHWH'), looks suspect.

3. On his way to Samaria, Jehu joins with Jehonadab and says: 'See my zeal for Yahweh' (וראה בקנאתי ליהוה, 10.16). His statement is strikingly similar to the words of Elijah at Horeb: 'I am very zealous for Yahweh' (קנא קנאתי ליהוה, 1 Kgs 19.10, 14). The parallelism appears to be purposeful: only one other text in the Hebrew Bible speaks of a person having 'zeal' for Yahweh (Num. 25.11-13).

4. Jehu commands his followers to 'seize' (תפשום) the princes of Judah, and then he 'slaughters' them (וישחטם, 10.14).[13] Later, in Samaria Jehu orders the execution of the prophets, priests, and worshippers of Baal. He warns his officers, 'Whoever allows to escape any of the men (האיש אשר־ימלט מן־האנשים) whom I am bringing into your hands' shall lose his own life (v. 24). The language here is reminiscent of Elijah's execution of the prophets of Baal at Mt Carmel (1 Kgs 18.40). There Elijah says to the people, 'Seize (תפשו) the prophets of Baal; do not allow one of them to escape' (איש אל־ימלט מהם). Elijah then 'slaughters them' (וישחטם).

In light of these parallels, 2 Kings 9–10 appears to present Jehu as a latter-day Elijah.[14] Both figures are 'zealous' for Yahweh; both speak Yahweh's word against the Omride kings; both oppose the cult of Baal in Israel; both 'seize' and 'slaughter' the enemies of God, 'letting not one of them escape'.

While comparing Jehu to Elijah, the account also contrasts Jehu with the negative picture of Ahab in 1 Kings 20. This text narrates two battles between the king of Israel and Benhadad of Syria.[15] Verses 26-43 locate the second battle at Aphek, and they present the episode as a holy war gone wrong. Yahweh 'gave' (ונתתי) Benhadad 'into the hand' (ביד) of Ahab (v. 28). However, when Benhadad appealed to Ahab for mercy, Ahab 'brought him up into the chariot' (ויעלהו על־המרכבה, v. 33b), made a covenant with him, and 'let him go' (וישלחהו, v. 34). Subsequently, a prophet denounced Ahab for allowing Benhadad to be

13. Reading the verb as a singular form departs only slightly from the MT's וישחטום. The singular form is attested in some manuscripts of the LXX (see *BHS*).

14. For a similar conclusion, see B.O. Long, *2 Kings* (FOTL, 10; Grand Rapids: Eerdmans, 1991), pp. 121, 138, 140-41.

15. As many scholars now argue, 1 Kgs 20 and 22.1-38 may have related originally to a later king of the Jehu dynasty, either Jehoahaz or Joash. (See, for example, Miller and Hayes, *History*, pp. 253-54, 262, 299-300.) The process by which the narratives came to be connected to the Omride period remains uncertain. Conceivably, the story in ch. 20 was associated with Ahab long before it attained its present place in 1 Kgs.

'missing' (יִפָּקֵד, v. 39), and he proclaimed Yahweh's judgment: 'Because you let go (שִׁלַּחְתָּ) the man under my ban (חֶרְמִי) from your hand (מִיָּדְךָ; cf. the MT מִיָּד), so your life shall be for his life (וְהָיְתָה נַפְשְׁךָ תַּחַת נַפְשׁוֹ) and your people shall be for his people' (v. 42).[16]

Much of the same language occurs in 2 Kings 10. Jehu, for example, met Jehonadab the Rechabite, made a covenant with him, and 'brought him up into the chariot' (וַיַּעֲלֵהוּ אֵלָיו אֶל־הַמֶּרְכָּבָה, v. 15).[17] The two of them rode to Samaria. There, Jehu ordered the people to summon all the adherents of Baal: 'Let no one be missing' (אִישׁ אַל־יִפָּקֵד, v. 19). When the worshippers of Baal assembled, Jehu ordered his officers to kill them: 'Whoever allows to escape any of the men whom I am bringing into your hand, his life will be for his life' (הָאִישׁ אֲשֶׁר־יִמָּלֵט מִן־הָאֲנָשִׁים אֲשֶׁר אֲנִי מֵבִיא עַל־יְדֵיכֶם נַפְשׁוֹ תַּחַת נַפְשׁוֹ, v. 24).

The verbal parallels between the stories of Ahab and Jehu are likely more than coincidence. This is especially true of the rare biblical idiom, 'a life for a life'(נֶפֶשׁ תַּחַת נֶפֶשׁ).[18] By means of this expression and the other shared vocabulary, 2 Kings 9–10 compares the two kings and suggests great differences between them. The writer implies that Jehu, unlike Ahab, entered an appropriate covenant with an adherent of Yahwism (Jehonadab); Jehu, unlike Ahab, carried out Yahweh's will by executing enemies/apostates taken 'in hand'.

The narrative elaborates on the thoroughness of Jehu's actions. Execution follows upon execution: first Jehoram, then Ahaziah, then

---

16. Commentators debate the compositional history of 1 Kgs 20, but most agree that vv. 35-43 do not belong to the original story. (For a convenient review of the redactional analyses, see B.O. Long, *1 Kings* [FOTL, 9; Grand Rapids: Eerdmans, 1981], p. 207.) Against this view, one may observe that v. 34 hardly brings the narrative to a satisfactory close. Ahab's covenant with Benhadad in vv. 31-34 can only appear as a violation of the rules of holy war (specifically, the custom of the ban), and the reader thus would expect the story to continue with a statement of condemnation. Verses 35-43 provide this statement, and the verbal links between the verses and the preceding narrative reinforce the impression that they are original to the story.

17. Verse 15bα states specifically that Jehonadab 'gave his hand' (וַיִּתֵּן יָדוֹ) to Jehu. Elsewhere this act signals a pledge of loyalty in the context of a treaty or covenant ceremony (see Ezek. 17.18; cf. 1 Chron. 29.24; 2 Chron. 30.8). Cf. 1 Kgs 20.34, where the covenantal relationship between Ahab and Benhadad is indicated more clearly by the use of the term בְּרִית.

18. Outside of 1 Kgs 20 and 2 Kgs 10, it occurs only twice, in the statements of talion law in Exod. 21.23 and Lev. 24.18.

Jezebel, then the 70 sons of Ahab, then the princes of Judah, then the rest of the house of Ahab in Samaria, and finally all the worshippers of Baal. Furthermore, in emphasizing the extensive slaughter, the text uses the specific terminology of 'leave/spare' (שאר), 'survivor' (שריד), 'wipe out' (שמד), and 'escape' (מלט).

10.11. Jehu killed 'all who were left (כל־הנשארים) of the house of Ahab...until he left him no survivor' (עד־בלתי השאיר־לו שריד).

10.14. Jehu 'did not spare one of them' (ולא־השאיר איש מהם).

10.17a. Jehu killed 'all who were left to Ahab (כל־הנשארים לאחאב) in Samaria until he had wiped him out' (עד־השמידו; cf. the MT's עד־השמידו).[19]

10.21. On Jehu's orders, all the worshippers of Baal came to the house of Baal in Samaria: 'no one was left who did not come' (ולא־נשאר איש אשר לא־בא).

10.24. Jehu warned his officers: 'Whoever allows to escape (האיש אשר־ימלט) any one of the men whom I am bringing into your hands' will forfeit his own life.

Significantly, the same language articulates the theme of annihilation in biblical stories of holy war (e.g. Num. 21.33-35; Josh. 8.18, 22; 11.14; Judg. 3.29; 4.16). These narratives typically tell how Yahweh 'gave' an enemy 'into the hands' of the Israelites, and how the Israelites then carried out the 'ban' (חרם) by 'wiping out' the enemy, 'sparing no one', 'allowing none to escape', 'leaving no survivor'. In light of these stories, the revolt of Jehu in 2 Kings 9–10 also appears as a holy war.[20] The text implicitly praises Jehu by suggesting that he, unlike Ahab, properly carried out the ban and 'spared no one'.

19. Schmitt, among others, regards 10.11 and 17 as late additions, but the argument rests largely on the assumption that the phraseology of the verses is distinctively deuteronomistic (*Elisa*, p. 23; see also G.H. Jones, *1 and 2 Kings*, II [NCB; Grand Rapids: Eerdmans, 1984], pp. 467-69). The language here may be simply part and parcel of the tradition of holy war that has shaped the entire story. Only the reference to Elijah in v. 17b should be regarded as secondary (cf. Noth, *The Deuteronomistic History*, p. 72).

20. See S. Niditch, *War in the Hebrew Bible: A Study in the Ethics of Violence* (Oxford: Oxford University Press, 1993), p. 73.

The Rhetorical Appeal of 2 Kings 9–10

The bias of 2 Kings 9–10 makes good sense against the background of the reign of Jeroboam II, c. 750 BCE. At this time, Rezin of Syria was encroaching on Israelite holdings in northern Transjordan and perhaps also in Galilee (see Amos 1.3-5; Isa. 9.11-12; Hos. 1.5).[21] A breakaway movement in Gilead, led by Pekah and supported by Rezin, may have been underway as well (see 2 Kgs 15.25, 27, 37).[22] Internally, there seems to have been widespread public sentiment against Jeroboam, and prophets like Amos and Hosea were calling for the overthrow of the regime (Amos 7.9, 11; Hos. 1.4). Support for Pekah perhaps was strong even west of the Jordan, specifically in the area stretching from Jericho and Gilgal up the 'Valley of Aven' (= Suweinit-Qelt valley; Amos 1.5).[23] In short, this was a time of extreme crisis for the Jehu dynasty, when the legitimacy of the regime was much in doubt. In this context, 2 Kings 9–10 would have served to shore up support for the dynasty by justifying its rise to power in the first place. The text attempts to legitimate the regime by demonstrating how its founder, Jehu, had seized the throne of Israel with the approval of Yahweh.

If this interpretation is right, it may be profitable to explore further the rhetorical force of certain claims of the Kings account in relation to Jeroboam's troubles. First, the narrative presents Elisha as the prophetic instigator of Jehu's revolt. Two observations cast light on this claim.

1. Several of the biblical stories about Elisha and the 'sons of the prophets' show a connection to the town of Gilgal (Khirbet Mefjir?) and the surrounding area (see 2 Kgs 2.1; 2.19-22; 4.38-41, 42-44; 6.1-7; 13.20-21). The Elisha tradition apparently was prominent at Gilgal, and it may have flourished there even in the mid-eighth century BCE.[24] The town was probably home to a community of prophets who viewed Elisha as their prophetic ancestor/founder and so told stories about him.

2. As suggested already, Pekah was challenging the authority of

21. See S.A. Irvine, 'The Southern Border of Syria Reconstructed', *CBQ* 56 (1994), pp. 21-41 (40).

22. See H.J. Cook, 'Pekah', *VT* 14 (1964), pp. 121-35; also J.H. Hayes, *Amos, the Eighth-Century Prophet: His Times and his Preaching* (Nashville: Abingdon Press, 1988), pp. 26-27.

23. See Hayes's interpretation of Amos 1.5; 4.4-5; and 5.4-5 (*Amos*, pp. 76-77, 143-44, 158-59).

24. See Schmitt, *Elisa*, pp. 109, 156-58.

Jeroboam and the Jehu dynasty as early as 750 BCE, and his domain west of the Jordan may well have encompassed Gilgal. If so, it is reasonable to suppose that the prophets and other citizens of Gilgal favored Pekah as their king.

In light of these considerations, the role of Elisha in 2 Kings 9–10 makes sense as a special appeal to prophets in Gilgal. On the one hand, they supported Pekah's kingship; on the other hand, they revered Elisha as their ancestor/founder. The Kings narrative perhaps aimed at persuading them to follow the example of Elisha and switch their allegiance from Pekah to Jeroboam and the Jehu dynasty.

Secondly, the Kings narrative presents Jehu's revolt as a holy war. The idea of holy war is also central to the Conquest tradition in the book of Joshua. Significantly, several of the Conquest stories there show a connection to Gilgal (see Josh. 4.19-24; 5.8-9, 10-12; 9.6; 10.6-7, 9, 15, 43). Whether any of them reflect a 'ritual conquest' in the Gilgal cultus, as some scholars have argued, remains debatable.[25] At a minimum, however, one might suppose that the Gilgal sanctuary was home to a cult that emphasized the Conquest tradition. If so, 2 Kings 9–10 again appears to have been composed in a way that would appeal especially to supporters of Pekah in Gilgal during the mid-eighth century BCE. The narrative perhaps intimated that they should accept the legitimacy of the Jehu dynasty because the dynasty had begun with a revolt very much like the ancient holy wars they remembered and celebrated.

If 2 Kings 9–10 glorifies Jehu's revolt as a holy war, it is reasonable to ask whether the account exaggerates the extent of the massacre. Undoubtedly the revolt was a bloody affair: in order to secure his rule, Jehu would have exterminated the remaining members of the Omride family and their supporters, including the cultic establishment in Samaria.[26] It is less certain, however, that he executed Jehoram and Ahaziah specifically, as the Kings narrative claims. The testimony of the Tel Dan stela raises doubt.

---

25. See H.-J. Kraus, 'Gilgal: Ein Beitrag zur Kultusgeschichte Israels', *VT* 1 (1951), pp. 181-99; F.M. Cross, *Canaanite Myth and Hebrew Epic: Essays in the History of the Religion of Israel* (Cambridge, MA: Harvard University Press, 1973), pp. 103-105.

26. According to 10.23, Jehu killed only the worshippers of Baal. However, one might guess that, historically, priests of Yahweh in the capital city also supported the Omride dynasty, and so they too might have been victims of the massacre.

The Testimony of the Tel Dan Stela

The Tel Dan stela is a ninth-century BCE royal inscription in the language of Old Aramaic.[27] The name of the author is missing, but most scholars attribute the inscription to a Syrian king.[28] The first part of the text reviews the reign and death of the author's father, as well as the author's own rise to kingship as the special choice of the god Hadad. Lines 6-9 then describe his battle with two kings of Israel and Judah, whose names are partially preserved as [...]*rm* and [...]*yhw*. The Hebrew Bible provides only one pair of possible candidates: Jehoram/Joram of Israel and Ahaziah of Judah. If these identifications are correct, the author of the inscription is likely Hazael of Damascus. 2 Kings 8.27 and 9.15 report that he was at war with Jehoram and Ahaziah in northern Transjordan on the eve of Jehu's revolt. The Tel Dan stela appears to narrate the outcome of this conflict.

6. of my kingdom. And I killed two [power]ful kin[gs],[29] who harnessed thou[sands of cha]/riots
7. and thousands of horsemen. [And I killed Jo]ram, son of [Ahab,]
8. king of Israel, and [I] killed [Ahaz]iah, son of [Joram, kin]/g
9. of the House of David; and I set [their towns into ruins?...the ci]/ties[30]

It is striking that Hazael takes credit for 'killing' (*qtl*) Jehoram and Ahaziah. The inscription thus appears to contradict a central claim of 2 Kings 9–10, namely, that Jehu executed the two kings at Jezreel. Scholars handle the problem in various ways.

27. See A. Biran and J. Naveh, 'The Tel Dan Inscription: A New Fragment', *IEJ* 45 (1995), pp. 1-18.

28. Cf. J.W. Wesselius, 'The First Royal Inscription from Ancient Israel: The Tel Dan Inscription Reconsidered', *SJOT* 13 (1999), pp. 163-86. He proposes Jehu as the author, but the interpretation is not convincing.

29. For this translation, see A. Lemaire, 'The Tel Dan Stela as a Piece of Royal Historiography', *JSOT* 81 (1998), pp. 3-14 (7-8). He restores the Aramaic as *ml[k]n.[tq]pn* and interprets *mlkn* as a dual form. Cf. the reading in the *editio princeps* of Biran and Naveh ('Tel Dan Inscription', pp. 12-13, 16): *ml[kn.šb]ʿn*, '[seve]nty kin[gs]'.

30. For the restored reading of the second half of this line, see W.M. Schniedewind, 'Tel Dan Stela: New Light on Aramaic and Jehu's Revolt', *BASOR* 302 (1996), pp. 75-90 (77-78).

According to A. Lemaire, the Tel Dan stela is a propagandistic memorial inscription from the later years of Hazael, and it glorifies the Syrian king by exaggerating his military accomplishments at the beginning of his reign, during the late 840s BCE.[31] The main narrative in 2 Kings 9–10 is nearly contemporary with the events it reports and thus is more reliable than the Tel Dan stela. Jehu, not Hazael, killed Jehoram and Ahaziah.

One might question Lemaire's assumption about the temporal priority of the Kings narrative. On the one hand, nothing in the Tel Dan stela clearly points to the late part of Hazael's reign as the time of the inscription's composition.[32] On the other hand, the early date of the Kings account is far from certain. It would be just as reasonable to accept the Tel Dan stela as a nearly contemporary and essentially reliable account and, on the basis of its report, to conclude that the Kings text probably dates long after the events of 841 BCE, when people no longer knew how Jehoram and Ahaziah actually had died.

A different approach to the problem involves harmonizing the two sources. S. Yamada, for example, re-examines the verb *qtl* in the Tel Dan stela and translates it as 'strike, defeat', rather than 'kill'.[33] The contradiction between the inscription and the biblical account thus disappears: Hazael 'defeated' Jehoram and Ahaziah in battle, and subsequently Jehu executed the two kings in Jezreel. Alternatively, W.M. Schniedewind resolves the contradiction by hypothesizing an alliance between Jehu and Hazael.[34] Jehu was supposedly subordinate to the Syrian king, and with the latter's approval—if not his assistance—Jehu killed Jehoram and Ahaziah. In his memorial inscription at Tel Dan,

31. Lemaire, 'The Tel Dan Stela', pp. 10-11; see also B. Margalit, 'The Old-Aramaic Inscription of Hazael from Dan', *UF* 26 (1994), pp. 317-20 (317 n. 3).

32. This is especially true if line 6 speaks only of Hazael killing 'two powerful kings', not 'seventy kings' (n. 29 above). See N. Na'aman, 'Three Notes on the Aramaic Inscription from Tel Dan', *IEJ* 50 (2000), pp. 92-104 (99-100).

33. S. Yamada, 'Aram–Israel Relations as Reflected in the Aramaic Inscription from Tel Dan', *UF* 27 (1995), pp. 611-25 (619-21).

34. Schniedewind, 'Tel Dan Stela', pp. 83-85; see also I. Kottsieper, 'Die Inschrift vom Tell Dan und die politischen Beziehungen zwischen Aram–Damaskus und Israel in der 1. Hälfte des 1. Jahrtausends vor Christus', in M. Dietrich and I. Kottsieper (eds.), *'Und Mose schreib dieses Lied auf': Studien zum Alten Testament und zum Alten Orient. Festschrift für Oswald Loretz zur Vollendung seines 70. Lebensjahres mit Beiträgen von Freunden, Schülern und Kollegen* (AOAT, 250; Münster: Ugarit-Verlag, 1998), pp. 475-500 (488-89).

Hazael simply claims credit for what his vassal in fact did: through Jehu, Hazael 'killed' the two kings.

Neither of these solutions is convincing. Against Yamada's proposal, one may note that, while *qtl* in Aramaic texts occasionally means 'defeat', the usual sense of the verb is 'kill'. Schniedewind's theory of an alliance between Jehu and Hazael is not impossible, but the evidence for this collusion is slim and open to different interpretations.[35] Enmity between the two seems more likely in view of their different policies toward Assyria. While Jehu submitted to Shalmaneser III in 841 BCE, Hazael chose to continue Syria's resistance. Moreover, 2 Kgs 8.11-12 remembers Hazael as a great oppressor of Israel, and 2 Kgs 10.32-33 speaks of him as 'attacking' Israelite territory in Transjordan during the reign of Jehu specifically. In light of these texts, the idea of cooperation between Hazael and Jehu seems doubtful.[36]

N. Na'aman represents a third approach to the problem.[37] According to him, the Tel Dan stela dates to the late 830s BCE and thus it is roughly contemporary with the events it reports. Despite its pro-Hazael bias, the inscription is probably reliable in claiming that the Syrian king killed Jehoram and Ahaziah in battle. 2 Kings 9–10, on the other hand, is a prophetic story that was handed down in oral tradition and eventually recorded in writing, many years after Jehu's revolt. In the course of this long history of transmission, historical memory perhaps blurred and certain details of the story may have changed. Thus Jehu erroneously got the credit for the deaths of Jehoram and Ahaziah.

This solution has much to recommend it, especially the general principle that a contemporary source should receive priority in historical reconstruction. The Tel Dan stela certainly aims to glorify Hazael, and its bias can be seen, for example, in the way it glosses over the

35. Schniedewind places great weight on 1 Kgs 19.15-18, which speaks of Hazael, Jehu and Elisha as sequential agents of divine judgment upon Israel ('Tel Dan Stela', pp. 83-84). However, the idea of their acting in concert with each other is far from obvious here. Even less convincing is Schniedewind's suggestion that the threat of Jezreel in Hos. 1.4-5 assumes an analogy between the Syrian–Israelite coalition c. 734 and the earlier alliance of Hazael and Jehu (p. 85). See S.A. Irvine, 'The Threat of Jezreel (Hosea 1:4-5)', *CBQ* 57 (1995), pp. 494-503 (496-98).

36. According to Kottsieper, 2 Kgs 10.32-33 indicates that the alliance between Jehu and Hazael collapsed soon after Jehu's revolt ('Die Inschrift vom Tell Dan', pp. 491-92). This proposal would be plausible if there were clear evidence for the alliance in the first place.

37. Na'aman, 'Three Notes', pp. 100-104.

king's irregular accession to the throne in Damascus.[38] However, the ninth-century BCE date of the inscription and its location in Dan probably limited the writer's ability to depart from certain essential facts. Historical propaganda may omit facts or twist them for the maximum 'spin' effect, but if it is to prove effective, it cannot flatly contradict what an audience otherwise knows to be true.[39] One might reasonably guess that, in the 830s and even 820s BCE, people in Dan, and in Palestine generally, knew how Jehoram and Ahaziah had died. If Jehu in fact had executed the two kings, Hazael (or his scribes) could hardly have hoped to persuade many that he had killed them. Thus, if the Tel Dan stela makes precisely this claim, it is probably true.

Although the late origin of the account in 2 Kings 9–10 cannot be proven, the circumstances in Israel during the mid-eighth century BCE have been seen to provide a plausible setting. Na'aman conceives of the story as taking shape over a long period of oral and written transmission, but it is just as likely that the basic account (i.e. apart from the few editorial accretions) stems from the court of Jeroboam II. If the narrative first arose c. 750 BCE, almost a century would separate it from the events it describes. Memory of Jehu's revolt certainly would have faded, and most Israelites at the time may have had only a vague idea of the massacre.[40] In these circumstances, the author of the Kings narrative would have been free to invent details, including the idea that Jehu killed Jehoram and Ahaziah.[41] If, historically, Hazael killed these two

---

38. Both 2 Kgs 8.7-15 and a summary inscription of Shalmaneser III (*KAH*, 30; see *ANET*, p. 280) indicate that Hazael was a usurper. The Tell Dan stela gives the general impression that his succession was without incident. However, the statement in line 4—'and Hadad made me myself king'—may hint at his need for special legitimation.

39. See P.M. Taylor, *Munitions of the Mind: A History of Propaganda from the Ancient World to the Present Era* (Manchester: Manchester University Press, 1995), pp. 4-15.

40. Scholars often assume that Hos. 1.4 attests the historicity of Jehu's revolt as described in 2 Kings (see H.G.M. Williamson, 'Jezreel in the Biblical Texts', *TA* 18 [1991], pp. 72-89 [79]). Possibly, however, the prophetic saying is not an independent testimony to the episode, but simply Hosea's response to the recently produced Kings account (see Irvine, 'The Threat of Jezreel', pp. 499-500, 503). In any case, even if the prophet had independent knowledge of the revolt, he may not have known specifically about the execution of Jehoram and Ahaziah. His expression, 'the blood of Jezreel', is quite vague.

41. See Taylor's comments on the 'perception gap' between reality and the

kings, why did the biblical writer think to attribute their deaths to Jehu? At least part of the answer may lie in the ideology of holy war that dominates 2 Kings 9–10. As has been indicated earlier, the author was concerned to depict Jehu as the zealous warrior who—unlike Ahab— fully carried out the practice of the ban. If this interpretation is right, it would hardly have served the writer's purpose to report that Jehoram and Ahaziah died by the hand of someone else. The glorification of Jehu as the righteous champion in holy war prompted the writer to exaggerate the bloodshed of Jehu's revolt so that it included the lives of the two kings as well.[42]

Conclusion

The main proposals of this essay can be summarized briefly. The basic story in 2 Kings 9–10 likely dates late in the reign of Jeroboam II. The account is royal propaganda for the purpose of shoring up support for the Jehu dynasty at a time when its legitimacy was widely questioned. The story justifies the regime by justifying the revolt with which it began. In this regard, three strategies of the narrative are especially noteworthy. First, the narrative claims that the prophet Elisha instigated the revolt. Second, the text portrays Jehu as a latter-day Elijah who, filled with a 'zeal for Yahweh', opposed the Omrides and worshippers of Baal and slaughtered them all. Finally, the account presents the revolt as a holy war in which Jehu, unlike Ahab before him, carried out the ban fully, killing all the enemies taken 'in hand'. The first and third of these strategies may have been aimed specifically at supporters of Pekah in Gilgal, who preserved and celebrated traditions of Elisha, the Conquest, and holy war.

There is little reason to doubt that, historically, Jehu's revolt involved a massacre. The Tel Dan stela indicates, however, that the executions did not include Jehoram and Ahaziah specifically. They had died already

claims of propaganda (*Munitions of the Mind*, p. 11). The gap, he explains, can be large in cases when the targeted audience stands at a great distance geographically or temporally from the reality in question and knows about the reality only through the propaganda.

42. This proposal contrasts sharply with the widespread view that the execution of the two kings was an embarrassing historical fact that 2 Kgs 9–10, as a nearly contemporary document, could not conceal but only justify. See, for example, Jepsen, *Nabi*, p. 73.

at the hand of Hazael in battle, and presumably it was their deaths that prompted Jehu to seize power in Jezreel and Samaria. If 2 Kings 9–10 erroneously credits Jehu with the deaths of the two kings, it is not just because the author was ignorant of the true facts. He was intent on glorifying Jehu as a righteous king who fully carried out the ban in a holy war. The writer thus extended the slaughter of the revolt to cover all the enemies of Yahweh, especially the Omride king and his Judean ally.

While the narrative remains 'one of the most brilliant pieces of Hebrew literary art', its value as an historical witness to Jehu's revolt turns out to be less than most scholars have supposed. The story reflects the circumstances of its origin c. 750 BCE as much as, if not more than, the ninth-century BCE events it purports to describe.

SOLOMON AT MEGIDDO?

Ernst Axel Knauf

Introduction

The question of the extent of Solomon's realm—controversial through-out the past decade of scholarship[1]—is not yet settled: did he rule from Dan to Beersheba (and even a bit further south),[2] or from Gibeon to Tamar?[3] Whether Solomon ruled in or over Megiddo would decide the case.[4] In the course of the discussion, the focus of the controversy pro-gressed from a qualitative question (Was there a state in tenth-century BCE Israel/Palestine?), always liable to degenerate from scholarly discourse to statements of dogmatic convictions, to the quantitative question: How much of a state can be observed in which regions of

---

1. The discussion was started, in a sense, by A.R. Millard, 'Texts and Archaeology: Weighing the Evidence, the Case for King Solomon', *PEQ* 123 (1991), pp. 19-27; and J.M. Miller, 'Solomon: International Potentate or Local King?', *PEQ* 123 (1991), pp. 19-27, and can be traced through and beyond in L.K. Handy (ed.), *The Age of Solomon: Scholarship at the Turn of the Millennium* (SHCANE, 11; Leiden: E.J. Brill, 1997).

2. Thus B. Halpern, 'The Gate of Megiddo and the Debate on the Tenth Century', in A. Lemaire and M. Sæbø (eds.), *Congress Volume: Oslo 1998* (VTSup, 80; Leiden: E.J. Brill, 2000), pp. 79-121, 86-88; 107-108.

3. Thus E.A. Knauf, 'Le roi est mort, vive le roi! A Biblical Argument for the Historicity of Solomon', in L.K. Handy (ed.), *The Age of Solomon: Scholarship at the Turn of the Millennium* (SHCANE, 11; Leiden: E.J. Brill, 1997), pp. 81-95.

4. Hazor is not decisive insofar as the alternative—whether it was Solomon or Omri who built Hazor X—is settled by the 'Low Chronology' *a priori*. It cannot be settled archaeologically by the 'traditional chronology', because pottery assemb-lages of the Iron IIA period (Solomon) and the early Iron IIB period (Omri) cannot yet be distinguished. Cf. A. Ben-Tor and D. Ben-Ami, 'Hazor and the Archaeology of the Tenth Century B.C.E.', *IEJ* 48 (1998), pp. 1-37; I. Finkelstein, 'Hazor and the North in the Iron Age', *BASOR* 314 (1999), pp. 55-70.

Syria–Palestine during the tenth century BCE?[5] As soon as one operates
with a general definition of 'state',[6] cross-culturally valid at least for the
ancient Near East and the eastern Mediterranean in antiquity, archaeology should provide the answer—one day. Being dedicated to the
pursuit of objective knowledge, that is the constructing of theories that
can be tested against empirical facts, the present argument departs from
Megiddo, a place with some of its history known, rather than from the
reign of king Solomon, a narrative construct (as long as not yet attested
in a contemporary document) the relationship of which to the past real
word is always laborious to establish, hypothetical and controversial.

The Objectivity of the Text

This is not to deny that texts are factual evidence of their own. Quite to
the contrary, they may not contain facts in every case, but they always
are facts—even artifacts. A text contains a specific number of sentences,
each constituted by a specific number of words. Syntactically as well as
macro-syntactically, texts are objectively structured. Semantically, they
always indicate whether they refer to the real word or another world of
imagination.[7] Under this point of view, texts are neither right nor
wrong, they just are. Statements within texts referring to the real world
are right or wrong, and historians want to know. Being part of empirical
research, history never leads beyond the level of probabilistic generalizations. It is more probable than not that a world exists beyond the
human perception of the world, but nobody knows for sure. Only
ideologues have absolute answers.

It is the objectivity of the texts, unaffected by its various readings,
that allows one to separate the text from its readings, traditional in

5.   Halpern, 'The Gate of Megiddo', pp. 120-21.

6.   Cultural relativism in the field of biblical studies sometimes claims that the
world of the Bible must be assessed on its own terms, and therefore one may call a
settlement of 1.4 ha a 'city' in ancient Israel (but does the Hebrew עִיר always
denote 'city' rather than 'fortified place of any size'?). Beyond the truism that each
and every culture is an individual synchronically and diachronically (the
individuality of which, however, is only recognizable by contrasting its features
that are shared with some or all other cultures), this argument might finally lead to
the claim that the Bible always addresses a world other than our real, empirical
world—a claim that would hardly be in the best interest of church and theology.

7.   Cf. E.A. Knauf, 'From History to Interpretation', in D.V. Edelman (ed.),
The Fabric of History: Text, Artifact and Israel's Past (JSOTSup, 127; Sheffield:
Sheffield Academic Press, 1991), pp. 26-64, esp. 48 n. 2.

religion or scholarships, and create new readings. It is part of the objectivity of the text that a textual element like 'Megiddo', by virtue of belonging to the class of toponyms, refers to a trans-textual reality, a place so named;[8] and even if 'Megiddo' were a virtual place created by an author's fantasy, it would tell the reader something about possible place names in the linguistic world of this author and something about the structure and nature of settlements in her or his imagination.

The textual evidence on Solomon leads to the objective statement that his court did not keep annals. First, there are no texts in 1 Kgs 1–11 that can be classified as excerpts from annals (as 2 Kgs 3.4-5), but this point might be debated. Second, the biblical authors do not cite the 'Annals of the Kings of Israel' or 'The Annals of the Kings of Judah' as their source for Solomon, but an evidently monographic work 'Book of the Affairs of Solomon' (1 Kgs 11.41). Finally, had there been annals and the accurate length of his reign known, one would not have attributed to him the formulaic 40 years for a long, but not superhumanly long, period.

The Objectivity of Archaeology
The objectivity of archaeology, on the first and factual level, is the product of a precision and intellectual discipline that is sometimes lacking in the work of textual analysis: a wall is 1.45 m thick and not 'very thick' or 'rather thick'; feature A is north, south, east, west of feature B and not 'right' or 'left' of it; a locus either contains charcoal and burnt mudbrick or not (and then, it is not 'destruction debris').

As a science based on statistics and measurements and the analysis of rather complex sets of data (instead of depending on aesthetics, intuition, interpretations and 'common sense'), the objectivity of archaeology may well be traced in the recent development of Iron Age chronology. Traditional chronology departed from an exodus under Ramesses II, the arrival of the Israelites in Canaan under Merneptah, and a united kingdom in the tenth century BCE. This was perfectly correct at a time when these historiographical constructs were commonly accepted as data.[9] By

8. J.M. Miller, 'Site Identification: A Problem Area in Contemporary Biblical Scholarship', *ZDPV* 99 (1983), pp. 119-29.

9. For the more recent view that an 'exodus' might well have happened after Merneptah and that Exod. 1.11 cannot possibly belong to a tradition deriving from the end of the second millennium BCE, see E.A. Knauf, *Midian: Untersuchungen zur Geschichte Palästinas und Nordarabiens am Ende des 2. Jahrtausends v. Chr.*

1990, it had become clear that traditional Iron Age chronology was a conventional rather than a rational construct.[10] In 1996, I. Finkelstein presented his 'Low Chronology' as a viable alternative, which proved itself superior in the subsequent discussion: more data could be more coherently synthesized, and objections raised could be invalidated.[11] By the summer of 2000, too much C-14 evidence was known to contradict the traditional chronology than could be easily dismissed.[12] The present contribution presupposes the 'Low Chronology', and for the convenience of readers not yet fully familiar with it, traditonal dates will be given in brackets.

	Low Chronology	Traditional Chronology
Iron I	1150±25–925±25	1200–1000
Iron IIA	925±25–875±25	1000–925/900
Iron IIB	875±25–725±25	925/900–734/700
Iron IIC	725±25–575±25	734/700–586

(ADPV; Otto Wiesbaden: Otto Harrassowitz, 1988), pp. 98-99, 104-105; *idem, Die Umwelt des Alten Testaments* (NSKAT, 29; Stuttgart: Katholisches Bibelwerk, 1994), pp. 103-106; K.W. Whitelam, ' "Israel is Laid Waste; his Seed Is No More": What If Merneptah's Scribes Were Telling the Truth?', *BibInt* 8 (2000), pp. 8-22.

10. See G.J. Wightman, 'The Myth of Solomon', *BASOR* 277-78 (1990), pp. 5-22; D. Ussishkin, 'Notes on Megiddo, Gezer, Ashdod, and Tel Batash in the 10th to 9th Centuries B.C.', *BASOR* 277-78 (1990), pp. 71-91.

11. See I. Finkelstein, 'The Stratigraphy and Chronology of Megiddo and Beth-Shan in the Twelfth–Eleventh Centuries B.C.E.', *TA* 23 (1996), pp. 170-84; *idem*, 'The Archaeology of the United Monarchy: An Alternative View', *Levant* 28 (1996), pp. 177-87; *idem*, 'Bible Archaeology or Archaeology of Palestine in the Iron Age? A Rejoinder', *Levant* 30 (1998), pp. 167-74; *idem*, 'Notes on the Stratigraphy and Chronology of Iron Age Ta'anach', *TA* 25 (1998), pp. 208-18; *idem*, 'Hazor and the North in the Iron Age: A Low Chronology Perspective', *BASOR* 314 (1999), pp. 55-70; E.A. Knauf, 'Kinneret and Naftali', in A. Lemaire and M. Sæbø (eds.), *Congress Volume: Oslo 1998* (VTSup, 80; Leiden: E.J. Brill, 2000), pp. 219-33; *idem*, 'The "Low Chronology" and How Not to Deal with It', *BN* 101 (2000), pp. 56-63.

12. Accumulated C14-evidence from the Feinan region dates the local Iron I period to the eleventh through the ninth centuries BCE; the data are published by T.E. Levy *et al.*, 'The Jabal Hamrat Fidan Project: Excavations at the Wadi Fidan 40 Cemetery, Jordan (1997)', *Levant* 31 (1999), pp. 293-308 (303, 305); see further A. Mazar, 'The 1997–1998 Excavation at Tel Rehov: Preliminary Report', *IEJ* 49 (1999), pp. 1-42 (40-41).

Absolute dates exist for the following Iron Age strata in Northern Israel:

—Samaria VI: destroyed by Sargon II in 720 BCE.
—Dan II, Hazor V, Kinneret II, Megiddo IVA: destroyed by Tiglathpileser III in 733 BCE.
—Dan III: built by Hazael, second half of the ninth century.[13]

1 Kings 9.15

Megiddo is mentioned twice in the story about Solomon, in 1 Kgs 9.15 and in 1 Kgs 4.12, but the two texts present the site in very different geographical and political contexts. For both texts, their pertinence to the tenth century BCE has been questioned.[14] As new evidence has to be considered—archaeological evidence in the case of 1 Kgs 9.15 and textual evidence in the case of 1 Kgs 4.12—the topic might be revisited.

a. *The Textual Evidence*

1 Kings 9.15-19 is hardly what an archaeologist would call a 'clean locus'. It is a 'fill', separating the introduction of the corvée in v. 15 from its elaboration in vv. 20-21. A stratified presentation of the English text (NRSV) should illustrate the literary stratigraphy most clearly:

> 9.15 This is the account of the forced labor that King Solomon conscripted to build the house of the LORD and his own house, the Millo and the wall of Jerusalem,
>> Hazor, Megiddo, Gezer
>>> 9.16 (Pharaoh king of Egypt had gone up and captured Gezer and burned it down, had killed the Canaanites who lived in the city, and had given it as dowry to his daughter, Solomon's wife;
>>>> 9.17 so Solomon rebuilt Gezer), Lower Beth-horon,
>>>> 9.18 Baalath, Tamar in the wilderness, within the land,
>>>> 9.19 as well as all of Solomon's storage cities, the cities for

---

13. The reused fragments of Hazael's inscription from Dan II at first do no more than attest Aramaean activity for one of the preceeding strata. Aramaic features, as stelae in and in front of the city gates, make the attribution of Dan III to Hazael certain.

14. Knauf, 'Le roi', pp. 91-92; *idem*, 'King Solomon's Copper Supply', in E. Lipiński (ed.), *Phoenicia and the Bible: Proceedings of the Conference Held at the University of Leuven on the 15th and 16th of March 1990* (StudPh, 9; OLA, 44; Leuven: Peeters, 1991), pp. 167-86 (178).

his chariots, the cities for his cavalry, and whatever Solomon
desired to build, in Jerusalem, in Lebanon, and in all the land
of his dominion.

9.20 All the people who were left of the Amorites, the Hittites, the
Perizzites, the Hivites, and the Jebusites, who were not of the people of
Israel—

9.21 their descendants who were still left in the land, whom the
Israelites were unable to destroy completely—these Solomon con-
scripted for slave labor, and so they are to this day.

'Hazor, Megiddo and Gezer' form a first insertion into the macro-
syntactical and logical sequence 9.15, 20-21; 16 is a scholion, adding an
interesting footnote on the history of Gezer. The insertion of 9.16 has a
third addition in its train, again following the catch-word 'Gezer', a
second town-list. 1 Kings 9.19 probably goes with the first insertion
rather than with the third: the Megiddo that the author had (and some
historians still have in mind) might well be characterized as a 'storage–
chariot–cavalry city';[15] even if it were not, the concept is at least
conceivable in this case, which it is not for Beth-horon, Baalath (Bet
Yearim) or Tamar (Ain al-Arus). The genesis of 1 Kgs 9.15-21 is quite
clear: to the original deuteronomistic account of the origin of the forced
labor needed to construct Solomon's projects at Jerusalem (15.20-21)
were first added three prominent cities other than Jerusalem (15.19),
then a gloss on Gezer, and finally another list of places that also
contained a reference to Gezer.

There are two lists of place-names in 1 Kgs 9.15-19, not one. Even if
one would not excise 9.16 as a stratigraphical divider (as the NRSV tries
to do by inserting its parentheses), the geographical scope of the list and
the political and economic weight of the places involved constitute
indisputable evidence for this. Are the major cities of the United States
New York, Chicago and Los Angeles, or New York, Ithaca and
Binghampton?

If there are two lists, a Megiddo–Hazor list and a Baalath–Tamar list,
one may still discuss the question of which of the two should be
attributed to Solomon. Does the sequence of the text, both in the
direction of the reading and in literary stratigraphy, reflect the decline
of Judah from the leading power in a 'United Monarchy' to a petty

15. There is no need to discuss the question of the 'stables' in Megiddo IVA in
the present context. It suffices for the argument that some people still think that
these structures were stables.

kingdom on the southern periphery of Syro-Palestine?[16] Unfortunately, the text of the Megiddo–Hazor-level contains an Assyrian loanword in Hebrew, ערי המסכנות 'storage-cities' (from Akkadian *maškantu* 'depot'),[17] which lends further support to the suspicion that 1 Kgs 9.15, 19 speaks about Hazor and Megiddo of the eighth, if not the seventh century BCE.[18] This observation, however, brings archaeology into the game.

b. *The Archaeological Evidence*
Archaeological information is arithmetic, geometric and visual rather than textual. It presumes that its recipients will think in four dimensions: to imagine the development of complex three-dimensional structures (such as a town or city) in the course of time.

Enough has been excavated to reconstruct the history of Megiddo in the Iron Age without recourse to written sources, not even those found at the site.[19] The chronological sequence is clear:

VIA (tenth century BCE, traditionally second half of the eleventh century BCE)
VB (late tenth/early ninth century BCE, traditionally early tenth century BCE)
VA/IVB (first half of the ninth century BCE, traditionally tenth century BCE)
IVA (eighth century BCE, traditionally ninth and eighth centuries BCE)
III (seventh century BCE).[20]

16. It goes without saying that the date of the stratigraphical context has no bearing on the dating of the (individual elements of the) 'fill'. The context (9.15, 20-21) presupposes the deuteronomistic ideology of the late seventh and sixth centuries BCE.

17. The reception of Akkadian *shin* as *samekh* betrays Assyrian rather than Babylonian pronunciation of Akkadian as the origin of the loan; cf. the names of Sargon and Asarhaddon in Hebrew, and E.A. Knauf, 'Aššur, Šuah und der stimmlose Sibilant des Assyrischen', *BN* 49 (1989), pp. 13-19.

18. The discussion of 1 Kgs 9.15-18 by Halpern ('The Gate of Megiddo', pp. 104-107) does not fully live up to the standard of his methodological principles as stated (p. 107)—which this author shares. There is no textual evidence that any material in 1 Kgs 9.15-19 formed part of the 'deuteronomist's' sources, quite to the contrary.

19. The reader might consult the plans in the most recent and most excellent synthesis of the archaeology of Israel/Palestine by Z. Herzog (*Archaeology of the City: Urban Planning in Ancient Israel and its Social Implications* [TAUMS, 13; Tel Aviv: Emery and Claire Yass Archaeology Press, 1997], p. 200, fig. 5.8 [VIA]; p. 213 fig. 5.15 [VA]; p. 227 fig. 5.21 [IVA]; p. 256 fig. 5.35 [III]) in order to visualize the following descriptions.

20. The dates are presented as based on C-14 evidence, or as if they were

Megiddo VIA was the last revival of Canaanite Megiddo, the independent city-state, if on a somewhat diminished level of prosperity. It is the last phase in which Temple 2048 was in use; it also was the last phase in which settlement covered the lower terrace,[21] abandoned thereafter when building activities were restricted to what now constitutes the tell. The ancient palace area in the north is still occupied by larger and more complex buildings than the domestic quarter in the south.

Megiddo VB was a village that gradually developed into the town of VA.[22] In VA, a palace (1723) and public buildings (1482, 6000) were added to structures of the grown town. The palace is separated from the town by an acropolis wall and a gate, marking itself as an intruder. Megiddo VA did not have a city wall,[23] not even a wall left uncompleted.[24]

Megiddo IVA was the first city to be walled in during the Iron Age, but it was no city: less than 25 per cent of its area was dedicated to domestic occupation. The rest consists of public buildings: courtyards, magazines and barracks (the so-called 'stables'). This Megiddo no longer served the needs of an indigenous population; it was nothing but a royal stronghold.[25]

(Megiddo III). For the date of Megiddo III, as based on the Assyrian documents, see B. Halpern, 'Centre and Sentry: Megiddo's Role in Transit, Administration and Trade', in I. Finkelstein, D. Ussishkin and B. Halpern (eds.), *Megiddo III: The 1992–1996 Seasons*, II (2 vols.; TAUMS, 18; Tel Aviv: Emery and Claire Yass Publications in Archaeology, Institute of Archaeology, Tel Aviv University, 2000), pp. 564-69.

21. See D. Ilan, N. Franklin and R.S. Hallote, 'Area F', in Finkelstein, Ussishkin and Halpern (eds.), *Megiddo III*, I, pp. 97-98; Halpern, 'Centre and Sentry', pp. 551-55; I. Finkelstein and D. Ussishkin, 'Archaeological and Historical Conclusions', in Finkelstein, Ussishkin and Halpern (eds.), *Megiddo III*, II, pp. 595-96.

22. See A. Kempinski, *Megiddo: A City-State and Royal Centre in North Israel* (MAVA, 40; Munich: C.H. Beck, 1989), pp. 87-90.

23. See Herzog, *Archaeology of the City*, p. 212, now confirmed by G. Lehmann, A. Killebrew and Y. Gadot, 'Area K', in Finkelstein, Ussishkin and Halpern (eds.), *Megiddo III*, I, p. 135; more evidence is forthcoming from the 2000 excavations.

24. Thus Halpern, 'Centre and Sentry', p. 558; *idem*, 'The Gate of Megiddo', p. 117. There is no point anymore in even trying to associate the notorious 'Solomonic gate' of Megiddo to any other stratum than to the one to which it belongs (IVA), simply because IVA was the only pre-Assyrian Iron Age Megiddo that had a city wall at all.

25. I cannot subscribe to the view of B. Halpern ('Centre and Sentry', p. 559) that the central administration had already exiled the population of Megiddo VA.

Under the Assyrians (stratum III) the site was resettled and became a thriving town again, well-planned and evidently well-organized. The Assyrian governor's palace(s) now occupy the region where once the palace of the Canaanite rulers had stood. Eighty per cent of the site serves domestic purposes.[26]

c. *Synthesis*

It is now possible to combine the textual and the archaeological evidence. No extra-mural king built Megiddo VIA. None of these built Megiddo VA either. All one can say is that somebody in control of Megiddo built *in* Megiddo (viz. Palace 1723 and concomitant structures). It is clear, however, that a king built Megiddo IVA (Jeroboam II) and another—or others (the Assyrian rulers from Sargon II through Asarhaddon) Megiddo III. Jeroboam II also refortified Hazor[27] and, in all probability, Gezer.[28] All three sites still were prominent, but less so under Assyrian rule: Megiddo was a provincial capital; Gezer produced economic cuneiform documents; and Hazor was the place of an Assyrian residence (Hazor IV).[29]

The only king presently known to have built Hazor, Megiddo and Gezer *as* cities of storage, chariots and horses is Jeroboam II. To explain 1 Kgs 9.15, 19, one might suggest that his building activities of an unprecedented scale became part of the popular (or scholastic) tradition about 'a great king of Israel', and that they were ascribed to Solomon when the name of Jeroboam was forgotten or suppressed.

1 Kings 4.12

a. *The Textual Evidence*

The list of Solomon's officials in 1 Kgs 4.7-19 presents more problems than most who treat it address. The opening v. 7 is nonsensical: there is no point burdening the northern tribe of Naphtali, for example, with provisioning the royal court for a month; the 300 fattened oxen

---

26. See J. Peersmann, 'Assyrian Magiddu: The Town Planning of Stratum III', in Finkelstein, Ussishkin and Halpern (eds.), *Megiddo III*, II, pp. 524-34.

27. See Finkelstein, , 'Hazor and the North', pp. 64-65 n. 27.

28. See I. Finkelstein, 'Penelope's Shroud Unravelled: Iron II Date of Gezer's Outer Wall Established', *TA* 21 (1994), pp. 276-82.

29. If the list of towns in 1 Kgs 9.15 derived from the Assyrian period, one might expect to find 'Megiddo, Dor and Shechem (instead of the detested Samaria)' instead of 'Hazor, Megiddo and Gezer'.

(required according to 1 Kgs 5.3) would have lost most of their fat on the way.[30] In addition, we will see that the original list contained fewer than 12 names. With 1 Kgs 4.7 lost for history, no evidence remains that the officials listed were tax-collecting governors and that the territories attributed to them, provinces. In addition, some verses in this list are heavily glossed (notably 4.12, 13 and 19).[31]

> 4.8   These were their names: Ben-hur, in the hill country of Ephraim;
>
> 4.9   Ben-deker, in Makaz, Shaalbim, Beth-shemesh, and Elon-beth-hanan;
>
> 4.10 Ben-hesed, in Arubboth (to him belonged Socoh and all the land of Hepher);
>
> 4.11 Ben-abinadab, in all Naphath-dor (he had Taphath, Solomon's daughter, as his wife);
>
> 4.12 Baana son of Ahilud, in Taanach, Megiddo, and all Beth-shean, which is beside Zarethan below Jezreel, and from Beth-shean to Abel-meholah, as far as the other side of Jokmeam;
>
> 4.13 Ben-geber, in Ramoth-gilead (he had the villages of Jair son of Manasseh, which are in Gilead, and he had the region of Argob, which is in Bashan, sixty great cities with walls and bronze bars);
>
> 4.14 Ahinadab son of Iddo, in Mahanaim;
>
> 4.15 Ahimaaz, in Naphtali (he had taken Basemath, Solomon's daughter, as his wife);
>
> 4.16 Baana son of Hushai, in Asher and Bealoth;
>
> 4.17 Jehoshaphat son of Paruah, in Issachar;
>
> 4.18 Shimei son of Ela, in Benjamin;
>
> 4.19 Geber son of Uri, in the land of Gilead, the country of King Sihon of the Amorites and of King Og of Bashan. And there was one official in the land of Judah.

The LXX adds further proof that the list underwent redaction between its origin at some king's court and its final form in the MT. As J. Böse-necker has observed, the position of v. 17 (M) *after* vv. 18-19 (M) in the Greek indicates a redactional fissure, edited out in M (as is quite

---

30. Such a system of royal provisioning worked fine in Egypt with its fast waterways. Therefore, the seeming parallel of an institution from the days of Sheshonq to 1 Kgs 4.7 confutes, rather than corroborates, the biblical narrative.

31. Where the MT has 'Gilead' instead of 'Gad' (thus the LXX), the NRSV rightly follows the Greek, because Gilead is already overpopulated by 4.13 and 14. On the other hand, 'Gad' poses an unsurmountable historical problem for the attribution of the whole list to Solomon. Cf. Knauf, 'King Solomon's Copper Supply', p. 178 n. 46. Recent treatments of 1 Kgs 4 that do not address this problem need not be considered.

frequently the case). In his opinion, an original list of ten officials has been enlarged by the last two.[32] It is to be assumed, then, that redactional activity is not only responsible for embellishing entries of the original list, but also for the addition of more entries. The list of ten entries (recognizable behind the LXX) does not necessarily represent the earliest version. A text-internal (and insofar objective) observation leads to a basic text consisting of 4.8-14*: from 4.8 to 4.14, the geographical sequence follows a clockwise movement, each successive region being adjacent to its preceeding one: the mountains of Ephraim—west—north—north—north and east—east—south. 1 Kings 4.15-18 jumps to the north, 4.18 to the south of Ephraim, and 4.19 to the southeast. It is safe to assume that an original list (covering only central and eastern Palestine) was later expanded in order to agree with the concept of a larger Israel.

Whether the basic document is Solomonic is a question that can only be adressed after the archaeological evidence has been taken into consideration. From a purely textual level one may observe that the 'incomplete names' (i.e. patronym without proper name, widely and rightly understood as indicating damage to the original document[33] before it entered the scribal tradition that transmitted it) are restricted to 4.8-13, that is the original list. The names Ben-Hur, Ben-Deker, Ben-Hesed, Ben-Abinadab, Ben-Geber and Ahinadab ben Iddo are not suspicious, because they do not occur elsewhere in the narrative about David and Solomon.[34] Formally, the note on a wife from the royal family is a gloss in both cases (4.11 and 4.15). The name Taphat (4.11), however, is inconspicuous, whereas Basemath (4.15) is not: her name ('the Balming One') presupposes Solomon's alleged involvement in the Arabian incense trade (1 Kgs 10.1-15, 22-25).[35] The name of her spouse comes from 1 Sam. 14.51 and/or 2 Sam. 15.27. The only name from the original list also known from other parts of the David–Solomon-tradition is Baana's father Ahilud (2 Sam. 8.16; 20.24; 1 Kgs 4.3), but

---

32. J. Bösenecker, 'Text und Redaktion: Untersuchungen zum hebräischen und griechischen Text von 1 Könige 1–11' (doctoral dissertation, University of Rostock 2000; to be published in the series OBO), p. 113.

33. Halpern, 'The Gate of Megiddo', p. 115 n. 48.

34. The same holds true for Joshaphat's father Paruah (4.17).

35. Which does not stand up to historical scrutiny; cf. Knauf, 'King Solomon's Copper Supply', p. 174 n. 26.

Baana (as Canaanite/Phoenician a name[36] as Taphat) is unlikely to have been invented. The same does not hold true for the second Baana (already one Baana too many in comparision with the distribution of the name) in 4.16. His father Hushai comes from 2 Sam. 15.32, a context where we already encountered Ahilud. It stands to reason that 4.16 is modelled after 4.12. Shimei (4.18) is probably the same person as in 1 Kgs 1.8. Geber (4.19) may be derived from his 'son' (4.13) and might be thought to be a brother of Solomon's mother, Bathsheba.

It is not necessary to investigate 1 Kgs 4.8-19 as the literary context of 4.12 in any more detail, but a closer look at 4.12 is in order. The geography of this verse is confused. The qualifier 'all' cannot precede the name of a city (Beth-shan); it must precede the name of a region. So the original tradition might be restricted to 'Baana son of Ahilud, in Taanach, Megiddo, and all Jezreel', being glossed twice by redactors who missed the important government stronghold of Beth-shan and the exact borders of its district. What is significant in this verse is the fact that Taanach takes precedence over Megiddo. Was there ever a constellation in the regional history of the Jezreel valley in which Taanach dominated Megiddo? This again is a question for archaeology.

b. *The Archaeological Evidence*
Taanach has four strata within the Iron I/IIA period (IA, IB; gap; IIA; IIB) that were equated with Megiddo VIIB through VA/IVB (W. Rast)[37] or Megiddo VIIA/VIB through VA/IVB (I. Finkelstein).[38] According to Finkelstein, Taanach IA covers the period between Megiddo VIIA and VIA (i.e. it corresponds at Megiddo to the gap after the destruction/abandonment of Megiddo VIIA and to Megiddo VIB). Contrary to Finkelstein, this synchronism is not hampered by the fact that there is no Philistine bichrome pottery at Taanach IA (and IB) that shows up in Megiddo VIB: Philistine imports in the North were few,

---

36. Ba'ana, also the name of a Sidonian king of the Persian period, is a hypocoristic for *Ben-'Anat, not for *Ba'alnatan, since the root NTN is replaced by YTN in Phoenician.

37. W.E. Rast, *Ta'anach I: Studies in the Iron Age Pottery* (Excavation Reports; Cambridge, MA: American Schools of Oriental Research, 1978); H.M. Niemann, 'Taanach und Megiddo: Überlegungen zur strukturell-historischen Situation zwischen Saul und Salomo', *VT* (in press).

38. I. Finkelstein, 'Notes on the Stratigraphy and Chronology of Iron Age Ta'anach', *TA* 25 (1998), pp. 208-18.

and the pottery evidence at Tanaach (especially for Taanach IB) is less.[39] Taanach IB developed out of IA without a break, as Megiddo VIA developed from VIB. Taanach IB ended in much the same sort of massive conflagration as did Megiddo VIA. For Finkelstein, Sheshonq is the culprit in both cases. But not every victim killed by the means of a Smith & Wesson 0.38 in New York City over the past 20 years was killed by the same person. The pottery assemblage of Taanach IB corresponds to Megiddo VIB and VIA,[40] and so the destruction of Taanach IB should slightly antedate the destruction of Megiddo VIA.

Taanach IA-B started to develop during the Iron I (eleventh century BCE)—well before Megiddo; then Megiddo sets in, as a village (VIB) that became a prosperous town (VIA). Might it be suspected that the people of Megiddo VIA knocked out their competition in the immediate neighborhood—Taanach IB?

The prosperous second half of the existence of Megiddo VIA corresponds to the gap at Taanach after IB. The people of Taanach, or the wider valley, however, might well have thought of revenge, and they may easily have gained Phoenician support (if the appearance of burnished red slip is an indicator of growing Phoenician influence). So they were most likely those who destroyed Megiddo VIA and founded Taanach IIA, to which corresponds the gap at Megiddo after VIA (the pottery of Taanach IIA falls between Megiddo VIA and VB).[41] Taanach IIA developed into Taanach IIB, at the same time as a new village sprang up at Megiddo: VB.[42] Then Sheshonq destroyed Taanach IIB, but he erected his victory stela at Megiddo VB,[43] thus designating the village for development as a regional center—a plan that was dually implemented by (Jeroboam I and) the dynasty of Omri, who trans-

39. See N. Na'aman, 'The Contribution of the Trojan Grey Ware from Lachish and Tel Miqne-Ekron to the Chronology of the Philistine Monochrome Pottery', *BASOR* 317 (2000), pp. 1-7 (4-5). Whether the *argumentum e silentio* (the absence of something in a context where this something is expected) is viable is always a question of quantities and statistics.

40. Finkelstein, 'Notes on the Stratigraphy and Chronology', p. 213.

41. Finkelstein, 'Notes on the Stratigraphy and Chronology', p. 215.

42. The occurrence of one collared rim-jar at Taanach IIB and Megiddo VB (Finkelstein, 'Notes on the Stratigraphy and Chronology', p. 216) argues for the contemporaneousness of these two strata, not of Taanach IIB and Megiddo VA/IVB.

43. It is unlikely that Sheshonq destroyed Megiddo; see Finkelstein and Ussishkin, 'Archaeological and Historical Conclusions', II, p. 599 n. 19.

formed the village of Megiddo VB into the regional center of Megiddo VA/IVB.

Taanach	Megiddo
	VIIA
IA	-gap-
IB	VIB
IB destruction	VIA
-gap-	VIA destruction
IIA	-gap-
IIB	VB
destruction by Sheshonq	Stela by Sheshonq → VA

According to this correlation, there are two periods when Taanach might have been more important than Megiddo: at the very end of the eleventh century BCE before the rise of Megiddo VIA, and in the third quarter of the tenth century BCE. Solomon's Megiddo—or rather, the Megiddo contemporary with Solomon, is Megiddo VB; and the list in 1 Kgs 4.12 and—by extension—4.8-14 contains information that cannot have entered the literary process except during the reign of Solomon.

c. *Synthesis*

H.M. Niemann has convincingly argued that Solomon's officials were not governors but royal representiatives vis-à-vis tribal or otherwise semi-independent areas outside the direct control of Jerusalem, constituting a sphere of influence that was basically inherited from the complex chiefdom of David.[44] On the basis of the foregoing literary analysis, it can be stated that this sphere of influence consisted basically of the central mountain range, the Sharon, the Jezreel, and northern and central Transjordan. Benjamin was not part of that sphere because it was under direct Jerusalemite rule.[45] Nor was the Galilee, already beyond the

---

44. See H.M. Niemann, *Herrschaft, Königtum und Staat: Skizzen zur soziokulturellen Entwicklung im monarchischen Israel* (FAT, 6; Tübingen: Mohr, 1993), pp. 27-41; *idem*, 'Megiddo and Solomon: A Biblical Investigation in Relation to Archaeology', *TA* 27 (2000), pp. 61-74; Halpern, 'The Gate of Megiddo', pp. 120-21.

45. This was necessary for geopolitical reasons, since Benjamin was a grain-

grasp of David, nor Issachar, Manasseh or Gad, tribes that did not yet exist by the time of Solomon.[46] It is entirely possible that Ben-Hur (4.8) represented Solomon at the court of a local dignitary whose name was Jeroboam.[47]

Conclusions

With 1 Kgs 9.15-19, a text has been dismissed from the tenth century BCE that previously had been detrimental enough for the dating and interpretation of Megiddo, as well as for the reconstruction of how large Solomon's kingdom was. With 1 Kgs 4.8-14*, another text has been gained for the historical approach to the same period.

At the beginning of his reign, Solomon tried to cover somehow the whole of David's inheritance. Since Megiddo VIA cannot have been destroyed before 950, the beginning of Solomon's reign, as attested in 1 Kgs 4.12, should be dated nearer 940 than 950. After Sheshonq's campaign, Solomon's rule was restricted to the area described in 1 Kgs 9.17-18.[48] The loss in territory was offset by advances in the

---

producing high plateau, thus forming the economic basis for any state that might exist around Jerusalem. Consequently, Jerusalem reached the nadir of its urban history during the Iron Age in the ninth century BCE, when most of Benjamin was lost to Israel and the Shephelah not yet been gained in compensation, as it was to be the case in the eighth century BCE. See E.A. Knauf, 'Jerusalem in the Late Bronze and Early Iron Periods—A Proposal', *TA* 27 (2000), pp. 75-90.

46. For David and Galilee, see Knauf, 'Jerusalem in the Late Bronze and Early Iron Periods'; for Issachar, Z. Gal, 'The Settlement of Issachar', *TA* 9 (1982), pp. 79-86 (commencing in Iron IIA, i.e. in the late tenth and early ninth centuries BCE); for Gad, Knauf, 'King Solomon's Copper Supply', p. 178 n. 46; Manasseh does not occur in any text that can confidently be attributed to the tenth century BCE (as the song of Deborah). Most probably, Manasseh split from Ephraim during the civil wars between Baasha and Omri. See notably 1 Kgs 15.33 and 16.21-22.

47. Even according to the pro-Solomonic account of the MT, Jeroboam was not a minor figure, but probably a high-ranking official (1 Kgs 11.26, 28); according to the LXX, 3 Kgdms 12.24b, Jeroboam had 300 chariots. Even if this number is exaggerated and even if the whole of 3 Kgdms 12.24a-z is basically midrashic in character, this piece of information deserves historical consideration. 1 Kings 9.17-18, being a third-level gloss within a rather late literary text, depicts (in the opinion of the present author) the borders of Solomon's kingdom correctly.

48. See Knauf, 'Le Roi', pp. 91-95. This reconstruction of Sheshonq's campaign(s) was elaborated independently of N. Na'aman, 'מסע שישק לארץ ישראל בראי הכתובות המצריות, המקרא והממצא הארכיאולוגי', *Zion* 63 (1998),

architectural manifestation of power. The north, in the beginning
loosely attached to Jerusalem by tribal alliances that had to be sustained
by special delegates, was now organized into a territoral state of its
own. The beginning and end of the Solomonic realm testify to the shift
of economic hegemony over Palestine from Philistia to Phoenicia,[49] and
the reappearance of Egypt on the scene, Phoenicia's traditional partner
and ally.

pp. 247-76 (title in English: Shishak's Campaign to Eretz Israel According to the
Egyptian Inscriptions, the Bible, and Archaeology).
   49. See Knauf, 'Jerusalem in the Late Bronze and Early Iron Periods', pp. 81-
87.

ŠAMŠI-ILU AND THE *REALPOLITIK* OF ISRAEL AND ARAM-DAMASCUS IN THE EIGHTH CENTURY BCE

Jeffrey K. Kuan

After the mid-ninth century BCE, that is from the time of the infamous Battle of Qarqar in 853 BCE, the Assyrians had a major influence in the political and commercial relations between the Israelites and the Arameans, especially those of Damascus. These relations were sometimes cooperative, sometimes antagonistic.

Following the final western campaign of Shalmaneser III in 838–836 BCE against Hazael of Aram-Damascus, there is no evidence of any Assyrian campaigns in the west until the time of Adad-nirari III. The absence of Assyria in the west meanwhile provided the occasion for Hazael of Aram-Damascus to expand his territory and dominate affairs in Syria–Palestine.[1] Biblical sources furnish evidence of Hazael's expansionist policy and his subjugation of Israel, Philistia and Judah. First, 2 Kgs 10.32-33 reports on the loss of Israelite Transjordanian territory to Hazael during the reign of Jehu. Second, 2 Kgs 12.17-18 recounts Hazael's aggression toward Philistia and Judah, capturing Gath and forcing the submission of Jehoash of Judah to Aram-Damascus's hegemony. W.T. Pitard, arguing against A. Jepsen and B. Mazar,[2] has noted that there is not enough evidence to support any claim that Hazael expanded his dominance north of Damascus.[3] Even without the northern expansion, he is probably right to conclude that

---

1. See W.T. Pitard, *Ancient Damascus: A Historical Study of the Syrian City-State from Earliest Times until its Fall to the Assyrians in 732 B.C.E.* (Winona Lake, IN: Eisenbrauns, 1987), pp. 151-58.

2. A. Jepsen, 'Israel und Damaskus', *AfO* 14 (1941–45), pp. 153-72; B. Mazar, 'The Aramean Empire and its Relations with Israel', *BA* 25 (1962), pp. 98-120 (108-16).

3. Pitard, *Ancient Damascus*, pp. 152-58.

the size of Hazael's empire was significant enough to make Damascus the capital of one of the most powerful states of Syria, an adversary with whom Assyria would have to deal when it began to stir once again at the end of the ninth century.[4]

With the accession of Adad-nirari III (810–783 BCE), Assyrian activities in the west resumed with a major campaign that lasted three or four years, was conducted to re-subjugate the states that had rebelled against Assyrian hegemony during the reign of Šamši-Adad V (823–811 BCE), and inaugurated a new policy of strength toward the west. This campaign, dated to 805–802 BCE, was carried out to suppress the north Syrian–Anatolian coalition led by Bar-Hadad of Aram-Damascus (so the Zakkur Stela) and Ataršumki of Arpad (so the Pazarcik Stela, obverse), a coalition that had made an unsuccessful attempt to force Zakkur, the king of Hamath and Lu'aš, to join the alliance in order to strengthen the resistance against Assyria throughout Anatolia and all of Syria. Adad-nirari's western campaign resulted in the capture of Arpad (so the Sheikh Hammad Stela, the Scheil and Millard Fragment, and the Pazarcik Stela, obverse) and the weakening of Aram-Damascus's military strength (so the el-Rimah Stela, the Calah Slab and the Saba'a Stela).

The period following the reign of Adad-nirari III, namely, during the reigns of Shalmaneser IV (782–773 BCE), Ashur-dan III (772–755 BCE) and Ashur-nirari V (754–745 BCE), is characterized by a weakening of the central Assyrian administration. Two major factors created this decline during the first half of the eighth century BCE. First, there was the Urartian expansion from their territory around Lake Van to the southeast toward Media and in the southwest toward Anatolia and Syria–Palestine. Urartu[5] had long been a major Assyrian opponent, struggling with Assyria for control of trade routes.[6] Urartu was at its

4.	Pitard, *Ancient Damascus*, p. 158.

5.	For studies on Urartu, see, e.g., B.B. Piotrovsky, *The Ancient Civilization of Urartu* (Ancient Civilizations; New York: Cowles, 1969); H.-J. Kellner, *Urartu: Ein wiederentdeckter Rivale Assyriens* (Prähistorische Staatssammlung München, Museum für Vor- und Frühgeschichte, Ausstellungskataloge 2; Munich: Buchdruckwerkstätte Pichlmayr, 1976); P.E. Zimansky, *Ecology and Empire: The Structure of the Urartian State* (SAOC, 41; Chicago: Oriental Institute of the University of Chicago, 1985).

6.	See R.D. Barnett, 'Urartu', in J. Boardman *et al.* (eds.), *The Cambridge Ancient History*, III/1. *The Prehistory of the Balkans, and the Middle East and the Aegean World, Tenth to Eighth Centuries B.C.* (Cambridge: Cambridge University

height of expansion during the reign of Argishtu I (about 786–764 BCE).[7] Numerous campaigns to expand its control and influence brought Urartu into direct confrontation with Assyria, putting the latter on the defensive. The eponym chronicle noted that several Assyrian campaigns were carried out against the Urartians between 781/780 and 774/773 BCE.

Second, and more importantly, there was a diffusion of authority and power in the hands of strong provincial governors, begun already in the reign of Adad-nirari III. These governors included such figures as Nergal-ereš, the governor of Raṣappa and Ḥindanu—provinces along the middle Euphrates—who was responsible for setting up the el-Rimah and Saba'a stelae of Adad-nirari. Two other officials of significance were Bel-tarsi-iluma, the governor of Calah, who set up two inscribed statues in honor of Adad-nirari and Semiramis,[8] and Bel-ḥarran-beli-uṣr, the *nāgir ekalli*, who built a city, named it after himself, and subsequently set up a stela to commemorate its founding.[9] However, the most important official appears to have been Šamši-ilu.

Who was Šamši-ilu? Information on Šamši-ilu comes predominantly from four non-biblical sources. First, the eponym chronicle lists Šamši-ilu as the *limmu* on three occasions, in 780/779, 770/769 and 752/751 BCE, appearing as *limmu* after those of three different Assyrian kings: Shalmaneser IV, Ashur-dan III and Ashur-nirari V.[10] While the eponym chronicle establishes that Šamši-ilu's career as *turtānu* spanned at least from 780–751 BCE, his tenure had begun already during the reign of Adad-nirari III. In the Antakya Stela, dating from the last decade of the ninth century BCE (807/806), Šamši-ilu is mentioned as the *turtānu*. His tenure, however, must have begun after 808/807 BCE, since Nergal-ilāya was identified as the *turtānu* for that year. It is therefore likely that he had a career that lasted more than half a century.

Press, 2nd edn, 1982), pp. 314-71 (333-56); H.W.F. Saggs, *The Greatness that Was Babylon: A Survey of the Ancient Civilization of the Tigris–Euphrates Valley* (Great Civilizations; London: Sidgwick & Jackson, rev. edn, 1988), pp. 98-100; L.D. Levine, 'East–West Trade in the Late Iron Age: A View from the Zagros', in *Le plateau iranien et l'Asie centrale des origines à la conquête islamique* (Colloques internationaux du Centre national de la recherche scientifique, 567; Paris: Editions du Centre national de la recherche scientifique, 1977), pp. 171-86.

7. On the reign of Argishtu I, see Barnett, 'Urartu', pp. 344-48.

8. *ARAB*, 1. §§744-45.

9. *ARAB*, 1. §§823-27.

10. See A.R. Millard, *The Eponyms of the Assyrian Empire, 910–612 BC* (SAAS, 2; Helsinki: Helsinki University Press, 1994), pp. 58-59.

A second source of information comes from the Stone Lion Inscription, discovered originally in 1908 at Tell Aḥmar, on the eastern bank of the Euphrates.[11] This site is identified with the ancient city of Til-Barsip, capital of Bit-Adini. In the inscriptions, engraved on two monumental lions, Šamši-ilu bore the titles of

> *turtānu* (commander), *nāgiru rabû* (great herald), *šatam ekurrāti* (administrator of the Temples), *rab-ummāni rapši* (chief of the vast army), *šāpir māt Ḫatti māt Guti u gimir māt Namri* (governor of the land of Hatti, the land of Quti, and all the land of Namri).[12]

In addition, he claimed to have subjugated Mushku and Urartu. These inscriptions bear striking resemblances to other neo-Assyrian royal inscriptions. With no mention of the name of the Assyrian king in the text,[13] Šamši-ilu must have seen himself as having 'the virtual authority of a king',[14] claiming Kar-Shalmaneser (that is, Til-Barsip) as his *āl bēlūtiya*. It is quite certain that Syria–Palestine fell under his jurisdiction and control.

The Antakya Stela is the third source of information on Šamši-ilu.[15] This is an inscription from the reign of Adad-nirari III, found in 1968 near the Orontes, between Antakya and Samandag in Turkey. The stela has two sculptured human figures at the top, one perhaps representing the powerful *turtānu* Šamši-ilu, who is featured prominently in the text. In all likelihood the stela was erected by Šamši-ilu.[16] The focus of the

---

11. See W.W. Hallo and K.L. Younger (eds.), *The Context of Scripture. II. Monumental Inscriptions from the Biblical World* (Leiden: E.J. Brill, 2000), p. 278; F. Thureau-Dangin and M. Dunand, *Til-Barsib* (Bibliothéque archéologique et historique, 23; Paris: Paul Geuthner, 1936).

12. Thureau-Dangin and Dunand, *Til-Barsib*, p. 146.

13. A. Malamat, 'Amos 1.5 in the Light of the Til-Barsip Inscriptions', *BASOR* 129 (1953), pp. 25-26.

14. A.K. Grayson, 'Assyria: Ashur-dan II to Ashur-nirari V (934–745 B.C.)', in J. Boardman *et al.* (eds.), *The Cambridge Ancient History*, III/1. *The Prehistory of the Balkans, and the Middle East and the Aegean World, Tenth to Eighth Centuries B.C.* (Cambridge: Cambridge University Press, 2nd edn, 1982), p. 278.

15. See V. Donbaz, 'Two Neo-Assyiran Stelae in the Antakya and Kahramanmaraş Museums', *Annual Review of the Royal Inscriptions of Mesopotamia Project* 8 (1990), pp. 5-24 (7).

16. On Šamši-ilu, see J.D. Hawkins, 'The Neo-Hittite States in Syria and Anatolia', in J. Boardman *et al.* (eds.), *The Cambridge Ancient History*, III/1. *The Prehistory of the Balkans, and the Middle East and the Aegean World, Tenth to*

text is a border dispute between Zakkur of Hamath and Ataršumki of Arpad along the Orontes, one that was settled most probably by the Assyrian *turtānu* rather than Adad-nirari himself, since Hamath and Arpad fell under the sphere of Šamši-ilu's influence and jurisdiction. The result was a border agreement that allowed both parties equal access to the Orontes.[17]

A fourth source of information on Šamši-ilu comes from the reverse of the Pazarcik Stela.[18] This stela, discovered at the village of Kizkapanli in the Pazarcik area (modern-day Kahramanmaraş) in Turkey, functioned as a boundary stone and contains two inscriptions. The obverse is an inscription of Adad-nirari III, while the reverse is an inscription from the reign of Shalmaneser IV. The stela must have originally been set up by Adad-nirari (or his *turtānu*, Šamši-ilu) as a 'boundary stone' to mark the border between Kummuḫ and Gurgum. The stela was reinscribed on the reverse during the reign of Shalmaneser IV (782–773 BCE) and given to Ušpilulume, king of Kummuḫ, by the *turtānu* Šamši-ilu as a sign of Assyrian commitment to helping Kummuḫ protect its boundary. Lines 4–13 of the reverse, following the introduction of the Assyrian king, read as follows:

> When Šamši-ilu, the *turtānu*, (5)marched to Aram-Damascus, the *madattu* of Ḥadiānu of Aram-Damascus—silver, gold, copper, his royal bed, his royal couch, his daughter with her enormous dowry, (10)the countless property of his palace—I received from him.
>
> On my return, this boundary stone to Ušpilulume, king of the Kummuḫites I gave...

Eighth Centuries B.C. (Cambridge: Cambridge University Press, 2nd edn, 1982), pp. 404-405.

17. The inscription reveals a situation when both Hamath and Arpad were loyal subjects of Assyria. The fact that this inscription was written on Ataršumki's behalf, identifying Arpad's border with Hamath, attests Arpad's alliance with Assyria at the time. The settlement of this dispute should be dated before 805/804 BCE, viz. to a time when Arpad was still a loyal subject of Assyria. The eponym chronicle notes that an Assyrian campaign was conducted in the west beginning in 805/804 BCE, with Arpad, which had rebelled against Assyrian hegemony, as its main target. On the other hand, the Antakya Stela cannot be dated earlier than 808/807 BCE, since the *turtānu* at that time was someone other than Šamši-ilu. The border dispute between Arpad (which was in rebellion against Assyria by 805/804 BCE) and Hamath (which remained loyal) probably indicates the beginning of friction between western pro- and anti-Assyrian kingdoms.

18. Donbaz, 'Two Neo-Assyrian Stelae', pp. 9-10.

That this was a campaign directed at Aram-Damascus is evident from the text. This campaign is most certainly to be correlated with the one mentioned in the eponym chronicle for the year 773/772 BCE, when the location of the army at the turn of the year was Damascus. In addition, it is quite certain that the campaign was led by the *turtānu* Šamši-ilu, rather than by Shalmaneser himself. This is supported by the usage of the third-person singular in the verbal form *illikūni* in line 5. Although the referent of the first-person singular in the term *amḫur* (line 10) is the king, without doubt it was Šamši-ilu who encountered Aram-Damascus and received the *madattu* on the king's behalf. Likewise, it must have been Šamši-ilu who reconfirmed the boundary of Kummuḫ (with Gurgum; see lines 11-13)—already established during the reign of Adad-nirari III (cf. Pazarcik stela, obverse lines 16-18)—even though the action was attributed to Shalmaneser. This text also reveals that it was Ḥadiānu, the king of Aram-Damascus, against whom the campaign was undertaken. Ḥadiānu must have begun to rebel against Assyrian hegemony and policies to warrant this attack from Šamši-ilu.

The western campaign that began in 773/772 BCE, the last regnal year of Shalmaneser IV, during which Šamši-ilu took direct action against Ḥadiānu of Aram-Damascus, continued into the following year, the first regnal year of Ashur-dan III (772/771 BCE). The eponym chronicle recorded the location of the main Assyrian army as Ḥatarikka for that year. During the period of Šamši-ilu's tenure as *turtānu*, two other western campaigns were mounted, one in 765/764 BCE and the other in 755–753 BCE. Both these campaigns were undertaken in northern Syria as the eponym chronicle for these years recorded Ḥatarikka and Arpad as the location of the main army. In all likelihood, these were campaigns led by Šamši-ilu as well.

To summarize, these Assyrian sources demonstrate that Šamši-ilu was the dominant authority in the west in the first half of the eighth century BCE, the de facto Assyrian king of Anatolia and Syria–Palestine. He was the one who led military campaigns to put down rebellions and establish firm control in the region. He claimed to have also led the campaigns against Urartu. He arbitrated border disputes between rival kingdoms as well.

The importance of Šamši-ilu has led scholars to identify him in non-Assyrian texts. A. Lemaire and J.-M. Durand have sought to identify

Bar-ga'yah of KTK in the Sefire inscriptions with Šamši-ilu.[19] More-over, A. Malamat, in his analysis of Amos 1.5 in light of the Til-Barsip inscriptions of Šamši-ilu, suggests identifying the Assyrian *turtānu* with 'the one who holds the scepter in Beth-Eden'.[20]

As important as a figure Šamši-ilu had been in Assyrian and Syro-Palestinian history, the role that he played in Syro-Palestinian politics has not been given due attention. One can hardly find even an index entry under his name in major histories of ancient Israel and Judah, including the latest history by G.W. Ahlström. Moreover, the recent works on Syrian history by W.T. Pitard and H. Klengel only make cursory mention of him.

Given the dominant role that Šamši-ilu played in the west, is there evidence from the Hebrew Bible that indicates his influence on Israelite–Damascene relations? It needs to be pointed out that during

19. A. Lemaire and J.-M. Durand, *Les inscriptions araméennes de Sfiré et l'Assyrie de Shamshi-ilu* (Hautes études orientales, 20; Geneva: Droz, 1984), esp. pp. 37-58. They argue that Bar-ga'yah was a dynastic name, equivalent to Bar-gush of the Zakkur stela and Bit-Agusi in Assyrian inscriptions. Moreover, נאיה is assumed to be an Aramaic variant of the Assyriann *ga'uni* in the Monolith Inscription (cf. *ARAB*, 1. §599). They further suggest that KTK should be identified with a royal city in Bit-Adini, which appears in the Monolith Inscription of Shalmaneser III (pp. 47-51). Although in the Monolith Inscription only two signs of the place-name are legible, namely, *ki...ka*, they note that Malamat had reconstructed the name to read *ki-[it]-ka*4 (see A. Malamat, 'A New Proposal for the Identification of KTK in the Sefire Inscriptions', in S. Bendor [ed.], *M. Razin Volume, Census Lists and Genealogies and their Historical Implications for the Times of David and Saul* [Haifa: University of Haifa, 1976], pp. 7-11 [Hebrew]). In addition, they note that Durand and Charpin have proposed restoring the name to read *ki-[tá]-ka*4 upon examination of photographs of the inscription. The city Kit(t)a/i/uka is, in turn, to be associated with Til-Barsip.

Lemaire and Durand's proposal is fraught with problems. First, there is no evidence that Šamši-ilu was descended from a royal family of Syrian stock. Moreover, it is unlikely that a Syrian would have been appointed to the very powerful position of *turtānu* in the Assyrian administration. Second, the association of נאיה with *ga'uni* is uncertain. Even if the identification is correct, Ga'uni is clearly distinguished from Bit-Adini in the Monolith Inscription. Lemaire and Durand do not explain how Ga'uni became Bit-Adini. Finally, the identification of KTK with *ki...ka* of the Monolith Inscription is based on the reconstruction of a place-name and is certainly questionable. Even if the name is correctly recon-structed, there is no evidence that the place later became known as Til-Barsip. In sum, the identification of Bar-ga'yah with Šamši-ilu cannot be sustained.

20. Malamat, 'Amos 1.5', pp. 25-26.

this period in the history of Israel and Judah, there is no evidence in biblical or non-biblical sources to suggest that Israel and Judah maintained other than a pro-Assyrian policy.

Two pieces of evidence on Israelite–Damascene relations from the Hebrew Bible may be offered. The first comes from Isa. 8.23, a text that may provide evidence that Šamši-ilu's campaign against Aram-Damascus in 773/772 BCE was undertaken to curb Damascus's encroachment upon Israelite territory in northern Galilee. Isaiah 8.23 may be translated as follows:

> Like the time (כעת) the former one (הראשון) treated contemptibly (הקל) the land of Zebulun and the land of Naphtali, so also the latter one (האחרון) has treated harshly (הכביד) the Way of the Sea, Beyond the Jordan, and Galilee of the Nations.

While there is scholarly agreement that Isa. 8.23 reflects Israel's loss of territories, there is no consensus regarding who was/were responsible for the losses. Both Assyrian and Israelite rulers have been suggested (see Appendix). My proposal in understanding the referents הראשון and האחרון rests on three assumptions. First, the terms refer to two separate persons. Second, the verse refers to territories that Israel lost, and third, as S.A. Irvine has rightly noted,[21] it was the Arameans of Damascus who were responsible for those losses. Since the verse is located in the context of the Syro-Ephraimitic crisis, Rezin must be its immediate referent, האחרון. Conversely, הראשון should be taken as a reference to Hadiānu, Rezin's predecessor, mentioned in the Pazarcik Stela. If this interpretation is correct, the biblical text provides evidence that Hadiānu harassed Israel during his reign in the second quarter of the eighth century BCE. The regions that were lost to Hadiānu included 'the land of Zebulun and the land of Naphtali', that is, Upper Galilee. Hadiānu's expansion of Aram-Damascus's territory most likely invited Šamši-ilu's campaign in 773/772 BCE. The successful campaign of the main Assyrian army led by Šamši-ilu was an effort to curtail Aram-Damascus's expansion in Syria–Palestine.

The second piece of evidence is the expansion of Israel under Jeroboam II. During this period of domination by Šamši-ilu, anti-Assyrian activities of Syro-Palestinian states were effectively curtailed. Pro-Assyrian Israel, now under the reign of Jeroboam II (788–748 BCE),

---

21. S.A. Irvine, *Isaiah, Ahaz and the Syro-Ephraimitic Crisis* (SBLDS, 123; Atlanta: Scholars Press, 1990), p. 224.

was able to continue its expansion,[22] begun already during the reign of Joash. 2 Kings 14.25 reports that Jeroboam 'restored the border of Israel from the entrance of Hamath as far as the Sea of the Arabah'. Hayes suggests that this statement 'denotes the territory from southern Lebanon to the area west of the Jordan at the northern end of the Dead Sea'.[23] Jeroboam's territory thus would have included all Galilee in the north and southward to the northern border of Judah. The reference to 'as far as the Sea of Arabah' probably implies that Jeroboam's territory included also the region of Gilead in Transjordan, territory already won back from Damascus by Joash (see 1 Chron. 5.17). The reclaiming of these territories would have come about at the expense of Hamath and Damascus, a factor possibly indicated by the enigmatic reference in 2 Kgs 14.28: ‏ואשר השיב את־דמשק ואת־חמת ליהודה בישראל‎.

The Galilean region was an area contested by Israel, Damascus, Tyre and perhaps Hamath. Aramean and Israelite control of the region seems to have varied from time to time; both states had vested interests in that region, since important trade routes passed through it to the coastal cities of Acco, Achzib, Tyre and Sidon. Thus, whoever controlled the region also enjoyed the possibility of improved trade relations with the Phoenicians. 1 Kings 15.20 indicates that Upper Galilee was taken by Ben-hadad I of Aram-Damascus during the reign of Baasha, king of Israel. Lower Galilee at the same time seems to have remained in the hands of Israel. 1 Kings 21 and 2 Kgs 9.14-26 indicate that during the Omride dynasty Israel continued to control part of the Jezreel Valley and thus perhaps at least portions of Lower Galilee, where the Omrides had a winter palace at Jezreel. No other biblical nor non-biblical inscriptional materials, however, indicate that the Omrides controlled territory north of Jezreel, making it uncertain whether the Omrides reclaimed any of Upper Galilee. Nevertheless, it has been argued that archaeological evidence from Hazor and Dan from this period, vis-à-vis architectural styles and construction techniques similar to those of the Ahab levels at Samaria and Megiddo, suggests that Upper Galilee—and Hazor in particular—had reverted to Israelite control.[24] Even if Israel

22. See E. Lipiński, 'Jéroboam II et la Syrie', in D. Garrone and F. Israel (eds.), *Storia e tradizioni di Israele: Scritti in onore di J. Alberto Soggin* (Brescia: Paideia, 1991), pp. 171-76.

23. J.H. Hayes, *Amos, the Eighth-Century Prophet: His Times and his Preaching* (Nashville: Abingdon Press, 1988), p. 22.

24. See Pitard, *Ancient Damascus*, pp. 109 and 120.

had controlled the whole of Galilee during the Omride dynasty, it was probably lost to Aram-Damascus again during the reign of Hazael, along with other Israelite, Judean and Philistine territories (so 2 Kgs 10.32-33; 12.17-18). While Joash had begun recovering territories for Israel, particularly in the Transjordan, it was Jeroboam II who retook Israelite territories in the Galilee, probably early in his reign.[25] Šamši-ilu's dominating presence in Syria–Palestine in no small part kept Damascus and other states under control and contributed to Israelite territorial expansion under Jeroboam.

2 Kings 14.22 mentions the restoration of Elath to Judah during the reign of Uzziah. Elath had come under the control of Aram-Damascus during the days of Hazael's empire (so 2 Kgs 16.6) with Aramean encroachment on Israelite and Judean territories. Thus, when Elath was restored to Judean control, it was taken from Aram-Damascus. It has been surmised that Uzziah ruled under the shadow of Jeroboam II,[26] possibly as a vassal of Israel.[27] Thus, the restoration of Elath to Judah was most likely carried out under Jeroboam's leadership.[28]

2 Kings 14.28 suggests that Israel dominated Hamath and Damascus during the reign of Jeroboam II. The MT וַאֲשֶׁר הֵשִׁיב אֶת־דַּמֶּשֶׂק וְאֶת־חֲמָת לִיהוּדָה בְּיִשְׂרָאֵל (literally, 'and how he returned Damascus and Hamath to Judah in Israel') is difficult. Emendations have been suggested, based not only on the difficulty of the text but also on

25. See M.F. Unger, *Israel and the Aramaeans of Damascus: A Study in Archaeo-logical Illumination of Bible History* (Grand Rapids: Zondervan, 1957), p. 90.

26. So J.M. Miller and J.H. Hayes, *A History of Ancient Israel and Judah* (Philadelphia: Westminster Press, 1986), p. 310; but cf. J. Bright, *A History of Israel* (Philadelphia: Westminster/John Knox Press, 4th edn, 2000), p. 258.

27. For much of its history, Judah was a subordinate state to Israel, beginning with the reign of Omri. This situation again existed after Amaziah of Judah challenged Israel's sovereignty and was soundly defeated by the forces of Joash of Israel (2 Kgs 14.8-14), reducing Judah to vassal status. Judah's vassaldom most probably continued during the reign of Uzziah. Cf. Hayes, *Amos*, pp. 23-24.

28. The referents in 2 Kgs 14.22 are not entirely clear. A straightforward reading would imply that Uzziah was designated as the one who rebuilt Elath and returned it to Judah. In addition, הַמֶּלֶךְ would refer to Amaziah (so NRSV). However, Amaziah met a violent death (cf. 2 Kgs 14.19-20) and thus the phrase 'slept with his fathers'—one that is often used to denote a king's peaceful death—is not applicable to him. The verse perhaps originally referred to Jeroboam II, whose father Joash 'slept with his fathers' (2 Kgs 14.16). It was he who recaptured Elath from Aram-Damascus but handed it over to the control of Judah.

historical considerations.[29] Most scholars see this verse as indicating that Israel and Judah were strong enough to subject Damascus (and possibly also Hamath) to vassalage.[30] While it is not impossible that Israel was strong enough to dominate Hamath and Damascus, particularly with the assistance of the Assyrian Šamši-ilu, it is doubtful that it did. First, Zakkur who reigned over Hamath beginning in the late ninth century BCE was a strong potentate involved in a border dispute with Ataršumki of Arpad, as mentioned in the Antakya Stela. In the first quarter of the eighth century BCE, Zakkur had extended his control to Luʿaš.[31] In addition, according to the account of the stela, Zakkur was strong enough to withstand a military expedition of a coalition of 16 Syrian–Anatolian states led by Bar-Hadad of Aram-Damascus. Thus, it was not likely that Israel would have been able to dominate Hamath during this period. Even less likely was Israel's ability to subjugate Damascus. While Aram-Damascus under Bar-Hadad may not have been as strong as the period of Hazael's reign, nonetheless, Bar-Hadad was still strong enough to assume leadership of the Syrian–Anatolian alliance (so the Zakkur Stela). Moreover, a kingdom (or empire) that was too strong would have posed a threat to Assyrian presence and interests in the region; thus it seems unlikely that Šamši-ilu would have permitted Israel's enormous expansion in southern and central Syria.

Relations between Israel/Judah and Aram-Damascus were obviously antagonistic during this period. Israel and Judah, as a consequence of

29. C.F. Burney, for example, emends the text to read ואשר נלחם את־דמשק ואשר השיב את־חמת יהוה מישראל ('and how he fought Damascus and how he turned back the wrath of Yahweh from Israel'). *Notes on the Hebrew Text of the Books of Kings* (Oxford: Clarendon Press, 1903), pp. 320-21. Burney's emendation has been followed by W.E. Barnes, *The Books of the Kings* (CBSC, 11a; Cambridge: Cambridge University Press, 1908), p. 254; and J. Gray, *I and II Kings: A Commentary* (OTL; Philadelphia: Westminster Press, 2nd edn, 1970), p. 616. M. Haran ('The Rise and Decline of the Empire of Jeroboam ben Joash', *VT* 17 [1967], pp. 266-97 [296]) suggests emending ליהודה וישראל to ליהודה בישראל, and so construing an alliance between Judah and Israel, who were able to exert direct control over Damascus and Hamath. Cf. K.D. Fricke, *Das Zweite Buch von den Königen* (BAT, 12/2; Stuttgart: Calwer Verlag, 1972), p. 190. T.R. Hobbs (*2 Kings* [WBC, 13; Waco, TX: Word Books, 1985], p. 175) omits 'Judah' and so translates, 'and how he restored to Israel Damascus and Hamath'.

30. See, e.g., Pitard, *Ancient Damascus*, p. 177.

31. So the Zakkur Stela (see J.C.L. Gibson, *Textbook of Syrian Semitic Inscriptions* [3 vols.; Oxford: Clarendon Press, 1971–82], pp. 8-13).

the restraining presence of Šamši-ilu, were strong enough to continue regaining territories after a lengthy period of subjugation by Aram-Damascus. Losing Elath to Israel and Judah meant not only Aramean loss of control of the Red Sea port, but also it allowed Israel to recover a major commercial ally in the Phoenicians. The Phoenicians needed Elath for access to the Red Sea trading route to carry on commerce with the Arabian and African coasts. With much of the Transjordan also under Jeroboam's control, the Phoenicians could only gain access to Elath through Israelite and Judean territories. Thus, it was only to Phoenician advantage to have cordial relations with Israel and Judah once Elath was restored to Uzziah's control. Such a commercial relation would undoubtedly have benefited both Israel and Judah economically as well.

The long career of Šamši-ilu came to an end, probably only as a result of his death, after 752/751 BCE, the last time he appeared as the *limmu* in the eponym chronicle. With his demise, new political conditions developed in Syria–Palestine, creating new international relations in the region. This new political reality was influenced also by the accession of Rezin (Ra'yān or Raqyān in Assyrian inscriptions) to the throne of Damascus. While it cannot be proven conclusively, in all likelihood Rezin's accession took place in the 750s,[32] during the final decades of Jeroboam's reign. In addition, in Israel, a rival claimant to the kingship appeared on the scene, namely, Pekah son of Remaliah.

With the death of Šamši-ilu, the strong Assyrian presence in the west no longer existed. Rezin of Aram-Damascus seized the opportunity to begin organizing an anti-Assyrian alliance. This alliance is most likely reflected in part in Amos 1.5, in the context of an oracle against Aram-Damascus.[33] According to Amos, the ruler of the Valley of Aven

32. See Pitard, *Ancient Damascus*, p. 189; and H.S. Sader, *Les états araméens de Syrie: Depuis leur fondation jusqu'à leur transformation en provinces assyriennes* (Beiruter Texte und Studien, 36; Beirut: Orient-Institut der Deutschen Morgenländischen Gesellschaft; Wiesbaden: Franz Steiner, 1987), p. 288. Hayes suggests the 760s (*Amos*, p. 26). The last king of Aram-Damascus mentioned in Assyrian sources before Rezin is Ḥadianu.

33. The superscription in Amos 1.1 provides two pieces of information for the dating of Amos's prophetic ministry, namely, the reigns of King Uzziah of Judah and King Jeroboam II of Israel and 'two years before the earthquake'. According to the chronology of J.H. Hayes and P.K. Hooker (*A New Chronology for the Kings of Israel and Judah and its Implications for Biblical History and Literature* [Atlanta: John Knox Press, 1988], pp. 50-55), Uzziah was king over Judah from 785 to 760

(יוֹשֵׁב מִבִּקְעַת־אָוֶן) and the ruler of Beth-Eden (וְתוֹמֵךְ שֵׁבֶט מִבֵּית עֶדֶן)
were members of the coalition. The ruler of the Valley of Aven may be
identified with Pekah.[34] Although the location of the Valley of Aven
remains uncertain, since it appears in only this text, Kallai-Kleinmann
has identified Beth-aven (mentioned in 1 Sam. 13.5; 14.23; Hos. 5.8)
with Tell Maryam in the Wadi es-Suweinit 1 kilometer west of
Mukhmas.[35] The Valley of Aven was thus probably the Suweinit Valley
and its continuation as the Wadi Qelt to the Jordan River. Pekah, with
the backing of Rezin, appears to have begun encroaching on territories
west of the Jordan after securing his hold in Transjordan.

That Beth-Eden in Amos 1.5 is to be identified with Bit-Adini is quite
certain. But who was the ruler mentioned? Malamat, as has been noted
earlier, suggests identifying Šamši-ilu, the Assyrian *turtānu*, with 'the
one who holds the scepter in Beth-Eden'.[36] He has been followed by
Hawkins[37] and Hayes.[38] Hayes, in particular, proceeds to suggest that
Amos 1.5 reveals the existence of a coalition made up of Rezin of Aram-
Damascus—the primary target of the oracle—Pekah, יוֹשֵׁב מִבִּקְעַת־אָוֶן,

---

BCE, but since he abdicated and died only in 734 BCE, he was assigned a reign of 52
years (see 2 Kgs 15.2). Jeroboam II reigned over Israel from 788 to 748 BCE.
Because of the long reigns of these two kings, the chronological data are too
general to be helpful. The other datum, 'two years before the earthquake', is
perhaps more helpful. Since earthquakes are not uncommon in Syria–Palestine (see
D.H. Kallner-Amiran, 'A Revised Earthquake-Catalogue of Palestine', *IEJ* 1
[1950/51], pp. 223-46; *IEJ* 2 [1952], pp. 48-65), this particular earthquake must
have been significantly powerful and unforgettable (cf. Zech. 14.4-5), and evidence
of it is attested in the remains of Stratum VI of Hazor, dated to the mid-eighth
century BCE (see Y. Yadin *et al.*, *Hazor II: An Account of the Second Season of
Excavations, 1956* [Jerusalem: Magnes Press, 1960], pp. 24-26, 36-37; cf. P.J.
King, *Amos, Hosea, Micah: An Archaeological Commentary* [Philadelphia:
Westminster Press, 1988], pp. 21, 38). The mid-eighth century BCE, thus, appears to
be the most probable date of Amos's ministry. However, if our interpretation of
Amos 1.5 in relation to the death of Šamši-ilu is correct, then Amos's ministry
could be dated more precisely to after 751 BCE.

34. So Hayes, *Amos*, p. 76.

35. Z. Kallai-Kleinmann, 'Notes on the Topography of Benjamin', *IEJ* 6
(1956), pp. 180-87; cf. P.M. Arnold, 'Beth-aven', *ABD* (1992), I, p. 682. See also
N. Na'aman, 'Beth-aven, Bethel and Early Israelite Sanctuaries', *ZDPV* 103 (1987),
pp. 13-21.

36. Malamat, 'Amos 1.5', pp. 25-26.

37. Hawkins, 'Neo-Hittite States', p. 404.

38. Hayes, *Amos*, pp. 74-79.

a rival king of Israel, and Šamši-ilu. Yet, it is precisely because the text speaks of an alliance that the identification of 'the one who holds the scepter from Beth-Eden' with Šamši-ilu is suspect. Contrary to Hayes, there is no reason why an Assyrian governor of Šamši-ilu's stature and power—and who was virtually the Assyrian king of the west—would enter into an alliance with Aram-Damascus, a state frequently opposed to Assyrian power in Syria–Palestine. Moreover, coalitions in the west were often formed in order to oppose Assyria's domination of the region and control of trade routes. Thus, Šamši-ilu's participation in the coalition would have meant rebellion against the Assyrian central administration, which seems unlikely. Therefore, while it is true that Beth-Eden in Amos 1.5 refers to Bit-Adini, the identification of the ruler with Šamši-ilu cannot be sustained.[39] Instead the reference is probably made to a native of Bit-Adini. With the death of Šamši-ilu, a rebellion broke out, leading to the defacement of his monuments at Til-Barsip and Arslan Tash.[40] A native of Bit-Adini, who was able to take over the throne, then joined the anti-Assyrian coalition headed by Rezin.

The new political situation following the death of Šamši-ilu also resulted in the loss of Israelite territory. I have argued that Isa. 8.23 is best interpreted against the background of Israel's loss of territory to Aram-Damascus. If הראשׁון refers to Ḥadiānu, the one who took 'the

39. F.I. Andersen and D.N. Freedman (*Amos* [AB, 24A; New York: Doubleday, 1989], p. 256) date this text to the reign of Ben-hadad son of Hazael and suggest that the king of Damascus was the one mentioned as the ruler of the Valley of Aven (identified as the Biq'ah Valley) and the ruler of Beth-Eden. Their interpretation assumes that Amos was talking about events already decades removed from his time, which seems unlikely. Moreover, there is no evidence that Aram-Damascus was able to extend its control as far north as Bit-Adini, especially during the reign of Ben-hadad when the power of Aram-Damascus was declining, due in large part to the presence of Šamši-ilu in Syria–Palestine. Cf. also S.M. Paul, who suggests understanding the reference along with בקעת און as representing the two polar extremes of Aram of an earlier period (*Amos* [Hermeneia; Minneapolis: Fortress Press, 1991], p. 54).

40. The defacement of the monuments is noted by Thureau-Dangin and Dunand, *Til-Barsib*, p. 142; J.E. Reade, 'The Neo-Assyrian Court and Army: Evidence from the Sculptures', *Iraq* 34 (1972), pp. 89, 93-94. It makes better sense to argue that the defacement was done deliberately by anti-Assyrian natives of Bit-Adini rather than by an Assyrian king. Although Šamši-ilu often assumed an independence from the Assyrian king in his inscriptions, there is no evidence that he ever opposed the Assyrian monarch.

land of Zebulun and the land of Naphtali' (i.e. Upper Galilee) from the Israelites, then הֲאָדְרוּן would refer to Rezin, under whose reign an attempt to create a 'Greater Syria'—paralleling that of Hazael—was launched. It was he who 'treated harshly the way of the sea, the land beyond the Jordan, and Galilee of the nations'. It has been noted that from his usurpation of the throne in Damascus sometime during the middle of the eighth century BCE, he began to encroach upon Israelite territories and supported Pekah as a rival king. In all likelihood, he wrenched away the coastal regions, Transjordan, and all Galilee from Jeroboam II and subsequently made Pekah his puppet over these territories. Amos 1 and 6.13 attest Jeroboam's troubles in the coastal regions and Gilead, while Hos. 1.5 may reflect his difficulties in Galilee.[41]

Third, the new political reality also led to the severing of the Israelite–Tyrian relationship.[42] This may be surmised from Amos's oracle against Tyre.[43] One of the two wrongdoings that Amos accuses Tyre of committing was forgetting the בְּרִית אַחִים, 'a covenant of brothers',[44] an expression used to describe treaty relationships. That בְּרִית אַחִים is used here in Amos as a reference to the relationship between Israel and Tyre has been proposed by earlier scholars.[45] Most of these scholars, however, see it as a reference to the treaty established at an earlier time,

41. So Irvine, *Syro-Ephraimitic Crisis*, p. 225.

42. See F. Briquel-Chatonnet, *Les relations entre les cités de la côte Phénicienne et les royaumes d'Israël et de Juda* (OLA, 46; StudPh, 12; Leuven: Peeters, 1992), pp. 132-37.

43. The question of the authenticity of this oracle as belonging to the prophet Amos has long been debated. For a discussion of the issues, see J. Barton, *Amos's Oracles Against the Nations: A Study of Amos 1.3–2.5* (SOTSMS, 6; Cambridge: Cambridge University Press, 1980), pp. 24, 32; K.N. Schoville, 'A Note on the Oracles of Amos against Gaza, Tyre and Edom', in G.W. Anderson *et al.* (eds.), *Studies on Prophecy: A Collection of Twelve Papers* (VTSup, 26; Leiden: E.J. Brill, 1974), pp. 55-63; M. Haran, 'Observations on the Historical Background of Am. I.2–II.6', *IEJ* 18 (1968), pp. 201-12.

44. See M. Fishbane, 'The Treaty Background of Amos I.11 and Related Matters', *JBL* 89 (1970), pp. 313-18. E. Gerstenberger ('Covenant and Commandment', *JBL* 84 [1965], pp. 38-51) and J. Priest ('The Covenant of Brothers', *JBL* 84 [1965], pp. 400-406) have pointed out the prominence of the concept of 'brotherhood' in treaty relationships in the ancient Near East.

45. See, e.g., A.S. Kapelrud, *Central Ideas in Amos* (Oslo: Aschehoug, 1956), p. 24; T.H. Robinson and F. Horst, *Die Zwölf Kleinen Propheten* (HAT, 1/14; Tübingen: J.C.B. Mohr [Paul Siebeck], 1938), p. 70; Priest, 'Covenant of Brothers', pp. 403-406. See also the discussion in Paul, *Amos*, pp. 61-63.

either during the Solomonic or the Omride period. It is more probable that Amos was referring to a situation that was closer at hand rather than one that was a century or more removed. As noted above, the Israelite–Phoenician relation, broken at the time of Jehu's extermination of the Omride dynasty, was restored sometime during the reign of Jeroboam II.[46] What Amos was condemning Tyre for, then, was the breaking of this 'covenant of brothers' during the final years of Jeroboam's reign.[47] This probably came about as the result of a new alignment between Tyre, Aram-Damascus and Pekah's rival kingdom, following the accession of Rezin to the Aramean throne. In addition, the expansion of Damascene control into Galilee, Transjordan and Elath make Damascus a more promising commercial partner. That Tyre was an ally of Rezin of Aram-Damascus is supported by an Assyrian inscription from the time of Tiglath-pileser III (ND 4301 + 4305). This cooperation, certainly in existence during the reign of Tiglath-pileser, probably began back in the 750s.[48]

The reason for Tyre to break with Israel and join Rezin and his anti-Assyrian coalition was commercial.[49] Elath was retaken by Rezin according to 2 Kgs 16.6. The annalistic note relating to Elath (reading with the MT), although placed in Ahaz's reign, most probably comes from the reign of Jotham in the 750s. The importance of Elath for access to the Gulf of Aqabah for commerce with the Arabian and African coasts has been already noted. As such, it was a vital port for the commercial interests of the Arameans and Phoenicians. Thus, it is not surprising that Rezin would have retaken it early in his reign. Since Tyre needed access to the trade route, it would not have hesitated to break off relations with Israel and to cooperate with Rezin in the anti-Assyrian coalition.

46. So already Hayes, *Amos*, pp. 88-89.

47. So also S. Cohen, 'The Political Background of the Words of Amos', *HUCA* 36 (1965), pp. 153-60. Cohen further suggests that Israel was on the defensive at this time.

48. Contra W.T. Pitard ('Rezin', *ABD* [1992], IV, pp. 708-709), who argues that the coalition was probably formed between 737 and 735 BCE. During Tiglath-pileser's campaigns in Syria–Palestine (743–740 and 738–737 BCE), the members of the coalition would have curtailed their anti-Assyrianism and, as we know, even offered *maddattu* to Tiglath-pileser.

49. See Briquel-Chatonnet, *Les relations*, pp. 136-37.

Appendix

Most scholars identify Tiglath-pileser III as the antagonist, who carried out these onslaughts in connection with the Syro-Ephraimitic crisis. C.F. Whitley ('The Language and Exegesis of Isaiah 8.16-23', *ZAW* 90 [1978], pp. 28-43 [41-42]) argues that it alludes to two separate campaigns against Israel, the first in 734 and the second in 733/732 BCE. J.A. Emerton, however, argues that the two lines are parallel reflections of Tiglath-pileser's annexation of the northern regions of Israel c. 732 BCE ('Some Linguistic and Historical Problems in Isaiah VIII 23', *JSS* 14 [1969], pp. 151-75 [156, 170]). On the contrary, A. Alt ('Jesaja 8, 23–9, 6. Befreiungsnacht und Krönungstag', in W. Baumgartner *et al.* [eds.], *Festschrift Alfred Bertholet zum 80. Geburtstag gewidmet von Kollegen und Freunden* [Tübingen: J.C.B. Mohr (Paul Siebeck), 1950], pp. 32-38, 45-49) and H. Barth (*Die Jesaja-Worte in der Josiazeit: Israel und Assur als Thema einer productiven Neuinterpretation der Jesajaüberlieferung* [WMANT, 48; Neukirchen–Vluyn: Neukirchener Verlag, 1977], pp. 141-66) suggest that the first line describes Tiglath-pileser's invasion of Israel during the Syro-Ephraimitic crisis, while the second anticipates the future liberation of Israelite territories. While it is true that 2 Kgs 15.29 describes the capture of territories in Gilead and Galilee by Tiglath-pileser during the reign of Pekah, less certain is the fact that they were taken from the Israelites and that as such the Assyrians were responsible for reducing Israel to a rump state in 734–732 BCE (so S.A. Irvine, *Isaiah, Ahaz, and the Syro-Ephraimitic Crisis* [SBLDS, 123; Atlanta: Scholars Press, 1990], p. 224; see also his chs. 2 and 3). Moreover, the likelihood that two different individuals are meant is stronger. (On the issue of the southern border of Aram-Damascus, see S.A. Irvine, 'The Southern Border of Syria Reconsidered', *CBQ* 56 [1994], pp. 21–41.) G.R. Driver contends that הראשון and האחרון refer to Tiglath-pileser III and Shalmaneser V respectively ('Isaianic Problems', in G. Wiessner [ed.], *Festschrift für Wilhelm Eilers* [Wiesbaden: Otto Harrassowitz, 1967], p. 48).

H.L. Ginsberg, on the other hand, identifies them as Pekah and Hoshea respectively, arguing that the verse bemoans Hoshea's failure to recover the Israelite territories that Pekah had lost ('An Unrecognized Allusion to Kings Pekah and Hoshea of Israel', in M. Avi-Yonah *et al.* [eds.], *Benjamin Mazar Volume* [ErIsr, 5; Jerusalem: Israel Exploration Society, 1958], pp. 61*-65*). Ginsberg's translation is problematic and hence his interpretation must remain questionable. According to Irvine, although הראשון and האחרון refer to Jeroboam II and Menahem, it was the Arameans who had actually encroached on and annexed Israelite territories (Irvine, *Syro-Ephraimitic Crisis*, p. 225). In other words, the two Israelite kings were only *passively* responsible for the losses. The text of Isa. 8.23, however, suggests, on the contrary, that the people mentioned were *actively* responsible, that is, they 'treated contemptibly and harshly' those territories. Irvine's interpretation is therefore untenable on this point.

THE TYPOLOGY OF THE DAVIDIC COVENANT

Steven L. McKenzie

Max Miller is that rare scholar whose work has effected significant advances in different trajectories of the discipline. Max has always been ahead of his time, and I have consistently found myself catching up to his conclusions. My own research has intersected with Max's in three specific areas. The first of these is *textual criticism*. In working on my dissertation I learned of J.D. Shenkel's demonstration of the superiority of the Old Greek chronology to that of the Masoretic text in sections of Kings,[1] only to discover later that Max's dissertation on the Omride dynasty had anticipated Shenkel's result.[2] Later in my career, I turned to the *redactional history* of Samuel and Kings and found myself in frequent agreement with Max's analyses of the *crux* in 1 Samuel 7–15 about the beginning of the monarchy[3] and of the Elijah–Elisha materials and the account of Ahab's reign.[4] Then, when I became interested in the reign of David and what, if anything, could be said about the *history* of his reign, I turned to Max's treatment in *A History of Ancient Israel and Judah*.[5] That such features as its treatment of David as a historical

---

1. J.D. Shenkel, *Chronology and Recensional Development in the Greek Text of Kings* (HSM, 1; Cambridge, MA: Harvard University Press, 1968).

2. J.M. Miller, 'The Omride Dynasty in the Light of Recent Literary and Archaeological Research' (PhD dissertation, Emory University, 1964). See his articles, 'The Elisha Cycle and the Accounts of the Omride Wars', *JBL* 85 (1966), pp. 441-54; and 'Another Look at the Chronology of the Early Divided Monarchy', *JBL* 86 (1967), pp. 276-88.

3. J.M. Miller, 'Saul's Rise to Power: Some Observations Concerning 1 Sam 9.1–10.16; 10.26–11.15 and 13.2–14.46', *CBQ* 36 (1974), pp. 157-74.

4. In addition to 'The Elisha Cycle and the Accounts of the Omride Wars' cited in n. 2, see J.M. Miller, 'The Fall of the House of Ahab', *VT* 17 (1967), pp. 307-24; and 'The Rest of the Acts of Jehoahaz (I Kings 20. 22,1-28)', *ZAW* 80 (1968), pp. 337-42.

5. J.M. Miller and J.H. Hayes, *A History of Ancient Israel and Judah* (Philadelphia: Westminster Press, 1986).

figure are sometimes cited today—usually without the same detailed and reasoned argumentation—as a conservative foil, only indicates the impact the book has had. Yet, for all that I have gained from Max's publications, I learned even more from him during one of his tours of Syria and Jordan, arranged by his gracious wife, Julene. The study that follows reflects on text-critical, redaction-critical and historical issues surrounding the Davidic covenant. It is with great appreciation for Max's gifts and for the experience of traveling with him that I offer it.

The Typologies of Cross and Weinfeld

Two typologies of the Davidic covenant have been proposed. That of Frank Cross finds three stages, the initial one of which dated back to David and conceived of the covenant as conditional upon the king's obedience to the deity's stipulations.[6] This understanding of the covenant of kingship was retained in the Northern kingdom and accounted for the series of royal houses, each overthrowing its predecessor. Thus, ideology determined history. A new stage developed under Solomon and continued in Judah after the division of the kingdoms. In this second stage, influenced by Canaanite traditions, the Davidic covenant became unconditional—the eternal decree of Yahweh dwelling on Zion. The language of divine sonship was adopted. Jerusalem was deemed inviolable. This theology furnished the basis for Judean royal propaganda, which was instrumental in maintaining the Davidic line on the throne. Again, ideology determined history, and the dynasty lasted until the kingdom itself fell. In the third stage, during and after the exile, both Northern and Southern royal ideologies were developed in various ways by different writers: the exilic Deuteronomist (Dtr[2]) explained the exiles of Israel and Judah via the Northern ideology as the execution of the curses of the covenant at Horeb, thus interpreting the Davidic covenant as both conditional and subordinate to the Mosaic covenant; Second Isaiah democratized the promise of an eternal Davidic house and anticipated its fulfillment in the people of Israel; P applied the expression 'eternal covenant', drawn from the Judean royal theology, to the patriarchal covenant; and apocalyptic thought looked for a new age

---

6.   F.M. Cross, *Canaanite Myth and Hebrew Epic: Essays in the History and the Religion of Israel* (Cambridge, MA: Harvard University Press, 1973), pp. 219-73, esp. 264-65.

in which a new David would reign in a new Jerusalem, thus fulfilling the Davidic promise.[7]

A second typology, proposed by Moshe Weinfeld, holds that there are two types of covenants in the Hebrew Bible: the obligatory type, represented by the Mosaic covenant, and the promissory type, represented by the covenants with Abraham and David.[8] The former was modeled after ancient Near Eastern vassal treaties, and the latter after land grants of ancient Near Eastern kings to their faithful subjects. The covenant with David, like these royal grants, was originally unconditional. It was the Deuteronomistic historian who conditionalized it and then built his theology around this conditionality in the early sixth century BCE, following the demise of both Israel and Judah. Weinfeld does not trace his typology beyond the exile. He is also not as explicit as Cross about the beginning point of the covenant, but he apparently agrees that the tradition began with David himself.

Gary Knoppers points to three serious problems with Weinfeld's proposal.[9] First, neither the land grants that Weinfeld cites nor the biblical texts referring to the Davidic covenant evince a typical structure or

7.   T.N.D. Mettinger (*King and Messiah: The Civil and Sacral Legitimation of the Israelite Kings* [ConBOT, 8; Lund: CWK Gleerup, 1976], esp. pp. 275-93) adopts a position close to Cross's, though Mettinger sees the conditionalizing of the covenant as a purely exilic and primarily Deuteronomistic phenomenon. Thus, the promise to David was originally unconditional and remained so even in the exile, except in redactional additions by the nomistic Deuteronomist (DtrN). Similarly, W.M. Schniedewind (*Society and the Promise to David: The Reception History of 2 Samuel 7.1-17* [Oxford: Oxford University Press, 1999]) finds the origin of the Davidic promise during Solomon's reign and holds that it represented the ideology required for the emerging monarchy. It was unconditional and remained so, except in certain late interpretations brought on by the exile. Schniedewind traces the development of the promise through the eighth and seventh centuries BCE, when it served to further the restoration efforts of Hezekiah and Josiah, and on to its democratization in the exile. He believes, incredibly in my view, that the promise was preserved and interpreted orally until the seventh century when it was finally recorded in writing in support of Josiah's centralization efforts.

8.   M. Weinfeld, 'The Covenant of Grant in the Old Testament and in the Ancient Near East', *JAOS* 90 (1970), pp. 184-203. Reprinted in F.E. Greenspahn (ed.), *Essential Papers on Israel and the Ancient Near East* (Essential Papers on Jewish Studies; New York: New York University Press, 1991), pp. 69-102 and 'בְּרִית', *TDOT*, III, pp. 253-79.

9.   G.N. Knoppers, 'Ancient Near Eastern Royal Grants and the Davidic Covenant: A Parallel?', *JAOS* 116 (1996), pp. 670-97.

common pattern. Secondly, the linguistic features of ancient Near Eastern sources that Weinfeld cites as parallels to the Davidic covenant in the Bible are drawn from a variety of genres and are not unique to land grants. Finally, close examination of land grants indicates that they were not predominantly unconditional. The biblical texts as well are not really unconditional but presume some obligation on the part of the Davidic line.[10] Knoppers concludes that the different biblical writers drew on a variety of genres and that each formulated the Davidic covenant differently. Knoppers's critique deals primarily with the ancient Near Eastern background of the Davidic covenant. But he also asks whether the Davidic covenant was ever really conceived of as unconditional in the sense posited by Cross and Weinfeld, and he raises the question as to whether the relevant biblical texts are better explained as the result of unilinear or independent development. I wish to focus more closely on these questions but especially on that of the date of origin of the Davidic promise or covenant.

Promise and Covenant

Apart from the conditional/unconditional divide, there are two types of reference to the Davidic covenant in the Hebrew Bible: those that actually use the term 'covenant' (ברית) and those that refer to it rather as a 'word' or 'promise' (דבר). Among the passages included in the latter category is 2 Samuel 7. In fact, the Deuteronomistic historian never uses the term ברית for God's word to David.[11] For the Deuteronomistic

---

10. A point developed further in G.N. Knoppers, 'David's Relation to Moses: The Contexts, Content and Conditions of the Davidic Promises', in J. Day (ed.), *King and Messiah in Israel and the Ancient Near East: Proceedings of the Oxford Old Testament Seminar* (JSOTSup, 270; Sheffield: Sheffield Academic Press, 1998), pp. 91-118.

11. Cf. L. Perlitt, *Bundestheologie im Alten Testament* (WMANT, 36; Neukirchen–Vluyn: Neukirchener Verlag, 1969), pp. 47-48. Two texts in Samuel–Kings that appear to contradict this statement require explanation. Solomon's prayer in 1 Kgs 8.23-24a contains the term ברית in what has been construed as a reference to the Davidic covenant. Thus, the NRSV translates: 'O LORD God of Israel, there is no God like you in heaven above or on earth beneath, keeping covenant and steadfast love for your servants who walk before you with all their heart, the covenant that you kept for your servant my father David as you declared to him...' The word ברית occurs in v. 23 (שמר הברית והחסד לעבדיך ההלכים לפניך בכל-לבם), but not in v. 24 where the NRSV again has 'covenant'. Verse 24 actually

Historian there is only one covenant—the one initially ratified on Mt
Horeb and then renewed by Moses in Moab.[12]

References to the Davidic 'Covenant'

The term ברית in reference to the Davidic covenant occurs in the
following biblical passages: 2 Sam. 23.5; Isa. 55.3; Jer. 33.20, 21, 25;
Ps. 89.4, 29, 35, 40; 2 Chron. 13.5; 21.7. The texts in Isaiah, Jeremiah
and Chronicles are relatively easy to date. Moving from the known to
the unknown, I shall therefore treat them first and save 2 Sam. 23.5 and
Psalm 89, which are more controversial, for last.

Isaiah 55.3

The late exilic date of 2 Isaiah, wherein this verse lies, is widely enough
acknowledged that it need not be defended here. The second half of this
verse is our primary concern. It reads: ואכרתה לכם ברית עולם
חסדי דוד האמנים ('I will make an eternal covenant with you, the sure
mercies of David').[13] The language is strongly reminiscent of 2 Sam.

---

begins with the relative אשר and is a continuation of the previous verse. It does not
refer to 'covenant' in v. 23 but is a more general reference to Yahweh's faithfulness
or חסד. The NRSV translation of the parallel verse in 2 Chron. 6.15, which is the
same in Hebrew as 1 Kgs 8.24, more accurately renders the sense: 'you who have
kept for your servant, my father David, what you promised to him'. Solomon, in
fact, goes out of his way to avoid referring to the word to David as a covenant.
Three times he uses the circumlocution אשר דברת לעבדיך דוד. Yahweh is
שמר הברית, '*the* covenant' being the Mosaic one, so that 'those who walk before
you with all their heart' are those who keep the law laid out in that covenant. The
second text is 2 Sam. 23.5 in the 'Last Words of David' (23.1-7), which I shall treat
in detail presently. For now it is enough to recognize that it falls within the
'Miscellany' at the end of 2 Sam. (20.23–24.25), 'a repository of diverse materials
pertinent to the reign of David' that 'is neither part of the Deuteronomistic history
nor related to the earlier literature it embraced' (P.K. McCarter, *II Samuel* [AB, 9;
Garden City, NY: Doubleday, 1984], p. 16) but is similar to materials that
accumulated immediately preceding the accounts of the deaths of other biblical
heroes, namely Jacob and Moses.

12. T.C. Römer (*Israels Väter: Untersuchungen zur Väterthematik im
Deuteronomium und in der deuteronomistischen Tradition* [OBO, 99; Freiburg:
Universitätsverlag; Göttingen: Vandenhoeck & Ruprecht, 1990]) has argued
convincingly that the 'fathers' in Deuteronomy referred originally to the exodus
generation and that the references to the patriarchs, Abraham, Isaac and Jacob
(including any promises or covenants with them), are secondary.

13. That is, 'mercies given to David'—probably an objective genitive, as argued

וחסדי לא־יסור ממנו...ונאמן ביתך וממלכתך עד־עולם לפניך 7.15-16
כסאך יהיה נכון עד־עולם. In addition to the name of David, three key words from 2 Sam. 7.15-16 occur in the brief half verse from Isaiah: עולם, חסד and נאמן. No other text about the Davidic promise or covenant shows greater affinity to 2 Samuel 7, except of course for the essential reiteration of it in 1 Chronicles 17. It seems likely, therefore, that 2 Isaiah is familiar with and is reinterpeting the Davidic promise in 2 Samuel 7 for his exilic audience.[14] This reinterpretation involves three points. First, the promise or 'word' of Yahweh through Nathan to David in 2 Samuel 7 has now become a covenant. The term ברית in Isa. 55.3 is used to mean a unilateral promise or pledge rather than a mutual agreement. This seems to be its sense elsewhere in 2 Isaiah: in 42.6, God gives Israel as a 'covenant to the people' (אור גוים // ברית עם); in 49.8, the same expression is used in the context of a guarantee of the return of the exiles; and in 54.10, ברית שלומי refers to Yahweh's promise never again to be angry with Israel. Second, it is called an 'eternal covenant' (ברית עולם), an expression typical of, if not exclusive to, late literature, as we will see. Third, the Davidic 'covenant' is now democratized. The plural suffix לכם, as well as the plural verbs earlier in the verse, show that the covenant is made not simply with David but with the returnees from Babylon, whom 2 Isaiah regards as Israel. The covenant with David is now renewed with the nation as a whole. The net effect of this reinterpretation is that 2 Isaiah herewith grounds the hope for the restoration of Israel in God's eternal covenant to David.

Jeremiah 33.14-26

Of the three occurrences of ברית in Jer. 33.20, 21, 25 only the one in v. 21 explicitly refers to the covenant 'with David'. The other two concern God's covenant with day and night. Nevertheless, all three convene to make the point that the Davidic covenant is as permanent as the covenant with day and night.

The unit in which these three verses occur is Jer. 33.14-26, which is a late addition to the book of Jeremiah, as is indicated by its absence from

by H.G.M. Williamson '"The Sure Mercies of David": Subjective or Objective Genitive?', *JSS* 23 (1978), pp. 31-49. Unless otherwise noted, all translations are the author's.

14. So also Williamson, 'Sure Mercies', pp. 41-43. The objective genitive accords with 2 Sam. 7.

the LXX. There are also internal indications of its lateness. The statement in v. 14, 'I will cause a righteous shoot to sprout for David', seems to allude to the re-establishment of the Davidic dynasty and hence to assume that it had been cut off. Similarly, v. 24 articulates the charge that God has rejected 'the two families whom Yahweh chose' (ויאמרם שתי המשפחות אשר בחר יהוה בהם), referring either to the nations of Israel and Judah or to the tribes of Judah (David's tribe) and Levi; in either case, the destruction of Jerusalem in 586 BCE is presupposed. The notion of a covenant with Levi appears elsewhere in post-exilic texts such as Mal. 2.4, 5, 8 and Neh. 13.29 (see also Num. 18.19 and 25.12-13, both P) as does the expectation of dual leadership under a Davidic king and a priest (Zech. 4.1-4; 6.13). The mention of the patriarchs Abraham, Isaac and Jacob by name in v. 26 seems to reflect familiarity with the Pentateuch more or less in its present form. Most scholars, therefore, date this passage to the post-exilic period.[15]

The version of the Davidic promise in Jer. 33.17 is nearly identical, *mutatis mutandis*, with David's and Solomon's recitations of it in 1 Kgs 2.4 and 8.25 (= 2 Chron. 6.16; cf. also 2 Chron. 7.18), respectively, and must have been borrowed from them.

---

15. See W.L. Holladay, *Jeremiah 2: A Commentary on the Book of the Prophet Jeremiah, Chapters 26–52* (Hermeneia; Minneapolis: Fortress Press, 1989), pp. 228-30, for other arguments. Holladay places this passage at about 400 BCE based on its style, anthological nature and content. T. Veijola (*Verheissung in der Krise: Studien zur Literatur und Theologie der Exilszeit anhand des 89. Psalms* [AASF B, 220; Helsinki: Suomalainen Tiedeakatemia, 1982], pp. 84-85) argues for an earlier, late exilic date for Jer. 33.14-26. Veijola asserts that the absence of the passage from the LXX may be due to a variety of factors and cannot be used to decide between an exilic and a post-exilic date. He also suggests that the references to Levi in vv. 18, 21b, 22bβ are not original to the passage but are later additions. But Veijola does not explain what possibilities he has in mind to account for the absence of vv. 14-26 from the LXX. There is no apparent mechanism (e.g. *homoioarchton* or *homoioteleuton*) that would indicate haplography, so the most likely explanation seems to be that the passage was a late addition to the proto-MT text. As for the references to the Levites, vv. 21b and 22bβ could well be later glosses. But I can see no literary reason for regarding v. 18 as secondary. Moreover, Veijola's argument is transparently motivated by his desire to locate Jer. 33.14-26 close to his DtrN. The usual, post-exilic date for the passage calls into question the precise differentiation and dating of Deuteronomistic redactional levels (DtrG, DtrP, DtrN) that Veijola posits on linguistic grounds.

Jeremiah 33.17	*1 Kings 2.4*	*1 Kings 8.25*
לא־יכרת לדוד איש ישב	לא־יכרת לך איש מעל	לא־יכרת לך איש מלפני
על־כסא בית־ישראל	כסא ישראל	ישב על־כסא ישראל

The two Kings passages are Deuteronomistic, and each makes direct
reference to Yahweh's promise to David in 2 Samuel 7. It is fair to
assume, therefore, that the author of Jer. 33.14-26 was familiar with the
version of the promise in 2 Samuel 7 and was essentially reinterpreting
it. It is striking, then, that Jer. 33.17 leaves out the condition expressed
in both versions of the promise in Kings:

אם־ישמרו בניך את־דרכם ללכת לפני באמת בכל־לבבם ובכל־נפשם :1 Kgs 2.4
רק אם־ישמרו בניך את־דרכם ללכת לפני :1 Kgs 8.25

The reason these statements of condition are omitted from Jer. 33.14-26
is that its author views the Davidic covenant as unconditional. The
point of this text is that the covenant with David cannot be broken by
humans, because it is not a mutual agreement but a unilateral promise
from God. Its permanence is guaranteed, like that of the sun and moon,
by Yahweh's very nature. The author evidently does not see the exile
with the accompanying interruption of the Davidid reign in Jerusalem
as annuling or infringing upon the promise to David. As with Isa. 55.3,
Jer. 33.14-26 is a text whose date after the fall of the Judahite kingdom
is indisputable. Yet both see the Davidic covenant as still in effect and
indeed find in it grounds for hope for restoration.

2 Chronicles 13.5; 21.7

Knoppers has shown how the Chronicler makes use of both unconditional and conditional versions of the Davidic promise from the Deuteronomistic History, recontextualizing and reinterpreting them for a variety
of purposes.[16] Above all, the Chronicler portrays Solomon's faithfulness on a par with David's as both the reason for the dynastic promise
or its reaffirmation and the standard for the relationship of future kings
with Yahweh. Most of the references to the Davidic promise in
Chronicles closely parallel those in Samuel–Kings, although there are a
few such references in the Chronicler's *Sondergut* (esp. 1 Chron. 22.10;
28.7). The Chronicler introduces his reinterpretation through subtle
changes in his *Vorlage*. Thus, the Chronicles version of Nathan's oracle
(1 Chron. 17.13) omits the possibility that David's heir might sin and be

16. Knoppers, 'David's Relation to Moses', pp. 101-106.

אֲשֶׁר בְּהַעֲוֹתוֹ וְהֹכַחְתִּיו בְּשֵׁבֶט אֲנָשִׁים וּבְנִגְעֵי בְּנֵי אָדָם) disciplined
2 Sam. 7.14b), because the Chronicler idealizes Solomon as much as
David, if not more so.

As we have seen, the Deuteronomistic historian does not use the term
בְּרִית in reference to the Davidic promise. Chronicles follows its
Vorlage in this regard for the most part, but there are two exceptions.
The first is in the speech of Abijah of Judah to Jeroboam of Israel
(2 Chron. 13.4-12), which is unique to Chronicles and widely recognized as the Chronicler's composition. In 13.5 Abijah asks, 'Do you not
know that Yahweh the God of Israel gave kingship over Israel to David
and his sons forever—a covenant of salt?' The term בְּרִית here obviously
means 'promise'. Knoppers rightly observes that the Chronicler's point
is that the divine promise to David includes all who go by the name of
Israel. Hence, the separate Northern kingdom and its rulers are illegiti-
mate and indeed in opposition to Yahweh's word. But the Northern
people are still a part of Israel and belong under a Davidic monarch.
The expression בְּרִית עוֹלָם does not occur here, but the perpetuity of
the covenant is indicated by its designation as a 'covenant of salt'[17] and
by the fact that the gift of the kingdom to the Davidids is לְעוֹלָם.

The second explicit reference to a Davidic covenant in Chronicles is
in the regnal formula for Jehoram in 2 Chron. 21.7, which parallels
2 Kgs 8.19.

2 Kings 8.19	*2 Chronicles 21.7*
וְלֹא־אָבָה יְהוָה לְהַשְׁחִית אֶת־יְהוּדָה	וְלֹא־אָבָה יְהוָה לְהַשְׁחִית אֶת־בֵּית דָּוִיד
לְמַעַן דָּוִד עַבְדּוֹ	לְמַעַן הַבְּרִית אֲשֶׁר כָּרַת לְדָוִיד
כַּאֲשֶׁר אָמַר־לוֹ לָתֵת לוֹ נִיר	וּכְאֲשֶׁר אָמַר לָתֵת לוֹ נִיר
לְבָנָיו כָּל־הַיָּמִים	וּלְבָנָיו כָּל־הַיָּמִים

The Chronicler has altered this statement so that its focus is no longer
the nation of Judah but the Davidic dynasty, which Yahweh refused to
destroy because of his covenant with David. The verse seems to equate
the content of the covenant with the promise 'to give David and his

17. The expression 'covenant of salt' is somewhat obscure, but it seems to mean
a permanent covenant and may have arisen from the properties of salt as a
preservative and/or from its use in ceremonial meals ratifying covenants. It occurs
elsewhere only in Num. 18.19 (P), though Lev. 2.13 mentions the 'salt of the covenant' (cf. also Ezra 4.14). It is not clear whether there is any relationship between 2
Chron. 13.5 and Num. 18.19, much less what the direction of dependence would
have been.

sons a fiefdom[18] forever'. It thus agrees with Isa. 55.3 and Jer. 33.14-26 in defining covenant not as a mutual agreement but as a unilateral promise from Yahweh to David.

The post-exilic setting of Chronicles is nearly universally affirmed by scholars and need not be defended here. There also remains a broad consensus, despite recent challenges, that the books of Samuel and Kings in the Deuteronomistic History were the Chronicler's principal source.[19] 2 Kings 8.19 is one of the Deuteronomistic texts that explain the endurance of the kingdom of Judah, despite wicked kings such as Abijah, as the benefit of David's faithfulness and Yahweh's promise to him. Thus, 2 Kgs 8.19 is an interpretation of 2 Samuel 7. The dependence of 2 Chron. 21.7 on 2 Samuel 7, therefore, can be traced in two directions. It takes one step further the interpretations of 2 Kgs 8.19 and 1 Chronicles 17, both of which are directly based on 2 Samuel 7. Hence, while 2 Chron. 13.5 may not be directly dependent on 2 Samuel 7, the latter is clearly the ultimate source of the Chronicler's reference to Yahweh's gift of the kingship to David and his sons forever.

Taken together, 2 Chron. 13.5 and 21.7 show that the Chronicler, as Second Isaiah and the author of Jer. 33.14-26, described Yahweh's word to David as a covenant (ברית) and conceived of this as a unilateral promise. Also as those authors, the Chronicler was aware of and interpreted 2 Samuel 7. The Chronicler's intent in these two verses can only be determined by considering his work as a whole. Among the major interests of Chronicles that are widely recognized by scholars are his inclusion of the Northern tribes within 'all Israel' and his portrayal

---

18. On this meaning of ניר see P.D. Hanson, 'The Song of Heshbon and David's *Nîr*', *HTR* 61 (1968), pp. 297-320; and E. Ben Zvi, 'Once the Lamp has been Kindled... A Reconsideration of the Meaning of the MT *Nîr* in 1 Kgs 11.36; 15.4; 2 Kgs 8.19 and 2 Chr 21.7', *AusBR* 39 (1991), pp. 19-30.

19. The challenge has come from A.G. Auld, *Kings without Privilege: David and Moses in the Story of the Bible's Kings* (Edinburgh: T. & T. Clark, 1994). See my critique in 'The Chronicler as Redactor', in M.P. Graham and S.L. McKenzie (eds.), *The Chronicler as Author: Studies in Text and Texture* (JSOTSup, 263; Sheffield: Sheffield Academic Press, 1999), pp. 70-90 (80-87); and Auld's response, 'What Was the Main Source of the Books of Chronicles?', on pp. 91-99 of the same volume. The Chronicler's text of Samuel was of a different type from that of the MT, but his text of Kings was essentially the same as the MT. See S.L. McKenzie, *The Chronicler's Use of the Deuteronomistic History* (HSM, 33; Atlanta: Scholars Press, 1985).

of David and Solomon as model kings.[20] Both of these interests surface in 2 Chron. 13.5, as has been noted above. Most scholars surmise that the Chronicler's interest in these topics (and in the cult as well) reflects an effort on his part to provide a program—however idealized—for the restoration of Israel in his day. To the extent that this is so, the Chronicler appears to agree with Isa. 55.3 and Jer. 33.14-26 that the Davidic covenant is still in effect and is a source of hope for the future.

2 Samuel 23.5

This passage is more difficult to date than the ברית דוד texts treated above. The 'Miscellany' in 2 Samuel 21–25 is widely recognized as an addition to the Deuteronomistic History, and the two poems in ch. 22 and 23.1-7 were probably the last insertions made into this material.[21] But 2 Samuel 22 is older than its date of insertion, and 23.1-7 may be as well. Still, a few internal features hint at the lateness of the second poem. The first of these is its use of the expression ברית עולם (v. 5), which occurs exclusively in literature from the exile and later: P (Gen. 9.16; 17.7, 13, 19; Exod. 31.16; Lev. 24.8; Num. 18.19; 25.13); late portions of Isaiah (24.5; 61.8), including Isa. 55.3, where we have already encountered it; Jer. 32.40; 50.5; Ezek. 16.60; 37.26; and the late Psalm 105 (v. 10), which is quoted in 1 Chron. 16.17.[22] In addition, McCarter observes that the word מלה and the image of David as a prophet in v. 2 are late, that the central metaphor of the poem in vv. 3-4 has close parallels to Mal. 3.19-20 and that the poem evinces various motifs common in Hebrew wisdom literature. However, he does not regard the latter two features as decisive and concludes that v. 2 is an insertion into a poem that otherwise exhibits early features.[23] He mentions three such features: (1) the opening of the poem using נאם

20. See R.W. Klein, 'Chronicles, Book of 1–2', *ABD* (1992), I, pp. 999-1001.

21. McCarter, *II Samuel*, pp. 16-19.

22. Veijola (*Verheissung*, p. 68 n. 48) points out further that the qualification of ברית by adjectives, as in 2 Sam. 23.5 with ערוכה and שמרה, is attested elsewhere only in Jer. 31.31 and Ps. 89.29 (ET v. 28). The latter is probably also exilic, as we shall see momentarily.

23. McCarter, *II Samuel*, pp. 480-86. McCarter states that Malachi envisions the coming of the Davidic king as an object of hope for the future in contrast to 2 Sam. 23.1-7, which speaks of the royal house as a living institution. He also notes that wisdom is 'timeless'. Of course, the wisdom literature in the Bible is predominately late, and the actualization of the dynasty in the poem may be due simply to its self-depiction as David's words.

('utterance'), best paralleled by the Balaam oracles in Numbers 24; (2) the absence of Deuteronomistic language; and (3) the use of divine epithets that are early. We may deal briefly with each of these features.

(1) The use of נְאֻם plus a human subject is rare; it occurs outside of the Balaam oracles and 2 Sam. 23.1 only in Prov. 30.1, where the text is problematic (cf. also Ps. 36.2, where the subject is פֶּשַׁע), and the denominative verb occurs in Jer. 23.31. Also, the word is so common in prophetic literature as the introduction of an oracle from Yahweh that its use in 2 Samuel 23 would make sense if the author were trying to cast David in a prophetic role.

(2) The use of 'house' in v. 5 referring to the Davidic line may not be exclusively Deuteronomistic, but it is in line with the usage in 2 Samuel 7 and Samuel–Kings generally. In addition, McCarter himself observes that to the extent that 'the fear of God' in v. 3 implies obedience to divine statutes and customs, it is best exemplified in Deuteronomistic usage.[24]

(3) The divine epithets in the poem were discussed by Freedman in a 1976 article that McCarter cites.[25] Freedman admits that the other occurrences of בְּרִית עוֹלָם are late and that it would be unusual to find the expression in an early poem. Hence, he reads עוֹלָם alone as an epithet: 'For the Eternal has executed a covenant in my behalf.' But this reading is obviously motivated by the assumption that the poem is early and is thus dependent on the assessment of the other presumed early epithets. Besides עוֹלָם the other epithets that Freedman finds in 2 Sam. 23.1-7 are עָל (v. 1), אֱלֹהִים (v. 3) and אֱלֹהֵי (in אֱלֹהֵי יַעֲקֹב, v. 1; and אֱלֹהֵי יִשְׂרָאֵל, v. 3), זְמִרוֹת (v. 1), צוּר (v. 3), יהוה (v. 2), and אֵל (v. 5). Of these, יהוה, אֱלֹהִים, אֵל and צוּר are common in material from all periods and are not indicative of an early date. עָל is otherwise attested in Gen. 49.26; Deut. 33.27; and 1 Sam. 2.10—all early poems. But its presence in 2 Sam. 23.5 is doubtful. 4QSam[a] reads אֵל, as do the Lucianic Greek witnesses, and both Cross and McCarter follow them, citing the frequent interchange of אֵל and עָל in the textual transmission of Samuel.[26] It is also uncertain whether זְמִרוֹת is a divine epithet. The

---

24. McCarter, *II Samuel*, p. 481.

25. D.N. Freedman, 'Divine Names and Titles in Early Hebrew Poetry', in F.M. Cross, W.E. Lemke and P.D. Miller (eds.), *Magnalia Dei: The Mighty Acts of God: Essays on the Bible and Archaeology in Memory of G. Ernest Wright* (Garden City, NY: Doubleday, 1976), pp. 55-107, esp. 73-75.

26. McCarter, *II Samuel*, p. 477; Cross, *Canaanite Myth*, p. 52 n. 31; p. 234 n. 66.

translation 'the sweet psalmist of Israel' or 'bard of Israel's songs'[27] makes perfect sense in context. It is true that the reading זמרת ישׂראל provides a better parallel to אלהי יעקב in the previous line. But the use of the term as an epithet (meaning 'stronghold') is only attested three other places—Exod. 15.2; Isa. 12.2; and Ps. 118.14—always in the stock expression עזי וזמרת יה.[28] In any case, the epithet itself cannot be regarded as indicative of an early date. Cross contends that Exod. 15.2a is an interpolation and deletes it from his reconstruction of the poem, noting that it was 'a familiar bicolon' because of its occurrence in Isa. 12.2 and Ps. 118.14.[29] The date of Psalm 118 is uncertain, but Isaiah 12 is widely recognized as the composition of the post-exilic editor of Isaiah 1–11.[30] In short, there is no compelling reason for seeing 2 Sam. 23.1-7 as early and several indications that it is late.

The brevity of the reference to the Davidic covenant makes it difficult to say much about how the author of the poem understands it. The expression ברית עולם and the exilic date indicated by its language suggest that the author sees the Davidic covenant as eternal and a basis for hope for the future and probably, therefore, as a unilateral promise. There is also little to go on as regards the poem's relationship to 2 Samuel 7. But again its exilic date and its use of the word 'house' to refer to the Davidic dynasty suggest dependence on 2 Samuel 7.

Psalm 89

The date and setting of Psalm 89 are also controversial, with proposals ranging from the Jebusite period[31] to that of the Maccabeans.[32]

---

27. F.M. Cross, *From Epic to Canon: History and Literature in Ancient Israel* (Baltimore: The Johns Hopkins University Press, 1998), p. 140.

28. So Exod. 15.2, Isa. 12.2 and Ps. 118.14 both read the construct זמרת without the suffix, but the suffixed form has textual support and is widely accepted as the correct reading in both cases.

29. Cross, *Canaanite Myth*, p. 127 n. 49; *idem, From Epic to Canon*, p. 146 n. 34.

30. See most recently H.G.M. Williamson (*The Book Called Isaiah: Deutero-Isaiah's Role in Composition and Redaction* [Oxford: Clarendon Press, 1994], esp. pp. 118-23), who argues for 2 Isaiah as the author of Isa. 12.

31. G.W. Ahlström, *Psalm 89: Eine Liturgie aus dem Ritual des leidenden Königs* (Lund: CWK Gleerup, 1959), pp. 182-83.

32. B. Duhm, *Die Psalmen* (KHAT, 14; Tübingen: J.C.B. Mohr, 1899), p. 224. Duhm added that the lateness of the psalm would have been evident long before, if

Fortunately, Veijola's 1982 study greatly facilitates our present task.[33] The present consensus seems to be that Psalm 89 is composite, consisting of sections from divergent settings.[34] Verses 6-19 (ET 5-18)[35] constitute the oldest section of the psalm. Its exact date does not concern us here, though it has been considered among the oldest pieces of literature in the Bible.[36] There is also little reason to doubt that the final section of the psalm (vv. 39-53) dates from the exile or later. To be sure, there have been attempts to connect these verses with earlier events in Judah's history—Shishak's (Sheshonq's) invasion, the Syro-Ephraimitic crisis, the deportation of King Manasseh and the death of Josiah—to name some of the more prominent suggestions.[37] But consideration of language and vocabulary, in addition to historical allusions, establish the exilic setting of these verses.[38]

only the Old Testament had been in the hands of impartial historians instead of theologians!

33. Veijola, *Verheissung in der Krise*, fully cited in n. 15.

34. A few have argued for the psalm's unity—notably J.M. Ward, 'The Literary Form and Liturgical Background of Psalm LXXXIX', *VT* 11 (1961), pp. 321-39; and R.J. Clifford, 'Psalm 89: A Lament over the Davidic Ruler's Continued Failure', *HTR* 73 (1980), pp. 35-47. Their case is largely form-critical, though Ward adds arguments from vocabulary. I see nothing from a form-critical standpoint that would preclude the possibility that a later writer adopted an older poem in vv. 6-19 as one of the constituent elements for a new psalm. Ward's arguments from vocabulary are superceded by the more recent treatment of Veijola (*Verheissung*, esp. pp. 47-91). N. Sarna ('Psalm 89: A Study in Inner Biblical Exegesis', in A. Altmann [ed.], *Biblical and Other Studies* [Philip W. Lown Institute of Advanced Judaic Studies, Brandeis University. Studies and Texts, 1; Cambridge, MA: Harvard University Press, 1963], pp. 29-33) also mounts a compelling case for unity.

35. The verse numbers for this psalm in English translations are one less than those in the Hebrew text. For convenience, I cite the Hebrew numbers.

36. So Cross, *Canaanite Myth*, pp. 45 n. 6; 144; 160-62. Veijola agrees in seeing vv. 6-19 as the oldest level of the psalm, but he does not date it, referring to it simply as 'the introductory hymn' ('der einleitende Hymnus') of the psalm (pp. 45-46). Based on metrical considerations he also includes vv. 2-3 as part of the initial hymn and sees vv. 17-19 as a later expansion of it (*Verheissung*, pp. 35-36).

37. For bibliography and other examples, see Veijola, *Verheissung*, pp. 15-17.

38. Veijola, *Verheissung*, pp. 47-118. To mention some of the more compelling evidence gathered by Veijola, the complaint in v. 40 that Yahweh has renounced the covenant with David strongly suggests an exilic setting. The other depictions of Yahweh's treatment of the Davidic king—defiling his crown (v. 40), removing his scepter (v. 45) and hurling his throne to the ground (v. 45)—support this suggestion

The real issue in Psalm 89, then, is the date and setting of its central section, vv. 20-38, and vv. 4-5, which are usually linked with it. This is especially so for our present concern, since three of the psalm's four references to the covenant with David (vv. 4, 29, 35, 40) occur within these verses. Veijola argues for the common authorship of these verses and vv. 39-46. He makes this case partly on metrical grounds: the poetic lines in vv. 6-19 are longer.[39] But more important, vv. 20-38

because of the occurrence of similar expressions in late prophetic texts for the end of national existence (Isa. 14.5, 9; 47.1; Jer. 48.17; Ezek. 19.11-14). In addition, these verses are full of language and images that are common in literature from the exile or later. For example, the reference to God renouncing the covenant with David in v. 40 uses the verb נאר (Piel), which occurs elsewhere only in Lam. 2.7, where it also parallels זנח. The motif of the passers-by in v. 42 is common in Deuteronomistic literature, especially in Jeremiah, where it usually refers to Jerusalem. The passers-by view the ruins and ask why the destruction has occurred, so that the city has become a reproach (חרפה) or an object lesson (משל) or the like (cf. Deut. 28.37; 29.23-27; 1 Kgs 9.7-8; 2 Kgs 22.19; Jer. 15.4; 19.8; 22.8-9; 24.9; 25.9; 34.17; Ezek. 5.14-15). The motif is used this way in Lamentations (2.15; cf. 1.12) as well. The exiles or refugees in foreign lands can also become a reproach, curse or object lesson (Jer. 29.18; 42.18; 44.8, 12). The dialogue about the cause for destruction occurs in other settings (Jer. 5.19; 9.11-15; 16.10-13), but it always revolves around the destruction of Jerusalem and the exile of Judah. In Ps. 89.42 it is the Davidic king who has become the reproach, and the passers-by are also plunderers. But the exilic setting is the same.

39. Following the approach of Loretz (cf. Veijola, *Verheissung*, p. 22 n. 2), Veijola counts consonants of individual stichoi. In vv. 6-16, the number of consonants per stichos runs from 13 to 19 with the average being 16.4. For vv. 17-19, the figures are 12–16 with an average of 14.2, and so Veijola regards these verses as secondary. For vv. 20-38, the number of consonants per stichos are between 11 and 16 with an average of 13. (I reckon v. 20aα as two separate stichoi of 12 and 13 consonants, respectively, rather than as a single stichos of 23 consonants as Veijola does; his division results in a slightly higher average of 13.3 consonants per stichos. These figures also exclude the סלה in vv. 38, 46.) For vv. 39-46, the numbers are 10–15 with an average again of 13. Variations in orthography, such as the inconsistent use of *matres lectiones*, raise questions about the usefulness of counting consonants as an analytical tool. A more reliable approach may be counting syllables. This technique also only indicates approximate comparative length of stichoi, because different sections of the psalm may have been written at different times, and conventions of vocalization and syllabification changed. I use the text supplied by Veijola, which is the MT except for a few emendations where there are textual problems. I attempt no reconstruction and follow the Masoretic vocalization and syllabification except where we know it to have been a post-biblical development (e.g. segholate forms and furtive vowels;

contain language and imagery that are just as late as those of vv. 39-46. A few examples from Veijola's comprehensive treatment must suffice.

First, these verses are quite similar in language to the passages about the Davidic covenant that we have just covered, especially Isa. 55.3 and Jer. 33.19-26. Indeed, we may now fairly say that the reference to a ברית with David occurs elsewhere only in late texts. Isaiah 55.3, has obvious commonalities with verses scattered throughout Psalm 89, exclusive of vv. 6-19 (vv. 2, 3, 4, 25, 29, 34, 35, 37, 38, 40, 50). In addition to the notion of Yahweh making (כרת) a covenant with David that is enduring (עולם), the two passages share the references to that covenant as an expression of Yahweh's חסד and faithfulness (forms of אמן). Jeremiah 33.19-26 also has vocabulary in common with Psalm 89, including the reference to David as 'my servant' (vv. 21, 22, 26).[40] But more important is the imagery that it shares with the psalm. Although Jeremiah 33 does not use the word עולם, it clearly agrees with Ps. 89.20-38 that the Davidic covenant is eternal and unbreakable. Both texts illustrate the point by comparison with natural phenomena: day and night, and heaven and earth in Jer. 33.20, 25; the heavens, and the sun and moon in Ps. 89.30, 37, 38.

There are also other linguistic features that suggest the lateness of this portion of Psalm 89. The word בחיר in 89.4 is always used to designate Yahweh's elect or chosen. Outside of 2 Sam. 21.6, where it is a textual error, the term occurs only in texts that are recognized as late; it is especially common in 2 and 3 Isaiah (Isa. 42.1; 43.20; 45.4; 65.9, 15, 22; Pss. 105.6, 43; 106.5, 23; 1 Chron. 16.13).[41] In these texts, it occurs frequently, as in Ps. 89.4 (cf. vv. 20-21), in parallel with עבד,

---

see A. Sáenz-Badillos, *A History of the Hebrew Language* [Cambridge: Cambridge University Press, 1993], pp. 69-70). A *shewa mobile* is counted as a full syllable. The results overall correspond to Veijola's consonantal count. In vv. 6-16, the range of syllables per stichos is 8–13 with an average of 10.3. For vv. 17-19, the range is 8–11 and the average 9.2. For vv. 20-38, the figures are 6–10 and 7.8 as an average, and for vv. 39-46, they are, strikingly, also 6–10 and 7.8.

40. Other common vocabulary are בחר, זרע, כסא and מאס. See Veijola, *Verheissung*, pp. 58, 82.

41. All of these texts are transparently late with the possible exception of Ps. 105, which is widely—though not universally—dated to the exile or later. Reasons for the late date include this psalm's acquaintance with the Pentateuchal story in its final form, the apparent connection with Ps. 106, whose scope clearly includes the exile, and the use of late vocabulary such as בחיר and late ideology such as the reference to the people of Israel as 'my anointed ones' (משיחי).

which is also a significant item. As Cross observes in his list of Deuteronomistic terminology in 2 Samuel 7,[42] the expression 'my servant David' is typically Deuteronomistic. It also occurs repeatedly, as we have seen, in Jeremiah 33 (vv. 21, 22, 26). The verb חלל (Piel) 'to profane', occurs three times in Psalm 89 (vv. 32, 34, 40), twice with God as its subject, which occurs elsewhere only in Isa. 23.9; 43.28; 47.6; Ezek. 24.21; 28.16; Lam. 2.2, almost all late texts, referring to the end of the kingdom of Judah and its institutions.[43]

Not surprisingly, Ps. 89.20-38 has strong affinities with 2 Samuel 7. These include: the reference to David as 'my servant' (Ps. 89.21; 2 Sam. 7.5), the statement that the evildoer(s) will not afflict or humble the Davidic king (Ps. 89.23; 2 Sam. 7.10), the statement that Yahweh's חסד will be with David or his son (Ps. 89.25, 29, 34; 2 Sam. 7.15), the reference to Yahweh as the Davidic king's father (Ps. 89.27; 2 Sam. 7.14), the promise to establish David's 'seed' and 'throne' forever (Ps. 89.30, 37; 2 Sam. 7.12-13), and the promise to discipline David's heir(s) as one would a child without removing חסד (Ps. 89.31-34; 2 Sam. 7.14-15). Thus, Ps. 89.20-38 follows the same structure as 2 Samuel 7 in its depiction of Yahweh's promise to David. There are good reasons to believe that the basis for these affinities is the dependence of this part of Psalm 89 on 2 Samuel 7 rather than the reverse, or their mutual reliance on an independent tradition. First, the similarity of this portion of Psalm 89 to the late texts discussed above strongly suggests that the direction of influence is from 2 Samuel 7 to Psalm 89. Second, Ps. 89.4-5, 20-38 is rich with terminology and ideology that is characteristically Deuteronomistic. I have already mentioned עבדי דוד in vv. 4, 21, but there are many more instances.[44] Among the more prominent are the following:

(a) the designation of David as Yahweh's chosen (בחיר in v. 4, בחור in v. 20) and his anointed (v. 21) (the latter evidently alludes to the story in 1 Sam. 16.1-13, which is a later addition to the David story in Samuel,[45] and thus further indicates the late date of Psalm 89);

---

42. Cross, *Canaanite Myth*, p. 253. See also Veijola, *Verheissung*, p. 50.

43. The date of the oracle against Tyre in Isa. 23 is disputed and is variously assigned by commentators to the late Assyrian (seventh century BCE), early Babylonian period (sixth century BCE) or even to the Persian period (fourth century BCE).

44. See Veijola, *Verheissung*, pp. 50-53.

45. The reasons for this judgment are laid out by J. Van Seters, *In Search of*

(b) the promise in v. 23 that the evildoer (בֶן־עוּלָה) would not afflict the Davidic king (לֹא יְעַנֶּנּוּ), which closely resembles 2 Sam. 7.10—וְלֹא־יֹסִיפוּ בְנֵי־עַוְלָה לְעַנּוֹתוֹ;[46]

(c) the use of כִּסֵּא to refer to the Davidic line or kingdom (vv. 5, 30, 37); and

(d) the idioms for faithfulness/apostasy in vv. 31-32: to abandon Yahweh's law (עָזַב תּוֹרָה), walk in his regulations (הָלַךְ בְּמִשְׁפָּטִים) and keep his commandments (שָׁמַר מִצְוֹת).

A third indication of the dependence of Psalm 89 upon 2 Samuel 7 is the developments in both terminology and ideology that it reflects.[47] The relatively rare word for 'vision', חִזָּיוֹן (nine occurrences in the Hebrew Bible), in 2 Sam. 7.17 is replaced in Ps. 89.20, as in 1 Chron. 17.15, with the more common חָזוֹן. The statement 'when he sins (בְּהַעֲוֹתוֹ) I will punishment him (וְהֹכַחְתִּיו) with a human rod and with stripes of mortals' (בְּשֵׁבֶט אֲנָשִׁים וּבְנִגְעֵי בְּנֵי אָדָם) in 2 Sam. 7.14 becomes וּפָקַדְתִּי בְשֵׁבֶט פִּשְׁעָם וּבִנְגָעִים עֲוֹנָם in Ps. 89.33. The change recalls the expression 'visiting the iniquity of the parents upon their children to the third and fourth generations' of Deut. 5.9 and elsewhere. Indeed, this change touches on the greatest ideological development between the two texts. In 2 Samuel 7 the references are all singular and refer specifically to David's son who will succeed him; only the generation immediately after David seems to be in view. The mention of discipline without the removal of divine חֶסֶד or loss of the throne serves to explain the continuation of the Davidic house despite Solomon's apostasy, albeit with the loss of the North. It is a Deuteronomistic theologoumenon and not the preservation of a form of royal grant, as Knoppers has made clear. But in Psalm 89, as elsewhere in the Hebrew Bible, the references are to David's heirs (plural), and the promise or covenant is seen as extending far beyond Solomon. In fact, according to Ps. 89.37 Yahweh's covenant with David, defined in the previous two verses as a unilateral oath, is understood to extend

---

History: Historiography in the Ancient World and the Origins of Biblical History (New Haven: Yale University Press, 1983), pp. 158-64; and Veijola, *Verheissung*, pp. 69-72.

46. Cross (*Canaanite Myth*, pp. 253-54) notes the similarity of these two verses, stating that it suggests 'that both stem from an oral formula of the early temple liturgy'. But this is hardly possible in light of the other Deuteronomistic language and signs of lateness in Ps. 89.20-38.

47. See Veijola, *Verheissung*, pp. 60-69, for more detail and further examples.

indefinitely into the future. Finally, Psalm 89 attests another ideological development in its use of the terms בחיר and בחור for David in vv. 4, 20. The root does not occur in 2 Samuel 7. Yahweh's choice of David is an important theme in the Deuteronomistic History, but it is not explicitly connected with the Davidic promise. However, in later literature, especially 2 Isaiah, the notion of the elect (בחיר) is more prominent, as we have seen. Psalm 89 identifies David as Yahweh's בחיר because of the covenant.

In sum, Psalm 89 in its present form is exilic and interprets 2 Samuel 7. As was the case with the texts treated earlier, it reflects an understanding of the ברית דוד as a unilateral promise. As in Jeremiah 33 in particular, this covenant is unconditional and eternal. The striking difference, of course, is that in Psalm 89, Judah's demise is interpreted, not as an indication of the covenant's conditional nature and the nation's violation of it, but as the result of Yahweh renouncing the covenant and, by implication, breaking his oath.[48]

Promise or Oath

A few passages concerning the Davidic promise do not use the word ברית: Psalm 132 and texts in the Deuteronomistic History, especially 2 Samuel 7.

Psalm 132

Psalm 132 is also quite difficult to date. However, a handful of expressions of Deuteronomistic origin or affiliation suggest a relatively late date for the psalm.[49] These include: 'for the sake of David your servant' (בעבור דוד עבדך) in v. 10,[50] 'the fruit of your body' (פרי [ה][בטן) in v. 11[51] and the reference to David's נר in Jerusalem in v. 17.[52] In

---

48. Even if vv. 20-38 and 39-46 are by different authors, they agree in seeing the covenant with David as unconditional and eternal. According to this under-standing of the Davidic covenant, vv. 20-38 could be read in isolation as finding hope for the future. But if they are by the same author, vv. 20-38 serve to describe the nature of the promise, which vv. 39-46 accuse Yahweh of breaking.

49. See Veijola, *Verheissung*, pp. 73-74; and Mettinger, *King and Messiah*, pp. 256-57.

50. The expression למען דוד עבי ('for the sake of my servant David') occurs repeatedly in Deuteronomistic texts in Kings (1 Kgs 11.12, 13, 32, 34; 15.4; 2 Kgs 8.19; 19.34; 20.6), occurs in Ps. 89 and Jer. 33, and is one of the Deuteronomistic expressions listed by Cross in 2 Sam. 7 (*Canaanite Myth*, p. 253).

51. Six of the ten occurrences of the expression outside of this verse are in

addition, the reference in v. 11 to the promise to David as an oath sworn (נשבע) by Yahweh occurs elsewhere only in Psalm 89 (vv. 4, 36, 50) and 2 Sam. 3.9-10, which is a Deuteronomistic expansion.[53] It stands beside the promise of the land as the other great oath sworn by Yahweh in the theology of the Deuteronomistic History (Deut. 1.8, 35; 19.8; 31.7; 34.4; Josh. 1.6; 5.6; 21.43, 44; Judg. 2.1).[54] The idea in v. 12 that David's descendants must keep Yahweh's covenant and laws (עדות, cf. Deut. 4.45; 6.17, 20) fits with Deuteronomistic ideology on two counts: there is only one covenant—the one on Horeb—and obedience to the law delivered to Moses on that occasion is essential. The use of the verb בחר in v. 13 to designate Jerusalem (Zion) as Yahweh's chosen dwelling place is part of a well-known motif in Deuteronomy (e.g. 12.5, 11, 14, 18, 21), which together with the choice of David forms Yahweh's great act of election in the Deuteronomistic History (1 Kgs 8.16; 11.13, 32, 36). Finally, Psalm 132 apparently agrees with 2 Samuel 6–7 that the ark was situated at Kiriath-jearim = Ja'ar[55] before its transfer to Jerusalem, and that the promise to David immediately followed his transfer of the ark.[56] To be sure, there may be seemingly archaic elements in the psalm,[57] but these must be considered archaisms, since it is possible for a later writer to use older language but not vice versa.

In light of the Deuteronomistic elements in Psalm 132 and the structure it shares with 2 Samuel 6–7, it seems fair to assume that the

Deuteronomy: Gen. 30.2; Deut. 7.13; 28.4, 11, 28, 53; 30.9; Isa. 13.18; Mic. 6.7; Ps. 127.3.

52. Cf. 1 Kgs 11.36; 15.4; 2 Kgs 8.19. Contrast 2 Sam. 21.17, where ניר seems to mean 'lamp' rather than 'fiefdom'. I am perplexed by Cross's statement that in Ps. 132.17 'we are to read *nīr*, 'mandate', parallel to *qéren*, a living use of *nīr*, in contrast to the frozen cliché of the Deuteronomist, parallel to *nīr* in Num. 21.30, as shown by Paul Hanson'. It is precisely the sense of 'mandate, fiefdom' that Hanson and Ben Zvi show נר to have in Deuteronomistic usage (see n. 18).

53. Cf. McCarter, *II Samuel*, pp. 113-14.

54. Veijola, *Verheissung*, p. 73.

55. On Ephrathah as a Calebite clan in the district of Kiriath-jearim, see Cross, *Canaanite Myth*, p. 94 n. 16.

56. Cross (*Canaanite Myth*, pp. 96-97) contends that there are strong differences between Ps. 132 and the Samuel account that indicate their bases in separate traditions. But his argument is entirely founded in his interpretation of משכנות as an archaic reference to a tent shrine. He does not consider the possibilities of archaizing and/or hyperbole on the poet's part.

57. See D.R. Hillers, 'Ritual Procession of the Ark and Ps 132', *CBQ* 30 (1968), pp. 48-55; and Cross, *Canaanite Myth*, p. 97 n. 24.

author of the psalm, as the authors of the previous texts we have discussed, knew and drew on the account of the Davidic promise in
2 Samuel 7. In agreement with 2 Samuel 7 but in contrast to the other
passages treated, Psalm 132 does not use the word ברית. As with those
passages, though, the Davidic promise (or better, 'oath') in Psalm 132
is unilateral, and it is also eternal, though Psalm 132 uses the expression
עדי עד (cf. לעד in Ps. 89.30) instead of לעולם. But unlike Jeremiah
33 and Psalm 89, in particular, Psalm 132 understands the promise to
David, at least in part, as explicitly conditional (v. 12). In this respect it
may be seen as very close to 2 Samuel 7. Both texts use an ambiguous
expression to refer to the succession of David: זרע in 2 Sam. 7.12; בטן
פרי in Ps. 132.11. Both immediately follow the promise with a
provision or condition (2 Sam. 7.14b; Ps. 132.12), but while 2 Sam.
7.13-15 makes clear that only one heir is in view ('when he commits
iniquity I will discipline him…but my *hesed* will not depart from him'),
Ps. 132.12 applies the condition of keeping the covenant to all of
David's ruling heirs. In short, Psalm 132, while still an interpretation of
2 Samuel 7, appears closer to it in thought than the texts that refer to the
Davidic promise as a ברית.

2 Samuel 7 and the Deuteronomistic History

2 Samuel 7 may be the most discussed passage in the Bible, with much
of the controversy swirling around the matter of its composition.[58]
There is a curious tension in most scholarly treatments of the chapter.
On the one hand, there is a conviction that the tradition of the Davidic
promise is ancient—dating back to David himself or at least to
Solomon—and that the chapter's narrative reflects this antiquity in its
unevenness. On the other hand, there is also widespread recognition of
the chapter's Deuteronomistic nature.[59] This tension has been implicitly

58. For bibliography and a survey of the issues, see W. Dietrich and T. Nau-
mann, *Die Samuelbücher* (ErFor, 287; Darmstadt: Wissenschaftliche Buchgesell-
schaft, 1995), pp. 143-56.

59. This tension is present in both the so-called 'Cross' or 'Harvard' and
'Smend' or 'Göttingen' schools. Thus, Cross (*Canaanite Myth*, pp. 252-54)
observes that the chapter 'fairly swarms with expressions found elsewhere in the
works of the Deuteronomistic school', and he finds such expressions in vv. 1, 3, 5,
6, 7, 8, 9, 10, 11, 13, 16, 23, 24, 25, 27 and 29. But he also finds a 'fundamental
dichotomy' between the opposition to the building of a temple in vv. 1-7 (esp.
vv. 5-7) and the pro-temple oracle of vv. 11b-16, which stems ultimately from the
distinct royal ideologies of Israel and Judah (*Canaanite Myth*, p. 241). The

recognized by Schniedewind,[60] whose solution to it is unacceptable. He limits the Deuteronomistic historian's contribution to v. 13a, without even considering the evidence presented by other scholars for extensive Deuteronomistic influence in the chapter,[61] and he argues that the tradition in the chapter, which was ancient, was preserved orally but not recorded in writing until the seventh century BCE. The other obvious solution to this tension is the exact opposite of Schniedewind's proposal, namely that the chapter is a Deuteronomistic composition, and that is the position I have advocated elsewhere.[62] I do not deny that there are tensions within the chapter that may indicate source material, but no underlying narrative or oracle can now be reconstructed, and no such reconstruction can bear the weight of the pre-exilic royal theology that has sometimes been placed upon it. We are dealing in 2 Samuel 7 with an author's (Deuteronomistic historian's) composition rather than an editorial supplementation.

There are two keys to understanding 2 Samuel 7: the reconstruction

---

Deuteronomistic historian's combination of the two reiterated the standard Judean royal ideology, which interpreted the covenant with David as the decree of an eternal dynasty. Similarly, T. Veijola (*Die ewige Dynastie: David und die Entstehung seiner Dynastie nach der deuteronomistischen Darstellung* [AASF B, 193; Helsinki: Suomalainen Tiedeakatemia, 1975], pp. 68-79) calls 2 Sam. 7 'a text heavily edited by the Deuteronomistic historian' ('[ein] stark dtr bearbeitete[r] Text') and 'the object of intensive Deuteronomistic editing' ('das Gegenstand intensiver dtr Überarbeitung'). But as with Cross, Veijola finds older material beneath this chapter—a prophetic veto of the plan to build the temple (vv. 1a, 2-5, 7) and a promise to David for the continuation of his house (vv. 8a, 9-10, 12, 14-15, 17)—that were combined by DtrG (vv. 11b, 13, 16, 18-21, 25-29) and then revised by DtrN (vv. 1b, 6, 11a, 22-24).

60. Schniedewind, *Society and the Promise to David*, esp. pp. 33-39.

61. In addition to the works of Cross and Veijola, see D.J. McCarthy, 'II Samuel 7 and the Structure of the Deuteronomistic History', *JBL* 84 (1965), pp. 131-38, who identified 2 Sam. 7 as a key structural passage in the Deuteronomistic History, and J. Van Seters, *In Search of History*, pp. 274-76, who surveys the pivotal connections between this chapter and the surrounding Deuteronomistic narrative. Cf. also the Deuteronomistic expressions noted by M. Weinfeld (*Deuteronomy and the Deuteronomic School* [Oxford: Clarendon Press, 1972], *passim*), especially for 2 Sam. 7.22b-24.

62. S.L. McKenzie, 'Why didn't David Build the Temple? The History of a Biblical Tradition', in M.P. Graham, R.R. Marrs and S.L. McKenzie (eds.), *Worship and the Hebrew Bible: Essays in Honour of John T. Willis* (JSOTSup, 284; Sheffield: Sheffield Academic Press, 1999), pp. 204-24 (esp. 204-16).

of its primitive text (particularly in v. 1) and its function in the Deuteronomistic History. McCarter's contention that 7.1b is a misplaced gloss
on v. 11 is compelling.[63] The statement in v. 1b that Yahweh has given
David rest from all his enemies is contradicted by both the account of
David's wars in the next chapter and by 1 Kgs 5.17-18 (ET 5.3-4). It is
also a contradiction of the entire scheme of the Deuteronomistic
History, going back to Deut. 12.9-11, that 'the place' of centralized
worship (i.e. the temple) would be established once Yahweh had given
Israel rest.[64]

With the removal of v. 1b the point of the chapter surfaces more
clearly. David proposes building a temple. Yahweh responds by telling
him, in effect, that the time is not right. Hence, Yahweh never requested
a temple from any of the previous leaders of Israel but moved about in
tent and tabernacle (vv. 6-7). Yahweh has now established David's
kingship (vv. 8-9a).[65] After Yahweh has used David to fix Israel's place
among the nations (vv. 9b-10), the temple may be built. However, it is
not David who will build it but his son (note the emphatic pronouns in
vv. 5b, 13). Interwoven with the motif of Yahweh's 'house', of course,
is that of the promise of a 'house' for David. With the new permanence
in the cult will come a new permanence in leadership.[66]

63. McCarter, *II Samuel*, p. 191.

64. The parallel in 1 Chron. 17 lacks v. 1b, either because the Chronicler's
Vorlage lacked it, or more likely, because the Chronicler recognized the problems it
caused and so deleted it. The references to rest in Josh. 21.44; 22.4; 23.1, which
also contradict the overall scheme in the Deuteronomistic History, are part of the
later addition identified by Noth in Josh. 13-22. See McKenzie, 'Why didn't David
Build the Temple?', pp. 211-12.

65. The reference in v. 9aβ to Yahweh cutting off all of David's enemies
'before him' must be taken in context to refer to those, as Saul, who stood in the
way of David's kingship and does not undermine the proposal that v. 1b is
secondary. Verse 9aβ also does not use the language of rest.

66. Cross (*Canaanite Myth*, p. 255) and McCarter (*II Samuel*, p. 226) are
troubled by the use of the verb ישׁב in vv. 1-7, and this is one of the factors leading
them to posit pre-Deuteronomistic source material here. But ישׁב is a key word
binding vv. 1-7 together, and its use here is in line with the Deuteronomic/
Deuteronomistic name theology. (Cf. S.D. McBride, 'The Deuteronomic Name
Theology', [PhD dissertation, Harvard University, 1969]). These verses do not say
that Yahweh dwells (ישׁב) on the earth and in fact use several different
circumlocutions to avoid saying this. In v. 2 it is the ark, not Yahweh, that dwells
(ישׁב) in a tent. In v. 5 ישׁב occurs in a rhetorical question, 'Will you build me a
house to dwell in?', whose answer is obviously 'no' (v. 6). T.N.D. Mettinger (*The*

The chapter serves an etiological function on at least two levels in the Deuteronomistic History.[67] First, it explains the tradition, scandalous by ancient Near Eastern standards, that the temple in Jerusalem was built not by the righteous founder of the dynasty but by his son.[68] The Deuteronomistic historian salvaged David's reputation by showing that his intentions were right and that it was Yahweh or his plan for Israel that prevented David from carrying them out. Later, the Deuteronomistic historian had Solomon commend David for his instincts (1 Kgs 8.18).

Second, the Deuteronomistic historian used this chapter to introduce the promise of a Davidic dynasty, which is a key motif in the Deuteronomistic History. Again, this promise is etiological on more than one level. It explains the succession of David by his son (contrast Saul, 7.15) and Solomon's continuation on the throne despite his apostasy (1 Kgs 11). It is important to note that the only unconditional part of the promise applies specifically to Solomon (7.14) and not to the entire Davidic line. It is this succession that is referred to in 7.16 as the establishment of David's house and kingdom and that is later recognized by Solomon as the fulfillment of the promise to David (1 Kgs 8.20). Outside of Solomon's succession of his father, the Davidic promise in the Deuteronomistic History is never unconditional. When it is reiterated to Solomon, its conditionality is explicit (1 Kgs 9.4-5). Solomon's unfaithfulness is the reason for the separation of the Northern tribes from the house of David (note the use of 'Israel' in 9.5), but it is Yahweh's devotion to David that explains why this takes place after Solomon and why the Davidids retain a domain (1 Kgs 11.12-13, 34-36).

Dethronement of Sabaoth: Studies in the Shem and Kabod Theologies [ConBOT, 18; Lund: CWK Gleerup, 1982], p. 60 n. 84) even characterizes vv. 5-6 as hostile to the idea. Then, v. 13 reveals that it is David's son who will build a house *for Yahweh's name*. Thus, Cross's perception of an older oracle behind vv. 1-7 that favored a temporary tent shrine over a permanent temple, though ingenious, is unnecessary and dubious in light of the thoroughly Deuteronomistic nature of the chapter and in the absence of any pre-Deuteronomistic reference to the Davidic promise.

67. Cf. S. Mowinckel, 'Natansforjettelsen 2 Sam kap 7', *SEÅ* 12 (1947), pp. 220-29. I am grateful to Dr Erik Aurelius of the University of Göttingen for translating this article for me.

68. On this connection especially in Mesopotamia, see T. Ishida, *The Royal Dynasties in Ancient Israel: A Study on the Formation and Development of Royal-Dynastic Ideology* (BZAW, 142; Berlin: W. de Gruyter, 1976), pp. 81-99.

Yahweh's devotion and promise also account for the prolongation of
the kingdom of Judah despite wicked kings (1 Kgs 15.4; 2 Kgs 8.19).[69]
But the Deuteronomistic historian is not clear about the duration he
envisioned for that promise. It is לעולם (2 Sam. 7.29; 1 Kgs 9.5),[70] but
this word is as ambiguous as its English counterpart 'forever'. There is
wide agreement that עולם does not refer to endless time or eternity in a
philosophical sense[71] but rather means 'long duration' or, in regard to
the future, 'most distant time', 'perpetual'.[72] In some cases in the
Deuteronomistic History (Deut. 15.16; 1 Sam. 1.22; 27.12; cf. Exod.
21.6; Lev. 25.46; Job 40.28 [41.4]) it refers 'merely' to an individual's
lifetime. Hence, the conception of the Davidic promise as לעולם is not
necessarily contradicted by the exile.[73] The Davidic dynasty did last for
a long time. Yahweh more than fulfilled his promise. The dynasty lasted
as long as it did because of Yahweh's love for David. But it was always
conditioned on the faithfulness of David's heirs, and eventually
Yahweh's patience gave out. Comparison of the similar promise to the
house of Eli is enlightening: 'Therefore Yahweh God of Israel said: "I
promised that your house and your father's house would walk before

69. The MT of 2 Kgs 8.19 reads: ולא־אבה יהוה להשחית את־יהודה למען דוד
עבדו כאשר אמר־לו לתת לו ניר (ו)לבניו כל־הימים. But LXX[B] does not reflect
לבניו, and its shorter reading must be considered primitive, all the more so since its
text at this point reflects the *kaige* recension. Thus, the verse does not define
כל־הימים as lasting as long as David has heirs, nor does it imply that the promise
applies unconditionally to all of David's line. The Davidic dynasty continues by
Yahweh's grace, not by his obligation to David.
70. Or עד־עולם (2 Sam. 7.16, 25; 2 Kgs 2.45) or כל־הימים (1 Kgs 11.36;
2 Kgs 8.19). There may be subtle differences in meaning between these expressions,
but the conclusions reached here apply to all three.
71. *HALAT*, III (1983), p. 755: 'usually eternal, eternity, but not meant in the
philosophical sense' ('gewöhnlich ewig, Ewigkeit, aber nicht im philosophischen
Sinn gemeint').
72. The classic study of עולם is that of E. Jenni, 'Das Wort *'ōlām* im Alten
Testament', *ZAW* 64 (1952), pp. 197-248; and 65 (1953), pp. 1-35. See also Jenni,
'עולם *'ōlām* eternity', *TLOT*, II, pp. 852-62. Jenni gives 'farthest time' ('fernste
Zeit') as the basic meaning of עולם, and he has been followed in this by more
recent treatments of the word. Cf. J. Barr, *Biblical Words for Time* (SBT, 33;
Naperville, IL: Alec R. Allenson, 1962); H.D. Preuss, 'עולם *'ōlām*', *TDOT*, X,
pp. 530-45; A. Tomasino, 'עולם', *NIDOTE* (1997), III, pp. 345-51.
73. Cf. Tomasino, 'עולם', p. 349: 'The use of *'ōlām*, in these cases does not
mean that the covenants could never be abrogated. Rather, it means that they were
made with no anticipated end point.'

me forever (לעולם)." But now Yahweh says, "Far be it from me, for I will honor those who honor me but those who despise me will be belittled" ' (1 Sam. 2.30). Certainly, the Davidic promise was never intended by the Deuteronomistic historian as a license for the kings of Judah to behave as they wished without reprisal. The Mosaic law remained the standard for judging their behavior. The Davidic promise was always subject to Yahweh, not the other way around.

The Origin of the Davidic Promise and of the
Deuteronomistic History

This study has indicated that the Deuteronomistic History, specifically 2 Samuel 7, is the fountainhead of all texts dealing with the Davidic promise or covenant in the Hebrew Bible. That is, there is no literary evidence independent of 2 Samuel 7 to support the existence of an older tradition in royalist propaganda or elsewhere of a promise or covenant with David, and 2 Samuel 7 is a Deuteronomistic composition. This conclusion receives confirmation from a comparison with prophetic texts. In the well-known oracle of Isaiah 7, which is related to the Syro-Ephraimitic crisis of 734, Isaiah reassures Ahaz that the plan of Pekah and Rezin will not succeed. But there is no mention of any promise to David. Moreover, if Clements is correct, those oracles that relate to Sennacherib's invasion of 701 are uniformly pessimistic about Jerusalem's future; only in later redactional material, perhaps from the time of Josiah, is Yahweh's protection promised for Jerusalem.[74] The other eighth century BCE Judahite prophet, Micah, also prophesied the destruction of Jerusalem without any reference to a Davidic promise. Only in the Deuteronomistic portions of the narrative about Sennacherib in 2 Kings 18–20 (esp. 19.34; 20.6) is it stated that Jerusalem will survive 'for sake of my servant David'.[75] Isaiah's oracles provide a *terminus*

---

74. R.E. Clements, *Isaiah and the Deliverance of Jerusalem: A Study of the Interpretation of Prophecy in the Old Testament* (JSOTSup, 13; Sheffield: JSOT Press, 1980), esp. pp. 28-51, 72-89.

75. Clements's perception of an ancient 'Davidic royal ideology of Jerusalem' as a root of the doctrine of the city's inviolability (*Isaiah and the Deliverance of Jerusalem*, pp. 81-89) fails to recognize the lateness of the motif of the Davidic promise and the Deuteronomistic nature of the statement that Yahweh would save Jerusalem 'for the sake of my servant David' (2 Kgs 19.34). Cf. S.L. McKenzie, *The Trouble with Kings: The Composition of the Book of Kings in the Deuteronomistic History* (VTSup, 42; Leiden: E.J. Brill, 1991), pp. 101-109.

post quem for the development of the Davidic promise. The doctrine of the promise may have developed in the seventh century BCE in tandem with that of the inviolability of Jerusalem, which itself was likely spurred by Jerusalem's survival of successive threats in 734, 721 and 701. Still, in the fallout from Jeremiah's temple sermon (Jer. 26) nothing is mentioned about the Davidic house; it is only the inviolability of the temple and city that appear to have become dogma. To be sure, these are considerations from silence and must be considered somewhat speculative. The evidence permits one to say only that the promise to David (as we have it) originated with the Deuteronomistic historian for etiological reasons, that is to explain the endurance of Judah and the Davidic dynasty beyond the royal houses and nation of Israel. In other words, it appears that ideology did not shape history but was abstracted from it.

Our study also has implications for understanding the composition of the Deuteronomistic History. In particular, it raises doubts about the theory of a pre-exilic (Josianic) edition of the Deuteronomistic History. According to Cross's classic formulation of this theory, one of the sources from which the Josianic editor drew was Judah's royal ideology of an eternal promise to David.[76] While the observation that the Davidic promise is an important theme in the Deuteronomistic History remains valid, the theory of a Josianic Deuteronomistic History is not supported by the reconstruction of a Judean royal theology. Nor is Noth's initial ascription of the Deuteronomistic History to an exilic author gainsaid by its inclusion of the Davidic promise לעולם, which may simply account for the extended duration of the Davidic dynasty. On the other hand, the ambiguity of the term leaves open the possibility that in the Davidic promise there remains a glimmer of hope for the future. This hope is certainly muted in the present ending of the Deuteronomistic History by the lack of any reference to the Davidic promise in the final three chapters of 2 Kings. It was left to the Deuteronomistic historian's interpreters in later books of the Bible to make this hope explicit in a variety of ways.

---

76. Cross, *Canaanite Myth*, pp. 278-85.

ABSALOM'S DAUGHTER:
AN ESSAY IN VESTIGE HISTORIOGRAPHY

Jack M. Sasson

No one ever lies. People often do what they have to do to make their story sound right.

William Ginsburg*

There is a notice about Absalom that is set half way between the two principal segments of his story: his murder of Amnon for the rape of Tamar (2 Sam. 13–14.24) and his attempt to usurp his father's throne (2 Sam. 14.28–18.18).[1] The Hebrew notice, dispensing heretofore undisclosed information about Absalom, translates as follows (2 Sam. 14.25-27).[2]

> Now in all Israel there was no one to be praised as much for being handsome as was Absalom; from the step of his foot to the crown of his head there was no blemish on him. When he cut his head hair—at specific intervals he needed to cut it; as it grew too heavy on him, he would cut it—he would weigh that head hair, about two hundred shekels, the king's weight. Three sons were born to Absalom and just one daughter, her name being Tamar; she was a beautiful woman.

---

* Quoted from the *New York Times*, 'Week in Review', 21 January 2001, p. 1.

1. Aside from consulting the commentaries on 2 Sam. and inspecting entries in dictionaries and encyclopedias *sub* 'David', 'Absalom' and 'Tamar', I have profited from (though I do not always cite) the following essays: V.H. Matthews and D.C. Benjamin, 'Amnon and Tamar', in G.D. Young *et al.* (eds.), *Crossing Boundaries and Linking Horizons: Studies in Honor of Michael C. Astour on his 80th Birthday* (Bethesda, MD: CDL Press, 1997), pp. 339-66; G.P. Ridout, 'The Rape of Tamar', in J.J. Jackson and M. Kessler (eds.), *Rhetorical Criticism: Essays in Honor of James Muilenburg* (PTMS, 1; Pittsburgh: Pickwick Press, 1974), pp. 75-84; J. Van Seters, 'Love and Death in the Court of David', in J.H. Marks and R.M. Good (eds.), *Love and Death in the Ancient Near East: Essays in Honor of Marvin H. Pope* (Guilford, CT: Four Quarters, 1987), pp. 121-24.

2. Unless otherwise noted, translations are mine.

The notice also signals a major change in the portrayal of the prince. The Absalom who meets a distraught Tamar is remarkably prudent (he advises her not to make a fuss), controlled (he shares no ugly words with Amnon), discreet (he keeps his counsel on his plans) and patient (he waits two years before exacting vengeance and three more years at the Geshur court of his grandfather).[3] Whether or not a metamorphosis was triggered by his father's moral blindness cannot be said, but the Absalom who resumes his life after the exile is markedly different in sensibility than heretofore.[4] He is rebellious and openly courts power; he cajoles, soothes, flatters, but also displays the common touch that his father once had but lost after years in palace living.

Yet, while the stories about Absalom themselves only inaugurate the disintegration of David's world that is so major a theme in the succession narratives (beginning with 2 Sam. 9), it is not at all obvious why the narrator has made the notice of 2 Sam. 14.25-27 so pivotal to his tale.[5] To label these verses 'secondary' or 'a later addition', as is done by many commentators, is a judgment that can hardly be useful.[6]

---

3.   We also wonder how Jonadab, perhaps with the sense that conspirators display about their opponents, knew exactly what Absalom had planned to do (see 2 Sam. 13.32-37).

4.   Such a change in posture is implied in the story of Keret in which his son Yassib (Yassub) openly proclaims his right to the throne, accusing his father of neglect of duty; translation by E. Greenstein in S.B. Parker (ed.) *Ugaritic Narrative Poetry* (Writings from the Ancient World, 9; Atlanta: Scholars Press, 1997), pp. 40-42; comments by S.B. Parker, *The Pre-Biblical Tradition: Essays on the Ugaritic Poems Keret and Aqhat* (RSB, 24; Atlanta: Scholars Press, 1989), pp. 197-203. The portrait of Absalom in 2 Sam. 13 has permitted Y. Amit to interpret the Tamar episode as a coherent and independent unit, meant to draw sympathy for the future usurper, 'The Story of Amnon and Tamar: Reservoir of Sympathy for Absalom', *Hasifrut* 32/9 (1983), pp. 80-87.

5.   A major feature of the biographical style of historiography adopted by the Hebrew is to have a hero overcome many obstacles to achieve his goals, only to have them compromised by fratricide and deaths. See my study, 'The Biographic Mode in Hebrew Historiography', in W.B. Barrick and J.R. Spencer (eds.), *In the Shelter of Elyon: Essays on Ancient Palestinian Life and Literature in Honor of G.W. Ahlström* (JSOTSup, 31; Sheffield: Sheffield Academic Press, 1984), pp. 305-12.

6.   There are suggestions, too, that the passage (or parts thereof) was moved from a later placement (most often suggested: just before 15.1); see C. Conroy, *Absalom, Absalom: Narrative and Language in 2 Sam. 13–20* (AnBib, 81; Rome: Biblical Institute Press, 1978), pp. 110-11. Reasons that are offered include the

To my good friend Max Miller I offer a study of these verses, making a proposal that, as solid a historian as he is, he is likely to question; but let it at least amuse him.

Absalom, the King

In the notice of 2 Samuel 14, we are told first that Absalom was an attractive presence. The vocabulary is rather fulsome and allocated to two phrases that together establish how physically exceptional Absalom was. The sequence follows a conventional Hebrew literary style in which the incomparability of individuals ('Now in all Israel there was no one to be praised as much for being handsome as was Absalom') is illogically stated *before* describing their features ('From the step of his foot to the crown of his head there was no blemish on him'...).[7] What is interesting to note here is that comparisons built on the formulation '...there was no one like...', when referring to men, generally is applied to kings and leaders.[8] In the case of Absalom, it is his beauty that is so beyond equal that an unusual phrase is applied to it, *lᵉhallēl mᵉ'ōd*. Aside from its uniqueness as a superlative construction that joins an adverb to an infinitive, it may be worth noting that *lᵉhallēl*, while commonplace with God as its object, is connected with kings (2 Chron. 23.12-13, acclamation of Joash).[9]

The narrator has waited until this juncture to praise Absalom for his beauty.[10] We should distinguish among praise to individuals for being

attribution of children to Absalom (despite 2 Sam. 18.18) and the reference to the 'king's weight', deemed by scholars to reflect the Persian period.

7. An excellent example is in 1 Sam. 9.2 (said about Saul), 'There was no one finer among the men of Israel; from his shoulders and up he was taller than any of the people.'

8. Said about Joseph's incomparable wisdom (Gen. 41.39), Moses' intimacy with God (Deut. 34.10), Saul's attractiveness (1 Sam. 9.2), Solomon's wisdom and wealth (1 Kgs 3.12,13; see 1 Chron. 29.2; 2 Chron. 1.12; Neh. 13.26), Ahab's wickedness (1 Kgs 21.25), and the faithfulness of Hezekiah (2 Kgs 18.5) and Josiah (2 Kgs 23.25). Somewhat similar is the statement about Daniel and his colleagues (Dan. 1.19-20). The phrasing can also be applied to inanimate objects (plagues, Exod. 9.18, 24, 26; 10.14) and to weapons (1 Sam. 21.10).

9. The formulation is also seldom attached to women: Sarai in Gen. 12.15, the king's favorite (Song 6.9), and a noble woman (Prov. 31.29, 31). Ironic uses are Prov. 27.2; Pss. 10.3 (modesty); 28.4 (evildoer); and Ezek. 26.17 (Tyre).

10. 'Only at the end of this affair does the narrator release the information about

handsome (using variations of the root **yph*), to the attractive features they are specifically said to display, and to their physique (referring to their attractive figure [*tō'ar*] or looks [*mar'eh* / *rō'î*]). To convey a generally handsome look, Hebrew creates a combination of the above vocabulary. Thus, Joseph is said to very very alluring (*yᵉpēh[-]tō'ar*, Gen. 39.6), and from the Philistine's perspective, David was good-looking (*yᵉpēh mar'eh*, 1 Sam. 17.42). David was also said (1 Sam. 16.12) to have had 'beautiful eyes' (*yᵉpēh 'ênayim*) and to be 'good-looking' (*ṭôb rō'î*). Adonijah was very nicely proportioned (*ṭôb-to'ar mᵉ'ōd*, 1 Kgs 1.6), but Saul was simply a fine adolescent (*bāḥûr wāṭôb*, 1 Sam. 9.2),[11] taller than most of his compatriots.[12] In the case of Absalom, however, we are told not just that he was very handsome, but that he had no bodily defect. Yet, we must also observe that the expression *mikkaf regel wᵉ'ad qodqōd* ('from the step of the foot to the crown of the head'; in one case, Isa. 1.16, simply *rō'š*, 'head') occurs exclusively in negative contexts, associated with punishment (Deut. 28.35; Job 2.7).[13] So a savvy listener to Scripture would have

Absalom's looks, with a perfect timing that the reader grimly smiles at in later recollection: just before the prince crosses the line separating the man of honor from the malcontent and rebel.' M. Sternberg, *The Poetics of Biblical Narrative: Ideological Literature and the Drama of Reading* (ILB; Bloomington: Indiana University Press, 1985), p. 358. See also his section, 'Good Looks in Samuel', pp. 354-64.

11. *Bāḥûr* is only the male equivalent of *bᵉtûlâ*, an adolescent; see Deut. 32.2 and Isa. 62.5. See Jer. 51.22; Ezek. 9.6; 2 Chron. 36.17; and especially Eccl. 11.9, with regard to the time of life of a *bāḥûr*. Still the accent here is not on his youth (as it was in the case of David) but on his readiness for the task that was to be his.

12. See also 1 Sam. 10.23. Hence God's admonition to Samuel to 'pay no attention to shape or height, for I have rejected him' (1 Sam. 16.7).

13. In fact all but two of a dozen references to the (largely) poetic term *qodqōd*, 'crown of the head', are similarly associated with negative consequences. We might notice how the expression goes from bottom (feet) to top (crown of head/head) in Deut. 28.5; 2 Sam. 14.25; Job 2.7; and (with *rō'š*) in Isa. 1.6. (Exceptional is Lev. 3.13, with head [*rō'š*] occurring before feet.) Such retrograde sequence is familiar from the Song of Songs (7.2-10), on which see my comments in 'A Major Contribution to Song of Songs Scholarship', *JAOS* 107 (1987), pp. 733-39. The sequence seems normal to King Zimri-Lim of Mari when he writes his wife, 'I am now sending you (potential) female weavers, among which there are priestesses. Sort out the priestesses and assign them to weaving establishments. Choose from among the weavers thirty—or as many as are worth selecting—handsome ones, who have no blemishes from toes to head hair, and assign these to Warad-ilishu.

recognized it as potentially a portent of trouble ahead for Absalom, kingly or otherwise.

We are told next about Absalom's luxuriant hair. It is often thought, at least since Josephus's day, that the narrator's focus on this aspect of the prince's anatomy foreshadows his ignominious manner of death.[14] However, as described in 2 Sam. 18.9, Absalom's head (not hair) got caught in the branches of an oak, and he was left suspended in mid-air, when the mule he was riding (as befits his royal status) continued on its way. Far-fetched is the view that the reference to hair was foreshadowed in David's reassurance to the woman of Tekoah that no harm would come to her son's hair, unintentionally applied to Absalom (2 Sam. 14.11).[15] So why hair is mentioned is not readily apparent. Conroy is not unique in thinking of hair as a symbol of pride.[16] But even in an age when bushy or curled hair was favored (Judg. 16.13, 19; Song 5.11),

Have Warad-ilishu teach them Subarean chant; but their quarters are not to be changed. Be careful with their ration so that their looks will not change...' (ARM 10.126 = J.-M. Durand, *Documents épistolaires du palais de Mari*, 3 [Littératures anciennes du Proche-Orient, 18; Paris: les Editions du Cerf], pp. 349-50 [No. 1166]). Retrograde listings are also known for genealogies. This is the case of Saul's line in 1 Sam. 9.1-2, for which see further J.M. Sasson, 'Generation, Seventh', *IDBSup* (1976), p. 355; cf. the retrograde sequence in the Assyrian King List; see R.R. Wilson, *Genealogy and History in the Biblical World* (YNER, 7; New Haven: Yale University Press, 1977), pp. 86-100. The pattern may be following a bottom-to-top sequence in the scanning of artistic depictions with multiple bands. For Mesopotamia, see I. Winter, 'After the Battle Is Over: The Stele of the Vultures and the Beginning of Historical Narrative in the Art of the Ancient Near East', in H.L. Kessler and M.S. Simpson (eds.), *Pictorial Narrative in Antiquity and the Middle Ages* (Studies in the History of Art, 16; Washington, DC: National Gallery of Art, 1985), pp. 11-32, especially from p. 19; H. Pittman, 'Unwinding the White Obelisk', in H. Waetzoldt and H. Hauptmann (eds.), *Assyrien im Wandel der Zeiten XXXIXe Rencontre assyriologique internationale, Heidelberg 6.–10. Juli 1992* (HSAO, 6; Heidelberg: University Press, 1997), pp. 347-54 (ref. courtesy B. Porter). For Egypt, see J. Baines, 'Temple Symbolism', *Royal Anthropological Institute News* 15 (1976), pp. 10-15.

14. *Ant.* 7.10.2, '... he entangled his hair greatly in the large boughs of a knotty tree that spread a great way, and there he hung, after a surprising manner...' I quote Josephus from the translation of W. Whiston, *Josephus: Complete Works* (Grand Rapids: Kregel, 1960).

15. See most recently, H.S. Pyper, *David as Reader: 2 Samuel 12.1-15 and the Poetics of Fatherhood* (BibInt, 23; Leiden: E.J. Brill, 1996), pp. 129-30.

16. Conroy, *Absalom, Absalom*, p. 44 n. 4. If there is pride, it was in weighing the hair, not having it.

what is told about Absalom's hair seems more about burden than pride: once each year, Absalom would produce hair that weighs 2.5 kilos (200 shekels at 11.5 each), equalling the wool production of a healthy ram.[17] One clue to the notice's significance may well be the reference to the 'king's stone [= standard]' by which Absalom's hair was weighed. While the phrase seems unexceptional (it is matched in Mesopotamian measures, from the Old Babylonian period on), it remains unique in Scripture, and it may not at all be surprising, if it were coined specifically to connect with Absalom's royal status.

Inspection of the two verses so far discussed have revealed that the physical attributes assigned Absalom are to be read as clues not so much of Absalom's vanity or ostentation, but of his presentation as a royal figure. In this respect, they serve the same role as the passages about Saul (1 Sam. 9.2-3) and David (1 Sam. 16.12-13) that foreshadow their rise to kingship. Even before his open rebellion, the verses imply that there were clues to his accession to power, aside from the pomp accompanying his moves (15.1) and his readiness to dispense justice (15.2–6). In fact, eventually Absalom's usurpation of the throne was so complete that after the failure of the rebellion his father had to campaign once more for it (2 Sam. 19–20).

The Children of Absalom

In 2 Sam. 14.27, the narrator dispenses information that ostensibly differs in goal from what immediately precedes. The focus shifts to Absalom's children. We are told that there were born to him three sons (none named) and a daughter, '...her name being Tamar; she was a beautiful woman'.[18] The reference to sons has meaning only as an issue

17. Josephus (*Ant.* 7.8.5), found a way to exaggerate on the exaggeration, '...and indeed such was the thickness of the hair of [Absalom's] head, that it was with difficulty that he was polled every eighth day; and his hair weighed two hundred shekels, which are five pounds'. On the amount of wool produced by a ram, see E. Firmage, 'Zoology', *ABD* (1992), VI, p. 1126.

18. About women, the following vocabulary describes their physical attributes: *yāpâ* ('pretty') is said of Tamar, sister of Absalom (2 Sam. 13.1), and of the Shunamite (1 Kgs 1.3; but *yāpâ 'ad-mᵉ'ōd* ['exceedingly pretty'] in 1 Kgs 1.4), and often of the beloved in the Song of Songs (1.15; 4.1, 7; 6.4, 10). In Prov. 11.22, it is said, 'As a ring of gold on a swine's nose is a beautiful woman who lacks sense.' Vashti and loose women are also said to be pretty (Est. 1.11; Prov. 6.25). *Yᵉpēh-piyyâ* (based on a reduplication of the root; 'very pretty') is said of Egypt (but a

concerning the continuity of Absalom's kingship, thwarted though his rule might have become. And this is confirmed by the other allusion to Absalom's progeny, albeit negative, coming at the conclusion of his story (2 Sam. 18.18) and so bracketing it:

> In his lifetime, Absalom took the pillar that was in the Valley of the King and erected it for himself, for he said, 'I have no son to keep my name alive'. So he dedicated the pillar to himself. It has been called 'Absalom's Memorial' ever since.[19]

Whether or not Absalom had sons has exercised scholars: some propose that he never did, others that he once did but was unable to father more after they died, or still others that they were executed during the rebellion. The suggestion is commonly met that one reference to sons (most often that of 2 Sam. 18.18) or the other (2 Sam. 14.27) is a later addition. But it must be noted that in 2 Sam. 18.18 Absalom is excusing his appropriation of a (previously installed) pillar, not because he did not have sons, but because during his lifetime no sons of his had enough prestige to set up a monument that honored their father. We recall that many commemorative stelae (for example Mesha's) are written in first-person mode by third parties.

Absalom's Daughter

The text insists that Absalom had only one daughter (*bat 'aḥat*), 'her name being Tamar' (*ušᵉmāh tāmār*, 2 Sam. 14.27). The formula *ušᵉmāh X* occurs about ten times in Scripture, introducing women who are either

---

horsefly is after her; Jer. 46.20). *Yᵉpat[-]mar'eh* characterizes a 'beautiful' woman, and it is applied to Sarai (Gen. 12.11, 14) and to Tamar, Absalom's daughter (2 Sam. 14.27). Pharaoh dreams of beautiful cows (Gen. 41.4). *Ṭōbat mar'eh* ('good-looking') were Rebekah (Gen. 26.7), Vashti (Est. 1.11), and a number of women against whom Esther competed (Est. 2.3). *Yᵉpat-ṭō'ar* ('shapely') is how a desirable captured slave is labeled (Deut. 21.11). *Yᵉpat-ṭō'ar wîpat mar'eh* ('shapely and beautiful') is said of Rachel (Gen. 29.17), while Esther is said to have been *yᵉpat-ṭō'ar wᵉṭôbat mar'eh* ('shapely and good-looking', Est. 2.7). Abigail, wife of David, while not beautiful, was *ṭôbat-śekel wîpat tō'ar* ('intelligent and shapely', 1 Sam. 25.3).

19. In other attestations, *maṣṣᵉbet/maṣṣᵉbat* is in construct: stone pillar (Gen. 35.14), pillar of Rachel's tomb (Gen. 35.20), pillar of Baal (2 Kgs 3.2; 10.27). The implication is that Absalom appropriated a pillar that was in the Valley of the King, naming it after himself.

featured in subsequent narrative or assigned a number of children.[20] In our case, however, except to be praised for her beauty, Tamar has no story attached to her. This is in contrast to 2 Sam. 13.1, which has a nearly duplicate vocabulary ('To Absalom, son of David, was a pretty sister, her name being Tamar'), but which proceeds with the story of her rape.[21] The anomaly was noted long ago, and there were efforts to give Tamar, daughter of Absalom, a future. Thus, while the majority of Greek versions agree with the MT in vv. 25 and 26 (with diverse spellings of the name Absalom [Abessalōm, Abesalōm]), for v. 27b, Vaticanus reads, '...and one daughter, and her name was Thēmar; she was a very beautiful woman, and she became the wife of Rehoboam, son of Solomon, and she bears to him Abiathar'. For the same section the 'proto-Lucianic' (Cross) or 'Antiochian' (Barthélemy) Greek reads, '...and one daughter, and her name was Maacha. And she was a very beautiful woman, and she became the wife or Rehoboam, son of Solomon, and she bears to him Abia'.[22] This last reading of her name as Maacah is itself likely inspired by 1 Kgs 15.2 and 10 in which an Abishalom (Absalom in 2 Chron. 11.20-21) was the father of Maacah,

---

20. Here is a rundown of the attestations: Gen. 16.1 (Hagar, surrogate for Sarai/Sarah, narrative follows); Gen. 22.24 (Reumah, concubine of Nahor; sons listed); Gen. 25.1 (Keturah, Abraham's wife; sons listed); Gen. 38.6 (Tamar, Judah's daughter-in-law; narrative follows); Josh. 2.1 (Rahab; narrative follows); Judg. 16.4 (Delilah; narrative follows); 2 Sam. 3.7 (Rispah, Saul's concubine; narrative fragments in later chapters); 2 Sam. 13.1 (Tamar, Amnon's sister; narrative follows); 2 Sam. 14.27 (Tamar, Absalom's daughter; no narrative); 1 Chron. 2.26 (Atarah, Jerahmeel's concubine; sons listed). Different formulation occurs for Naamah, Tubal-cain's sister (*'aḥôt tûbal-qayin*) in Gen. 4.22, also with no narrative or listing of sons.

21. The commentaries commonly explain that Absalom named his daughter after his raped sister. Given that 2 Sam. 14.27 is chronologically set within five years of the rape, it would have been premature to describe any daughter of his as a beautiful 'woman', because the term applied to her (*'iššâ*) is not normally used when describing young children or adolescents (as was, for example, *na'arâ* or *'almâ*).

22. For these versions see S. Pisano, *Additions or Omissions in the Books of Samuel: The Significant Pluses and Minuses in the Massoretic, LXX and Qumran Texts* (OBO, 57; Freiburg: Universitätsverlag, 1984), pp. 55-57. Qumran fragments read this passage essentially the same as in MT, see E.C. Ulrich, '4Qsamᶜ: A Fragmentary Manuscript of 2 Sam. 14–15 from the Scribe of the *Serek hayyaḥad* (IQS)', in E. Tov (ed.), *The Hebrew and Greek Texts of Samuel* (Jerusalem: Academon, 1980), pp. 170, 176.

the wife of King Rehoboam and mother of his successor Abija(m). The reference itself has allowed some scholars to suggest that Absalom had two daughters, one named after his sister, the other after his mother. Other scholars have proposed that Maacah was Tamar's daughter.

What is obvious from the above is that the 'tradition' about the name and identity of the daughter of Absalom leaked badly, and I would resist hunting for an 'original' (presumably a truer) version.[23] Luckily, in this essay we are not reconstructing historical truths but are fleshing out literary traditions, in which minor characters are brought in to fulfill other than annalistic purposes. The seemingly gratuitous and undeveloped reference to Tamar in 2 Sam. 14.27 has all the earmarks of being vestigial, that is a remnant from a fuller exposition, much like the mention of Naamah, sister of Tubal-Qayin in Gen. 4.17-22. But unlike Naamah who is mentioned in a starkly unpromising context (midrashic lore has her as Noah's wife), interesting speculation can be proposed for Tamar.[24]

The Rape of Tamar

Biblical tradition in 2 Samuel and Chronicles gives names for 19 sons that David's many wives bore him. Although notices say that his concubines also bore him sons and daughters (2 Sam. 5.13; 1 Chron. 14.3), the birth of no daughter is specifically mentioned. That Absalom was a uterine brother of Tamar is inferred only from 2 Samuel 13, where the narrator invokes 'brother' and 'sister' almost 20 times, occasionally also very gratuitously, especially when the terms follow a proper name.[25] Thus, when Jonadab inquires into Amnon's distress, he is told,

23. Pisano's conclusion (*Additions or Omissions*, p. 56) is typically rational, but also with room for doubt: 'Thamar is thus proto-MT, for if Maacha had been in the text originally [*sic*], it is not likely that it would have been modified to Thamar in the face of so many texts which give the contrary.' See also the brief overview by G.H. Oller, 'Tamar', *ABD* (1992), VI, p. 315.

24. Vestigial information must not be confused with obtrusive information, such as the unexpected introduction of a character (e.g. the man who tells Joseph where to find his brothers, Gen. 37.15-17), for vestigial characters are not played as *dei ex machina*.

25. This point is nicely worked out in Ridout, 'The Rape of Tamar', pp. 75-78. See also J.P. Fokkelman, *Narrative Art and Poetry in the Books of Samuel: A Full Interpretation Based on Stylistic and Structural Analyses*. I. *King David (II Sam. 9–20 and I Kings 1–2)* (Assen, NL: Van Gorcum, 1981), pp. 99-114.

'I am in love with Tamar, the *sister* of my *brother* Absalom' (13.4). In this context, we notice that the spelling of Absalom's name here is defective (written without the *waw*). This is conspicuous, for the name Absalom is written *plene* over 70 times but only a score of times is it spelled defectively (without a *waw*), all but one occurring after 2 Sam. 15.37.[26] This forlorn example seems to stick out and may betray a later insertion.

Obtrusive too is how Amnon calls his future victim *'aḥōti*, and Tamar calls her potential tormentor, *'āḥî* normally terms of endearment in erotic literature, but here obviously alerting us to incest as potential. Finally, embedding four references to 'brother' and 'sister' in Absalom's advice to Tamar (13.20) is much too conspicuous a deployment of crucial vocabulary, 'Her brother Absalom said to her, "Has Aminon [*sic*] your brother been with you? Yet now, my sister, keep quiet. He is your brother. Don't be consumed with this matter". So Tamar, forsaken, lived in the house of Absalom, her brother.'[27] While a sensitive reader of texts might justify the 20 references to 'brother' and 'sister' in this episode, the cumulative effect of this surfeit succeeds in exhibiting a royal family about to become dysfunctional. Yet, the story of Amnon's assault on his [half-]sister continues to mystify readers, addressing questions that are answered, in articles and commentaries, but with mixed success:

— What could Jonadab, a courtier in his uncle's (David) circles hope to gain by advising Amnon to seduce his sister (vv. 4-5)?
— What was the nature of the activities that Tamar was asked to perform (v. 7)? [28]

---

26. Incidentally, defective spellings of *šālōm* are but a handful (e.g. at Gen. 37.4; 1 Sam. 16.4; 1 Kgs 2.5, 6; 5.26; Jer. 15.5; Ezek. 13.16 [2×]). Almost 200 examples of plene *šālōm* are known.

27. Tamar is described as *šōmemâ*, the root of which has to do with devastation or the like (often applied to land). Isa. 54.1 offers hopes that a *šōmemâ* will produce more sons than a married woman, so referring to a woman who will never acquire husbands and family. As a result of Amnon's double abuse (rape and abandonment; contrast with Shechem who rapes but wants to wed Dinah [Gen. 34]), Tamar must live her life beyond the palace, in utter humiliation.

28. The *lᵉbibôt* Tamar shaped for Amnon may or not be 'heart-shaped' (Hebrew *lēb*, *lᵉbāb*), but people listening to the story will no doubt make the connection. They may also realize that the verb Amnon used for baking (*lᵉlabbēb*) evokes a homonym that belongs to the language of love (Song 4.9). At any rate, the acts of kneading, shaping and baking of food by an attractive woman can be highly erotic.

— Did David expect Tamar to enter Amnon's bedchamber (v. 7)?[29]

— Was rape or incest the $n^e b\bar{a}l\hat{a}$ against which Tamar warned Amnon (v. 12)?[30]

— How could Tamar suggest (and expect Amnon to believe) that their father would allow the union of siblings (v. 12)?[31]

— After the rape, why would Tamar beg her brother not to send her away (v. 16)?

—Why did Tamar move to Absalom's home after her rape (v. 20)?

— Why did David allow this outrage to go unpunished (v. 21)?[32]

— Why did Absalom wait two years to take his revenge (vv. 23-29)?

The Rape of Absalom's Daughter

The outrage itself is not precisely fixed within David's 40-year rule, occurring after his move to Jerusalem and after his marriage to Bathsheba. Given that Solomon was but a teenager when he succeeded David (see 1 Kgs 3.7; 1 Chron. 22.5; 29.1), we must imagine that everything about Absalom and about his revolt occurred toward the end of David's reign.[33] Since the rape occurred a maximum of seven to

A.J. Bledstein makes the interesting suggestion that Tamar was being asked to perform a healing ceremony that includes the baking of food magically sympathetic: 'Was Habbirya a Healing Ritual Performed by a Woman in King David's House?', *BibRes* 37 (1992), pp. 15-31. Conroy (*Absalom Absalom!*, pp. 29-30 n. 43), cites somewhat similar notions.

29. Normally unmarried princesses remain in the palace (see 13.7) and do not venture unaccompanied beyond it.

30. For $n^e b\bar{a}l\hat{a}$ as a sexual outrage, see also Judg. 19.23, 24; 20.10.

31. Despite all the learned speculation in the commentaries, nothing in Hebrew or Canaanite culture would allow marriage between brothers and sisters. Hebrew law (whatever their age) is firmly opposed to it (Lev. 18.9 [from same mother], 11 [from different mothers]; 20.17; and Deut. 27.22). In antiquity, such marriages were found only in a few royal houses (Egypt, Elam, some Anatolian tribes), and they would have shocked the mores of people in Canaan and Israel.

32. B. Halpern argues that David thought that Yahweh inspired Amnon's rape of Tamar, and consequently, he could not punish the prince. *David's Secret Demons: Messiah, Murderer, Traitor, King* (Grand Rapids: Eerdmans, 2001). I find the explanation too accommodating.

33. It is possible that the MT of 2 Sam. 15.7 ('After forty years had gone by,

eight years before the revolt, Amnon and Absalom, who were born in
Hebron, would have been adults, and likely to have had children of
their own.[34] We presume that their sister Tamar would have been
slightly younger in age than both of her brothers. While we know from
other tales that biblical women kept their charm deep into old age
(Sarai/Sarah for example), it is difficult to imagine Amnon's violent
passion for a spinster he has known most of his life. To the contrary, the
story reads as if Amnon was struck by the freshness, youth and
inviolability of Princess Tamar. It is tempting to imagine, therefore, that
the object of Amnon's lust was not a sister of Absalom, but the
daughter mentioned in 2 Sam. 14.27.

As far as I know, this suggestion has been made just once previously.
In commenting on 2 Sam. 14.27, P.R. Ackroyd says about Tamar,
'...she could have been named after his sister (ch. 13), though it is
possible that this isolated note contains a hint of an alternative tradition
that it was his daughter rather than his sister whom Amnon raped'.[35]
The suggestion is hesitant, fleeting and unsubstantiated; so far it has
elicited little response.[36] It might be worth developing this notion. I find
it economical to do so by rehearsing the activities of those involved in

Absalom told the king, "I wish to go to Hebron and fulfill the vow I made to the
Lord"') fixes the revolt in David's last year; but other witnesses (Greek, Josephus)
read 'four years', presumably after Absalom was brought back to Jerusalem. R.
Althann reads 'forty days', a more conventional number. 'The Meaning of
ארבעים שנה in 2 Sam. 15.7', *Bib* 73 (1992), pp. 248-52. Absalom waited two years
after the rape before murdering his brother (2 Sam. 13.25). He lived three years in
exile (2 Sam. 13.38) and was two years (2 Sam. 14.28; four years, if one accepts the
Greek for 2 Sam. 15.7) brewing a revolt while away from his father's presence. The
interval shrinks appreciably if fractions of years are involved. See also R.E. Merrill,
'The "Accession Year" and Davidic Chronology', *JANESCU* 19 (1989), pp. 101-
12.

34. This inference is supported by the narrator's willingness to assign Absalom
three sons and a daughter just as he ended his exile, so within five years of the rape
(2 Sam. 14.27).

35. *The Second Book of Samuel* (CBC; Cambridge: Cambridge University
Press, 1977), p. 135. I made the same proposal in 1987, unaware of Ackroyd's
proposal. See my 'Who Cut Samson's Hair? (And Other Trifling Issues Raised by
Judges 16)', *Prooftexts* 8 (1988), pp. 333-39 (339 n. 3).

36. A.A. Anderson (*2 Samuel* [WBC, 11; Waco, TX: Word Books, 1989],
p. 190) writes, 'It is unlikely that the mere occurrence of the name "Tamar" points
to a tradition to which Amnon raped Absalom's *daughter* [italics there] rather than
his *sister* (cf. Ackroyd, 135)'.

the sordid tale, with the victim being Absalom's *daughter* rather than his *sister*.

Amnon had a powerful desire for his niece Tamar that needed immediate satisfaction. He was frustrated that the object of his passion lived in the palace, where her movement was likely restricted. A beautiful young woman, Tamar was a valuable asset to her grandfather the king, and she wore the type of clothing that warned others about her status. As the heir apparent, Amnon could have sued for his niece's hand, and she likely would have been his wife. But he was loath to compromise so early in his career his choice of queen. In the protocol of antiquity, the decision normally cemented political connection with nearby powers. Moreover, Amnon could not have been eager to have his own brother, Absalom, as father of the queen, if only because it would have given undue prestige to an ambitious prince, himself next in line to the throne of Israel.

So Amnon obsessed about his niece; he may even have sensed that his was carnal lust that would die once quenched. (Hebrew uses *'āhab* for infatuation, love, passion, even worship [of God].) When Jonadab suggested a ploy by which to bring Tamar into his personal compound, Amnon promptly acted on it. Amnon may not have imagined that his enjoyment of Tamar would turn so quickly into violent hatred; but the psychology is apt, especially in someone who was after momentary gratification and had no intention to be permanently attached to the girl. Before the rape, Amnon was enraged by Tamar's attempt to frustrate his goals and, afterwards, by her pleas for him to keep her. Amnon may have realized that Tamar was not likely to keep the assault quiet; yet—and this is psychologically also very true—he could only think of ridding himself of her. Whether Amnon ever worried about Absalom's reaction cannot be known, but he had such confidence in his father's affection for his firstborn that he decided to take his chances.

Jonadab was a courtier, practicing in the palace his reputation for intelligence and good counsel, for he was an 'exceedingly wise man' (*'îš ḥākām me'ôd*).[37] Jonadab had every hope to continue his privileged position, and so he befriended Amnon, the crown prince, and was solicitous about his welfare ('Prince, why are you in such a sorry state morning after morning? Won't you tell me?' v. 4). What exactly Jonadab was advising Amnon to do is open to debate. Taking their cues

---

37. The term *ḥākām* describes a 'wise' person [including Solomon] as well as skilled artisans. It is not used pejoratively, but whether to read it ironically is up to us.

from what ensued in the story, some translations simply deem him a conspirator in the ensuing rape, and so mistranslate *ḥākām* as 'a crafty man', 'clever', 'subtle' or 'shrewd'. There is even speculation that he was a dupe of Absalom, goading Amnon into a rape that would lead to assassination.[38]

Yet Jonadab never urged Amnon to rape Tamar, daughter of Absalom. He did indeed suggest deception, but to bring the two in contact, recalling that princesses were not likely to circulate freely beyond the women's quarters. It is also probable that he had expressed the same suggestion he offered Amnon directly to the king, for in instructing Tamar on what to do (v. 7), David adopted a partial version of Jonadab's advice (v. 5) rather than Amnon's request (v. 6). From Jonadab's perspective, even if Amnon had forced himself on his niece, it would only have guaranteed Absalom's acceptance of her marriage to her uncle. In ancient Israel, while not endorsed, marriage though violence was tolerated (Exod. 22.16; Deut. 22.28-29).

What must have shocked Jonadab, as it did others, was not so much the rape of Tamar (Jonadab may even have anticipated it, given Amnon's confession of his inflamed libido), but Amnon's refusal to keep her in his own compound once he abused her. Dishonoring Tamar was also dishonoring Absalom her father, so that when Jonadab heard of murders in Baal-Hasor, he knew that Amnon would be the sole victim. And so it seems that no one else but Amnon, not even Jonadab, was responsible for Amnon's humiliation of an entire household.

David was no longer the shrewd person of yore, who accurately read people's intents and charmed them into doing his will. David felt maneuvered into a marriage with Bathsheba, and in the death of their first son he had learned to prize the life of his children above all gifts. He was undoubtedly concerned about Amnon's illness, and when the latter asked that his niece prepare before him the food that would heal him, he readily consented. He might have had some qualms about it all, because when he voiced his version of the request to Tamar, he omitted that she should serve the food to Amnon, as suggested by his son (v. 6) and for that matter, by Jonadab as well (v. 5). We need not guess

---

38. N. Arrarat, 'The Story of Amnon and Tamar', *BethM* 95 (1983), pp. 331-57; A.E. Hill, 'A Jonadab Connection in the Absalom Conspiracy?', *JETS* 30 (1987), pp. 387-90. Because Jonadab was close to David, there has even been speculation that the king was an accomplice to the crime against Tamar, see Conroy, *Absalom Absalom!*, pp. 24-25 n. 18.

whether David feared what eventually came to pass. From his perspective, he was sending Tamar to a sickly person who was surrounded by servants and attendants.

For David, as for Jonadab, the assault was bitter news; not just because Tamar was robbed of her virginity, but because she was cast aside by her tormentor. The David of old could have forced Amnon to marry Absalom's daughter, perhaps even have punished Amnon by exiling him from his presence. But he did neither. 'When King David heard about all these events, he was furious', the Hebrew text says (v. 22), and the Greek version adds 'but he did not rebuke his son Amnon, for he loved him since he was his firstborn'. David must have realized that in denying justice to Tamar, he was also aggrieving Absalom, and he must have suspected that the matter would not end there. When against his better judgment he allowed Amnon to attend Absalom's banquet, he made sure to surround him with brothers, just to be safe. Still, David was so conscious of his own inadequate response to the rape and felt so guilty about the consequent dishonor of Absalom's household, that when he heard about Absalom's vengeance, he—and all but Jonadab among his courtiers—were certain that an angry Absalom was retaliating by usurping power (vv. 30-36). In this, David was eventually correct.

Tamar had every reason to dream of a bright future. Daughter of Absalom and praised for beauty, she lived in her grandfather's palace, wearing the robes of a princess, for David himself apparently had no daughters from primary wives (see above). The king commanded her to go to the compound of her uncle Amnon. She was only to prepare for him healing food. (She may, as suggested above, have had special culinary knowledge.) She prepared and set out the food and was ready to leave. But because she was raised to obey men, even after her uncle dismissed his servants, she readily agreed to feed him in his inner chamber.

When her uncle seized her, Tamar kept her senses throughout the ordeal. Before the rape, she warned that the squalid crime would leave her dishonored and him disgraced. Amnon needed only to ask the king for her hand to enjoy her sexually. After the rape, when he was forcing her out, Tamar struggled to keep her dignity. If she might remain in his compound, as a wife or even as a concubine, the crime would not be beyond repair.

Tamar could have quietly gone back to the palace, stifling all evidence of the outrage against her. But her double humiliation (and possibly other consideration, cf. Deut. 22.13-21) would not permit it. And so, with grief publicly displayed, Tamar made Amnon's crime known to all (v. 19). But she also condemned herself to a secluded life, no longer as a palace princess but as a pariah. In her father's house (v. 20), Tamar became as one of the 'living widows' that survived Absalom's capture of Jerusalem (2 Sam. 20.3).

Absalom had no expectations that he would rule after David. He had three sons and a daughter. As she reached puberty, Tamar was moved to the palace, to enjoy the status of a marriageable princess. Although his permission was not needed when Tamar was ordered to attend to Amnon, Absalom must certainly have known of the commission, for when he witnessed his daughter's anguished behavior, he knew that Amnon was its cause (v. 19). Absalom tried to quiet his daughter, perhaps hoping that the king would right the matter. But David never did, and as Amnon was escaping his responsibility, Absalom could develop murderous hatred toward him.

Conjectures

Once we accept that Amnon raped his niece rather than his sister, the roster of queries raised above will find natural solutions. This version does indeed 'enhance' Amnon's character. A pervert in the old version for raping his sister, in the new version Amnon becomes merely a scoundrel for abandoning the niece he assaulted. David too 'improves' in the new version. From a king who had lost his moral compass by condoning incest, David turns into a milquetoast, incapable of forcing his son Amnon to do right by Tamar. In this rendering, too, Tamar would not be counselling Amnon toward incest, but toward a licit connection between an uncle and his niece. Jonadab, too, would no longer be a partner in a sordid crime, but a counsellor who misjudged the man he sought to influence.

But in this version, it is Absalom who gains most in stature. As a *brother* of a raped woman in the old account, Absalom had cause to be indignant. Yet, beyond wrecking the life of Tamar, Amnon's offense was against their father David, and so any retaliation or punishment was the king's to make. (Let us recall the curse Simeon and Levi received from their father for taking matters in their own hand after the rape of Dinah in Gen. 34.) As the *father* of Tamar, however, Absalom was amply justified in his hatred of Amnon and in his frustration with David. Murdering a brother may be a heinous crime, but psychologically not beyond a father's reaction to the crippling of a beloved daughter's future. Very likely, Absalom was ready to pay for his own crime through permanent exile in Geshur. But once he was permitted to return to Jerusalem, his contempt for the king, his father, only increased, for David compounded the offense of condoning rape by absolving a fratricide. Absalom quickly placed himself on a course to unseat his father. What Absalom could not have known is that his ambition was fueled by a God who was displeased with David's behavior in the Bathsheba affair. Through the prophet Nathan, David had been warned, 'Thus said the Lord, "I am about raise evil against you from your own house. Before your own eyes, I will take your wives and give them to your associate (r^e'*êkā*). He will sleep with your wives under this very sun. You have acted secretively, but I shall make this happen before all Israel and under the sun"' (2 Sam. 12.11-12).

Despite the narrator's stunning control of verisimilitude, we are obviously dealing with tales whose connection with real events are beyond recovery. Moreover, their editing has gone through so many phases that any original goals the narrative may have had become murky at best. Therefore, despite the competing scholarly ascriptions to the Deuteronomists of quasi-mathematical stages in the development of the David narratives, it is nearly impossible to set the diverse Absalom episodes into a chronological sequence or to establish motivations for their presence. Whether or not we owe the presentation of Absalom as a royal figure (2 Sam. 14.25-26) to the same narrator who was responsible for the rape story (2 Sam. 13), we are still burdened with the need to justify the brusqueness with which his daughter Tamar is mentioned in 2 Sam. 14.27. In ancient as well as in contemporary scholarship, the notice about Absalom's daughter has prompted the speculations I mentioned above.

In treating the mention of Absalom's daughter as vestigial of an alternate version of Tamar's rape, I propose that the notice about Absalom's regal posture, as well as about his children (2 Sam. 14.25-27), may in fact have launched the series of Absalom tales.[39] With minimal editing, we may insert these verses at the opening of 2 Samuel 13, to read:

---

39. Many commentators, in fact, move these verses just before 2 Sam. 15.

Now in all Israel there was no one to be praised as much for being handsome as was Absalom; from the step of his foot to the crown of his head there was no blemish on him. When he cut his head hair—at specific intervals he needed to cut it, as it grew too heavy on him, he would cut it—he would weigh that head hair, about two hundred shekels, the king's weight. Three sons were born to Absalom and just one daughter, her name being Tamar; she was an attractive woman. Amnon son of David became infatuated with her...

Most references to 'sister' and 'brother' in the remaining tale need not be removed, for the terms were conventional among people of close kinship and among those courting each other. The gratuitous references to this vocabulary, such as at vv. 4 and 22, however, will need excision, for under this conjecture, they were added by a narrator intent on sharpening Amnon's repulsiveness, heightening David's oblivion to moral justice, and exposing the rotten core within David's family. Ultimately, however, whether we connect the aggrieved Tamar as a sister or as a daughter of Absalom, we will not evade the powerful lesson the Hebrew writer wanted us to learn from this engrossing tale of lust, moral lapses, vengeance, but also of redemption.

Part III

ARCHAEOLOGY AND GEOGRAPHY

NEW EVIDENCE ON EDOM IN THE NEO-BABYLONIAN AND PERSIAN PERIODS[*]

Piotr Bienkowski

This paper is offered to Max Miller in friendship and respect, with thanks for his help and generous hospitality over the years, and with the hope that this paper will bring back pleasant memories of his participation in Crystal Bennett's excavations at Busayra in 1972.

Current Status of Research

The Iron Age kingdom of Edom in southern Jordan flourished in the late eighth and seventh centuries BCE, the period when it is recorded as paying tribute to Assyria. Current evidence shows that the earliest Iron Age settlements date to the ninth century BCE, possibly to be identified as small mining camps in the Faynan copper-mining area (Khirbat en-Nahas and Barqa el-Hetiye; cf. Fig. 1 for location).[1] By the late eighth century BCE, settlement had intensified all over Edom, and the main excavated sites—Busayra, Tawilan, Umm el-Biyara, Tell el-Kheleifeh and Ghrareh—have been dated essentially between the eighth and sixth centuries BCE.[2] However, the date of the end of settled occupation at

[*]   The writer thanks Andrea Berlin and Jane Waldbaum for their identifications of Attic and Hellenistic pottery at Busayra.

1.   V. Fritz, 'Vorbericht über die Grabungen in *Barqa el-Hetiye* im Gebiet von *Fenan, Wadi el-'Araba* (Jordanien) 1990', *ZDPV* 110 (1994), pp. 125-50; *idem*, 'Ergebnisse einer Sondage in *Hirbet en-Nahas, Wadi el-'Araba* (Jordanien)', *ZDPV* 112 (1996), pp. 1-9; P. Bienkowski, 'Iron Age Settlement in Edom: A Revised Framework', in P.M.M. Daviau and M. Weigl (eds.), *The World of the Aramaeans. II. Studies in History and Archaeology in Honour of Paul-E. Dion* (Sheffield: Sheffield Academic Press, 2001), pp. 257-69.

2.   P. Bienkowski, 'The Edomites: The Archaeological Evidence from Transjordan', in D.V. Edelman (ed.), *You Shall Not Abhor an Edomite for He is your Brother: Edom and Seir in History and Tradition* (ABS, 3; Atlanta, GA: Scholars Press, 1995), pp. 41-92 (44-45).

these sites has been problematic: there was firm proof only for a seventh-century BCE date and no real evidence for how much later the settlements and their associated pottery might date. Circumstantial evidence suggested that the pottery might date as late as the Persian period, but there was no definitive proof.

The lack of a firm archaeological anchor for the end of Iron Age settlement in Edom was compounded by a dearth of historical sources following the Assyrian period. After the references to Edom in the inscriptions of the Assyrian king Ashurbanipal (c. 667 BCE),[3] there is no unambiguous reference to the kingdom of Edom. It has thus been unclear when, how and why Edom ceased to exist as an independent state.

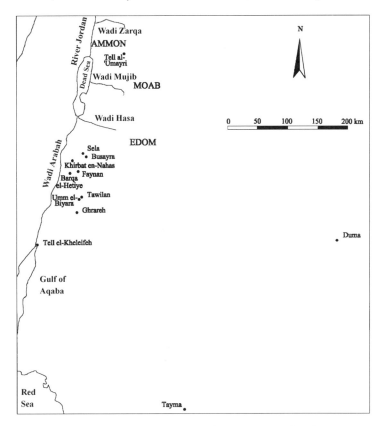

Figure 1. *Map showing location of sites mentioned in the text*

3.   Cf. A.R. Millard, 'Assyrian Involvement in Edom', in P. Bienkowski (ed.), *Early Edom and Moab: The Beginning of the Iron Age in Southern Jordan* (SAM, 7; Sheffield: J.R. Collis, 1992), pp. 35-39.

There have been two main theories regarding the end of the Edomite state and of settlement in the area. Bennett argued that the Edomite 'capital' of Busayra was destroyed and abandoned in the sixth century BCE, and her final published view[4] attributed this to the Neo-Babylonian armies (despite her previous attempts[5] to identify Persian-period pottery at Busayra). Lindsay and Bartlett both suggested that the Neo-Babylonian king Nabonidus (555–539 BCE) brought about the end of the independent kingdom of Edom during the campaigns of his third year in 553 BCE; Bartlett further commented that Nabonidus may have been responsible for the destruction of Edomite sites, but with the intention of subjugation rather than annihilation, and so argued for continued settlement under direct Neo-Babylonian rule.[6] Indeed, Bartlett suggested that, following the departure of the Babylonians, Busayra probably remained the centre for any Persian administration.[7]

New evidence from Crystal Bennett's excavations at Busayra, which the present writer is preparing for final publication, now proves beyond doubt that settlement at the site continued into the Persian period and provides an opportunity for reviewing the archaeological and historical evidence for the end of Edom within this revised chronological framework.

New Evidence from Busayra

Busayra is a modern village situated about 10 km south of Tafila and 45 km north of Petra in Jordan. The ancient site, as excavated, lies at the north end of the village, on a spur running northwest along the 1100 m contour line. Crystal Bennett excavated four main areas (A–D) on the upper part of the site during 1971–74 and in 1980 (Fig. 2). Area A was the central and highest point (the so-called 'acropolis'), with walls built of huge stones that suggested the presence of an important structure.

---

4. C.-M. Bennett, 'Excavations at Buseirah (Biblical Bozrah)', in J.F.A. Sawyer and D.J.A. Clines (eds.), *Midian, Moab and Edom: The History and Archaeology of Late Bronze and Iron Age Jordan and North-west Arabia* (JSOTSup, 24; Sheffield: JSOT Press, 1983), pp. 9-17 (17).

5. C.-M. Bennett, 'Excavations at Buseirah, Southern Jordan, 1974: Fourth Preliminary Report', *Levant* 9 (1977), pp. 1-10, Pls. I-III (8).

6. J. Lindsay, 'The Babylonian Kings and Edom, 605–550 B.C.', *PEQ* 108 (1976), pp. 23-39 (32); J.R. Bartlett, *Edom and the Edomites* (JSOTSup, 77; Sheffield: JSOT Press, 1989), pp. 159-61.

7. Bartlett, *Edom and the Edomites*, p. 166.

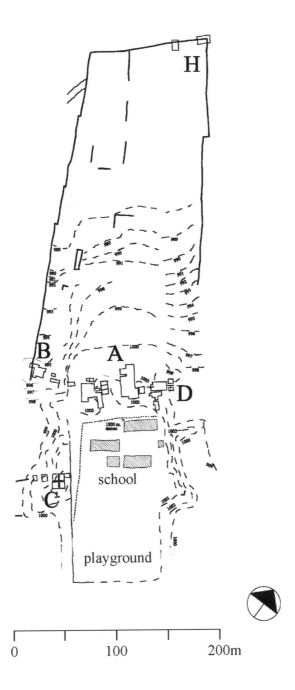

Figure 2. *Site plan of Busayra, showing location of excavated areas*

Already by the end of the first (1971) season, Bennett proposed that Area A was the site of a palace and/or temple.[8] Her final hypothesis, following the last (1980) season, was that there were two distinct building periods on Area A: her 'Building B' (earlier) and her smaller 'Building A' (later), possibly with an intermediate period, the whole of which was constructed on a deep earth fill.[9] She dated these to Iron II, with the final phase ('Building A') ending either in the sixth century BCE[10] or continuing into the Persian period.[11]

Revised Stratigraphy

Work on the stratigraphy and pottery by the present writer has modified Bennett's conclusions and proved the continuity of the Area A building into the Persian period. There were five occupational/structural phases in Area A. Phase 1 is poorly represented by a wall and two plaster floors on bedrock. In Phase 2, a series of stone walls and associated earth, stone and plaster fill deposits—incorporating the Phase 1 walls and deposits—created a stone and earth platform. On this platform was constructed a single large building in Phase 3, rectangular in plan and measuring 76.50 by 38.00 m, with traces of other structures against it (Fig. 3).

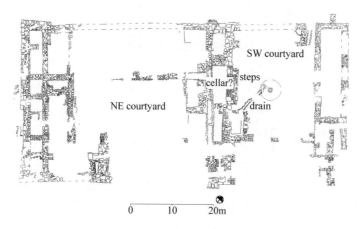

Figure 3. *Busayra Area A: plan of Phase 3 'temple'. The outer walls shown on the plan are Phase 4, but they are a rebuild of Phase 3 walls*

8.   C.-M. Bennett, 'Excavations at Buseirah, Southern Jordan, 1971: A Preliminary Report', *Levant* 5 (1973), pp. 1-11 (11).

9.   Bennett, 'Excavations at Buseirah (Biblical Bozrah)', p. 13.

10.   Bennett, 'Excavations at Buseirah (Biblical Bozrah)', p. 17.

11.   Bennett, 'Excavations at Buseirah, Southern Jordan, 1974', p. 8.

The building consisted of two wings, each with rooms around an inner courtyard. The courtyard of the northeastern wing contained a stone-lined cistern associated with two drains, one emerging from a small room with plastered floor and walls. At one end of the courtyard stone paving led to shallow stone steps that were flanked by two circular stone bases, each bearing the imprint of columns, statues or cult objects. The steps led up to a long narrow room with a plastered floor, associated with two low stone podia and copper-alloy chair fittings, perhaps suggesting that it originally contained an impressive chair or throne. There was no direct access between the two courtyards, and it is possible that the two parts of the building functioned separately.

Bennett and Reich both proposed that this building was very suggestive of a temple, with the small plastered room, from which one drain exited, identified as a 'purification room', before entering the long narrow plastered room reached by the steps, described as a 'cella' or 'holy of holies'.[12] The rooms surrounding the courtyard and the series of small rooms in the southwestern wing might be interpreted as storerooms, in which case the southwestern wing might have functioned as a storage and perhaps administrative annexe to the temple proper. There were some traces of fire at the end of Phase 3, particularly in parts of the plastered courtyard, around the steps and in the narrow plastered room ('cella'), but no evidence of widespread destruction.

In Phase 4 many parts of the Phase 3 building were rebuilt and some new walls were added, partitioning rooms to create smaller spaces (Fig. 4). Two of the new major walls had a concave construction, producing a 'winged' effect and giving the southwestern wing the appearance of a separate building, further evidence that perhaps the two wings of the building functioned as separate activity areas. With a few minor changes, the plan seems to have remained the same as in Phase 3 (*contra* Bennett, who reconstructed the Phase 4 building [= her 'Building A'] on a different, smaller plan than that of Phase 3 [her 'Building B']).[13] There

12. Bennett, 'Excavations at Buseirah, Southern Jordan, 1974', pp. 4-6; *idem*, 'Excavations at Buseirah (Biblical Bozrah)', p. 15; R. Reich, 'Palaces and Residencies in the Iron Age', in A. Kempinski, R. Reich *et al.* (eds.), *The Architecture of Ancient Israel from the Prehistoric to the Persian Periods, in Memory of Immanuel (Munya) Dunayevsky* (Jerusalem: Israel Exploration Society, 1992), pp. 202-22 (219).

13. Bennett, 'Excavations at Buseirah, Southern Jordan, 1974', pp. 4-5; *idem*, 'Excavations at Buseirah (Biblical Bozrah)', pp. 12-14.

is nothing to suggest a change in function from Phase 3, that is possibly a temple with a storage/administrative annexe. The Phase 4 loci were overlain by thick black ash and fallen stones, evidence of an intense fire that ended Iron Age occupation in Area A.

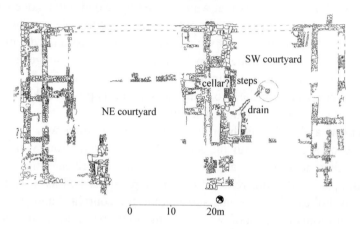

Figure 4. *Busayra Area A: plan of Phase 4 'temple'. Many of the walls were rebuilt and some areas were partitioned into smaller rooms*

Evidence of activities post-dating the burning and collapse deposits of Phase 4 has been assigned to Phase 5, but it is not clear if these activities were connected and dated to the same period. A possible threshing floor might date to the Roman period, based on a tentative dating of an associated quern. Several elliptical walls might be interpreted as having an agricultural connection, but no evidence for their date was found (they may or may not be connected with the threshing floor). A poorly recorded burial against one wall clearly cut through a Phase 4 floor, but it may have predated the final Phase 4 burning and collapse layers.

The structural phases in Area A more or less correlate with those in Area C, which also yielded a single building, probably to be identified as a palace or residency (Figs. 5 and 6). However, they cannot easily be correlated with the sequences in Areas B and D, which were excavated in small squares whose individual sequences could not be fitted into an overall phasing scheme for the areas.

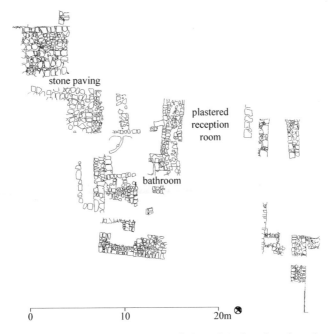

Figure 5. *Busayra Area C: plan of Phase 3 'palace/residency'*

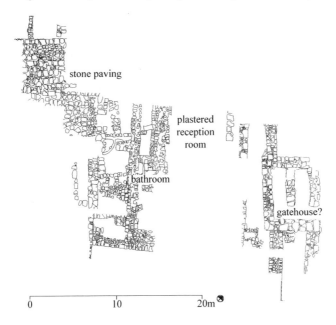

Figure 6. *Busayra Area C: plan of Phase 5 'palace/residency'; the areas were partitioned into smaller rooms, and a 'gatehouse' was added*

Revised Chronology

The key new ceramic dating evidence all comes from Phase 4 deposits in Area A. From two separate, stratified loci within Phase 4 came two imported Attic sherds dated to the late fourth century BCE. Another late fourth-century BCE Attic sherd came from topsoil. These sherds were discovered already in the first season of excavations (1971) but have remained unidentified until now. These Attic sherds are evidence that Phase 4 was in use up to the late fourth century BCE, at least to the end of the Persian period (traditionally 332 BCE). Not a single Attic sherd was found in earlier deposits. The 'local' pottery in Phases 1–4, both the painted 'Edomite' pottery and the coarse ware, is identical, and it is only the presence of the Attic sherds that proves a late fourth-century BCE date, rather than an earlier one. At present, it is not possible to distinguish between 'Assyrian', 'Babylonian' and 'Persian' periods on the basis of the local pottery. No Attic sherds were found in the other excavated areas at Busayra; thus Area A is the key to the chronology of the site.

It may be possible to correlate the sparse historical data with this new archaeological evidence to propose—or perhaps to speculate on—dates for the phases on Area A. Clearly, the dating of Phase 4 hinges around the late fourth-century BCE Attic pottery, while Phases 1–3, according to the local pottery, appear to date between the late eighth (at the very earliest) and sixth centuries BCE. Two working hypotheses are proposed here: (1) that the selective destruction at the end of Phase 3 should be attributed to Nabonidus in 553 BCE; and (2) that the subsequent Phase 4 dates from 553 BCE until at least the late fourth century BCE. Clearly caution is necessary, since such a small amount of chronologically diagnostic imported pottery is involved. Furthermore, one possibly third-century BCE black-slipped sherd was found in what is identified as a Phase 4 deposit at Busayra. While a single third-century sherd may be a stray (and other Hellenistic third/second-century BCE sherds were found in insecure contexts postdating the destruction of the site), it cannot be totally excluded that occupation continued into the third century BCE. Nevertheless, for the sake of argument, this paper's working hypothesis is that the Attic sherds are indeed evidence of continued occupation at Busayra into the late fourth century BCE.

Four arguments can be advanced in support of these two hypotheses. First, Edom, or perhaps even specifically Busayra, may have been the objective of an attack by Nabonidus, according to the Nabonidus

Chronicle for his third year, 553 BCE, but the signs are broken and the exact reading is not certain.[14] The relevant text reads:

> In the month Kislimu, the king [mustered?] his army [and ... ...] and to Nabû, Bel-dan, brother [... ... ...] of Amurru, to [... ...] he/they encamped [against? the land of E]dom. [... ... ...] the large armies [... ... ...the g]ate of the city Rugdini (Šindini?) [... ... ...he ki]lled him [... ... ...] x [... ... ...] his army.[15]

Beaulieu restores the name *[u]du-um-mu* here as 'Edom', and the restoration of the relevant passage can be either 'he/they encamped against the land of Edom' or 'against the city of Edom', and this is usually understood as meaning a siege of Busayra and the annexation of Edom.[16] Beaulieu dates this action more specifically to December 553 BCE.[17] However, *[u]du-um-mu* could refer to either Edom or Duma in northwest Arabia,[18] although Smith already argued in 1944 that, if this event occurred while Nabonidus was on his way to Tayma in Arabia, then Duma seems to be too far east and out of the way.[19] There is certainly no evidence that Edom was attacked or annexed earlier by the Neo-Babylonians. According to Josephus (*Ant.* 10.9.7), Nebuchadnezzar conquered Ammon and Moab—but not Edom—in 582 BCE, and this is usually interpreted as meaning that Ammon and Moab were annexed at this point and were henceforth ruled directly from Babylon.[20]

Second, further evidence for the presence of Nabonidus in the vicinity of Busayra is the relief at Sela, just to the northwest of Busayra.[21] This shows a standing king, above him a crescent and a star, and an illegible

14. P.-A. Beaulieu, *The Reign of Nabonidus, King of Babylon: 556–539 BCE* (YNER, 10; New Haven: Yale University Press, 1989), pp. 166, 169; A.K. Grayson, *Assyrian and Babylonian Chronicles* (TCS, 5; Locust Valley, NY: J.J. Augustin, 1975), pp. 105, 282.

15. Beaulieu, *The Reign of Nabonidus*, p. 166.

16. Lindsay, 'The Babylonian Kings and Edom', p. 36; Bartlett, *Edom and the Edomites*, pp. 157-61.

17. Beaulieu, *The Reign of Nabonidus*, pp. 168-69.

18. Lindsay, 'The Babylonian Kings and Edom', pp. 33-34.

19. S. Smith, *Isaiah Chapters XL–LV: Literary Criticism and History* (Schweich Lectures, 1940; London: British Academy, 1944), pp. 37-38, 139-40 nn. 86, 87.

20. E.g. L.G. Herr, 'The Ammonites in the Late Iron Age and Persian Period', in B. MacDonald and R.W. Younker (eds.), *Ancient Ammon* (SHCANE, 17; Leiden: E.J. Brill, 1999), pp. 219-37 (232).

21. S. Dalley and A. Goguel, 'The Sela' Sculpture: A Neo-Babylonian Rock Relief in Southern Jordan', *ADAJ* 41 (1997), pp. 169-76.

inscription. Analysis of the style of the relief identifies the figure almost certainly as Nabonidus. Dalley and Goguel propose that the relief was carved to commemorate Nabonidus's journey through Edom towards Tayma, perhaps in years three or four of his reign (i.e. c. 553–552 BCE).[22] They further suggest that the presence of the relief in Sela implies that Edom was under (direct?) Babylonian administration at that time and that Nabonidus's campaign might have been responsible for the destruction of Busayra.

Third, the selective destruction at Busayra Area A at the end of Phase 3 appears to be concentrated in the 'cella' and main courtyard of the building tentatively identified as the temple. Similarly, in the contemporary phase of the Area C palace or residency, also raised on a stone platform, the fire was concentrated in the 'reception room/courtyard'. Thus, in both these major buildings, probably the most important public buildings at Busayra, the fire was concentrated in what have been identified as the key symbolic areas: the 'cella' of the temple and the 'reception room' of the palace. This might suggest that the destructions were not random outbreaks of fire, but deliberate and focused messages left by a conqueror intent not on annihilation but on subjugation.[23] This would fit the hypothesis that the attack was the work of Nabonidus.

Fourth, following the destruction of parts of Area A at the end of Phase 3, there was a rebuilding in Phase 4, characterized especially by the partitioning of rooms to create smaller spaces (Fig. 4). Exactly the same pattern was repeated in the Area C 'palace/residency', with spaces subdivided and new doorways added (Fig. 6). Although this suggestion is pure speculation, such rebuilding (following partial destruction) is not incompatible with a slightly different usage for the buildings following a conquest of Busayra and an annexation of Edom by Nabonidus. Despite the lack of any specific evidence, the possibility cannot be excluded that the 'palace/residency' was redesigned for use by a governor appointed by the Babylonians, and later, the Persians.

Although the late fourth-century BCE Attic pottery in the Area A Phase 4 deposits is evidence that this phase continued to the end of the Persian period, there are no ancient written sources that refer to Transjordan during the Persian period that can help provide a historical framework. Eph'al proposes that Persian rule in southern Transjordan collapsed after the death of Darius II in 404 BCE, when there were anti-

---

22. Dalley and Goguel, 'The Sela' Sculpture', pp. 174-75.
23. Cf. Bartlett, *Edom and the Edomites*, p. 159.

Persian activities fomented by Egypt in the Levant and Cyprus, and rebellions and internal struggles within the central government.[24] However, clearly occupation at Busayra continued beyond that date, for at least another hundred years or so (bearing in mind the presence of a possibly third-century BCE sherd; see above), perhaps quite independently of Persian rule. In any case, by 344 BCE the Phoenician revolt against Persia had been defeated, and Persia reconquered Egypt in 342 BCE. It is likely that Transjordan was under Persian rule at that time, although the situation remains unclear.

Taking the Area A building as a framework for Iron Age occupation at Busayra, Phases 1–3 date from the late eighth century (at the earliest) to 553 BCE, and Phase 4 dates 553–c. 300 BCE, if the hypotheses outlined above are accepted.

Other Sites in Edom
The only other sites in Edom with some evidence of Persian-period occupatiom are Tawilan and Tell el-Kheleifeh. The cuneiform tablet discovered at Tawilan, but drawn up in Harran in Syria, was dated to the accession year of one of the Achaemenid kings named Darius.[25] However, it was impossible to attribute the tablet with certainty to Darius I (521 BCE), Darius II (423 BCE) or Darius III (335 BCE). Dalley thought that Darius III was unlikely, given the extreme rarity of cuneiform documents at the end of the Persian period.[26] Attribution to Darius I or II could be seen in the context of military movements in the Harran region in the accession years of both kings, which would explain the presence of the Babylonian scribe who drew up the tablet. However, Eph'al has discounted Darius I on the basis of the royal title on the tablet, 'King of the Lands', which Darius I is not known to have taken up so early in his reign.[27] This would leave Darius II and a date of 423 BCE for the tablet, but none of the three kings can be definitely excluded.

---

24. I. Eph'al, *The Ancient Arabs: Nomads on the Borders of the Fertile Crescent 9th–5th Centuries B.C.* (Jerusalem: Magnes Press, 1984), p. 205.

25. S. Dalley, 'The Cuneiform Tablet', in C.-M. Bennett and P. Bienkowski, *Excavations at Tawilan in Southern Jordan* (BAMA, 8; Oxford: Oxford University Press, 1995), pp. 67-68.

26. Dalley, 'The Cuneiform Tablet'.

27. I. Eph'al, 'Syria–Palestine under Achaemenid Rule', in J. Boardman *et al.* (eds.), *Cambridge Ancient History. IV. Persia, Greece and the Western Mediterranean, c. 525 to 479 BC* (Cambridge: Cambridge University Press, 2nd edn, 1988), pp. 139-64 (151 n. 30).

The tablet was found in a context following the end of Iron Age settlement at Tawilan. After a fire the site was abandoned, with many of the walls collapsing. The surviving network of walls acted as a catchment for the accumulation of silts and soils, and the tablet was found next to a pillar within these fill-accumulation deposits.

The new evidence from Busayra is perhaps a further hint that the Tawilan tablet dates to either Darius II (423 BCE) or even Darius III (335 BCE). The chronology of Tawilan is not entirely clear; the pottery is very similar to that at Busayra[28] and the possibility was left open that the final Iron Age deposits at Tawilan continued into the Persian period.[29] Since Busayra now appears to continue into the late fourth century BCE, it is possible that Tawilan can be similarly dated, at least up to 423 BCE (if we accept the attribution to Darius II) or even as late as 335 BCE (Darius III), despite the fact that the tablet was found in a post-abandonment context.

At Tell el-Kheleifeh, most of the pottery associated with the two major Iron Age phases reconstructed from Glueck's excavations—casemate fortress and fortified settlement—has been dated between the eighth and sixth centuries BCE.[30] This pottery came from what Glueck called his Period IV corpus. Pratico allows for the possibility that some of the pottery may have continued into the fifth century BCE.[31] Fifth- and fourth-century BCE Greek sherds and Aramaic ostraca came from Glueck's Stratum V, which was poorly preserved,[32] and this pottery is therefore normally disassociated from the main Iron II settlement at Kheleifeh. However, its association with the Iron II/?Persian settlement should not be totally excluded, since we now know that stratified late fourth-century BCE Greek pottery is associated with the Iron II/Persian settlement at Busayra; also, renewed excavations at Kheleifeh are drastically revising Glueck's stratigraphy and plans, and it is conceivable that

28. S. Hart, 'The Pottery', in C.-M. Bennett and P. Bienkowski (eds.), *Excavations at Tawilan in Southern Jordan* (BAMA, 8; Oxford: Oxford University Press, 1995), pp. 53-66.

29. P. Bienkowski, 'Conclusions', in C.-M. Bennett and P. Bienkowski (eds.), *Excavations at Tawilan in Southern Jordan* (BAMA, 8; Oxford: Oxford University Press, 1995), pp. 101-105.

30. G.D. Pratico, *Nelson Glueck's 1938–1940 Excavations at Tell el-Kheleifeh: A Reappraisal* (ASORAR, 3; Atlanta: Scholars Press, 1993), pp. 49-50.

31. Pratico, *Tell el-Kheleifeh*, p. 50.

32. Pratico, *Tell el-Kheleifeh*, p. 50.

his original division into strata will not survive this reappraisal.[33] Therefore, the possibility cannot be excluded that the settlement at Tell el-Kheleifeh, like Busayra, continued from the Iron II to the end of the Persian period.

A New Framework for Edom in the Neo-Babylonian and Persian Periods

The evidence considered above allows us to propose tentatively a revised framework for the Neo-Babylonian and Persian periods in Edom. The earliest Iron Age settlements so far discovered are possibly to be identified as small mining camps in the Faynan copper-mining area, dating to the ninth century BCE. Settlement had expanded over most of Edom by the late eighth century BCE. By this time Edom was recognized as an independent state with its own king, probably ruling from Busayra. From the campaign of the Assyrian king Tiglath-pileser III in 732 BCE, Edom regularly paid tribute to Assyria and appears to have been a loyal tributary state.[34]

Following the fall of Nineveh in 612 BCE, the Neo-Babylonians took over the Assyrian empire. While Ammon and Moab appear to have been annexed by Nebuchadnezzar in 582 BCE, Edom probably survived as an independent state.[35] It is suggested above that the selective destruction of the temple and palace at Busayra was the work of Nabonidus during his campaign of December 553 BCE. Evidence of fire at other sites, such as Umm el-Biyara and Tell el-Kheleifeh, might also be attributed to Nabonidus. It is likely that Edom was annexed at this point into the empire and henceforth ruled directly from Babylon. Occupation continued at Busayra, and probably at Tawilan and Tell el-Kheleifeh; the temple and palace at Busayra were rebuilt, the latter conceivably to house a Neo-Babylonian governor.[36]

33. M.-L. Mussell, 'Tell el-Kheleifeh', *ACOR Newsletter* 11.1 (1999), pp. 5-6.

34. Cf. P. Bienkowski, 'Transjordan and Assyria', in L.E. Stager, J.A. Greene and M.D. Coogan (eds.), *The Archaeology of Jordan and Beyond: Essays in Honor of James A. Sauer* (HSM; Studies in the Archaeology and History of the Levant, 1; Winona Lake, IN: Eisenbrauns, 2000), pp. 44-58.

35. Bartlett, *Edom and the Edomites*, pp. 150-57.

36. Similarly, for Ammon Herr has proposed that the administrative buildings at Tell al-'Umayri date initially to the Neo-Babylonian period and were built by the Ammonite monarchy to administer outlying farmsteads that produced wine to pay the tribute or tax to Babylon. These buildings continued to be used in the Persian period. See Herr, 'The Ammonites in the Late Iron Age and Persian Period', p. 232.

After the fall of Babylon in 539 BCE, the Persians took over the empire. The discovery of imported late fourth-century BCE Attic pottery at Busayra is evidence that settlement there continued to the end of the Persian period, and it is likely that Tell el-Kheleifeh and possibly Tawilan were occupied at the same time.

In the Persian sources the area from the Euphrates to southern Palestine (including Transjordan) is known by the territorial term 'Beyond the River' (though the term had already been used in Neo-Assyrian and Neo-Babylonian times).[37] During the fourth year of the rule of Cyrus in Babylonia (535 BCE), a united province was created consisting of Babylonia and 'Beyond the River'.[38] There appears to have been little administrative change in the transition from Neo-Babylonian to Persian rule. Since the entire Neo-Babylonian empire came under the rule of a single governor, this suggests that for the time being Persian rule in the Levant maintained the same administrative patterns as in the Neo-Babylonian period.[39] After 486 BCE, 'Beyond the River' became a satrapy in its own right.[40] Therefore, Edom probably came under the overall rule of the Persian satrap of 'Beyond the River'. A sub-unit of a satrapy was a province, ruled by a governor. The only certain provinces within the satrapy of 'Beyond the River' in the sources are Judah and Samaria in Palestine.[41] At present there is no evidence that Edom became a separate province within the satrapy of 'Beyond the River', although there is now evidence that Ammon was a separate province.[42]

37. Eph'al, 'Syria–Palestine under Achaemenid Rule', p. 141.

38. M.A. Dandamaev, *A Political History of the Achaemenid Empire* (Leiden: E.J. Brill, 1989), pp. 60-61; Eph'al, 'Syria–Palestine under Achaemenid Rule', p. 153.

39. K.G. Hoglund, *Achaemenid Imperial Administration in Syria–Palestine and the Missions of Ezra and Nehemiah* (SBLDS, 125; Atlanta: Scholars Press, 1992), p. 5; E. Stern, 'New Evidence on the Administrative Division of Palestine in the Persian Period', in H. Sancisi-Weerdenburg and A. Kuhrt (eds.), *Achaemenid History IV: Centre and Periphery. Proceedings of the Groningen 1986 Achaemenid History Workshop* (Leiden: Nederlands Instituut voor het Nabije Oosten, 1990), pp. 221-26 (221); Y. Aharoni, *The Land of the Bible: A Historical Geography* (London: Burns & Oates, 2nd edn, 1979), p. 411.

40. Eph'al, 'Syria–Palestine under Achaemenid Rule', pp. 153-55; A. Lemaire, 'Histoire et administration de la Palestine à l'époque perse', in E.-M. Laperrousaz and A. Lemaire (eds.), *La Palestine à l'époque perse* (Etudes annexes de la Bible de Jérusalem; Paris: Cerf, 1994), pp. 11-53 (13).

41. Eph'al, 'Syria–Palestine under Achaemenid Rule', p. 158; A. Lemaire, 'Histoire et administration de la Palestine à l'époque perse', pp. 16-24, 41-46.

42. Herr, 'The Ammonites in the Late Iron Age and Persian Period', pp. 233-34.

The evidence presented above indicates that settlement at Busayra and Tell el-Kheleifeh, and possibly Tawilan, continued into the late fourth century BCE. The Attic pottery at Busayra dates to the late fourth century BCE, with one stratified (stray?) sherd possibly later. At Tell el-Kheleifeh Greek pottery and Aramaic ostraca also date to the fifth/ fourth centuries BCE, although it is not clear whether they can be associated with the Iron II/?Persian settlement. The cuneiform tablet from Tawilan may date to the accession year of Darius II (423 BCE) or even of Darius III (335 BCE). If Busayra and Tell el-Kheleifeh, two of the most important centres in Edom—one the 'capital', the other a trading centre on the Red Sea—survived until the late fourth century BCE, it cannot be excluded that some sort of political entity called Edom also survived throughout the whole of the Persian period.[43]

43. It is interesting that the first historical mention of the Nabataeans dates to 312 BCE, according to Diodorus (19.94.1), who describes an attempt by Athenaios, a general of Antigonos Monophthalmos, one of the successors of Alexander the Great, to conquer the Nabataeans, at that time still essentially nomads. The year 312 BCE is intriguingly close to the likely date of the destruction of Busayra, and thus two possible agents for this destruction who can now be considered are the Nabataeans or Antigonos. Diodorus describes the Nabataeans as having a rocky stronghold with only one easily defensible access. This description is often applied to Umm el-Biyara, inside Petra, but some scholars claim that Sela or even Busayra would fit better the geographical description and distances given by Diodorus; for references, see S. Schmid, 'The Nabataeans: Travellers between Lifestyles', in B. MacDonald, R. Adams and P. Bienkowski (eds.), *The Archaeology of Jordan* (Sheffield: Sheffield Academic Press, 2001). The sparse 'classic' Nabataean finds at Busayra postdate the Phase 4 destruction or are out of context, and probably date to the first centuries BCE/CE.

ASSYRIAN INFLUENCE AND CHANGING TECHNOLOGIES
AT TALL JAWA, JORDAN

P.M. Michèle Daviau

Introduction

The search for evidence of occupation and settlement patterns on the
plateau of central Jordan is essential for historical and cultural research
concerning the Iron Age kingdoms of Ammon and Moab. The contribution of Max Miller to the archaeology of Jordan is like a pearl without
price, the centrepiece of a circlet of small excavation projects that now
illuminate various corners of the large territory that he surveyed.[1] His
research also throws light on problems encountered at other sites in
Ammon to the north and Edom to the south. Of greatest value is the
awareness that there are few real tells with deep deposition of superim-
posed occupation layers.[2] Instead, there are sites with only a few phases

1. Such projects include the excavations of Mattingly (G.L. Mattingly *et al.*,
'Al-Karak Resources Project 1997: Excavations at Khirbat al-Mudaybi'', *ADAJ* 43
[1999], pp. 127-44) at Khirbat al-Mudaybi'; B. Routledge ('Seeing Through Walls:
Interpreting Iron Age I Architecture at Khirbat al-Mudayna al-'Aliya', *BASOR* 319
[2000], pp. 37-70) at Khirbat al-Mudayna al-'Aliya in central Moab; and P.M.M.
Daviau ('Moab's Northern Border: Khirbat al-Mudayna on the Wadi ath-Thamad',
BA 60 [1997], pp. 222-28) at Khirbat al-Mudayna on the Wadi ath-Thamad, in
northern Moab. Other current excavation projects in Moab include the work of
U.F.Ch. Worschech and F. Ninow ('Preliminary Report on the Third Campaign at
the Ancient Site of el-Balu' in 1991', *ADAJ* 38 [1994], pp. 195-203) at Bālū', and
of D. Homès-Fredericq ('Excavating the First Pillar House at Lehun [Jordan]', in
L.E. Stager, J.A. Greene and M.D. Coogan [eds.], *The Archaeology of Jordan and
Beyond: Essays in Honor of James A. Sauer* [Harvard Semitic Publications: Studies
in the Archaeology and History of the Levant, 1; Winona Lake, IN: Eisenbrauns,
2000], pp. 180-95) at Lahūn.
2. N. Glueck ('Explorations in the Land of Ammon', *BASOR* 68 [1937], pp.
13-21 [21]) had already noticed the paucity of sites with a typical tell shape; in his
survey area, he considered Khirbat al-Mudayna on the Wadi ath-Thamad in northern
Moab to be an exception to the rule.

of occupation within the same chronological horizon. Such is the case for the site of Tall Jawa, where Iron II and late Iron II buildings were all footed on bedrock across the walled settlement. Changes between the two phases can be seen in the rise of new building types, new ceramic fabrics, and certain high-status artifacts, favoured by the Assyrians. This paper is a contribution to the cultural study of Jordan in appreciation of the contributions, friendship and support of Max Miller over many years.

Assyrian Influence in Palestine[3]

The influence of Assyria on neighbouring states, especially those in the Levant, has been documented on the basis of texts, architectural traditions,[4] ceramic styles[5] and artifacts, although the exact nature of that influence may vary from one small state to another. Open court style buildings at Megiddo (Stratum III), Hazor (Stratum III) and at Buseirah (Area A) in Edom are defined as Assyrian in inspiration[6] and dated to the seventh century BCE. Such identification is relatively easy for tell sites occupied for hundreds or even thousands of years with a refined stratigraphic sequence. More difficult is the understanding of the chronological setting for sites in Transjordan that did not have comparable occupation histories or were one-period sites, occupied only during the Iron Age. This difficulty is more complex when the material-culture

---

3.   This paper is a revised version of my presentation at the Annual Symposium of the Canadian Society for Mesopotamian Studies, Toronto, Ontario (P.M.M. Daviau, 'Technological Change and Assyrian Influence at Tall Jawa, Jordan', *Bulletin of the Canadian Society of Mesopotamian Studies* 32 [1997], pp. 23-32); it is re-published here with the permission of Michel Fortin, editor of the *Bulletin*.

4.   R.B.K. Amiran and I. Dunayevsky, 'The Assyrian Open-Court Building and its Palestinian Derivatives', *BASOR* 149 (1958), pp. 25-32; C.-M. Bennett, 'Some Reflections on Neo-Assyrian Influence in Transjordan', in P.R.S. Moorey and P. Parr (eds.), *Archaeology in the Levant: Essays for Kathleen Kenyon* (Warminster: Aris & Phillips, 1978), pp. 164-71; *idem*, 'Neo-Assyrian Influence in Transjordan', in A. Hadidi (ed.), *Studies in the History and Archaeology of Jordan I* (Amman: Department of Antiquities, 1982), pp. 181-87.

5.   R.H. Dornemann, *The Archaeology of the Transjordan in the Bronze and Iron Ages* (Milwaukee Public Museum Publications in Anthropology and History, 4; Milwaukee: Milwaukee Public Museum, 1983), pp. 178-79.

6.   Amiran and Dunayevsky, 'The Assyrian Open-Court Building'; Bennett, 'Neo-Assyrian Influence'.

remains do not have close parallels from well-published sites that represent continuous occupation. Such is the case for Tall Jawa, a site in central Jordan, which appears to have been a settlement within the Ammonite kingdom during Iron Age I and II.

Tall Jawa is a 2.0 ha site, 10 km south of Amman, that overlooks the plain of Madaba to the south and west (Fig. 1). Located on a rise where it commands a strategic position, this mound was heavily fortified during Iron Age II (1000–600 BCE). During six seasons of excavation (1989, 1991–1995), 90.00 m of the casemate wall system were exposed, enabling us to study its building materials, construction techniques and associated features, such as towers, drains and gate complex.[7] Repairs to this fortification system, the introduction of new building types and the development of new ceramic styles and fabrics during the late Iron Age II period suggest both chronological and cultural change, possibly related to increased Assyrian influence in the area. This paper will examine changes in fortification strategy, building plans, ceramic manufacture and certain high-status artifacts, in order to identify elements of Assyrian influence on Ammonite material culture and life style.

Fortification Strategy
Evidence for occupation at Tall Jawa suggests the presence of an Iron Age I village (Stratum X)[8] that was replaced in Iron II by a town (Stratum IX) with a solid fortification wall. This settlement was subsequently surrounded by a casemate wall system (Stratum VIII), formed of two parallel walls with cross walls at intervals that created rooms and towers within the thickness of the defences. Typical Ammonite pottery, comparable to finds from Rabbat-Ammon (Humbert, personal communication, July 1994), filled the domestic buildings (B113, B300) constructed up against these defences. This evidence suggests that the Iron II fortifications represent a central government initiative,[9] probably related to state formation on the part of the Ammonites (Benê 'Ammon).

---

7.   P.M.M. Daviau, *Excavations at Tall Jawa I: The Iron Age Town*, in preparation.

8.   The Iron Age I settlement was previously identified as Stratum IX (Daviau, 'Technological Change', p. 23).

9.   Z. Herzog, 'Settlement and Fortification Planning in the Iron Age', in A. Kempinski and R. Reich (eds.), *The Architecture of Ancient Israel: From the Prehistoric to the Persian Periods. In Memory of Immanuel (Munya) Dunayevsky* (Jerusalem: Israel Exploration Society, 1992), pp. 231-74 (248).

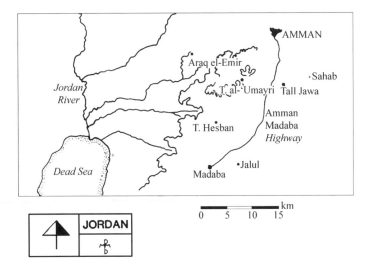

Figure 1. *Central Jordan, showing location of Tall Jawa south of Amman*

Later changes to the wall system are most apparent in the south-eastern part of the town where a terrace is protected by a single, solid wall (Stratum VII) that is attached to the casemate system. At Tall Jawa, the solid wall (W9000) surrounds a domestic complex (Building 900) and two distinct structures (B700,[10] B800), each built independent of the defensive wall. At the same time, a gate complex (B910) was built (VIIB) on the terrace, and later remodelled (B905, VIIA) with the result that the central roadway[11] was converted into a series of industrial rooms.[12] Such changes may have been one of those refashionings of an

10. B700 is the siglum for the Iron Age house; B600, used in earlier publications (P.M.M. Daviau, 'Excavations at Tell Jawa, Jordan [1993]. Preliminary Report', *ADAJ* 38 [1994], pp. 173-93; *idem*, 'Tell Jawa: A Case Study of Ammonite Urbanism during Iron Age II', in W.E. Aufrecht, N.A. Mirau and S.W. Gauley [eds.], *Urbanism in Antiquity: From Mesopotamia to Crete* [JSOTSup, 244; Sheffield: Sheffield Academic Press, 1997], pp. 156-71 [167]) represents a later phase, that dates to the late Byzantine–early Islamic period.

11. The location of the Stratum VII road and entryway is uncertain due to the presence of a modern cemetery to the east of Gate Complex 910 in Squares C83–85 and C91–95.

12. The same occupation sequence is evident at the site of Khirbat al-Mudayna on the Wadi ath-Thamad where a six-chambered gate complex was remodelled some time during the late Iron Age II. This gate was excavated (1996–99) under the direction of the author (R. Levesque and R. Chadwick were field supervisors). See

existing town under Assyrian supervision, as described by Mazzoni.[13]

Building Plans: Residential Structures
The construction of two, large residential buildings (B700, Fig. 2; B800, Fig. 3) and a gate complex on the southeast terrace during Stratum VII (late eighth–seventh centuries BCE) suggests major changes in town planning. These new houses were not built up against the wall system or incorporated into it,[14] as were the domestic units of Stratum VIII (B300, B113), but were located a short distance north of solid Wall 9000. Both Buildings 700 and 800 show evidence of extensive domestic activity, but appear to be larger than what might be expected for modest housing. Building 800 measured 13.50 × 16.50 m[15] and Building 700 was at least 12.20 × 16.00 m. In both houses, there are monolithic stone pillars standing 1.80 m in height, and stone-built staircases that lead up to the second storey.[16] In Building 800, there would have been approximately 22 rooms on two storeys, while in Building 700 there could have been as many as 18 rooms.

R. Chadwick, P.M.M. Daviau and M. Steiner, 'Four Seasons of Excavations at Khirbat al-Mudayna on the Wadi ath-Thamad, 1996–1999', *ADAJ* 44 (2000).

13. S. Mazzoni, 'Settlement Pattern and New Urbanization in Syria at the Time of the Assyrian Conquest', in M. Liverani (ed.), *Neo-Assyrian Geography* (Quaderni di geografia storica, 5; Roma: Università di Roma, 1995), pp. 1-11, Pls. I–III. Although he is confident that Assyrian influence penetrated all of the small states in Transjordan during the Iron Age, Kh. Yassine ('Tell el-Mazar, Field I: Preliminary Report of Areas G, H, L, and M', in *idem* (ed.), *Archaeology of Jordan: Essays and Reports* [Amman: Department of Archaeology, University of Jordan, 1988], pp. 75-135 [88]) assumes that there were no Assyrian provincial governors in these states as there was at Megiddo.

14. See Beer-sheba, Stratum II (Y. Aharoni, 'Excavations at Tel Beer-sheba, Preliminary Report of the Fifth and Sixth Seasons, 1973–1974', *TA* 2 [1975], pp. 146-68 [Fig. 1]); and Tell Beit Mirsim, Stratum A (W.F. Albright, *The Excavation of Tell Beit Mirsim.* II. *The Bronze Age* [AASOR, 17; New Haven: American Schools of Oriental Research, 1938], Pl. 47).

15. Building 800 is irregular in shape with a maximum length on the west side of 17.8 m.

16. Daviau, 'Excavations at Tell Jawa, Jordan (1993). Preliminary Report', Fig. 13; *idem*, 'Domestic Architecture in Iron Age Ammon: Building Materials, Construction Techniques, and Room Arrangement', in R.W. Younker and B. MacDonald (eds.), *Ancient Ammon* (SHCANE, 17; Leiden: E.J. Brill, 1999), pp. 113-36 (Fig. 5.2).

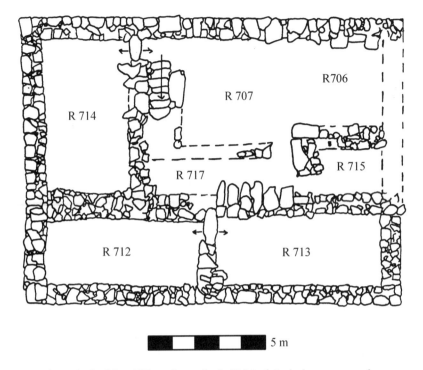

Figure 2. *Building 700, redrawn by B. Holthof; includes room numbers of Late Iron II (Stratum VII)*

A search for parallels to this building plan leads directly to the discussion of 'open-court style' buildings represented at several Israelite sites after the conquest by Assyria. The best examples are at Megiddo (Buildings 1052, 1369 = Stratum III) and Hazor (Area B = Stratum III), where these structures resemble residential units of Neo-Assyrian palaces, such as Residence L at Khorsabad,[17] and certain houses in Mesopotamia at Assur, Tell Halaf and Babylon.[18] Some characteristics of these building plans appear at Tall Jawa in Buildings 700 and 800:

17. D. Milson, 'On the Chronology and Design of "Ahab's Citadel" at Hazor', *ZDPV* 107 (1991), pp. 39-47 (42, Fig. 3).

18. Amiran and Dunayevsky, 'The Assyrian Open-Court Building', Figs. 6a, 6b; 7; 9.

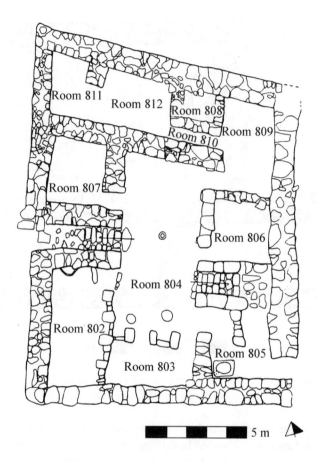

Figure 3. *Building 800, two-storey building dating to Late Iron II (Stratum VII)*

(1)   both are detached and rectangular with the exception of some
       corners that are not precisely 90°;
(2)   both have well-built inner and outer walls, sufficient to carry a
       second storey (0.65–1.00 + m thick);
(3)   B800 has a central hall with rooms on four sides, and B700
       has rooms on at least three sides of a central hall;
(4)   Building 800 has a small side entrance (R805); and
(5)   a corridor (R810) runs along one side of the central hall (in
       B800) with a series of rooms along one side of this corridor.[19]

19. See parallels in Amiran and Dunayevsky, 'The Assyrian Open-Court Building', p. 29.

Characteristics that are specific to the Tall Jawa buildings include:

(1)   doorways into rooms are usually positioned at the ends of walls;

(2)   staircases lead up to the second storey; and

(3)   evidence of a ceiling over the central hall was present in B800.[20]

With this in mind, there remain several additional factors that should be studied to ascertain the best functional parallels for the Tall Jawa structures. Primary among these factors is that of size. Although the Tall Jawa buildings are larger than most Palestinian houses of the period, they are only half the size of the Hazor Citadel (Area B) building that was 26.00 × 30.00+ m.[21] This difference is also seen in room size and the width of doorways; the widest entrance at Hazor was 2.50 m,[22] while at Tall Jawa it was 1.65 m. These differences are clearly related to a fundamental difference in function.

A closer parallel to the Tall Jawa buildings may be the Neo-Assyrian houses at Assur, which continued a long Mesopotamian tradition.[23] In

20.   The discussion of roofed space versus open courtyards in the central space continues, although both P.M.M. Daviau (*Houses and their Furnishings in Bronze Age Palestine: Domestic Activity Areas and Artefact Distribution in the Middle and Late Bronze Ages* [JSOT/ASOR Monograph Series, 8; Sheffield: Sheffield Academic Press, 1993]) and C. Foucault-Forest ('Modèles d'organisation de l'espace dans l'habitat du Bronze Moyen et du Bronze Récent en Palestine', in C. Castel, M. Maqdisi and F. Villeneuve [eds.], *Les Maisons dans la Syrie antique du IIIe millénaire aux débuts de l'Islam: Pratiques et représentations de l'espace domestique, Actes du Colloque International, Damas 27–30 juin 1992* [Bibliothèque archéologique et historique, 150; Beyrouth: Institut Français d'archéologie du Proche-Orient, 1997], pp. 151-60), have demonstrated that this style was not often used in Palestine. In B800 at Tall Jawa, there was no open court.

21.   Y. Yadin *et al.*, *Hazor*. I. *An Account of the First Season of Excavations, 1955* (Jerusalem: Magnes Press / The Hebrew University, 1958), p. 45.

22.   Yadin *et al.*, *Hazor*, I, p. 46.

23.   In C. Preusser's publication (*Die Wohnhäuser in Assur* [Ausgrabungen der Deutschen Orient-Gesellschaft in Assur, A; Die Baudenkmäler aus assyrischer Zeit, VI; Wissenschaftliche Veröffentlichung der Deutchen Orient-Gesellschaft, 64; Berlin: Gebr. Mann, 1954]) of the domestic structures uncovered in the excavations of the Deutsche Orient-Gesellschaft, he presents a study of central-court-style houses beginning with the Old Akkadian period houses under the Sin-Shamash Temple (Pl. 2) and the house southeast of the Ziggurat (Pl. 3). Such houses continued through the Middle Assyrian period, where it is best seen in the plan of the house in Area fE,gA9,10I (Pl. 6).

the Neo-Assyrian period, houses with a central court and rooms on four sides continued to be built, although their rectilinear plan was somewhat compromised due to the lack of space in the domestic quarter of Assur. One of the closest parallels is House No. 4,[24] which measured approximately 15 × 20 m and had ten rooms. In this house and in the Red House, one of the largest (approximately 28 × 30 m) in the domestic quarter with 23 rooms,[25] the tendency was to build all rooms on the ground floor (Room 23 in the Red House may have been a staircase), whereas the smaller houses (Nos. 8, 12, 21) show evidence of stairs, probably leading to the roof.[26]

While there is no doubt that the Tall Jawa residences served domestic and craft-related purposes,[27] both Stratum VII Buildings produced seals, while Building 800 also contained an ostracon suggesting economic and administrative activities.[28] While these finds point to administrative activities, it is important to note that neither the seals nor the Aramaic ostracon contain cuneiform script suggestive of Assyrian presence; they appear to be local in design and in manufacture. The same can be said for the ceramic evidence, although significant changes appear here as well, indicative of overall cultural change.

Ceramic Manufacture

Within the Stratum VII buildings, the most common find that serves as an indication of culture, chronology and human activity is the pottery. At Tall Jawa, the ceramic repertoire is also a prime indicator of technological change in that it bears witness to continuity in certain formal types, along with changes in form, fabric and firing techniques.[29]

24. C. Preusser, *Die Wohnhäuser in Assur*, Pl. 9.

25. The Big House in Area b,c6 with at least 28 rooms and walls almost 2.00 m thick is clearly in a different class (Preusser, *Die Wohnhäuser in Assur*, Pl. 17).

26. Comparison of construction techniques and specific features such as staircases between the houses at Assur and at Tall Jawa does not appear to be productive at present. More examples of local Ammonite architecture are needed before the degree of influence can be determined.

27. Loom weights were present in two rooms (R802, R804) in B800, as well as in B700. Daviau, *Excavations at Tall Jawa I: The Iron Age Town*, in preparation.

28. P.-E. Dion, 'The Ostracon from Building 800', in P.M.M. Daviau (ed.), *Excavations at Tall Jawa, Jordan*. II. *The Iron Age Artifacts* (forthcoming).

29. Continuity in the form of jugs and storejars, with slight changes over time, can also be documented. One such change is the use of the ring base instead of the disk or double disk base, which were characteristic of earlier Ammonite sites.

Surface Treatment

Continuity in Stratum VII is best seen in the occurrence of a vertical neck, red-slipped carinated bowl, that was common in Field E of Stratum VIII. At the same time, a study of the percentage of red-slipped vessels represented by both reconstructed forms and sherd material shows a marked difference between Stratum VIII and Stratum VII remains. Of the material recovered from B300 in Field E (VIII) during 1992 and 1993,[30] 36.3 per cent is red slipped.[31] In Building 800 (VII), there was only 11.2 per cent red slipped, while 5 per cent of the 445 registered sherds were black burnished, a ceramic ware that is missing in Field E.[32]

Vessel Forms

Although continuity of vessel form is apparent in certain types that were common to both Stratum VIII and Stratum VII, more significant are the new forms that make their appearance. For example, the hemispherical bowls from Stratum VIII were the most common small bowl form of the earlier occupation phases. These vessels, which range in size from 12–14 cm in diameter and are 6–7 cm deep were heavily red slipped, inside and out, and the slip had been burnished to a high polish. No such bowls have been identified in the finds from the Stratum VII buildings. Instead, a shallow saucer bowl is the most common form in Building 800, where a stack of saucers all have the same diameter (17–18 cm, Fig. 4.1, 2). The most common surface treatment consists of red slip and spiral burnishing. While the dominant colour was red (10R 4/6),[33]

30. These statistics were prepared for a paper entitled, 'Intrasite Distribution of Red Slipped and Black Burnished Wares at Tell Jawa, Jordan', presented to the Annual Meeting of the American Schools of Oriental Research, Washington, DC, 20 November 1993.

31. A slightly different picture appeared when the wares were quantified on a room-by-room basis. In Room 303, 41.4 per cent were red slipped, while in Room 302, where storage and food preparation took place, only 28.4 per cent were red slipped. A few vessels, recovered outside the activity areas in Square E65, were red slipped and decorated with black and white paint. Although these vessels are not directly relevant to the current study, they may lead to a further refinement of our analysis of surface treatment of ceramic wares in central Transjordan during the Iron Age.

32. Only a handful of black burnished sherds, out of a corpus of many thousands, appear in Field E. A discussion of black burnished wares will be presented below along with our analysis of new fabric types.

33. All pottery from Tall Jawa is colour-coded using the Munsell Soil Color charts, rev. edn, 1994.

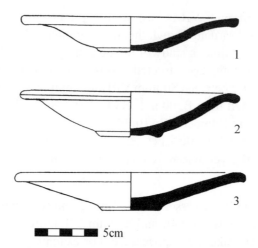

5cm

Figure 4. *Shallow saucer bowls: (1) V808, (2) V812, (3) V803*

two saucer bowls (V810, and C17:45/116.4-6[34]) appear in a lighter red slip (2.5 YR 5/6), and one saucer (V803) (Fig. 4.3) is almost yellow (5RY 6/6, reddish yellow), suggesting a change in the chemistry of the slip. Saucers, similar in shape, appear at Megiddo, where Assyrian control is marked by the presence of courtyard-style buildings in Strata III and II.[35]

The introduction of carinated bowls at Iron Age sites in Palestine, long believed to be either imports or local imitation of Assyrian palace ware,[36] also occurs at Tall Jawa in Stratum VII. In her study of pottery from Fort Shalmaneser at Nimrud, Oates reserves the term 'palace ware' for eggshell thin, fine wares, usually 'greenish buff' in colour.[37] At Tall

34. Vessel numbers are assigned where several sherds can be mended to form a sufficient part of a discrete vessel to distinguish its type and subtype. Sherd registration is in the form of Field+Square: Locus/Pail number.item number.

35. R.S. Lamon and G.M. Shipton, *Megiddo*. I. *Seasons of 1925–1934, Strata I–IV* (Oriental Institute Publications, 42; Chicago: University of Chicago Press, 1939), Pls. 23.4, 24.42; Fig. 89.

36. W.M.F. Petrie, *Gerar* (British School of Archaeology in Egypt, Publications of the Egyptian Research Account, 43; London: British School of Archaeology in Egypt, 1928), p. 7; and R. Amiran, *Ancient Pottery of the Holy Land: From Its Beginnings in the Neolithic Period to the End of the Iron Age* (Jerusalem: Masada Press; New Brunswick, NJ: Rutgers University Press, 1969), p. 291.

37. J. Oates, 'Late Assyrian Pottery from Fort Shalmaneser', *Iraq* 21 (1959), pp. 130-46, Pls. XXXV–XXXIX (p. 136 n. 13; Pls. XXXV.18, 20, XXXVI.27, 28, 29).

Jawa, shallow carinated bowls appear in the traditional clay fabric, well known from Stratum VIII, and are red slipped and burnished (B800; V869, Fig. 5.1; V870, Fig. 5.2). In addition, the rims of these TJ bowls are shorter than those from Nimrud and have more in common with the bowls depicted in the stone carved relief of Esarhaddon's banquet.[38] The introduction of several styles of thin-walled simple-rim bowls with red slip also appear at this time, probably in imitation of another common palace ware bowl style.[39]

Another bowl style common at Neo-Assyrian sites, such as Aššur,[40] are also carinated but have finger depressions in imitation of metal bowl forms. At Tall Jawa, a red-slipped (2.5YR 5/6) bowl with finger depressions (V215, Fig. 6.1) and black, or very dark gray (2.5YR N3) painted bands, was present in a Stratum VIII building (B102), while a red-slipped chalice (V920; Fig. 6.2) from Stratum VII has the same style of finger depressions in imitation of a metal prototype.[41]

38. R.D. Barnett and A. Lorenzini, *Assyrian Sculptures in the British Museum* (Toronto: McClelland and Stewart, 1975), Pls. 169, 170.

39. Parallels for carinated bowls with red slip are numerous, for example at Tell el-Far'ah (N) where 13 examples are published (A. Chambon, *Tell el-Far'ah I. L'âge du fer* [Mémoire, 31; Paris: Éditions Recherche sur les Civilisations, 1984], Pls. 57.1–3; 61.2–11); at coastal sites such as Tell Jemmeh where G.W. van Beek ('Digging up Tell Jemmeh', *Archaeology* 36/1 [1983], pp. 12-19 [16, 18]) suggests that the finds of such bowls represent imported vessels; and Tawilan, with parallels from other Edomite sites (S. Hart, 'The Pottery', in C.-M. Bennett and P. Bienkowski [eds.], *Excavations at Tawilan in Southern Jordan* [British Academy Monographs in Archaeology, 8; Oxford: Oxford University Press, 1995], pp. 53-68, Figs. 6.1–39 [57, Fig. 6.3:1-12]). By contrast, few clear examples of imitation palace ware (and no imports, cf. G.A. London, H. Plint and J. Smith, 'Preliminary Petrographic Analysis of Pottery from Tell el-'Umeiri and Hinterland Sites, 1987', in L.G. Herr *et al.* [eds.], *Madaba Plains Project*. II. *The 1987 Season at Tell el-'Umeiri and Vicinity and Subsequent Studies* [Berrien Springs, MI: Andrews University Press, 1991], pp. 429-39 [437] concerning black burnished wares) were present in the assemblages from Tall al-'Umayri (L.G. Herr, 'The Pottery Finds', in L.T. Geraty *et al.* [eds.], *Madaba Plains Project*. I. *The 1984 Season at Tell el-'Umeiri and Vicinity and Subsequent Studies* [Berrien Springs, MI: Andrews University Press, 1989], pp. 299-354 [308, Fig. 19.16.7]), at least in the Iron II–Persian horizon. Examples from Nimrud (J. Lines, 'Late Assyrian Pottery from Nimrud', *Iraq* 16 [1954], pp. 164-67, Pls. XXXVII–XXXIX [165-66]) are described as 'greenish-buff' in colour.

40. L. Jakob-Rost, *Das Vorderasiatische Museum* (Berlin: Staatliche Museen zu Berlin, 1992), Pl. 124.

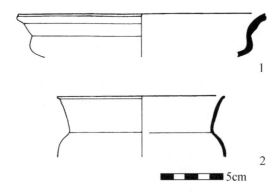

Figure 5. *Carinated bowls in imitation of Assyrian palace ware forms:*
(1) V869, (2) V870

Also significant is the occurrence of a new form of small container, the carrot-shaped bottle, present in the Stratum VII domestic quarter (Building 900) in Field C-East and in B700. This bottle is very common in Transjordan[42] during the late Iron Age II period (seventh century before 630 BCE), and the same vessel type is identified at Tel Batash in Stratum II[43] as an 'Assyrian painted bottle'. Whether this identification can be sustained is uncertain, although this form appears in numerous exemplars in tombs of the late Iron II, especially in the area of 'Amman.[44]

41. Assyrian palace ware beakers (Oates, 'Late Assyrian Pottery', Pl. XXXVII. 60-62, 64-67) from Fort Shalmaneser have finger depressions in the lower body, below the neck. One such beaker appeared at Megiddo in Stratum III (Lamon and Shipton, *Megiddo. I. Seasons of 1925–1934, Strata I–IV*, Pl. 9.12). Locally made bowls from Tawilan have the same type of finger depressions (Hart, 'The Pottery', p. 54), suggesting that the fine Assyrian palace wares were widely imitated.

42. Dornemann (*The Archaeology of the Transjordan*, p. 178) sees a stronger connection of this vessel form to Syrian sites than to sites in western Palestine, where it occurs rarely.

43. G.L. Kelm and A. Mazar, *Timnah: A Biblical City in the Sorek Valley* (Winona Lake, IN: Eisenbrauns, 1995), Fig. 8.24.

44. Dornemann, *The Archaeology of the Transjordan*, Fig. 39.1-38. For other examples from Palestine, see Bethel (W.F. Albright and J.L. Kelso, *The Excavation of Bethel [1934–1960]* [AASOR, 39; Cambridge, MA: American Schools of Oriental Research, 1968], Pl. 79.4) and Tell el-Far'ah (N) (Chambon, *Tell el-Far'ah I*, Pl. 61.13), although this example has red paint rather than black bands.

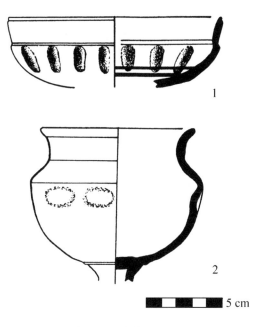

Figure 6. *Carinated bowl with finger depressions (1) V215;*
chalice with finger depressions, (2) V870

Ceramic Fabric

The vessel types discussed so far were all manufactured from clays in common use at Tall Jawa throughout Stratum VIII. More interesting is the introduction of a group of new ceramic fabrics that were used with some of the traditional forms and, at the same time, were reserved for new forms present only in Stratum VII.[45] The distinguishing element in these fabrics is the reduction of inclusions, primarily of limestone, basalt and recycled ceramic material, which was evident in Stratum VIII wares. Smooth creamy wares for small vessels appear to have been levigated, removing natural inclusions and reducing the amount and type of organic temper added for strength and flexibility.[46] For storejars and jugs, potters

45. Dornemann (*The Archaeology of the Transjordan*, p. 179) saw 'a complete overlap' in both forms and fabrics used for red-slipped, black-slipped and creamy wares. This was not the case at Tall Jawa, where the new fabrics of Stratum VII were used for a limited number of traditional Stratum VIII forms and for almost all of the new vessel types.

46. In his definition of 'levigation', Franken (D. Homès-Fredericq and H.J. Franken, *Pottery and Potters—Past and Present: 7,000 Years of Ceramic Art in*

used both the levigated clays and a thin grainy ware that has larger inclusions, but is different in composition and in chemistry from the Stratum VIII fabrics.

These new fabrics went along with the use of a fast wheel,[47] evident in the sharp rills on the interior surfaces of the closed vessels and, most likely, of a higher firing temperature. The fast wheel would necessitate a change in clay fabric to preserve the potter's hands from injury caused by large inclusions. A higher firing temperature is apparent in the fully oxidized cores and hard finish of the cream ware vessels. Five vessel types were present in this ware: (1) very thin walled carinated bowls with grooved rims (A93.60.2; A93.121.1), (2) everted, square rim bowls (see below), (3) oblong or cylindrical juglets, (4) small amphorae and (5) cylindrical jars. Here we will discuss only the most representative types.

Oblong/Cylindrical Juglets
Four almost complete examples of oblong or cylindrical juglets (V702, 703, 861, 860, Fig. 7.1-7.4)[48] from B700 and B800 were all made of the same pink (7.5YR 8/3) clay with few inclusions. The clay had certainly been levigated, and the exterior surfaces were in the same colour range of pink to very pale brown (10YR 7/3); the surfaces were smoothed or burnished at the leather hard stage, although no distinct burnishing

Jordan [Ausstellungskataloge der Universität Tübingen, 20; Tübingen: ATTEMPO Verlag, 1986], p. 26) limits the use of levigated clay to the fine wares of Petra in the late Hellenistic–early Roman period. However, analysis of Assyrian palace wares from Nimrud describes the clay as either naturally washed or 'artificially levigated'. This 'drab' clay, used in fine wares, was high in alumina inclusions and fired a light colour with pink colouration where heat was less intense. P.S. Rawson, 'palace wares from Nimrud: Technical Observations on Selected Examples', *Iraq* 16 (1954), pp. 168-72, Pls. XL–XLII (170).

47. Dornemann, *The Archaeology of the Transjordan*, p. 49. He also (p. 48) notes that there has been 'little attention…to the technical aspects' of late Iron Age II pottery from Transjordan. For a study of forming methods for Iron Age II pithoi from Tall Jawa, see P.M.M. Daviau, 'Iron Age II Pithoi from Tall Jawa, Jordan: Construction Techniques and Typology', in *Studies in the History and Archaeology of Jordan V* (Amman: Department of Antiquities, 1995), pp. 607-16.

48. Vessel 702 = V602; V703 = V603 (n. 8, above; Daviau, 'Technological Change', Fig. 5); V861 = TJ A83.42.1; V860 = TJ C27.179.1). A fifth example (V862 = A93.81.1) could not be completely mended. Sherds of this same juglet type also appear in B905.

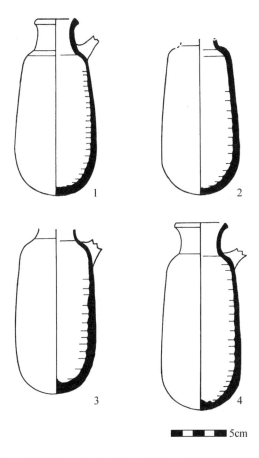

Figure 7. *Oblong juglets from B700 and B800: (1) V703,
(2) V702, (3) V860, (4) V861*

marks were evident. The juglets have an everted profile rim and a single
loop handle rising slightly above the rim.[49] While this form does not

49. Parallels to the oblong juglets appear at Hazor (Y. Yadin, *Hazor. II. An
Account of the Second Season of Excavations, 1956* [Jerusalem: Magnes Press/
Hebrew University, 1960], Pl. LVIII.5-7) = Stratum VIII = ninth century BCE, in
various clay fabrics; the form continued into Stratum VI = eighth century (Pl. LXX.2,
3, 5, 6) in pink to yellow clay (item 6 is levigated clay!); at Beth Shan (F.W. James,
The Iron Age at Beth Shan: A Study of Levels VI–IV [Museum Monographs; Philadelphia: University Museum, University of Pennsylvania, 1966], Figs. 10.13; 45.6);
at 'Amman in the Tomb of Adoni Nur (Dornemann, *The Archaeology of the Transjordan*, Fig. 38.9; in Tomb A, Fig. 38.10; and in sherds from the Citadel Sounding,
Fig. 60.737); at Maqabalain (Dornemann, *The Archaeology of the Transjordan*,

appear at Nimrud, Oates's description of one of the palace ware fabrics types is significant: 'the core becomes salmon to brick red in colour, and the surface becomes a pinkish-buff, in some cases so pale as to be almost white'.[50] Without chemical analysis we cannot know whether these oblong juglets were imported or locally made. Because of the number of vessels of this same fabric at Tall Jawa, local production seems more likely.

Other vessels that appear in the same ware consist of a small amphora (V701, Fig. 8.1)[51] with fabric in the range of light red (2.5YR 7/6) to reddish yellow (5YR 7/6), with the interior surface fired to the same colour as the fabric (5YR 7/6). By contrast, the highly polished exterior surface fired a very pale brown (10YR 8/2), with areas that were pink (5YR 7/4). Painted bands on the body are worn but were originally very dark gray (10YR 3/1) to dark grayish brown (10YR 4/2). A second vessel is unique in shape; it is a cylindrical jar (V901, Fig. 8.2)[52] with handles.[53] Its fabric (7.5YR 8/3) and interior surface (7.5YR 8/4) are pink in colour, while its exterior surface is a very pale brown (10YR 8/2),[54] with areas that were pale red (2.5YR 7/4). Very dark gray bands of paint decorated this jar.[55]

Jugs formed of levigated clay or of grainy wares with large inclusions are common in Stratum VII, whereas they occur in only rare examples in Stratum VIII. The typical shape is that of a globular vessel with a wide neck and rim. Great experimentation in clays is evident in the range of wares and the various colours that result from firing: pale pink, bright orange (2.5RY 6/6, light red), and gray–green (V837; 2.5Y 6/2, light brownish gray).

Fig. 38.7, 8), at Tall Dayr 'Alla (Homès-Fredericq and Franken, *Pottery and Potters*, Fig. 479), and at Tell Mazar (Yassine, 'Tell el-Mazar', Pl. XI.5).

50. Oates, 'Late Assyrian Pottery', p. 131.

51. Vessel 701 = TJ D21.20.14 from B700.

52. Vessel 901 = TJ C43.1.6 from B900.

53. Only one handle is preserved, but there is no reason to suppose that there was not a matching handle on the other side.

54. Oates ('Late Assyrian Pottery', p. 131) points out that the palace ware vessels from Nimrud were not slipped. The surface colouring and appearance was the result of wet smoothing before firing and the firing process itself.

55. A similar vessel type, without handles but with the same grooves near the base, was reported from Maqabalain (Dornemann, *The Archaeology of the Trans-jordan*, Fig. 40.7, 8).

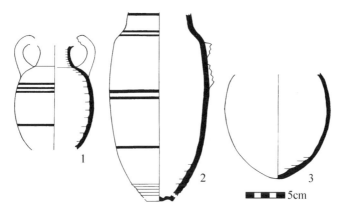

Figure 8. *Creamy-ware amphoriskos (1) V701: cylindrical jar, (2) V901; green ware goblet, (3) V852*

Unique Fabric Types

Three vessels, each with a unique fabric, appear at Tall Jawa.[56] Vessel V852 (Fig. 8.3) is the body of a small jug/goblet with a distinctive light greenish gray (Gley-10Y 7/1) ware that was levigated, showing no interior core and no slip or decoration on its exterior surface.[57] Jug V851 is a cylindrical vessel with a light red (2.5YR 7/6) fabric that feels like sand.[58] On the exterior, it was covered with a thin tan or very pale brown (10YR 8/3) slip, while on the interior, the surface had flaked away almost completely, leaving a very rough surface. The last vessel in this group (V850) is a large decanter with a hard, gray (5YR 5/1) fabric and a dark red (10R 4/6, red) slip that was ring burnished on the shoulder. The slip did not adhere properly to the fabric and tends to come off in water. This is extremely rare, as a slip is usually fired onto the vessel.

Black Burnished Bowls

A special case is black burnished pottery, which appears predominantly in Ammonite sites.[59] This ware contains small amounts of fine grain in-

56. The wares of these vessels are not represented at sites under excavation by the Madaba Plains Project (Herr, personal communication, 25 January 1996) or at sites surveyed in central Moab (Routledge, personal communication, 25 January 1996).

57. While the description of this vessel is reminiscent of Assyrian palace ware beakers (Oates, 'Late Assyrian Pottery', Pl. XXXVII.61, 64, 68), only chemical analysis could determine the origin of the Tall Jawa jug (V 852).

58. It is possible that this vessel was slightly overfired; however, the fabric is almost devoid of temper and thus remains unique in composition, colour and texture.

59. Dornemann (*The Archaeology of the Transjordan*, p. 49) notes, without

clusions and has a dearth of voids within the fabric, which indicates a lack of organic material.[60] At Tall Jawa the ware is found in fine wares in the forms of bowls (Fig. 9.1, 2) and small juglets.[61]

Bowls with Everted Square Rims

Four examples of bowls, each with an everted square rim, were present in the assemblages from B800, while three more such bowls come from Building 905. These bowls are very regular in size, all with a diameter of approximately 25 cm. Three bowls were of black burnished ware, while one bowl was red slipped on the rim and exterior surface and burnished all over (C17.21.1). Three unslipped bowls were yellowish red on their exterior surfaces. The interiors received various treatments, smudging or irregular burnishing with a (manganese?) burnishing tool. No examples of this bowl were recovered from Field E in Stratum VIII, although one bowl from Fields A–B has this rim style. In this case, the bowl was covered with a yellowish red slip (5YR 5/6) and burnished.

Bowls with a Bar Below the Rim

Inverted rim bowls with a bar or thickening below the rim is distinct from bar-handle bowls, which also appear in the Tall Jawa corpus. In the case of the bowls chosen for this study, no evidence for the bulb at the end of the bar has been found. It appears that the bar totally encircles the bowl immediately below the rim. The rim diameter ranges in size from 17–23 cm, and the bowl stands about 9–13 cm high. From B800, six examples of this bowl form occur in black burnished ware (e.g. V893, Fig. 9.3; and V816), while two other examples were red slipped, one on the inside (C27.78.5) and the other on the outside (C27.26.1); both were

specific references, that both cream wares and black burnished wares appear at the same time in the Amuq. Such similarities may suggest the arrival of potters with the same traditions in widely separated regions of the Assyrian empire. To date, there is no textual evidence that would suggest their presence in Ammon or in contemporary towns of southern Syria.

60. For a petrographic analysis of black burnished wares from Tall al-'Umayri, see London *et al.*, 'Preliminary Petrographic Analysis', p. 437; Fig. 23.3. London suggests that two samples may in fact be Assyrian palace ware, but there is at present insufficient evidence for confirmation.

61. Gray bowls that imitate basalt have also been found at Tall Jawa. These vessels do not have the same fabric as black burnished wares (*pace* Dornemann, *The Archaeology of the Transjordan*, p. 49), and these will be considered separately below.

burnished.[62] A second deep-bowl form (V816, Fig. 9.4) appears only in black burnished pottery.

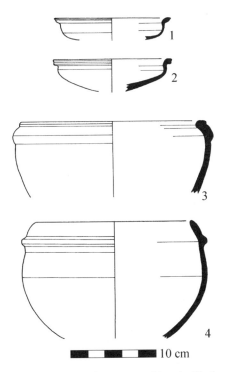

Figure 9. *Black burnished bowls, carinated bowls (1) sherd, (2) V873;*
bar-ribbed bowl, (3) V893; deep bowl, (4) V816

While the large number of black burnished wares at Tall Jawa argues for local production, there is insufficient evidence at present to determine the extent of this tradition. All that we can affirm at this stage in the study of ceramic traditions of Transjordan is that black burnished pottery is one of the new fabric types that appears in late Iron Age II.[63]

62. One sherd (TJC17.31.4), which originated in a locus not under study here, was a very delicate example of this same vessel and rim form. The ware is reddish yellow (5YR 6/6), unslipped and unburnished.

63. Only two mendable sherds belonging to a small black burnished-ware bowl (MT A17:4/18.1) were recovered at Khirbat al-Mudayna on the Wadi ath-Thamad in the upper debris layers of Temple 149 (MT pottery registration). This ware is extremely rare, 0.001 per cent of sherds from four seasons of excavation (1996–99) and one brief surface survey in 1995.

Wedge-incised Bowls/Graters

Among utilitarian wares such as mortar bowls or graters,[64] there is also a new type that appears at Tall Jawa in Stratum VII. This type has thick walls that are stepped on the exterior in the form of a shallow basalt mortar bowl.[65] In both of the Tall Jawa examples (V828, V845, Fig. 10.1, 2), there is a thick ring base.[66] The clay is levigated, comparable to that used in the oblong juglets. The core is almost completely oxidized with a pinkish-gray (7.5YR 7/2-7/3) colour. On the outside there is a dark gray (1 Gley N 4/) slip, with a brown slip (10R 4.2, weak red) on the interior.[67] The slip and interior surface of V845 was very worn,[68] while its twin (V828) had relatively well-preserved wedge- or cuneiform-shaped depressions impressed in the centre. Although there were only two such bowls recovered at Tall Jawa, the clay fabric suggests that the graters themselves[69] were not imports, although the incised wedges were produced with a tool that resembled a stylus used for writing cuneiform script. Their position in the archaeological record is very secure, making it clear that they date to late Iron Age II.[70]

64. G.A. London, 'Reply to A. Zertal's "The Wedge-shaped Decorated Bowl and the Origin of the Samaritans"', *BASOR* 286 (1992), pp. 89-92 (90).

65. Shallow ceramic mortar bowls with tripod feet (e.g. V827) were in use in Stratum VIII and continued in Stratum VII. The wedge-incised graters are slightly more shallow; none have feet.

66. Vessel 845 retains a vestige of the double-disk base that was common on inverted-rim bowls in Stratum VIII. While this base continues to appear throughout Stratum VII on certain bowl forms, a greater variety of base forms makes its appearance: simple flat bases, disk bases and ring bases.

67. It is not certain that the colour was intended as an imitation of basalt commonly used to produce mortar bowls (TJ 35+1741), since these were simultaneously in use at Tall Jawa with ceramic tripod mortars (V827).

68. Only the lower part of several wedge-shaped depressions are visible, making it impossible to determine the pattern of incisions.

69. A. Zertal ('The Wedge-shaped Decorated Bowl and the Origin of the Samaritans', *BASOR* 276 [1989], pp. 77-84 [82]) suggests that it is only the decoration that originated in Mesopotamia, although he does not make it clear that the bowls themselves were locally produced.

70. *Pace* U.F.Ch. Worschech, 'Rectangular Profiled Rims from el-Bālūʿ: Indicators of Moabite Occupation?', in L.E. Stager, J.A. Greene and M.D. Coogan (eds.), *The Archaeology of Jordan and Beyond: Essays in Honor of James A. Sauer* (Harvard Semitic Museum Publications; Studies in the Archaeology and History of the Levant, 1; Winona Lake, IN: Eisenbrauns, 2000), pp. 520-24 (532), who dates a sherd of one such vessel found at al-Baluʿ to the late Persian period, without

In a recent discussion of deep bowls with the same wedge incisions, Zertal has suggested that this decoration originated in Mesopotamia and came to the hill country of central Palestine[71] with deportees from Babylonia. In Palestine, the bowls were a common local form made of a 'metallic' ware; the bowls had a dark gray core and were fired orange on their exterior surface. It was clear that the wedges had been incised before firing.[72] For Zertal, these bowls are evidence of the presence of a new people in the central hill country. However, this does not explain the presence of the shallow, mortar-style bowls found at Tall Jawa, or a sherd (TJ-C71.15.9) with wedges from a bowl similar in shape to those from Tell el-Far'ah(N). While there is as yet insufficient evidence for Zertal's interpretation of cultural change at Transjordanian sites, the introduction of these graters certainly reflects a change in food processing techniques or diet, which was probably part of the technological and cultural changes resulting from increased Assyrian influence in the region.[73]

Special Artifacts
In the case of high-status or distinctive artifacts appearing at Tall Jawa, trade can account for their distribution throughout Transjordan. At the

providing any stratigraphic evidence for this allocation.

71. Zertal ('The Wedge-shaped Decorated Bowl', p. 81, Fig. 3) locates the majority of bowls with wedge decoration in the region between Shechem and Taanach.

72. Chambon, *Tell el-Far'ah I*, Pl. 56.21, 22, description.

73. Sherds from similar bowls appear also at Tall al-'Umayri (R.D. Low, 'Field F: The Eastern Shelf', in L.G. Herr *et al.* [eds.], *Madaba Plains Project. II. The 1987 Season at Tell el-'Umeiri and Vicinity and Subsequent Studies* [Berrien Springs, MI: Andrews University Press, 1991], pp. 170-231 [Fig. 8.22.22, 23]), a site 5 km northwest of Tall Jawa, at Balu' in Moab (U.F.Ch. Worschech, 'Eine keilalphabetische Inschrift von el-Bālū'?', *UF* 23 (1991), pp. 395-99; *idem*, 'Rectangular Profiled Rims') and at Tell es-Sa'idiyeh (J.B. Pritchard, *Tell es-Sa'idiyeh: Excavations on the Tell, 1964–1966* [University Museum Monograph, 60; Philadelphia: University Museum, University of Pennsylvania, 1985], Fig. 16.14) in the Jordan Valley. At Tall al-'Umayri the wedge-incised bowls are assigned to Field F Phase 3 (Low, 'Field F', Fig. 8.22.22-23), the early Persian period, along with three mortar bowls (Fig. 8.22.3-5) without wedges, which had grooved rims similar to the tripod mortar bowls from Tall Jawa. It would not be unexpected to see such forms continuing into the Persian period, especially at a site where occupation was not interrupted.

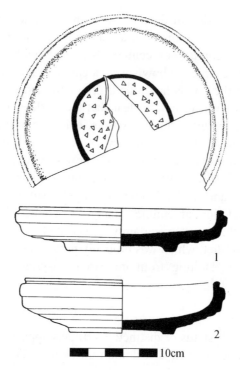

Figure 10. *Wedge-decorated bowls: (1) V828, (2) V845*

same time, the introduction of these objects as valuable items certainly reflects changes in taste and availability. One such find is a *Tridacna* shell (TJ A83.34.1471), present in the second-storey collapse of Room 807 in Building 800. Comparable shells, such as the decorated *Tridacna squamosa* shell from Busayra in Edom, appear to be characteristic of the Neo-Assyrian period, especially during the seventh century BCE.[74] Of course, such trade was not a new phenomenon in Jordan. Already in Stratum VIII at Tall Jawa there was a silver earring (TJ E53.21.1755), which has parallels among the earrings in the gold hoard from Tawilan in Edom[75] and in the jewellery from the Nimrud tombs of the queens,[76] although details from this great find are still lacking.

74. Bennett, 'Neo-Assyrian Influence', p. 187; Fig. 3a.

75. J. Ogden, 'The Gold Jewellery', in C.-M. Bennett and P. Bienkowski, *Excavations at Tawilan in Southern Jordan* (BAMA, 8; Oxford: Oxford University Press, 1995), pp. 69-78 (Fig. 8.17).

76. Ogden, 'The Gold Jewellery', p. 72.

Utilitarian ceramic basins having a triangular shape and rounded corners also appear in Stratum VII assemblages. One which can be partially reconstructed (V831) is a large container, with thick (3.0–6.0 cm) vertical walls and a flat bottom. This basin has a thickened rim and handles, the only characteristic to distinguish it from Assyrian style coffins, which are usually without handles.[77] While the exact function of these basins is still under discussion,[78] they could have been multifunctional, serving both an industrial and a domestic function, as at Megiddo.[79] That they were reused as coffins appears to be directly related to Assyrian presence in Israel, at such sites as Tel Jezreel,[80] where a basin contained a skeleton. Their occurrence in the late Iron Age at sites in ancient Israel is consonant with the date of Building 800 at Tall Jawa.

Conclusions

Technological change during the late Iron Age II is most clearly seen in the introduction of new ceramic wares, a fast wheel and higher firing temperatures. These techniques produced a great variety of new vessel forms, ranging from fine wares to food-processing utensils. As at Busayra,[81] imported ceramic items from Assyria proper cannot be identified with certainty. Nevertheless, the changes in the ceramic corpus point to changes in diet, and possibly to the introduction of new food stuffs through expanded trade networks. Such trade may also explain the presence of a number of unique ceramic vessels without parallel at neighbouring sites. Increased trade also accounts for the presence of high-status artifacts such as the *Tridacna* and the silver earring. Such items at the outlying site of Tall Jawa clearly show that it was within a network of towns sharing the benefits of Assyrian influence.

77. J.P. Free, 'The Sixth Season at Dothan', *BASOR* 156 (1959), pp. 22-29 (Fig. 3).

78. J.R. Zorn, 'Mesopotamian-Style Ceramic "Bathtub" Coffins from Tell en-Naṣbeh', *TA* 20 (1993), pp. 216-24.

79. Lamon and Shipton, *Megiddo*. I. *Seasons of 1925–1934, Strata I–IV*, p. 63; Fig. 74; Pl. 18.91; G. Loud, *Megiddo*. II. *Seasons of 1935–1939* (Oriental Institute Publications, 62; Chicago: University of Chicago Press, 1948), Pl. 256.6.

80. D. Ussishkin and J. Woodhead, 'Excavations at Tel Jezreel, 1994–1996: Third Preliminary Report', *TA* 24 (1997), pp. 6-72 (Figs. 32-33).

81. Bennett, 'Neo-Assyrian Influence', p. 187.

This same influence may have had an impact on social and political structures in Ammon. Evidence of change in fortification strategies, such as the remodelling of the chambered gate and the casemate wall, suggest a new political order that reduced the risk of enemy attack. Whether this order involved direct administration of the region by a local governor who inhabited the larger (B800) of the two central-hall-style buildings remains unclear. It appears that Tall Jawa was abandoned at the end of Stratum VII and not resettled during the Persian period, although its neighbour, Tall al-'Umayri, served as a Persian administrative centre.[82] What we can affirm about Tall Jawa is that a significant amount of manpower and expertise was expended in the construction of the impressive central-hall buildings, the gate and the solid terrace wall. Such changes represent the influence of an ever-expanding Assyrian empire on a small town in the Ammonite hinterland.

82. L.G. Herr, 'Wine Production in the Hills of Southern Ammon and the Founding of Tall al-'Umayri in the Sixth Century BC', *ADAJ* 39 (1995), pp. 121-25 (124).

THE INTELLECTUAL, THE ARCHAEOLOGIST AND THE BIBLE*

Philip R. Davies

Biblical Archaeology as an Incompetent Reading of the Bible

The title of this paper is not meant to imply that biblical archaeologists are not intellectuals. It does, however, suggest that biblical archaeology quite specifically implies one rather narrow approach to biblical interpretation: the view of the Bible as a description of a real past world. Not merely the reflection or product of an ancient real world, which biblical literature clearly must be—however indirectly—but a generally reliable portrait of a past reality that can now be reconstructed with the help of the spade, the trowel and the bulldozer, or with the surface survey or indeed with the tools of social anthropology. This 'search for ancient Israel' on which I have already written,[1] dominates discourse about the Bible in the media and remains very influential even within the discipline of biblical studies. The Hebrew Bible/Old Testament is still widely understood as essentially a historical record, and history is still widely seen as the proper perspective from which to understand it. This perspective not only rules out much of the Bible's literature that is not historically focused, creating a 'canon within a canon', but also, as I shall argue in this essay, largely misunderstands even the biblical literature that does seem devoted to history.

I am particularly happy to dedicate this essay to Max Miller, whose competence in archaeology and biblical criticism and whose experience as a historian of ancient Israel and Judah have endowed him with a breadth of perspective on the issue at hand. Even more importantly, he

* The substance of this essay was delivered as a lecture in November 2000 at a 'Bible and Archaeology Fest' sponsored by the Biblical Archaeology Society in Nashville, TN.

1. P.R. Davies, *In Search of 'Ancient Israel'* (JSOTSup, 148; Sheffield: Sheffield Academic Press, 2nd edn, 1995).

is a man whose open-mindedness, generosity and loyalty to friends, colleagues and students are widely known and acknowledged. However much he will find to disagree with in this essay, I know that he will at least understand and appreciate its arguments and implications, and I can think of no more appropriate context for my assault on biblical archaeology than in a volume in his honour.

The idea that history is the natural 'meaning' of the Bible, that is the external reality to which it refers, and the canon by which its 'truth' can be 'attacked' and 'defended', is a fairly modern one. It is certainly not the mode of exegesis dominant in the rabbinic literature, since on the whole the rabbis were *not* much interested in their scriptures as history. When faced with arguments about chronology, they were likely to respond, 'There is no before or after in the Bible.'[2] There was little place for contingent history in a theology of eternal Torah. History was Haggadah: it taught moral principles, not facts, and to understand the Bible required not credulity but intellectual effort, perpetual study, questioning and the elaboration of rules of exegesis to determine the will of God for human behaviour. In a word, the rabbis cultivated intellectual agility in the service of Jewish piety.

The early Christian fathers likewise preferred to see allegory rather than history in the Old Testament, because allegory was a productive means of Christianizing the Jewish scriptures. Insofar as it was history, that history was a mere 'preparation for the gospel' (cf. Gal. 3.23-26). The Old Testament scriptures were not read for their historical reliability but for their confirmation of the truth of the gospel.

Of course, rabbinic and patristic exegesis was determined by theological agendas: the history of Israel, it might be said, was a victim of theology. Still, any mode of biblical exegesis is dictated by some theological (or ideological, if you prefer) framework. Why is it that nowadays we do not follow the rabbis in an intellectual engagement with the ideas of the Bible?[3] Why do we instead treat the Bible as a record of history, textbook of (Christian) theology or a collection of wonderful *stories*. Should it be reduced to an anthology of proof-texts, a code of regulations for daily life or perhaps a component of the

---

2.   The quotation may be found, *inter alia*, in Genesis Rabbah 22.1-7.

3.   Study of the Bible, as is well known, is minimal in the Yeshiva, where the Talmud fulfils something of the same function as the New Testament in Christian seminaries: dictating the mode of exegesis and obscuring direct vision of the biblical text.

world's great literature? All these reductions (and every interpretative method is a reduction) imply a certain *appropriation* of the scriptures, and each appropriation is inevitably driven by ideological interests. Naturally, each of these interests will regard its own way of reading the Bible as the *natural* one, and none more so than the 'historical' reading.

I am not so naive as to call for a non-reductionist way of reading the Bible, but I am concerned with *competent* readings. And a reading that takes biblical descriptions of Israel as historical portraits, as sketches of a society that can be historically retrieved by archaeology, is incompetent, because it is not based on a detailed and critical reading of the literature, preferring the naive assumption that biblical 'historiography' is intended to describe Israel as it really was. The hold that archaeology has over our understanding of the Bible is unjustified, harmful and leads to a monumental distortion of the intellectual agenda of the writers of the biblical literature. The Bible is not devoid of historical information, but it is not history. Its writing about history is a vehicle for ideas, and the ideas need to be recognized in order for the various 'Israels' of the Bible to be comprehended.

The Archaeologist and the Intellectual

What I mean by distinguishing between 'intellectuals' and 'archaeologists' in my title is this: artifacts are the typical domain of the archaeologist, and 'ideas' the typical domain of the intellectual.[4] Ideas and materials have a long history of warfare. In our Western philosophical tradition there has always been a distinction between 'idealism' and 'materialism': the first asserting the primary reality of idea (as in Plato), the other the primary reality of matter (as in Epicurus). Now, these two approaches also afford different ways of looking at the Bible. One focuses on its relationship to the authentic ancient world, emphasizing its rootedness in a past culture; the other focuses on its ideas, regardless of when, where and by whom they were expressed. For 1500 years, it was an idealist approach that dominated our understanding of the Bible, both in Judaism and Christianity. The Bible was the word of God, put

4. I am aware of the argument that archaeology can retrieve ideas, e.g. about afterlife. But all such inferences are always drawn from material data. Inscriptions are not a special case: the deciphering and interpretation of inscriptions is not, unlike their recovery, an archaeological procedure, but an epigraphic, linguistic and historical one.

into words and writing by inspired persons. The historicity, authorship and chronology of the Bible were not important, and the historical origins of the Bible were in any case largely irretrievable.

It is the materialist approach that has subsequently set the pace, and it was born of several parents: one was the pre-eminence of literalistic readings that developed more or less after the Reformation. One of the results of this development was that statements in the Bible about historical events were taken to be primarily just that: historical reports about events. The plain sense of the Bible was primary. Accordingly, since the inspiration and authority of the Bible were unquestioned, its statements about the past assumed the mantle of inerrancy. The Bible's historical statements were inspired in being correct. If they were not correct, how could they be inspired and authoritative?

Another parent of the materialist trend was the birth of historical science, an awareness of a retrievable past that could be scientifically recovered and described, different from the simple recording of stories that were handed down or the plagiarizing of earlier authors. Enlightenment history aimed to recover the past 'as it really was', separating fact from story, tradition and memory. And in this task historical science was quickly aided by archaeology, which demonstrated the presence of the past in a material form. The past lay beneath our own feet. Biblical archaeology replaced holy relics with genuine artifacts, taken directly from their original location, and holy stories were replaced by scholarly reconstructions of these data, sometimes, it must be said, not much different and no less fanciful. But archaeology represented science and scientific knowledge and still does. Only archaeologists themselves usually appreciate how provisional and subjective its interpretation often is. A few even admit it publicly.[5]

Another political and social impetus to the archaeological enterprise has been Zionism, because archaeology could demonstrate a historical link of the Jewish people to the land of Israel. Since this link does not require religious belief, secular Jews can use it as well. The Bible, taken as history, is testimony that Israel was born in the land it now occupies, and to a people whose historical existence was threatened with extinction in Nazi Europe, this demonstration was not merely comforting, but reclaimed a land and a history from the threat of annihilation. Clearly, Zionism has been a powerful force and fundamental to most Jews, but

5. See, e.g., J.M. Miller, *The Old Testament and the Historian* (GBSOT; Philadelphia: Fortress Press, 1976), pp. 40-48.

its effects on the practice of archaeology have not always been helpful. Fifteen hundred years of non-Jewish occupation of Palestine have been subordinated to a thousand years of Israel and Judah, because Palestinian archaeology is still very largely biblical archaeology. Despite the contributions of Israeli archaeologists to non-Jewish periods of Palestinian habitation, Israeli archaeology has been overwhelmingly concerned with the Iron Age.[6]

At the beginning of the twentieth century biblical scholarship on the whole balanced the idealist and the materialist. The emphasis on materialist readings culminated in the mid-twentieth century in the 'biblical theology' movement of the Albright school, which replaced ideas by events in its theological system. But subsequently the pendulum has swung back in a revival of so-called 'literary criticism', which began with a strong anti-historicist bias and remains on the whole uninterested in who wrote the literature, or when and why. But this literary criticism seems to me largely to have focused on the poetic, rhetorical and aesthetic aspects of the literature and often fails to engage the ideational and intellectual content—as if such engagement would tread on the toes of theology. In its anti-historicist bias it has placed the Bible in the category of 'fiction', which is where 'literature' belongs. In doing so, the emphasis is placed on technique, not substance, and where substance is confronted, the issues are rarely framed in terms of a philosophical agenda on the part of the authors.

Where the *ideas* of the Bible are addressed is in the area of biblical theology. But what passes for theology in biblical studies is generally inferior, since biblical theology is still largely (and perhaps even essentially) a Christian enterprise, yet the ideas of the Hebrew Bible are not conceived as Christian ones. The overlay of Jewish and Christian canonizing makes it difficult for us to separate what the Bible says from what it has been understood or made to say by those for whom it is scripture. This leaves a gap: where will the modern agnostic intellectual find an exegetical agenda? And where will the voice of the ancient author escape the muzzle of canonicity?

---

6.   Allowance must be made, of course, for the interest in the 'New Testament' period, though such archaeology also serves to underline the 'Jewishness' of that era and thus of the origins of Christianity. Might one suggest that the Bronze Age is relatively well preserved, perhaps because it was not necessary to destroy or remove such strata in order to expose the Iron Age remains?

It is just such an intellectual agenda that I want to contrast with the agenda of biblical archaeology. If we are able to identify and strip away from the ancient writings (to the extent possible) the overlay of centuries of Jewish and Christian interpretation, we can still see some remarkable ideas. And if we eschew the idea that these came revealed verbatim from heaven, the alternative is that the ideas are of human intellectual construction.

The Bible is *intellectually* both ambitious and compelling. It makes its way towards the idea of one male god, who is also the embodiment of justice and virtue, who made the world and chose one people from the world population. This philosophical framework (you may indeed call it theological if you wish—and then you can call Plato a theologian as well) is not based on revelation, but on human reason, and so I would happily call it philosophy. It is not a revealed framework, and it does not appear fully fledged or completely articulated. There are traces in the Bible of differing viewpoints, and we can see very clearly that the ancient populations of Israel and Judah did not subscribe to this framework, though as all nations they might have thought their own ethnic or national or city god—if they had one—was best. The Bible itself makes it perfectly clear that Israel and Judah did *not* adhere to the religious system it expounds and that this system is *not* descriptive of what was generally practised. Here is a biblical warning, if you like, to biblical archaeologists: you will not find a *biblical* Israel in the bones and stones of the Holy Land! You will find instead a population behaving culturally as 'Canaanites'. What is essential about the 'Israel' of the Bible is its religious ideas, but these ideas do not find expression in history, at least not in the Iron Age. The philosophical or theological ideas of the Bible are rather *expressed in the biblical writing about history*. 'Historiography' (if that is the right term) is a mode of writing about ideas, not of describing facts. To this a critic might reply: why cannot it be both? Is not all ancient history-writing a vehicle for ideology? To which I reply: indeed there is historical information in the Bible's 'historiography', but that hardly means that this genre was developed in order to describe historical reality. We are not talking about history-writing with an ideological agenda. We are talking about an ideological agenda that merely assumes the form of historiography. Such 'historiography' gives no warrant to biblical archaeology to search for historical counterparts.

If not from the history of the Holy Land, then what is the origin of biblical Israel? The direct answer is: from inside people's heads. But we can be more precise: from within a community, an academy in the loose sense, a philosophically inclined community; a small, influential, literate, privileged and largely urban community, comprising what we would now call the intelligentsia of ancient Judah. Its members worked mostly in and around the temple of Jerusalem and had a near-monopoly on reading and writing. (Hence, while the thoughts of the illiterate are not directly preserved for us, those of the literate are.) The literature of the Bible emerged from their thoughts, discussions, arguments, their writing and rewriting. To be sure, their everyday life *affected* what they wrote, but not in such a way that archaeology will ever fundamentally explain. Archaeology can help us understand how the economic system worked; how people lived, died and were buried; their religious artifacts; and their social structures. But it cannot explain them, far less demonstrate these ideas in reality.

So the ideas of the Bible are not the ideas of most ancient Israelites or Judaeans, the village farmers. These people largely worshipped fertility gods, as you would expect farmers to do. They are, it can be argued, culturally indistinguishable from Canaanites. Indeed, the populations of the ancient monarchies of Israel and Judah comprised the farmers in the hill country, whom some archaeologists and historians want to identify as 'Israel', but one should also include areas and populations beyond these villages: lowland farmers, urban residents and 'Canaanites'. One of the brilliant inventions of the writers of the biblical literature was to posit two cultures: that of their own philosophical and monotheistic Yahwism and that of the indigenous culture with its fertility religion. This philosophical difference was expressed in the form of a division between 'Israel' and 'Canaan'. What the populations of Israel and Judah in fact practised was 'Canaanite', and what the philosophers of the Bible were developing was the 'religion of Israel'. The archaeologist will readily find this Canaan, but not this Israel. For in reality, the biblical distinction is not a historical one. Here already we have an idea mistaken for a fact and an archaeological search for a distinction that does not exist. The biblical Israel is an idealization, the vehicle for a philosophical or religious system. More precisely, however, I should speak not of *one* 'biblical Israel' but of several, each of which was the vehicle for ideas.

Demonstration: Some Biblical Israels

The accusation has been made and the case expounded. Now comes the moment for demonstration. I will concentrate the bulk of this on the books of Moses, the Pentateuch, because it is here that the case can most easily be argued and least easily misrepresented (though misrepresentation can confidently be predicted). Within the Pentateuch we find several idealized Israels. Indeed, unlike what is found in the books of Kings, we don't find an 'Israel' and a 'Judah' in the Pentateuch, just an 'Israel'. Just as the category 'Canaanite', the biblical category 'all Israel' (the 12-tribe entity, as distinct from a kingdom based in Samaria of that name) *is an intellectual construction and not an historical fact*. This *idea* has deliberately confused the categories of 'Judaean' and 'Israelite' in such a way that even today we call the religion 'Judaism' and the state 'Israel'.[7]

Now here I must be careful. The religion of Judaism and the community that calls itself 'Israel' are real. The ancient kingdoms of Israel and Judah were also real. The Bible is real. But the Israels described in the books of Moses, in the books of Joshua to Kings and in the books of Chronicles, are *not* real. They do not pretend to be real and were not conceived as realistic portraits. Idealized histories don't reflect reality; they certainly can and do, however, create it.

It is the foundation and structure of this artificial 12-tribe entity with which the books of Moses deal. There is an important tradition in human thought and literature that concerns itself with the ideal nature of society. Writers of this genre usually feel that there is such a thing as an ideal society, and they seek to establish it on logical (sometimes theological) foundations. We may not have read, but we will have heard of, Plato's *Republic*, Augustine's *City of God* and Thomas More's *Utopia*. There is also the satirical tradition found in Jonathan Swift's *Gulliver's Travels* and Samuel Butler's *Erewhon*. George Orwell's *1984* or Aldous Huxley's *Brave New World* represent the modern version of a dystopia, a bleak vision of the future. Hollywood has provided many

---

7.   A lucid and compelling account (though I disagree about the historical context) of the invention of a 12-tribe 'Israel' binding Israel and Judah can now be found in I. Finkelstein and N.A. Silberman, *The Bible Unearthed: Archaeology's New Vision of Ancient Israel and the Origin of its Sacred Texts* (New York: Free Press, 2001).

more, often reflecting the clash between the values of totalitarianism and personal freedom, the system versus the individual, a conflict which, I dare suggest, says a lot about the underlying nature of US society.

But this genre is also part of a Jewish tradition. The best-known example is the Mishnah, which recreates a new Israel from the death of an old one: from the ashes of the temple, cult and priesthood the rabbis created—by intellectual more than political effort—a new Israel, defined by obedience to law, purity in social life, the separation of clean and unclean and the regulation of property and persons in an orderly social and domestic life. In creating this vision, Mishnah also retrojects an Israel into the land of Israel, where tithing was performed, the temple rites were scrupulously enumerated and a Sanhedrin full of Pharisees ruled. On these matters the Mishnah is a mixture of reliable historical memory and sheer invention. The Israel it remembered is a utopia, but one that generates a potentially realistic programme for the present. A new and real Israel is created through a historical fiction.

The Mishnah's idealized Israel, though, is already based on a scriptural tradition, and it is this tradition that must now be unearthed. While modern writers, as I said, tend to set their utopias in the future, the ancient writers of Judah set them in the past. Specifically, in the case of the Pentateuch they used the wilderness. Why? Probably because it was geographically outside their own land, and this gave a certain spatial distance to go with the temporal distance. They also placed the period chronologically in the time of Moses, the great lawgiver and prophet and the traditional founder of the nation. In the wilderness, outside the land and outside the present, there is a place for ideal Israels. Most biblical scholars accept that there was no historical counterpart to this epoch, and most intelligent biblical archaeologists accept this too. So it should not be difficult for me to argue that the wandering Israels are an ideal and not a reality.

No respectable biblical archaeologist today would be looking for evidence that three million people lived thousands of years ago for 40 years in the Sinai *en route* from Egypt to Canaan.[8] Let us look instead at the *intellectual* programme of the literature that describes such a trek, beginning with the narrative framework of the books of Genesis to

8.   This assertion stands apart from the fact that archaeological remains would not necessarily have remained. But see Finkelstein and Silberman, *The Bible Unearthed*, pp. 351-52, on Kadesh-barnea for a refutation of the historicity of Israelite presence there.

Deuteronomy. These books tell the story of the birth of a nation: the idea of a nation is formed by dividing humans into races; a biological ancestor is chosen; his descendants become numerous by their rapid multiplication in Egyptian servitude; this people is chosen by its deity; a constitution is bestowed on the nation in the form of a treaty between their god and his chosen people; and finally, this new nation acquires its own land.

Here, then, we find enumerated all the things any nation needs in order to qualify as a nation: ancestor, constitution and land—and of course, its very own god(s). So the narrative framework of the Pentateuch presents the story of the birth of the nation, an idealized story of an idealized (12-tribe, single-ancestor, ex-Egyptian slaves) nation, of course.

But the narrative is interspersed with large non-narrative blocks of legal and cultic material, typically set in the mouth of God or Moses. The second part of Exodus, nearly all of Leviticus, bits of Numbers and most of Deuteronomy are not narrative at all. Rather, they describe in varying degrees of detail how this nation is to be structured and how it is to live. One way of understanding the books of Moses—and I have no way of discovering the processes of this construction—is to see it as a story interspersed with essays in *how that chosen nation should be constituted*. The narrative and the non-narrative portions, together, answer the question: what is Israel and what should it be? What is the best way to understand the relationship between the one god and his chosen people? How will that election be expressed and reflected in everyday life in a way that is appropriate to the character of its god? These are, I would say, the fundamental questions of Judaism from its birth, whenever we want to place that birth. The nature of the perfect society is also an ancient philosophical problem.

But Leviticus, Numbers and Deuteronomy each offer a distinctly *different* portrait of an ideal Israel. Leviticus constructs not just an Israel but a world, in which God, priests, Israel and the nations symbolize concentric areas of order, holiness and cleanness. Israel is a camp, at the centre of which is the holy tent of the god, attended by priests. Contact with this god requires a state of holiness to which Israel cannot always attain, though this is required for the people to maintain communion with God. So Israelite life is governed by the rites of transition between states of uncleanness, cleanness and holiness. Outside the 'camp' of Israel is defilement, chaos, a realm beyond the possibility of approach to God. This realm is non-Israel and starkly defines the limits of Israel and of God's election.

Israelite society, according to Leviticus, is based on the preservation of the holiness necessary to accommodate the presence of God within society. It is not difficult to draw a profile of the author responsible for a vision in which the priesthood remains closest to God, maintains the contact between God and chosen people, and guards the divine holiness from the people and vice versa. The structure of this society is invisible; that it is invisible and that the priests alone can control it underline the authority and power of the priesthood. The priests not only mediate between God and Israel, but they also ensure the maintenance of cosmic order. Time and space within Israel are all sacred and represent the natural, created order. The author's social world, and indeed his cosmic world, reflect the interests of a priestly caste.

This portrait of Israel is no historical reconstruction of a wilderness people, but a sketch of the true nature of Israel as the priestly author understands it. It reflects a sanctuary-centred view of an agricultural society able to sustain a large number of priests with a large number of sacrificial animals. God owns the land, its people and its produce, and on his behalf the priests order its agricultural economy, including first-fruits, tithing and sabbatical and jubilee years. One might ask about the real historical setting of the author and his work, but not about the real historical setting of his Israel.

A quite different portrait of Israel emerges from Deuteronomy. Here holiness is not at all the issue, and priests have much less prominence. Israel is, rather, a nation bound to its deity by a legal contract. The continued existence of the nation depends on observing the 'small print' as well as the 'big print' of that contract. The 'big print' prescribes keeping away from Canaanites and other foreigners and not worshipping their gods. The 'small print' requires maintaining a just society, one that protects the poor, constrains the powerful and treats slaves and women relatively well. The Israel of Deuteronomy, run by elders and priests, is a society of villages and cities in a territory notionally conquered but still rife with foreigners. There is one sanctuary, somewhere, and although the sanctuary does not dominate as it does in Leviticus, the ceremony of Passover is centralized. In Deuteronomy it is the framework of a legal agreement that keeps Israel and God connected, and the bonds of society are also expressed in the form of laws, laws that sometimes may reflect actual common practice, but also include some utopian measures, such as executing rebellious children and not pursuing fleeing slaves. The king, according to Deuteronomy, rules literally 'by the book' and so is a true constitutional monarch. This too is, of course, utopian.

As with Leviticus, this ideal Israel of Deuteronomy lies not in the wilderness. It implies a land with settled villages and cities and a population in which we have a nation within a nation. It is Deuteronomy that is responsible for inventing the category of 'Canaanite' to designate all those in the land who do not live under the covenant agreement. As with Leviticus, Deuteronomy has a well-defined (though invisible) boundary between Israel and non-Israel: the ethnic distinction between 'Israelite' and 'Canaanite'. Moreover, it is not difficult to conclude that the author of Deuteronomy's Israel was a legal scribe. His inspiration for the idea of religion as legal contract was probably drawn from the political vassal treaties of the Assyrians, but he made a creative leap and invented the notion of Israel's covenant with its god on a similar basis. As with Leviticus's Israel, we can argue about the real social world of the author, but not the real social world of his 'Israel'.

Finally we turn to Numbers. Here we are dealing not with a portrait in exclusively legal or ritual form but one that includes a narrative. The book opens directly with a census of those 'able to go to war', and from that point on the portrait of the nation offered is a military one. Such a portrait suits well the narrative context chosen for it, in which the nation is, as a campaigning army, on the march towards a destination to be conquered, living off the terrain and constantly on the alert for attack. Space is devoted to the disposition of the camp and the order of marching. Even after details of priestly and cultic matters, we arrive at instructions for the priests to blow the trumpets in time of war as well as on cultic occasions, linking the two kinds of activity. The Israelite army marches from Sinai, following its divine leader's cloud. The heart of this army is the central cultic object, the ark, *and its deity*, carried into action with the words, 'Arise, Yahweh, let your enemies be scattered and your foes flee before you', and on its resting, 'Return, Yahweh of the massed armies of Israel.'

The organization of Israel then, according to Numbers, is military. The nation is divided into families and tribes, but these are all reconfigured as military units, and their social groupings provide specified numbers of young men to fight. The spatial arrangement of Israel is also important, for it assumes the form of a military camp: on each of the four sides is a group of three tribes. Towards the close of the book attention moves to the imminent occupation of the land. Its divisions and the disposition for the tribal allotments are given, followed by allotments for the levites, as the geography of the camp is converted in anticipation into the geography of the land. Military men, I suspect, prefer to deal with maps, something they can see and mark.

The attitude of Numbers towards discipline also reflects the military point of view. The rebellion of the people, who wish to go no further in the wilderness, is a constant theme, and the issue of Moses' leadership clearly stands as a motif of the entire book, climaxing in a challenge by Miriam and by Korah, Dathan and Abiram. Such disobedience to the appointed leader is, naturally, harshly punished.

So in the books of Moses we have more than a narrative of the founding of the nation. We have an exercise in social philosophy. Historical description is a transparent vehicle for something more important. What has often misled scholars, however, is that the ancient Judaean philosophers did not use the genre of the treatise, the letter, the dinner conversation, the debate or the novel. They used genres familiar to them—lawcodes, annals, chronicles, legends and myths—though not necessarily for the purposes that these genres traditionally served.

The 'Deuteronomistic History'

Can this demonstration that the Pentateuchal biblical 'Israels' are intellectual constructions be extended to other books? The case of Chronicles would be too easy: there is already a respectable consensus for the view that its 'Israel' and that Israel's history are highly idealized, if not ideal.[9] More crucial, perhaps, is the work extending from Joshua to Kings. The so-called 'Deuteronomistic History' looks at first sight much more like a reliable historical account than do the books of the Pentateuch. But as with the books of Moses, we should begin our analysis with a review of its structure and plot. Narratively, it deals with the story of the relationship between the people (its 'Israel') and the land, from acquisition to loss. Within this we find several intellectual issues running: what is the ideal leadership for the chosen people in its land—military dictator, charismatic leader, dynastic monarch? (All certainly fail, leaving perhaps open the question of whether imperial and/or hierocratic rule is best.) Another issue is the relationship between history, human behaviour and divine decree. As a whole, it is the Israel

---

9. See, for example, the summary by R.W. Klein, 'Chronicles, Book of 1–2', in *ABD* (1992), I, pp. 992-1002 (997-98).

of Deuteronomy that seems to predominate here, with the 'covenant' functioning as the cement bonding deity, people and land; the temple signifies not so much holiness as a defence against idolatry. The history of this 'Israel', a single nation divided into two kingdoms, is a history of adherence to and apostasy from the covenant. It corresponds, on the national scale, to the wisdom theology of retribution.

With this narrative and these philosophical issues in mind, we can now explore the books of Joshua–Kings as literature in which history is a vehicle for philosophy. The intellectual agenda behind Joshua is, among other things, to assert that the land belongs to 'Israel' (the writer's idealized 'Israel', that is) and not to 'Canaan' (those not adhering to the religious–philosophical system represented by the 'covenant'); the divine intention for 'Canaanites' is extermination; and the land is a divine gift, not an acquisition ('Israel' acquires it by virtue not of birth or possession, but divine gift). To understand the point of this, we would have to consider the place of the immigrant elite in Persian Yehud, who considered the 'people of the land' as non-Israel and saw themselves as having been (re-)given the land in return for loyalty to their god.

The debate in Judges is about charismatic leadership and the unity of 'Israel'. The fiction of an Israelite institution of 'judgeship' underlies the narrative sequence of a judge from each tribe acting in a localized fashion. Did such an Israel and such a period ever exist? Several scholars have suggested that this portrait is among the most realistic of all, reflecting a pre-monarchic stage in the evolution of the Israelites. But whatever the source of some of the original tales of the 'judges', national 'judgeship' was never a real institution. Nor was there a time when a distinct grouping of 12 'tribes' felt reciprocal obligations to each other. The formal structuring of the 'major judges' and the structural programme of cyclical oppression and deliverance are not the basis for any serious historical reconstruction. At best we can argue over whether some of the material has been quarried from folktales. An affirmative answer in any case would not make the Israel of Judges into something with which archaeology could deal.

The case for the books of Samuel being a reflection of a historical reality depends on whether one accepts that there was a 'United Monarchy' and that Jerusalem was the capital of a state. Archaeology can make a contribution here but has yet to do so definitively. What archaeology cannot decide is how far the 'David' of these books is a real character or a fictional hero (or anti-hero). If the phrase *bytdwd* in the Tel Dan inscription really is to be translated 'house of David', at best this explains how the biblical 'David' became the founding hero of the Judaean dynasty. It may or may not point to a historical individual of that name (if it is a name and not a title), and whether such a person or his deeds or his realm or his Jerusalem—as portrayed in Samuel— bears any resemblance to historical reality cannot be proved. What can be proved is that the Davidic empire and that of Solomon is also *ideal* and has no counterpart in Palestinian history. To date, however, this point has not been acknowledged by most.

One strand of the intellectual agenda in the books of Samuel and Kings is the relationship between prophecy and monarchy. Biblical prophecy is not a real social *institution* from Israel and Judah's past. Certainly, these societies had intermediaries. But the idea of a discrete and visible succession of recognized speakers of the word of God, distinguishable from false prophets—that is an idealized notion. I do not mean that all the individual prophets who are identified necessarily never existed. I mean rather that prophecy as a clearly defined, quasi-hereditary (i.e. comprising a 'succession' of prophets) institution, similar but alternative to monarchy, is not an historical reality at all. 'Prophecy' is an intellectual construction for the purpose of presenting a political debate about how religious leadership will be exercised. Accordingly, since kingship shows itself incapable of sustaining a theocracy, and rule by charisma is (as Judges shows) unrealistic, it may therefore be necessary to represent the kingship of God by a separate institution, which itself enforces the treaty or covenant between God and Israel. So Samuel and Saul clash, as do Nathan and David, Elijah and Ahab, Isaiah and Ahaz, and Jeremiah and Jehoiakim.

And how was this debate concluded? It was not. Neither side won. The intellectuals knew very well that a theocracy was undesirable and impractical, just as the rabbis forbade charisma to override consensus. But the issue remains: if politics is about the will of God, how is that will communicated? Can there be a righteous monarch who has no need of such communication? And how (here is a Deuteronomic intervention) would one recognize a true prophet anyway, other than after the event?

My claim that the history of Israel and Judah in the books of Samuel and Kings is also not the history of a real society but a vehicle for the articulation of philosophical ideas cannot be conclusively demonstrated. It can, nevertheless, be shown that to a large extent the history in

Samuel–Kings does not conform to the real experiences of a real people, although there are undoubtedly real historical events exploited by the author, just as Deuteronomy includes laws and customs that were probably taken from actual practice or decree. I have shown that ideal Israels are present elsewhere in the Pentateuch and Former Prophets. The 'Israel' and 'Judah' of Samuel and Kings are based on the ideal notion of a 12-tribe, covenant-bound, chosen people of the one God Yahweh. The scheme of 'good' and 'bad' kings in Samuel–Kings is also transparently artificial. What remains, however, is that the names of the kings (and possibly their lengths of reign) are correct and that some of the events mentioned are corroborated in other independent sources. Do these observations make the case that the societies of Israel and Judah, whose history these books narrate, are recoverable by archaeology? Biblical archaeologists will probably answer in the affirmative. I would say, however, that two societies are occupying the same time and space, and both witness some of the same events. Each also has its own experiences. They are not identical, though, and only one ever existed to be recovered by archaeology.

Postscript

So, does archaeology retrieve the Israel of the Bible? No. Does it retrieve the Israel and Judah of history? No. This cannot be *retrieved*; it has to be reconstructed without biblical presuppositions. Is biblical archaeology fit for the task? By definition, no. Can archaeologists write a real history of Israel? Yes. And once this task is underway, biblical scholarship can finally exorcize the evil influence of biblical archaeology and revert to its task of understanding the Bible as a literature whose intellectual content needs also to be retrieved from theology and welcomed as a contribution to contemporary discussion of the nature of an ideal society, of its leadership, of the notion of 'history' and of the basis of morality. Take the Bible off the 'religion' shelf, off the 'fiction' and 'ancient mysteries' shelf, and put it next to Plato.

THE GEOGRAPHY OF THE EXODUS

John Van Seters

The geography of the exodus story has played an important role in the discussion of the historicity and historical reconstruction of the Egyptian sojourn and liberation event as recounted in Exodus 1–15 for over a century. The reason for this is that only in the names of places in Egypt does the story give us any hope of establishing a firm connection with Egyptian historical texts and monuments. This has also involved a continuing interaction between Egyptologists and biblical scholars, often without the competence or training to fully appreciate the discussion in the other's discipline. The history of the debate has created a great confusion of issues that has thoroughly muddled the debate and left a curious residue of errors in biblical studies, still evident in biblical atlases and histories.

What has made obsolete much of the earlier discussion of the geographical names of Exodus is the archaeological activity in the last 30 years at the two sites of Tell ed-Dab'a-Qantir and Tell el-Maskhuta in the eastern Delta of Egypt. The full impact of these excavations and their significance for re-evaluation of the older epigraphic materials has not yet been felt within the discipline of biblical studies. There is still considerable effort by both Egyptologists and biblical scholars to try to fit the exodus story into the older way of viewing things, viz. to understand the biblical scenario within the context of the 19th Dynasty of Egypt. The location of the exodus event within this period of Egyptian history is based upon two major considerations. The first is the reference to the city (or land) of Rameses (Exod. 1.11; 12.37; cf. Gen. 47.11), which is identified with Piramesse, the capital city built by Ramesses II. The second consideration is the dating of the 'conquest' of Canaan by the Israelites to the period of the late 19th or early 20th Dynasties with the exodus event preceding this by '40 years' of wilderness wanderings. In current discussion of the origins of Israel the conquest scenario may be ruled out as largely irrelevant to the discussion for the dating of the exodus. This leaves only the reference to Rameses, which is embedded within the geography of the sojourn–exodus story and must be considered within this context. It cannot be used as the sole basis for reconstructing an historical event and then eliminating elements that do not fit the reconstruction by labeling them as redactional.

Consequently, an important issue that must be faced in this discussion is literary, and this has usually been ignored. The biblical sources that make up the account of the sojourn in Egypt and the exodus in Exodus 1–15 were not contemporaneous with the events that they sought to portray. Even the earliest source, the so-called Yahwist (J), is variously dated from the tenth to the sixth centuries BCE (or even later), which by any reckoning of the date of the exodus is a long time afterwards. Furthermore, there is an increasing tendency towards the later dating of J, and it seems very likely that the geography of J's exodus account will reflect his familiarity with the Egypt of his own day rather than preserve hoary traditions of place-names from the second millennium. One cannot simply use the geography of the exodus uncritically as a way of dating the exodus. Nor can one fit the place-names into a predetermined historical period and make sense of them in that way. The possibility must be left open that the geographic background of the exodus story is Egypt in the time of the writer. Yet there has scarcely been any serious consideration of this possibility in the whole discussion about the exodus.[1] With this in mind, we will begin by reviewing the two major archaeological sites related to Pithom and Rameses (Exod. 1.11) that have been at the center of the discussion for so long.

Pithom and Succoth

In the winter of 1883, Edouard Naville conducted his excavations at Tell el-Maskhuta, the first project of the Egypt Exploration Fund.[2] Naville left no doubt about the object of his explorations in the Eastern Delta: it was to illuminate the geography of the Exodus. In this regard he considered his mission as highly successful, for he identified Tell el-Maskhuta with biblical Pithom, one of the store-cities which, according

---

1.   An exception is the work of D.B. Redford that will be discussed below.
2.   E.H. Naville, *The Store-City of Pithom and the Route of the Exodus* (Memoir of the Egyptian Exploration Fund, 1; London: Egypt Exploration Fund, 4th edn, 1903).

to Exod. 1.11, the Israelites built during a period of Egyptian servitude. Naville came to this conclusion by examining the monuments in the museums of Ismailia and Cairo that had been found at Tell el-Maskhuta, as well as the inscribed objects that came to light in his own excavations there. What convinced Naville of Tell el-Maskhuta's identification with Pithom was the fact that on many of these monuments the god Atum was given special honor and reference was made to his temple, Per Atum (or Pithom). It is clear from one monument, the so-called Pithom stela of Ptolemy II, that the temple of Atum gave its name to the city itself—Pithom, the Patoumos mentioned by Herodotus (2.158). At the same time, the city was also called *Tjeku* (biblical Succoth), because it was the chief city of the region of *Tjeku*. In the Greek sources of the Hellenistic and Roman periods the town was known as Heroo(n)polis, which was often shortened in Latin texts to Ero. Both forms were found by Naville on Latin inscriptions on the site. The large building in which Naville found monuments bearing the god's name, Atum, he identified as the temple itself. He also cleared parts of another large structure that he interpreted as a store-house. This he believed confirmed the biblical designation of 'store-city'. Finally, he traced the outlines of the large fortification walls that dominate the central portion of the site.

In spite of this rather impressive array of materials, Naville's identification of Tell el-Maskhuta with Pithom was challenged by Alan Gardiner,[3] who preferred to identify Pithom with Tell er-Retaba, about 8 miles to the west, while retaining the identity of Succoth with Tell el-Maskhuta as a separate town (see map, Fig. 1). Gardiner's views were popularized by T.E. Peet in *Egypt and the Old Testament* (1924), and as a consequence they became widely accepted by Old Testament scholars, including the influencial W.F. Albright. In the context of remarks on an expedition that he made to the Egyptian Delta and the Sinai in 1948, Albright states,

---

3. A.H. Gardiner, 'The Geography of the Exodus', in *Recueil d'études égyptologiques, dédiées à la mémoire de Jean François Champollion à l'occasion du centenaire de la lettre à M. Dacier relative à l'alphabet des hiéroglyphes phonétiques, lue à l'Académie des inscriptions et belles-lettres le 27 Septembre 1822* (Bibliothèque de l'École des Hautes Études, Sciences historiques et philologiques, 234; Paris: E. Champion, 1922), pp. 203-15.

A flying visit to the vast site of Tell el-Maskhuta and the smaller (but still large) site of Tell Ertabeh convinced me that Gardiner's identification of them with Sukkoth and Pithom of Exodus, respectively, is correct. The geography of the Egyptian phase of the exodus thus approaches a definite solution.[4]

Albright never says anywhere exactly what it was during this 'flying visit' that led him to such conviction, but it has become the standard view nevertheless. Yet there are Egyptologists who continue to support Naville's original identification of Tell el-Maskhuta with Pithom and Succoth.[5]

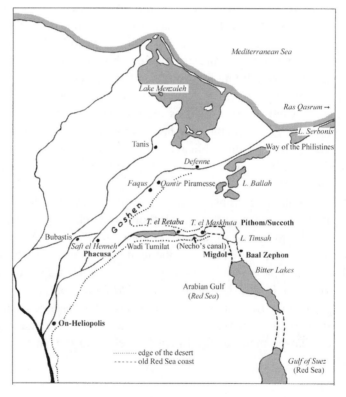

Figure 1. *Map of the Eastern Delta, with details drawn from M. Bietak, Tell El-Dab'a II, p. 108 and Naville,* The Store-City of Pithom, *opposite p. 40; the reconstruction of the old Red Sea coastline follows L. de Bellefonds*

4. W.F. Albright, 'Exploring in Sinai with the University of California African Expedition', *BASOR* 109 (1948), pp. 5-20 (15).

5. D.B. Redford, 'Pithom', in W. Helck and W. Westendorf (eds.), *Lexicon der Ägyptologie* (Wiesbaden: Otto Harrassowitz, 1982), cols. 1054-58.

It is now generally agreed that from the time of the 19th Dynasty of Egypt onwards, the region of the Wadi Tumilat, or the eastern end of it, was known as *Tjeku*. This is to be identified almost certainly with biblical Succoth, and for convenience I will use this name henceforth. The principal god of the region was Atum of Succoth, and he may have had a temple or estate in the Wadi Tumilat called Per-Atum as early as the 19th Dynasty, but that is entirely uncertain. A text from the time of Merneptah that mentions a Per-Atum in connection with this region has called forth a lot of discussion. It is contained in a border report that states,

> We have finished letting the Bedouin tribes (Shasu) of Edom pass the fortress of Merneptah Hotep-hir-Maat, l.p.h. which is in Tjeku (Succoth), to the pools of Per-Atum of Merneptah Hotep-hir-Maat, which are in Tjeku, to keep them alive and to keep their cattle alive.[6]

This text is often viewed as significant, because Merneptah is frequently considered to be the pharaoh of the exodus. The text is thought to refer to two towns of the period, the fortress of Tjeku, which is identified with biblical Succoth, and Per-Atum, which would correspond to biblical Pithom. Furthermore, the fortress of Succoth would need to be situated to the east of the pools of Per-Atum, although how far east is not clear. However, it must be noted that both the fortress and the pools are said to be in Tjeku (Succoth) so that Succoth must be the name of a region and not that of a city.

Naville argued that since a large statuary group honoring Ramesses II and the god Atum of Succoth (and the god Seth) was found at Tell el-Maskhuta, as well as a large temple to Atum, it was reasonable to assume that Ramesses built Pithom at Tell el-Maskhuta.[7] For him also the towns of Pithom and Succoth were identical, based upon the occurrence of their names together in the later texts. Thus he interpreted the Merneptah text quoted above to refer to a fortress, as yet unidentified, just to the east of Pithom (= Tell el-Maskhuta). Gardiner countered this by suggesting that Tell el-Maskhuta should be regarded as the fortress of Succoth referred to in the above text and that the 'pools of

---

6. This rendering is based on the translation of J.A. Wilson in *ANET*, p. 259. See also R.A. Caminos, *Late-Egyptian Miscellanies* (Brown Egyptological Studies, 1; London: Oxford University Press, 1954), p. 293.

7. E.H. Naville, 'The Geography of the Exodus', *JEA* 10 (1924), pp. 18-39, esp. pp. 32-39.

Atum' lay beyond in the region of Tell el-Retaba, the actual site of Pithom.[8] He rather cavalierly dismissed all of the monumental and documentary evidence for a temple of Atum at Tell el-Maskhuta and the fact that no such temple to Atum could be identified at Tell er-Retaba. Gardiner's view was adopted by Albright and is still generally reflected in maps of the exodus route. Naville's protests against Gardiner's views were largely ignored.

A new phase in the discussion was introduced by D.B. Redford,[9] who raised two important points in the discussion of Pithom and Succoth. First, there is no evidence before the mid-first millennium BCE (the Saite period) in Egyptian records of either name being identified as *towns*. Per Atum is the name used for a number of different temples to the god Atum in various locations, but none receives the town determinative in Egyptian until the inscriptions of the late period. Similarly, Tjeku (Succoth) appears as the name of a district by the time of the Ramesside period and must be understood as a district in the Merneptah text cited above. It only receives the town determinative, signifying the name of the principle town of the region, in the late (Saite) period. This means that references to these places in the biblical record could only reflect the geography of a mid-first millennium BCE dating at the earliest. Secondly, the Merneptah text must also be understood in an entirely different way. The fortress of Tjeku can only refer to some guard post within the district of Succoth and not to the town of Succoth. The pools of Per Atum, likewise, does not refer to some body of water connected with a town of Pithom but as belonging to the temple estates of the god Atum, who was the god of the region. The temple of Atum could be situated somewhere else and the epithet 'Atum of Merneptah-Content-with-truth' strongly suggests its location in the capital of Piramesses. Thus there is no basis for finding in the two names of this text two distinct towns of Succoth and Pithom, separated from each other by several miles and therefore no basis for the positions of Gardiner and Albright.

It is true that Redford's position was challenged by W. Helck, and his

8. A.H. Gardiner, 'The Geography of the Exodus: An Answer to Professor Naville and Others', *JEA* 10 (1924), pp. 87-96.

9. D.B. Redford, 'Exodus I 11', *VT* 13 (1963), pp. 401-18; *idem*, 'An Egyptological Perspective on the Exodus Narrative', in A.F. Rainey (ed.), *Egypt, Israel, Sinai: Archaeological and Historical Relationships in the Biblical Period* (Tel Aviv: Tel Aviv University Press, 1987), pp. 137-61.

article is often cited as a way of dismissing Redford's challenge.[10] Helck does accept the identity of Per Atum with Tjeku, against Gardiner, to be located at Tell el-Maskhuta. However, against Redford he argues that the lack of the town determinative with the name Tjeku (Succoth) does not necessarily mean that a town of that name did not exist in the district of Tjeku. This means that he interprets the Merneptah text differently also. He takes the temple of Atum to be in Tjeku, which he understands as a town with a fortress just to the east of it as part of the whole complex, and this town he locates at Tell el-Maskhuta as a Ramesside construction. His position that Tjeku represents a town with a temple to Atum in the 19th Dynasty rests entirely upon his acceptance of the archaeological evidence as set forth by Naville.

A new and quite decisive factor in the discussion of Pithom and Succoth is the result of the Wadi Tumilat project of the University of Toronto, directed by J.S. Holladay, Jr. The project carried out a ceramic survey of several sites in the Wadi Tumilat, including Tell er-Retaba and Tell el-Maskhuta in 1977 and 1983 and conducted five seasons of excavations at Tell el-Maskhuta in 1978, 1979, 1981, 1983 and 1985.[11] This expedition added an important critical correction to Naville's earlier work in terms of controlled stratigraphy and ceramic chronology. It also raised serious objections to the views of Gardiner and Albright about their location of Pithom and Succoth. It is now clear from the archaeological evidence that Naville was wrong about assigning to Ramesses II the founding and building of Pithom. Naville excavated in the days before the use of ceramic chronology and dated the site solely on the basis of the inscribed objects found there. The recent excavations at Tell el-Maskhuta under Holladay make it abundantly clear that this city was built only at the end of the 7th century BCE, in the time of Pharaoh Necho II. In fact, the city was probably built in conjunction with Necho's work on the great canal that Herodotus tells us the

10. W. Helck, 'Ṯkw und die Ramses-Stadt', *VT* 15 (1965), pp. 35-48. See Redford's own response in 'The Literary Motif of the Exposed Child', *Numen* 14 (1967), pp. 209-28 (221 n. 52).

11. J.S. Holladay, Jr, *Cities of the Delta*. III. *Tell el-Maskhuta: Preliminary Report on the Wadi Tumilat Project, 1978–1979* (American Research Center in Egypt Reports, 6; Malibu, CA: Undena, 1982); *idem*, 'Maskhuta, Tell el-', in *ABD* (1992), IV, pp. 588-92; B. MacDonald, 'Excavations at Tell el-Maskhuta', *BA* 43 (1980), pp. 49-58. The writer participated as a field supervisor and associate director during the 1978 and 1981 seasons.

pharaoh attempted to dig from the Nile to the Red Sea (*Histories* 2.158). Yet this revised dating of the site does not dispute the fact that Tell el-Maskhuta must be identified with Pithom, the name of the place from c. 600 BCE down to Roman times.

Naville had argued that Ramesses II was probably the founder and builder of Pithom and its store-houses, using Israelite labor, since this king's statue was found at Tell el-Maskhuta. But the ceramic evidence and dateable stratigraphy clearly exclude such a possibility. How then can we explain those Ramesside and other pre-Saite monuments found at Tell el-Maskhuta? We know from examples of other sites that fine statuary and other monuments were often transported from one place to another to adorn new palaces and temples. It seems likely that some pharaoh, perhaps Nectanebo I, adorned the temple at Tell el-Maskhuta with monuments taken from various places in the eastern Delta that bore the name of Atum of Succoth.[12] Once the canal was built and Pithom established as the religious and commercial center of the region, the whole character of the Wadi Tumilat changed. It was now the primary commercial access and trade route between Lower Egypt and the Red Sea.

Furthermore, Gardiner's identification of Pithom with Tell er-Retaba is not possible because—on the basis of the Wadi Tumilat expedition's ceramic survey of the site in 1977 and all the published materials to date—Tell er-Retaba was largely unoccupied from the Saite to Roman times, precisely the time when the monuments attest the existence of the *town* of Pithom. There were many Per-Atum temples and estates in Egypt in the Ramesside period but no indication that any gave their name to a particular town. The most important temple of Atum was the one in Heliopolis (= biblical On), and for that reason E.P. Uphill identifies it as the site of Pithom.[13] The biblical tradition, however, regards the city of On (Gen. 41.50) as quite distinct from the city of Pithom and few have followed his suggestion. It is also true that there was an important Ramesside town at Tell er-Retaba, but we do not know its name from any inscriptions on the site. Tell el-Maskhuta replaced Tell er-Retaba as the most important town of the region and the latter dwindled to a village.

This archaeological dating of the site of Tell el-Maskhuta confirms

12. See Redford, 'Pithom', col. 1055.
13. E.P. Uphill, 'Pithom and Raamses: Their Location and Significance', *JNES* 27 (1968), pp. 291-316; 28 (1969), pp. 15-39.

the observations made by Redford, long before the recent excavations, about when Succoth–Pithom became a town.[14] Against Helck who depended entirely upon Naville's dating of Pithom to Ramesses II, Redford had argued that the use of the town determinative in hieroglyphic writing with either the name Succoth or Pithom after c. 600 BCE is significant for dating the founding of the town. The inscriptions also make clear that these are not two separate towns, as the maps so often suggest, but the same place. It would appear that Necho built Tell el-Maskhuta as a great frontier fortification—witness the great walls around the town—and placed a large temple there to honor the principal god of the region. The result was that the town acquired the name Pithom, because of the temple (a very common occurrence in Egypt), and also the name Succoth, because it was the major town of the region by that name.

It is now possible to suggest a somewhat different interpretation of the Merneptah texts with its mention of the 'pools of Per-Atum'. M. Bietak has recently undertaken a study of the ancient geography of the eastern Delta region.[15] He concludes that in the western part of the Wadi Tumilat there was once an ancient lake that was supplied by the overflow from the Nile (see the map, Fig. 1). It is this lake region that is referred to in the Merneptah papyrus, and the fort that the bedouin had to pass to get to the lake region may well be Tell er-Retaba, situated at the eastern end of the lake.[16] Since Tell el-Maskhuta was not occupied

---

14. Redford, 'Exodus I 11', pp. 403-408.

15. M. Bietak, *Avaris and Piramesse: Archaeological Exploration in the Eastern Nile Delta* (Mortimer Wheeler Archaeological Lecture, 1979; London: The British Academy, 1981), p. 277 (initially published in the *Proceedings of the British Academy* 65 [1979], pp. 225-96). For more detailed treatment, see his *Tell el-Dab'a II: Der Fundort im Rahmen einer archäologisch-geographischen Untersuchung über das ägyptische Ostdelta* (Österreichische Akademie der Wissenschaften, Denkschriften der Gesamtakademie, 4; Vienna: Österreichischen Akadamie der Wissenschaften, 1975).

16. It is not possible to identify the fort in Succoth with Tell el-Maskhuta as Gardiner and Albright did, because it was not yet in existence. See also S. Herrmann (*Israel in Egypt* [SBT, 2nd series, 27; London: SCM Press, 1973], p. 26), who follows Naville in identifying Pithom with Tell el-Maskhuta in the Ramesside period. His description of the region around Tell el-Maskhuta in the 19th Dynasty as fertile could hardly be correct. Until the building of the canal it could hardly have been much more than a desert track with the fertile region lying much further to the west in the wadi.

during the Ramesside period, there is no other candidate east of Tell er-Retaba that fits the description of this text. The text makes clear that both the pools and the fort are in the district of Succoth, but it hardly warrants identifying the fort either with a *town* of Succoth or with Per-Atum, though it is possible that there was a temple to the god Atum of Succoth at this site. Furthermore, Redford has argued that while the pools of the region of Succoth are said to belong to the estate of the god Atum, this does not mean that the temple of the god was in this region as well. He considers it much more likely that the temple of Atum of Merneptah referred to here is that belonging to the capital Piramesse. It remains very doubtful, without further evidence, that there was a specific site or temple with the name Per-Atum in the region of Succoth in this period.[17]

Rameses–Piramesse

The identification of Rameses, the other 'store-city' mentioned in Exod. 1.11 as built by the Israelites, was a matter of controversy for several years. Most scholars accept the equation of Rameses with Piramesse, the capital of the 19th Dynasty built by Ramesses II. While many locations for Piramesse have been proposed, the excavations at Tanis (San el-Hagar), especially those conducted by Pierre Montet, seemed to put the matter to rest, because so many and so impressive were the monuments and inscriptions naming Ramesses II, his successors, and the gods of Piramesse.[18] Most biblical atlases and histories identified Tanis with Piramesse, and biblical scholars argued that since the name of the city was changed from Piramesse to Tanis with the rise of the 21st Dynasty, c. 1100 BCE, the biblical references to Rameses must preserve an old tradition from the time of the sojourn in Egypt.[19]

The presence of these monuments and the inscriptions at Tanis,

17. Redford, 'An Egyptological Perspective on the Exodus Narrative', pp. 140-42.

18. P. Montet, 'Tanis, Avaris et Pi-Ramses', *RB* 39 (1930), pp. 5-28; *idem, Les enigmes de Tanis* (Bibliotheque historique; Paris: Payot, 1952); A.H. Gardiner, 'Tanis and Pi-Ramesse: A Retraction', *JEA* 19 (1933), pp. 122-28; H. Cazelles, 'Les localisations de l'Exode et la critique littéraire', *RB* 62 (1955), pp. 321-64. Cazelles's otherwise useful review of earlier literature on the subject is controlled entirely by his identification of Piramesse with Tanis.

19. J. Bright, *A History of Israel* (Philadelphia: Westminster Press, 3rd edn, 1981), p. 121; also Herrmann, *Israel in Egypt*, p. 75 n. 42.

however, has proven deceptive, because it is clear that they did not originate at the site.[20] They were all brought to it from elsewhere. Nowhere is the matter of careful stratigraphic evaluation more important than at Tanis. The fact is that there is no 19th and 20th Dynasty stratigraphy at Tanis. It was a new city built by the pharaohs of the 21st Dynasty. The real capital site is about 30 kilometers south in the vicinity of the modern town of Qantir. This fact seems to be well established now, since the stratified ruins of a fine palace with thousands of glazed tiles were found *in situ*, as well as other monuments. The identification of Avaris with Tell ed-Dab'a, just to the south of Qantir, through the excavations of M. Bietak further confirm this identification of the capital of the Ramessides beyond any reasonable doubt.[21]

The city of Piramesse was largely abandoned at the end of the 20th Dynasty, probably because of the silting-up of the waterway on which it was located[22] and the shift of the marine traffic to a new watercourse through Tanis. It was at this time that Tanis became the new capital of the 21st Dynasty. Piramesse became a quarry for valuable stone blocks and monuments to be used at Tanis and other sites, especially Bubastis. Yet the name and remembrance of Piramesse did not entirely disappear. It appears in a list of place-names of the 21st Dynasty date, along with Tanis.[23] Under Sheshonq I (Shishak) of the 22nd Dynasty the city of Piramesse seems to have had a brief revival by a king who emulated Ramesses II's career.[24] It is no longer justified to say that the reference to Rameses in the exodus story must preserve an ancient tradition from the time of the sojourn if it was the capital of Egypt in the tenth century BCE.

How long the ruins of Piramesse continued to retain the name is a matter of some debate. What complicates the situation is the fact that

---

20. See J. Van Seters, *The Hyksos: A New Investigation* (New Haven: Yale University Press, 1966), pp. 127-55; Bietak, *Avaris and Piramesse*, pp. 278-83.

21. M. Bietak, *Avaris and Piramesse*; idem, *Avaris, the Capital of the Hyksos: Recent Excavations at Tell el-Dab'a* (Raymond and Beverly Sackler Foundation Distinguished Lecture in Egyptology, 1; London: British Museum Press, 1996). The latter has an extensive and current bibliography.

22. See Bietak, *Avaris and Piramesse*, pp. 271-83.

23. A.H. Gardiner, 'The Supposed Egyptian Equivalent of the Name Goshen', *JEA* 5 (1918), pp. 218-23 (198); idem, 'Tanis and Pi-Ramesse: A Retraction', p. 126.

24. D.B. Redford, *Egypt, Canaan, and Israel in Ancient Times* (Princeton: Princeton University Press, 1992), pp. 314-15.

monuments from the original site of Piramesse that were transplanted in both Tanis and Bubastis led to the establishment of cults to the gods of (Per) Ramesses.[25] This, in turn, may have encouraged the notion that the region from Bubastis to Tanis and eastward was known as the 'land of Rameses', as we find it used in the Joseph story (Gen. 47.11). Yet it seems unlikely to me that either Bubastis or Tanis, cities otherwise known to the biblical writers, were ever confused with Rameses. There is late testimony from the sixth century CE that the name of Ramesses was still associated with the ruins of the original Piramesse.[26] Furthermore, the shortened form of the name Rameses, with the loss of the initial element pi = per, is probably derived from the time when the cults of the gods of Piramesse flourished in the Delta cities in the first millennium BCE, because it is precisely in these texts that the name of the city has the shortened form of Ramesse (Rameses).[27]

The designation of Rameses as a 'store-city' in the exodus story, instead of the royal city, is also quite curious. The meaning of the Hebrew phrase *'arē miskᵉnôt* is not entirely certain, but judging from the reference in 1 Kgs 9.19 and its context, it suggests supply depots and fortresses on the frontier of the land. While this would be quite appropriate for Pithom/Tell el-Maskhuta from the sixth century BCE onwards, it is hardly suitable as a designation for the residence of the king's palace and temples of the Ramessides, anymore than it would be for Jerusalem under Solomon. Only after the original significance of Piramesse was long forgotten could the extensive ruins of the region be interpreted as a fortress on Egypt's northeastern frontier corresponding to that of Tell el-Maskhuta in the Wadi Tumilat.

The exodus story relates that it was the Israelites who had settled down in the 'land of Rameses', also known as Goshen, that were pressed into corvée labor in order to build these two cities. Now there is a tendency to identify the Shasu bedouin who entered the Wadi Tumilat to graze their flocks, as reflected in the text of the Merneptah papyrus

25. M. Bietak, *Tell el-Dabʿa II*, pp. 219-21.

26. J. Van Seters, *The Hyksos*, pp. 148-49. Redford ('Exodus I 11', p. 409) also points to a Ptolemaic inscription from Tanis with the name of Piramesse on it in the title of 'a prophet of Amun of Ramesses from Piramesse'. Whether this attests to the cult of Amun in Piramesse at that time or merely its transplant in Tanis is not clear.

27. Redford, 'An Egyptological Perspective on the Exodus Narrative', p. 139; cf. *idem*, 'Exodus I 11', pp. 409-10.

quoted above, as proto-Israelites and the ones who served as the labor force in Ramesses II's extensive building activities.[28] This is most unlikely, however, as W. Helck has acknowledged.[29] Egypt had many prisoners of war and their descendants, taken from the urban centers of Syria–Palestine, who were already skilled construction workers, and so it was hardly necessary to press into service those who had no such skills and training. The livestock of the bedouin, grazing on the marginal lands of the Wadi Tumilat, were a source of food supply for the frontier towns like Tell er-Retaba.

Goshen

In the Joseph story of Genesis and during the sojourn in Exodus, the Israelites live in the land of Goshen. This region is described in rather ambiguous terms as being separate from the rest of Egypt and thus a border region, but also as part of Egypt, indeed the best of the land (Gen. 46.28-34; 47.1-10). It is suitable for the grazing of livestock, but also for the cultivation of crops. The location of Goshen and its particular Egyptian identity was another subject of controversy between Naville and Gardiner, and Egyptologists have subsequently taken up positions on one side or the other. Naville identified Goshen with a region located in the eastern Delta corresponding to the 20th nome of Lower Egypt[30] (see the map, Fig. 1). The name of the region, which occurs in a number of late geographic texts, he read as Kesem or

28. See M. Bietak, 'Comments on the "Exodus"', in A.F. Rainey (ed.), *Egypt, Israel and Sinai: Archaeological and Historical Relationships in the Biblical Period* (Tel Aviv: Tell Aviv University Press, 1987), pp. 163-71 (168-69); also Herrmann, *Israel in Egypt*, pp. 25-26. Herrmann admits that in his interpretation of the Merneptah text the 'proto-Israelites' were being admitted into the Wadi-Tumilat peacefully in the region that he identifies with the land of Goshen long after the date of their supposed enslavement and exodus.

29. W. Helck, 'Die Bedrohung Palästinas durch einwandernde Gruppen am Ende der 18. und am Anfang der 19. Dynastie', *VT* 18 (1968), pp. 472-80 (480 n. 1). Helck, however, still looks for a historical fit of the exodus tradition in the 19th Dynasty.

30. E.H. Naville, *The Shrine of Saft el Henneh and the Land of Goshen (1885)* (Memoir of the Egyptian Exploration Fund, 5; London: Egyptian Exploration Fund, 1887); *idem*, 'The Geography of the Exodus', pp. 18-32. See also P. Montet, *Géographie de L'Égypte ancienne* (Paris: Imprimerie nationale, 1957), I, pp. 205-12. Montet supports Naville's position.

Gesem. Its district capital was Pisoped (Saft el Henneh). The Septuagint renders the name Goshen as 'Gesem of Arabia', and Arabia was the name that Greco-Roman sources gave to the 20th nome. The Greek and Roman geographers called Pisoped 'Phakusa', which Naville argues is derived from the name of the region, Gesem. Inscribed on a shrine dedicated to the god Soped by Nechtanebo II[31] is the name of the place, given as the town of Kus, as well as the land of Kus.[32] The town of Kus or Phakusa (Kus with the article 'pha') refers to the chief city of the land of Kus (Goshen or Gesem), just as the town of Succoth is the political name for the chief city of the region of Succoth.

Gardiner, however, disputed Naville's reading of the name Gesem, because the initial hieroglyph could be read šs as well as g.[33] He associated the name with a region known as šsmt (Shesmet), the name for the mining region of the Sinai of the Old and Middle Kingdoms. However, the only point of connection between the two place names is their common association with the god Soped, Lord of the East, but that alone hardly warrants their identity. Against the identity of these two names are a number of important considerations:

1) The names of the two places are separated by at least 1000 years. There is no continuity of usage between them.

2) They represent two quite different regions, the one in the mountains of the eastern Sinai peninsula and the other in the eastern Delta, centering in a site just a few miles east of Bubastis. This is the 20th nome that does not even include the area of the 8th nome (Succoth) that is immediately adjacent to the Sinai. The fact is that the Egyptians stopped mining in the eastern Sinai many centuries before the late form of the name *gsm* appears.

3) The orthography of the two names is completely different.[34] It is true that there is one text of the 12th Dynasty that contains a possible

31. Montet attributes this shrine to Nectanebo I.

32. Naville, *Shrine of Saft el Henneh*, pp. 9, 12, 14-20 and pls. iv, vi. The spelling Kes (Kus) is merely a defective rendering of the name Kesem, which appears elsewhere in connection with Per-Soped.

33. Gardiner, 'The Supposed Egyptian Equivalent of the Name Goshen', pp. 218-23; *idem*, 'The Geography of the Exodus: An Answer to Professor Naville and Others', pp. 87-96. H. Gauthier (*Dictionnaire des noms géographiques contenus dans les textes hiéroglyphiques* [Cairo: Société royale de Géographie d'Égypte, 1925-31], V, pp. 145-46) supports the position of Gardiner.

34. Gesem is written ⟨hieroglyphs⟩ and Shesmet is ⟨hieroglyphs⟩.

reference to *šsm/gsm* in hieratic that is similar to the later forms and that Gardiner interprets as an alternate form of the older name, giving him his only connection between the two forms of the name. The text is variously understood by different scholars and may or may not be related to either place.[35]

4) Finally, there is one unambiguous rendering of the name Gesem with an initial hieroglyph which must be read g or k.[36]

In my view there is no good reason to question Naville's identification of Goshen with the 20th nome of Lower Egypt.

As the name of a specific region or nome, Gesem appears in the Egyptian texts rather late. Naville's mistake was to read all of this evidence back into the Ramesside period. The region, however, probably originated as a princedom that arose in the Delta during the eighth century BCE with its capital at Pisoped. With the reunification of Egypt under the Saite rulers, it became a district or nome. The land of Goshen (Gesem) covered the western end of the Wadi Tumilat as far as Bubastis, the eastern part of the wadi being the district of Succoth with its chief city Pithom. Goshen extended north along the eastern Nile branch as far as the ruins of Piramesse. The Bible seems, in fact, to equate the 'land of Rameses' with Goshen (compare Gen. 47.6 and 11), and this is made especially clear in the LXX. The northern extent of the region may perhaps be confirmed by the fact that in later Christian times the town of Faqus rose to prominence as a bishopric and displaced Pisoped as Phaqusa—the district center of Goshen. Faqus is only 5 kilometers south of Qantir, the site of Piramesse. Within its geographic limits there was both fine agricultural land between Saft el Henneh and Qantir, and marginal grazing land in the Wadi Tumilat. The district of Goshen/Gesem would fit all the requirements of the biblical texts.[37]

35. See Naville, 'The Geography of the Exodus', p. 28 n. 2; also Montet, *Géographie*, pp. 207-208.

36. Naville, 'The Geography of the Exodus', p. 29. Cf. Gardiner's rather weak rejoinder on this point in 'The Geography of the Exodus: An Answer to Professor Naville and Others', p. 94.

37. Redford has an alternate explanation for the name of Goshen ('Perspective on the Exodus', pp. 139-40). He derives it from the Qedarites who occupied the eastern Delta in considerable numbers from the seventh century BCE onwards. The name Goshen would then be related to the dynastic name of Gasmu (Gesem) by the royal family of the Qedarites. This seems to me most unlikely. There is no evidence that the Qedarites actually controlled the Wadi Tumilat or gave their name to the

The Red Sea and the Israelites' Egyptian Itinerary

The oldest source of Exodus, the Yahwist, describes the route of the exodus in the following terms (Exod. 12.37a; 13.17-18, 20):

> The people of Israel set out from Rameses towards Succoth... And moreover, a large group of bedouin left with them, along with a great number of livestock, both sheep and cattle... When Pharaoh expelled the people, God did not lead them along the route to the land of the Philistines, even though it was shorter...but God brought them around on the desert route towards the Red Sea... They set out from Succoth and encamped in Etham on the edge of the desert.[38]

On the basis of our earlier discussion of geography, these texts suggest that the people set out from the region of Qantir (Rameses) and traveled through the Wadi Tumilat to Succoth/Pithom (Tell el-Maskhuta). As the author explains, this is not the direct route towards the northeast and the coastal road to Canaan. Instead, they had to go 'around' by traveling up the Nile southwest, until they came to the mouth of the Wadi Tumilat and then turn east through the Wadi Tumilat.[39] The language of the itinerary suggests that Succoth here refers to the town of Succoth (Tell el-Maskhuta) and not just the region that stretched over the eastern half of the Wadi Tumilat. Succoth, both town and region, is outside of Goshen.

The remark about the large group of bedouin (*'ereb*) with their animals accompanying the Israelites is of interest. It adds an element of color that is very distinctive of this route. During our excavations at Tell el-Maskhuta it was common to see groups of bedouin moving

region. Their base of power was the northern Sinai, and this was never known as Goshen. The Israelites have left Goshen long before they reach the region of the Sinai Peninsula. It seems to me much more likely that the biblical author would use an Egyptian name for the region within Egypt, as he did for the rest of his geographic terms.

38. Author's translation.

39. The various routes for the exodus proposed in the biblical atlases, such as H.G. May, *Oxford Bible Atlas* (rev. by J. Day; New York: Oxford University Press, 3rd edn, 1984) whose maps are also used in the various editions of the *Oxford Annotated Bible*—NRSV or the *Oxford Study Bible*—REB version, simply ignore the basic elements of the region's geography. They draw a straight line from Qantir to Tell el Maskhuta—right through the desert sand dunes! They are entirely misleading.

through the wadi with their flocks and livestock, often in rather large numbers, some even camping temporarily at the site of our excavations.[40] There was both a supply of water from the canal and marginal grazing land. The local villagers called them ' *'arab*', the same term that is used in the text above, a terms that the villagers did not apply to themselves. It was, and remains, the primary access route from the Sinai into Egypt from time immemorial. As we saw above, the region of the Wadi Tumilat from Pi-Soped (Saft el-Henneh) to Pithom in the Greco-Roman period and in the LXX was known as Arabia.

From Succoth they moved east to a place called Etham, whose identity and location is uncertain. It would appear to be at or near the sea and at the same time to mark the edge of the Sinai desert. Some have tried to associate the name Etham with the Egyptian word for fort, *ḥtm*, but the initial laryngeal *ḥ* would rule this out.[41] Redford suggests deriving the name from *ḥwt-itm*, which would be phonetically possible, and this is supported by its location in the 8th nome.[42] Yet this name, which means the temple estate of Atum, is the direct equivalent of Per-Atum and very likely refers to the same place, Pithom. This may suggest that the author was familiar with the names Succoth and Etham and their association with the eastern Wadi Tumilat, but he understood them as two separate places with Etham (Pithom) east of Succoth. He simply used the two names as stops on his route. If Etham is Pithom, is it near the sea and on the border of the desert?

The sea is not identified in the story of the crossing itself in Exodus 14, but from the itinerary in 13.18 and 15.22 (both J) it is named as the Red Sea. Yet if the Red Sea is the Gulf of Suez, then it is too far from the direction of travel to be seriously considered (see map, Fig. 1). The sea directly east of Succoth/Pithom at the end of the Wadi Tumilat is Lake Timsah. One common solution to the problem of identifying the sea is to interpret the Hebrew *yam suf* as meaning 'sea of reeds', since Hebrew *suf* does mean 'reeds' in some texts (Exod. 2.3-5) and seems closely related to Egyptian *tjwf* 'papyrus'. There is, in fact, a reference

40. See Holladay, *Tell el-Maskhuta*, Pl. XLVI. It pictures a small bedouin encampment on the tell.

41. See Redford, 'An Egyptological Perspective on the Exodus Narrative', p. 153 n. 9; G.I. Davies, *The Way of the Wilderness: A Geographical Study of the Wilderness Itineraries in the Old Testament* (SOTSMS, 5; Cambridge: Cambridge University Press, 1979), pp. 79-80.

42. Davies, *The Way of the Wilderness*, pp. 79-80.

in some Egyptian texts to a papyrus marsh somewhere east of Piramesse, and this has led to the suggestion of identifying the body of
water along the northeastern exit in the vicinity of Lake Ballah.[43] The
obvious objection to this is that this proposal would involve the
rejection of the itineraries that contradict such a northern route, but to
do so would also get rid of Rameses as the starting point. The fact of
the matter is that *yam suf*, in all of the instances in the Hebrew Bible
outside of the exodus story, clearly designates the Red Sea and its
extensions in the Gulf of Aqaba and the Gulf of Suez. There are no
'reeds' in the Red Sea since the papyrus in question is a freshwater
plant. A solution that proposes the same geographic term for two
entirely different things does not seem to me to be acceptable.[44]

Naville proposed a different solution to the problem of the Red Sea.[45]
He pointed out that studies done by a French geologist, Linant de
Bellefonds, prior to the building of the Suez Canal, found evidence that
the Gulf of Suez extended much further north in antiquity to include
the Bitter Lakes and Lake Timsah, and in fact to reach quite close to Tell
el-Maskhuta.[46] It would also explain the rather high incidence of Red
Sea shells, particularly oyster shells, that were found in the recent
excavations under Holladay. This would hardly be likely if the Red Sea
were 80 kilometers away. In fact, the French geologists in their
investigation of the Isthmus of Suez between Lake Timsah and the Gulf
of Suez found many deposits of shells and other evidence of the
existence of the sea in that region. As Naville points out, this geological
position agrees with classical sources that gave this extension of the
Red Sea north as far as lake Timsah the name Arabian or Heroopolitan
Gulf, because it ended close to Heroopolis, the Greek name for Pithom.
Herodotus, in his description of the canal built by Necho (2.158) says,
'The water [of the canal] is derived from the Nile and leaves it a little

43. Bietak, 'Comments on the Exodus', p. 167; *idem*, *Avaris and Piramesse*,
p. 280. For a general discussion of the various proposals, see Davies, *The Way of
the Wilderness*, pp. 70-74.

44. A summary of the various views may be found in J.R. Huddlestun, 'Red
Sea', *ABD* (1992), V, pp. 633-42. For an earlier review, see Cazelles, 'Les
localisations', pp. 328-29, 340-43.

45. *The Store-City of Pithom*, pp. 15-39; *idem*, 'The Geography of the Exodus',
pp. 36-39.

46. See also the review of L. de Bellefonds's work in J. Mazuel, *L'Oeuvre
géographique de Linant de Bellefonds étude de géographie historique* (Cairo:
Société Royale de Géographie d'Égypte, 1937), pp. 243-59.

above the city of Bubastis. Flowing alongside of Patoumos (Pithom), the city of Arabia, it then enters into the Red Sea.' He elsewhere refers to the Red Sea end of the canal as the Arabian Gulf, so that it is most reasonable to interpret his description of the fresh-water canal as extending from a point near Bubastis on the west to Pithom on the east, the point at which it empties into the Red Sea.[47] Herodotus also tells of Necho's establishment of a navy in the 'Arabian Gulf', very likely in support of Red Sea and East African trade.[48] This is especially the case after the construction of the canal by Necho. Tell el-Maskhuta (Pithom) was the final terminus for the canal, and this fact would help explain its location and importance as a port and trans-shipment site, where goods coming by canal from inland could be collected and stored and then transferred to sea ships that traveled through the Red Sea and beyond. This same pattern of shipping activity in the Red Sea through the canal and the Arabian Gulf was also attested for Ptolemy II in a detailed description of his construction and expeditions in this region in the famous Pithom Stele.[49] The very close association between the main center of the region at Pithom and the point from which the sea-going expeditions set out and brought back their goods make this proximity of the Red Sea extension to Pithom obvious. In spite of some objections that have been raised against this view, none of which seem to me to be very persuasive,[50] this explanation is still the best possibility (see map, Fig. 1). A biblical reference to the Arabian Gulf may be seen in Isa. 11.15 with its designation of the crossing point of the sea as the 'tongue of the Egyptian sea', which is almost certainly a reference to a narrow gulf of the Red Sea.[51]

If the Red Sea was so close to Pithom/Etham and in the direct line of march by the Israelites through the Wadi Tumilat, then the event as portrayed in the J source has to do with Lake Timsah, the northern part of the Arabian Gulf. What the author has in mind is an encampment at

47. See Naville's extended discussion of this text in *The Store-City of Pithom*, pp. 34-39.

48. See A.B. Lloyd, 'Necho and the Red Sea: Some Considerations', *JEA* 63 (1977), pp. 142-55.

49. See Naville, *The Store-City of Pithom*, pp. 18-21.

50. See Davies, *The Way of the Wilderness*, pp. 73-74. Davies allows for the possibility of this explanation and retains the designation 'Red Sea' for *yam suf*. Nevertheless, he gives very little attention to Naville's views.

51. Cazelles ('Les localisations', p. 343) argues that 'tongue' means 'gulf' but tries to identify the Egyptian Sea with the Mediterranean, which is unlikely.

the northwestern end of the lake in which a strong wind drove the water back so that the Israelites crossed this stretch on dry ground during the night. When the Egyptians tried to follow the next morning, they were caught by the returning waters and drowned.[52]

The later Priestly Writer modified this account by having the Israelites turn back from Etham at the border of the wilderness and head further south to a point more centrally on the west side of the sea (Exod. 14.1-2, 9b). This was presumably to avoid the impression that the Israelites did not just go around the northern end of the lake and to enhance the miracle of the walls of water on either side as they crossed. P specifies the geography rather carefully by mention of the place-names Pihahiroth, Migdol and Baal-Zephon. It is these names, however, that have given rise to the conjectures about a northern route out of Egypt, even though they occur in the latest source. Furthermore, the remarks by P are built into the prior itinerary of J and cannot be divorced from it.

Nevertheless, northern locations have been given for Baal-Zephon either at Tell Defenne, which is not near the sea, or with Mount Casios (Ras Qasrun) on the Mediterranean coast, a route that is difficult to reconcile with the rest of P's itinerary through the desert.[53] Migdol is usually situated at Tell el-Her on the northern route several kilometers from the Mediterranean coast and a long distance from Tel Defenne or Ras Qasrun. Furthermore, the name 'Migdol' means a fortress, and it could represent any number of sites on the eastern frontier, including the eastern end of the Wadi Tumilat. What is often overlooked in the discussion is the fact that there is evidence for all three place-names being situated at the eastern end of the Wadi Tumilat, although their exact locations are not given in the texts.[54] This seems much more likely to me, since P did not contradict his earlier source by proposing

---

52. For a discussion of J's account, see J. Van Seters, *The Life of Moses: The Jahwist as Historian in Exodus–Numbers* (Louisville, KY: Westminster/John Knox Press, 1994), pp. 128-39.

53. See a review of these sites in Davies, *The Way of the Wilderness*, pp. 80-82; Huddlestun, 'Red Sea', *ABD* (1992), V, pp. 639-40; Cazelles, 'Les localisations', pp. 321-64.

54. See Redford, 'An Egyptological Perspective on the Exodus Narrative', pp. 142-44; also Davies, *The Way of the Wilderness*, p. 82; Naville, *The Store-City of Pithom*, pp. 30-31.

an entirely different northerly route. He merely modified J's route by including a few additional geographic and narrative details.

The Geography of the Exodus Story and History

The geography of the sojourn and exodus, as it is presented in Exodus 1–15 does not provide us with any evidence of the historicity of the events in the time of the Ramessides. On the contrary, the earliest version of the story's geography, as presented by the Yahwist, presents the biblical author's understanding of the region of the Eastern Delta, which corresponds with the sixth century BCE. His portrayal of Goshen as the region in which the Israelites sojourned, his references to the town of Pithom/Succoth, and the construal of the site of Rameses as the ruins of an ancient 'store-city', all of this fits only the later period. This also agrees closely with the perceived threat on the northeastern border, expressed in Exodus 1, because from the time of the late Assyrian and the Babylonian periods onward invasions from this direction were a constant threat. As a consequence, it is precisely in the Saite period that narratives expressive of xenophobia make their appearance in Egypt and become a staple of the Egyptian self-consciousness.[55] The Goshen region also contained a large number of settlers from Asia, including Jews, and there was increasing tension between such foreign settlers and the native Egyptian population.

In the past biblical scholars have used the argument that the close fit between the traditions of the exodus, as preserved in the oldest source of the Pentateuch in Exodus 1–15, and the time of Ramesses II was a firm basis for maintaining the great antiquity of these traditions. They could in turn be used as a means by which to reconstruct the early history and religion of the people. The few place-names of Rameses, Pithom and Succoth became the key to the whole historical enterprise. However, the demise of efforts to understand early Israelite history in the context of the Middle and Late Bronze Ages should have encouraged the same caution towards the geographic details in the story of the exodus.

55. See D.B. Redford, *Pharaonic King-Lists, Annals and Day-books: A Contribution to the Study of the Egyptian Sense of History* (SSEA Publication, 4; Mississauga, ON: Benben, 1986), p. 295; *idem*, 'Studies in Relations between Palestine and Egypt during the First Millennium B.C.', *JAOS* 93 (1973), pp. 3-17 (17).

What I would suggest by this analysis is that all of the colorful details of the exodus story are the work of the Yahwist, including his presentation of the geography. Since there is much throughout his work that suggests a date in the exilic period, these details, especially the geography, fit this period better than any other. There is no way of dating any 'hisorical' exodus event. Prior to the Yahwist, there are only rather vague references to the tradition about an origin in Egypt and an exodus brought about by divine deliverance. Such notions about national origins are too common and too stereotyped to be very helpful to the modern historian. If this seems 'minimalist' to some, it is the only option for the cautious historian to take. To such a cautious and dedicated historian, geographer and archaeologist, Max Miller, I am happy to offer this piece.

Part IV

MANUSCRIPTS AND EPIGRAPHY

The Qumran Scrolls and Textual Reconstruction

Phillip R. Callaway

Frequently scholars have experimented with reconstructing texts found in the Qumran caves. In the days before computer software was available, one could search in lexica and concordances for a brief contextual framework for an identified word or phrase. These days a computer word or phrase search could easily produce the text one needs to support a reconstruction. The underlying assumption is that once we identify the text we can rapidly postulate the most likely readings within the brackets. In order to do this the scholar of the scrolls needs to keep a copy of the MT, the LXX, the Samaritan Pentateuch, perhaps the Vulgate, and others books within reach. All of the editors of the Qumran scrolls, especially those who have worked on biblical manuscripts, begin with these simple steps. Now, however, even their editorial reconstructions have become the foundational texts for further research.[1]

While many scholars continued to fill in the gaps in their assigned biblical manuscripts, the question arose in Qumran studies about the extent to which it was possible to reconstruct a non-biblical text, as it may have originally read in antiquity. The same procedures apply in principle from biblical to non-biblical texts. Based on the notion of predictability, one searches in presumably related fragmentary manuscripts for regularities that might apply at least to a portion of the imagined text. For instance, one might expect '*first* x happened, *then* y and *finally* z'. The presence of any of these time variables would permit one to attempt a reconstruction of before and after scenarios. At a minimum one of these time elements must be present. Two are much better. These cornerstones enable one to establish a rough timeframe, but they are not sufficient to fill in the narrative. One does best if a literary or documentary model exists for the type of text one hopes to reconstruct.

---

1. E. Tov reports that the publication of the scrolls will be completed during the year 2001 (e-mail to author, 26 November 2000).

Imagine trying to reconstruct a person's daily, weekly, monthly or yearly activities based on an appointment book from which numerous pages are missing and others are stuffed in between the covers with no apparent rhyme or reason. If a few verbal patterns representing the person's likely habits are discovered, one then has concrete support for meaningful reconstructions of missing dates and activities, especially if these occasions involve some regular ritual or formality. While searching for more verbal patterns, one discovers that some damaged pages contain words that make sense when juxtaposed with what is still intact. So much the better if another appointment book turns up that confirms the reconstruction. If the withered and perhaps shredded pages are lying around loose on the floor and their margins have been destroyed, the reconstructive process has taken a dramatic turn.

In essence, this is how reconstruction of fragmentary manuscripts from the Qumran caves occurs. After an editorial team was set up in the 1950s to deal with the thousands of scraps of leather and papyrus lying around in the caves, scholars rather easily determined that a particular piece came from this or that biblical work. Only in cases where two or more separate works shared identical or very similar wording might one be mistaken about the correct source. At least one had reduced the possibilities. One could imagine confusing passages in Samuel–Kings with Chronicles or Isaiah and Jeremiah with Kings, especially Exodus with Deuteronomy and Jubilees with Genesis. The possibilities for ambiguity are certainly much greater than these few examples suggest, but they should suffice to make the point. In the case of a damaged non-biblical work for which there may be no other complete copy the ambiguities are greatly reduced, but so are the possibilities for comparison. One searches among the collected fragments for formal verbal principles such as 'day 1 precedes day 2', 'morning precedes or follows evening', 'month 1 precedes month 2 and the last month of the previous year', even an acrostic or traditional story sequence. If some verbal clues are found, the journey toward reconstruction may begin. But can one fill in or account for the gaps? Some scholars have tried.

Hartmut Stegemann describes the process more exactly.[2] After collecting related fragments based on physical features such as writing material, scoring, script and topic, one looks for material and topical

2. H. Stegemann, 'How to Connect Dead Sea Scroll Fragments', in H. Shanks (ed.), *Understanding the Dead Sea Scrolls: A Reader from the Biblical Archaeology Review* (New York: Random House, 1992), pp. 245-55.

joins. Stegemann compares this with assembling a crossword puzzle. Yet this approach goes only so far with the Qumran fragments. Stegemann also noticed that some fragments, the vestiges of larger scrolls, were discovered in stacks or little piles. This is nothing more or less than discovering a scroll *in situ*, Stegemann realized. Based on these observations he began to align similarly shaped fragments horizontally on a table with back-lighting. Within varying stretches of time one could work out the sequence. In order to determine the length of the original scroll, he considered the thickness of the fragments and the increasing diameter of the scroll as it was rolled up.

Although Stegemann applied his method to the 4Q fragments of the Thanksgiving Hymns (1QH) years ago, his method was first publicized widely in Carol Newsom's book on the *Songs of the Sabbath Sacrifice* (4Q400–407)[3] and at a Qumran conference in New York in the mid-1980s.[4] Newsom's *Songs* provided some of the formulaic verbal clues needed to give rein to his imagination. Occasionally Stegemann and Newsom found the expression 'To/for the *maskil*, song of the *x*-numbered sabbath on such and such a date'. Other formulaic phraseology recurred referring to the seven chief princes. Beyond that, much of the phraseology could be postulated to fill in gaps. Stegemann factored in the thickness of the parchment, its increasing width as it was rolled up, and estimated the distance of one fragment to the next as well as the length of the original work. Instead of a disjointed array of apparently unrelated fragments, now one could envision how these *Songs* might have looked in antiquity. When Stegemann applied his method to the Songs of the Sage (4Q510–511), the formulaic language enabled him to offer a successful reconstruction, aided by the formulaic language of the *Songs*.[5] In both cases the secret was in large part the discovery and

3.   C.A. Newsom, *Songs of the Sabbath Sacrifice: A Critical Edition* (HSS, 27; Atlanta: Scholars Press, 1985), pp. 101-102. See now Newsom, 'Shirot 'Olat HaShabbat', in E. Eshel *et al.* (eds.), *Qumran Cave 4. VI. Poetical and Liturgical Texts, Part 1* (DJD, 11; Oxford: Clarendon Press, 1998), pp. 173-401 (172-240; 249-50, for formulaic language; and 310, for the calculation of distances and the resulting chart of sequences).

4.   H. Stegemann, 'Methods for the Reconstruction of Scrolls from Scattered Fragments', in L.H. Schiffman (ed.), *Archaeology and History in the Dead Sea Scrolls: The New York University Conference in Memory of Yigael Yadin* (JSPSup, 8; JSOT/ASOR Monographs, 2; Sheffield: JSOT Press, 1990), pp. 189-220; Stegemann, 'How to Connect', pp. 249-55.

5.   See Stegemann, 'Methods for the Reconstruction', pp. 249-50.

use of repeated formulaic language along with measurements between fragments.

Stegemann also applied his method to the non-canonical psalms published by Eileen M. Schuller. While appending Stegemann's suggestions to her work, Schuller had reservations about the juxtaposition of fragments 1, 14 and 76 in order to reconstruct a single psalm.[6] She also questioned the combination of fragments 33, 45 and 79 to form a prayer of Manasseh, as well as the combination of fragments 48 and 78 and the placement of fragments 24B, 28 and 29 in col. ii. In all these questionable cases, Stegemann's association of fragments was based on the similarity of language among fragments or their shared themes. Speculative connections of fragments can easily be made based on common phraseology. The problem for later researchers is to disjoin the fragments once their combination has become part of textbook truth.

4QMMT (4Q394–399), as reconstruction, provides an example of how easy it is to misjoin fragments.[7] The editors have created a composite text that is clearly weak at the seams. VanderKam and Callaway demonstrated conclusively that 4Q394 1–2 have no material connection to 4Q394 3–7.[8] 4Q394 1–2 are properly placed together because of their calendric theme. The orthography of 4Q394 3a–4 is not consistent with that of 4Q394 1–2, and palaeographically they are distinct. The placement of fragment 5 after fragment 4 is at least questionable. If the editors' placement of fragments 4–5 is correct, this seems to create problems for fragments 3b and 6, which were penned in a smaller script. Study of plate II suggests that the fragments are not in alignment. The editors also have problems with 4Q395 1. One expects line widths

6. E.M. Schuller, *Non-Canonical Psalms from Qumran: A Pseudepigraphic Collection* (HSS, 28; Atlanta: Scholars Press, 1986), pp. 267-77 (positive comments) and 277-78 (her critique).

7. E. Qimron and J. Strugnell, *Qumran Cave 4. V. Miqsat Ma'ase Ha-Torah* (DJD, 10; Oxford: Clarendon Press, 1994), pp. 44-63 (composite text).

8. J.C. VanderKam, 'The Calendar, 4Q327, and 4Q394', in M.J. Bernstein, F. García Martínez and J. Kampen (eds.), *Legal Texts and Legal Issues: Proceedings of the Second Meeting of the International Organization for Qumran Studies, Cambridge 1995. Published in Honour of Joseph M. Baumgarten* (STDJ, 23; Leiden: E.J. Brill, 1997), pp. 181-89; P.R. Callaway, '4QMMT and Recent Hypotheses on the Origin of the Qumran Community', in Z.J. Kapera (ed.), *Mogilany 1993: Papers on the Dead Sea Scrolls, Offered in Memory of Hans Burgmann* (Krakow: Enigma Press, 1996), p. 19.

to be fairly consistent when offering reconstructions: the editors' line-widths range from 9 to 30 to 55 spaces (see ll. 4, 1, 6). A larger problem between the two editors is the proper placement of 4Q398 14–17.[9] These problematic details may be obvious to the specialist, but it is likely that the editors' composite text, not the fragments themselves, will be the focus of interested students in the future.

The so-called 'Rewritten Pentateuch' (4Q364–367) represents another case of almost tacit acceptance of scholarly suggestions. The editors have written, following the estimates of Stegemann, that the original Rewritten Pentateuch was 22 to 27 meters in length,[10] although one of the editors had noted elsewhere that both the length and the content of such a scroll was speculation.[11] 4Q364 preserves parts of Genesis 25–27; an addition; 34–35; 37–38; 44–45; 48; Exodus 21; 19; 24; an addition; 25–26; Numbers 14; 33; Deuteronomy 1; Numbers 20 (Samaritan) and Deuteronomy 2–3; 9–11 and 14. 4Q365 consists of portions of Genesis 21; Exodus 8–10; 14–15; an addition; 17–18; 26–30; 35; an unidentified piece; Exodus 36–39; Leviticus 11; 13; 16; 18; 23–24; an addition; 25–27; Numbers 3–4; 7–9; 13; 15; an unidentified piece; Numbers 17; 27; 36; Deuteronomy 2; 19–20. 4Q366 entails Exodus 21–22; Leviticus 24–25; Numbers 29–30; Deuteronomy 16; 14. 4Q367 preserves Leviticus 11–13; 15–19; an addition; Leviticus 20 and 27.[12] If one puts all the fragments together, they constitute a little less than parts of 134 chapters of the Pentateuch (approximately 38 per cent, if these were complete chapters). Treated separately, each manuscript tells its own story.

One should keep in mind that these are only partial chapters, perhaps a handful of verses or less. No single fragment or certain juxtaposition of fragments of 4Q364–367 includes more than two contiguous columns

---

9. Qimron and Strugnell, *Miqsat Ma'ase Ha-Torah*, pp. 201-11.

10. E. Tov and S. White, 'Reworked Pentateuch', in H.W. Attridge *et al.*, *Qumran Cave 4. VIII. Parabiblical Texts, Part 1* (DJD, 13; Oxford: Clarendon Press, 1994), pp. 187-351 (187); H. Stegemann, *Die Essener, Qumran, Johannes der Täufer und Jesus: Ein Sachbuch* (Freiburg: Herder, 1994), p. 62.

11. E. Tov, 'Biblical Texts as Reworked in some Qumran Manuscripts with Special Attention to 4QRP and 4QparaGen–Exod', in E.C. Ulrich and J.C. VanderKam (eds.), *The Community of the Renewed Covenant: The Notre Dame Symposium on the Dead Sea Scrolls* (CJA, 10; Notre Dame: University of Notre Dame Press, 1994), p. 126.

12. Tov and White, 'Reworked Pentateuch', pp. 188-351.

of writing. Besides that, the editors pointed out at least five additions, omissions and rearrangements. Such compositional features distinguish the work under investigation from a control text (such as *BHS*). In fact, there may once have been more additions to and omissions from the text than one can detect in the fragments. So much has been written about these fragments, now enshrined as a sensationally long Rewritten Pentateuch, that it will probably be difficult to view them in any other light.

Theoretically, one should be able to reconstruct a biblical work to some extent, if it is not qualified as a rewritten or modified text. This is precisely the principle followed by Julio Trebolle Barrera, the editor of 4QKgs. After a rather traditional analysis of fragments 1–7, which consist roughly of 1 Kgs 7.19–8.19, Barrera presents Stegemann's reconstruction.[13] Fortunately, he clearly separates his comments into 'factual' and 'speculative'. Among Stegemann's facts are: (1) fragment 6 lay above fragment 5 among a stack of 'similarly shaped' fragments; (2) fragment 4 preserves 1 Kgs 7.31-42, and fragment 6 preserves 1 Kgs 7.51–8.9; and (3) reconstruction to the left of fragment 5 and to the right of fragment 6 resulted in a column width of about 21 cm. Then Barrera emphasizes that he is moving to the more hypothetical part of his discussion. He estimates that two columns of 4QKgs (fragments 1–7) equal roughly four pages of *BHS*; thus one column equals two pages of *BHS*. Then he calculates that the rest of 1–2 Kings would have measured roughly 100 pages. Noting that the Temple Scroll was written on thin parchment that increased its diameter by 1 mm for each turn, the editor states that 4QKgs was a bit thicker and each roll must have increased its diameter by 1.5 mm. 4QKings measured according to these calculations 50 columns or 6.25 meters beyond fragment 5.

Barrera points out that most of the scrolls from the caves were badly damaged, leaving relatively few fragments. Statistically, he says, roughly half of the extant fragments of a scroll came from the middle, since the outside columns were easily ruined by humidity (hence, being in the middle is a safeguard). Based on the premise that 1 Kgs 7.19–8.19 came from the middle of the scroll, Barrera argues that this scroll must have been a lengthy one encompassing Joshua, Judges, 1–2

13. J.T. Barrera, '4QKgs', in E.C. Ulrich *et al.* (eds.), *Qumran Cave 4. IX. Deuteronomy, Joshua, Judges, Kings* (DJD, 14; Oxford: Clarendon Press, 1995), pp. 171-83.

Samuel and 1–2 Kings.[14] Using *BHS* as his control text, he estimates that this volume would have measured 20 meters in length.

The chief problem with Barrera's speculation derives from the claim that the extant fragments came from the middle of the scroll. He admits that the other half of fragments that survived did not come from the middle. In fact, before attempting to reconstruct a massive work from Joshua to Kings, it makes more sense to account for 1 Kings itself. The editor notes by way of conclusion (and on the basis of a lacuna in the 4Q text) that 4QKgs must have preserved an original reading of 1 Kgs 8.16: this reading found in the Old Greek of this verse comes from the parallel text of 2 Chron. 6.5b-6a. This is another case of a more lengthy reading affecting the length of the book.

The chief difficulty in reconstructing many texts is that we depend heavily on certain control texts (MT, LXX, Samaritan Pentateuch) to support our readings. The creative scribal work witnessed in many of the scrolls certainly enhances our understanding of the ancient Jewish approaches to reading and writing scripture. But these texts often demonstrate unexpected creativity that may or may not be repeated by other scribes. In the case of the Temple Scroll, for example,[15] the last few columns (cols. 52-66) quote extensively from select chapters of Deuteronomy. The author/redactor was choosing the material he needed to complete his thematic survey. Suddenly, he changed styles and extended biblical legislation by applying a simple principle of analogy to a previously quoted biblical passage. This can hardly be expected and certainly cannot be predicted. If only those sections of the Temple Scroll that quote Deuteronomy verbatim had survived, one could hardly reconstruct the preceding 50 columns. Outside of the calendar section (cols. 13-29), very little of the Temple Scroll is predictable.

One would also expect that a major Psalms scroll would look very much like the Masoretic Psalms. 11QPs[a], which has been described as a liturgical scroll, disproves that in several ways.[16] This scroll preserves roughly the last third of the HB's book of Psalms. However, it presents an unusual ordering of chapters along with the inclusion of several new

14. Barrera, '4QKgs', p. 183.

15. Y. Yadin, *The Temple Scroll*, II (Jerusalem: Israel Exploration Society, 1983), pp. 131-300.

16. J.A. Sanders, *The Psalms Scroll of Qumran Cave 11 (11QPs[a])* (DJD, 4; Oxford: Clarendon Press, 1965), p. 5.

or non-Masoretic pieces. The order is as follows: Psalms 101–103; 109; 105; 146; 148; 121–32; 119; 135–36; 118; 145; Syriac Psalms 2; a plea for deliverance; Psalms 139; 137; 138; Sir. 51.13-23, 30; an apostrophe to Zion; Psalms 93; 141; 133; 144; Syriac Psalms 3; Psalms 142; 143; 149–50; a hymn to the creator; 2 Sam. 23.7; a piece entitled 'David's Composition'; Psalms 140; 134; and 151A and B. This creative psalter appeared rather unique until other Qumran Psalms manuscripts demonstrated similar reorderings and the use of non-Masoretic pieces (4QPs[d]; 4QPs[e]; 4QPs[f]; 11QPs[b]).[17]

Even the more sectarian scrolls make a similar point. For a long time one has read about the many copies of the Community Rule in Cave 4.[18] The control text is 1QS with 1QS[a] and 1QS[b]. No other manuscripts preserve 1QS[a] and 1QS[b]. Qualifications must be made when comparing 1QS with the 4Q manuscripts.[19] 4QS[d] or 4Q258 (1) begins at 1QS 5,1; (2) the first two columns are said to be shorter and smoother; (3) 1QS 8,24–9,10, 15 comes after 9,6-21; and (4) the words 'the *harabbim*' stand where 1QS has 'priests, sons of Zadok'. 4QS[e] or 4Q259 provides another example based on 1QS. It presents an abridgment of 1QS 8,4–9,11, which lacks the interlineal additions.

These examples should suffice to show that textual reconstruction has its limits. When one can be sure that the text under reconstruction is practically identical to its control text, the task of reconstruction is easy. Once we realize that scribes were more creative with one manuscript than another, we must exercise caution in postulating reconstructions. Even in the exciting field of textual reconstruction, one must be careful not to recreate too much of the lost text, and what is reconstructed must be checked for correctness and probability by other researchers. Whenever possible, one should base textual reconstructions on what is

---

17. P. Flint, 'The Psalms Scrolls from the Judaean Desert: Relationships and Textual Affiliations', in G.J. Brooke with F. García Martínez (eds.), *New Qumran Texts and Studies: Proceedings of the First Meeting of the International Organization for Qumran Studies, Paris, 1992* (STDJ, 15; Leiden: E.J. Brill, 1994), pp. 31-52 (40).

18. P.S. Alexander and G. Vermes, *Qumran Cave 4. XIX. Serekh Ha-Yaḥad and Two Related Texts* (DJD, 26; Oxford: Clarendon Press, 1998).

19. G. Vermes, *The Complete Dead Sea Scrolls in English* (New York: Penguin Press, 1997), pp. 97-98, 118 and 123. S. Metso, *The Textual Development of the Qumran Community Rule* (STDJ, 21; Leiden: E.J. Brill, 1997), pp. 36-54.

actually known or extant. Hypothetical reconstructions maintain enduring soundness, when evidence can actually be adduced. If scholars continue to study the additions, omissions, conflations and creative pieces in the Qumran manuscripts and other versions, the field of textual reconstruction will make significant progress in the future.

MESHA' AND SYNTAX

Anson F. Rainey

In the summer of 1967, Max Miller and I were digging at Arad. Many of our colleagues on the staff of that expedition are no longer with us: Yohanan Aharoni, Bernie Boyd and Immanuel Ben-Dor. It was a memorable season for the spirit of cooperation that prevailed between the American and Israeli excavators. Several epigraphic finds made the season a doubly exciting time in our lives. I shall never forget the day we found Arad Letter 24, the detailed account of reinforcements being ordered from Arad and Kinah to defend Ramat-negeb 'Lest Edom come there'. My own interest in Hebrew and Northwest Semitic epigraphy has never flagged since that time.

Max Miller has, of course, had a long-standing interest in the Mesha' text[1] and has made a lasting contribution to the archaeology and history of Moab.[2] So it is hoped that he will find something of interest in the ensuing remarks on this fascinating text.

The Mesha' inscription is a display text dating to the mid-ninth century BCE.[3] It gives the Moabite version of the conflict with Israel and with Judah thus supplementing the information provided by the biblical books of Kings and Chronicles. In spite of some difficulties, it is possible to reconstruct a coherent picture[4] of the relationship between Israel, under the dynasty of Omri, and Moab on the one hand, and

---

1. J.M. Miller, 'Moab and the Moabites', in J.A. Dearman (ed.), *Studies in the Mesha' Inscription and Moab* (ABS, 2; Atlanta: Scholars Press, 1989), pp. 1-40.

2. J.M. Miller (ed.), *Archaeological Survey of the Kerak Plateau* (ASORAR, 1; Atlanta: Scholars Press, 1991).

3. J.K. Drinkard, 'The Literary Genre of the Mesha' Inscription', in J.A. Dearman (ed.), *Studies in the Mesha' Inscription and Moab* (ABS, 2; Atlanta: Scholars Press, 1989), pp. 131-54.

4. Y. Aharoni and M. Avi-Yonah, *The Macmillan Bible Atlas* (rev. by A.F. Rainey and Z. Safrai; New York: Macmillan, 3rd edn, 1993), pp. 97-98.

between Moab and Judah on the other (especially thanks to Lemaire's important discovery in line 31; see below).

The dialect of this inscription bears numerous affinities to Hebrew narrative prose in the Bible.[5] There are, of course, some morphological differences, for example the masculine plural in -*n* rather than -*m,* but the remarkable thing is that the syntax includes certain syntagmas typical only of pre-exilic Judean Hebrew. Hurvitz[6] has made a special study of the differences between pre- and post-exilic Hebrew and today there can be no doubt about the main lines of diachronic development between the first- and the second-temple periods. The purpose of the present study is simply to point out some of the more interesting syntagmas in the Mesha' text and their parallel usages in biblical Hebrew prose of the pre-exilic period.

First-Person Narrative Preterit

The narrative preterit of biblical Hebrew has long been a special interest of mine,[7] but in spite of my efforts and those of some colleagues, the full implications of this syntactical and morphological usage has not attracted the attention it deserves. This is probably because, as my teacher H.J. Polotsky once lamented,[8] Hebrew remained the province of theological rather than orientalist faculties. Too many Hebrew scholars have never studied Akkadian, where the prefix preterit is a basic component to the verbal system. Arabists, on the other hand, do not recognize the one survival of the *yaqtul* preterit in their language.[9] Therefore, one still reads about the so-called '*waw*-conversive', which

5.   K.P. Jackson, 'The Language of the Mesha' Inscription', in J.A. Dearman (ed.), *Studies in the Mesha' Inscription and Moab* (ABS, 2; Atlanta: Scholars Press, 1989), pp. 96-130.

6.   A. Hurvitz, 'The Historical Quest for "Ancient Israel" and the Linguistic Evidence of the Hebrew Bible: Some Methodological Observations', *VT* 47 (1997), pp. 301-15.

7.   'The Ancient Hebrew Prefix Conjugation in the Light of Amarnah Canaanite', *Hebrew Studies* 27 (1986), pp. 4-19; 'Further Remarks on the Hebrew Verbal System', *Hebrew Studies* 29 (1988), pp. 35-42.

8.   H.J. Polotsky, 'Semitics', in E.A. Speiser and B. Netanyahu (eds.), *At the Dawn of Civilization: A Background of Biblical History* (World History of the Jewish People, First Series, Ancient Times, 1; New Brunswick, NJ: Rutgers University Press, 1964), pp. 99-111 (100).

9.   Polotsky, 'Semitics', p. 110.

introduces a supposed imperfect form and gives it past-tense meaning. One of the reasons that the *yaqtul* (with zero suffix) preterit is not universally recognized is that first-person forms often do not conform to the same pattern as the second and third persons. The seconding of the first-person cohortative into the preterit paradigm was seen already by Müller[10] but largely ignored. Since the cohortative for third weak verbs is outwardly identical to the imperfect (-v*yu* and -v*ya* both being reduced to -*e^h*),[11] scholars have thought that cohortative forms from third weak verbs serving in the preterit paradigm were simply 'converted' imperfects.[12] However, there are some short first-person forms in the narrative preterit, and in fact, the Mesha' inscription attests such forms, thus lending support to my contention that the zero form, including the short form in third weak verbs, was the original preterit pattern. Four very important examples from the Moabite dialect are:[13]

(3) ---------- ואעש . הבמת . זאת . לכמש-----

(3) - - - And I made this altar platform for Chemosh - - -

(7) וארא . בה . ובבתה - - -

(7) but I was victorious over him and his house - - -

(9) ואבנ . את . בעלמענ - - -

(9) and I (re)built Ba'al- me'on - - -

(12) --- ואשב . משמ . את . אראל . דודה . ---

(12)---and I captured (confiscated?) from there its Davidic altar hearth---

Identical forms from these same verbs are also documented in biblical Hebrew prose, for example:

Deut. 10.3	ואעש ארון עצי שטים
So I made an ark of acacia wood,	
Gen. 41.22	וארא בחלמי
and I saw in my dream	

However, D. Talshir[14] made a special study of first-person forms in

---

10. A. Müller, *Hebräische Schulgrammatik* (Halle: Max Niemeyer, 1878), p. 73.

11. Rainey, 'The Ancient Hebrew Prefix Conjugation', pp. 9-10.

12. S.R. Driver, *A Treatise on the Use of the Tenses in Hebrew and some Other Syntactical Questions* (Clarendon Press Series; Oxford: Clarendon Press, 3rd edn, 1892), pp. 52-53.

13. The translations that follow are the author's unless otherwise noted.

14. 'Syntactic Patterns in Late Biblical Hebrew', in *Proceedings of the Ninth*

the narrative preterit and discovered that one can trace the diachronic progress from the short form to the seconded cohortative to the regular long forms. This process in turn influenced the Masoretes to vocalize original short forms as if they were long. In the following passage (1 Kgs 3.17-21), compare the third-person וַתֵּלֶד in v. 18 with first-person וָאֵלֵד in v. 17 and third-person וַתָּקָם in v. 20 with first-person וָאָקֻם in v. 21. This latter form is especially instructive. As Talshir had noted, the consonantal orthography suggests a short form *wā'āqŏm, but the Masoretes—unwilling to add a *waw* to the consonantal text— nevertheless pointed the form with *kubbuṣ* and accented the second syllable, intending it to be read wā'āqûm.

1 Kgs 3.17-21

וַתֹּאמֶר הָאִשָּׁה הָאַחַת בִּי אֲדֹנִי אֲנִי וְהָאִשָּׁה	17
הַזֹּאת יֹשְׁבֹת בְּבַיִת אֶחָד וָאֵלֵד עִמָּהּ בַּבָּיִת	
וַיְהִי בַּיּוֹם הַשְּׁלִישִׁי לְלִדְתִּי וַתֵּלֶד גַּם־הָאִשָּׁה הַזֹּאת	18
וַאֲנַחְנוּ יַחְדָּו אֵין־זָר אִתָּנוּ בַּבַּיִת זוּלָתִי שְׁתַּיִם־אֲנַחְנוּ בַּבָּיִת	
וַיָּמָת בֶּן־הָאִשָּׁה הַזֹּאת לָיְלָה אֲשֶׁר שָׁכְבָה עָלָיו	19
וַתָּקָם בְּתוֹךְ הַלַּיְלָה וַתִּקַּח אֶת־בְּנִי מֵאֶצְלִי וַאֲמָתְךָ יְשֵׁנָה	20
וַתַּשְׁכִּיבֵהוּ בְּחֵיקָהּ וְאֶת־בְּנָהּ הַמֵּת הִשְׁכִּיבָה בְחֵיקִי	
וָאָקֻם בַּבֹּקֶר לְהֵינִיק אֶת־בְּנִי וְהִנֵּה־מֵת	21

The one woman said, 'Please, my lord, this woman and I live in the same house; and I gave birth while she was in the house. Then on the third day after I gave birth, this woman also gave birth. We were together; there was no one else with us in the house, only the two of us were in the house. Then this woman's son died in the night, because she lay on him. She got up in the middle of the night and took my son from beside me while your servant slept. She laid him at her breast, and laid her dead son at my breast. When I rose in the morning to nurse my son, I saw that he was dead'.

The true long form with full orthography is found in late compositions of the second temple period, for example:

Dan. 8.27 וָאָקוּם וָאֶעֱשֶׂה אֶת־מְלֶאכֶת הַמֶּלֶךְ

So I arose and I went about the king's business

Such forms had developed through shortening of the seconded cohortative forms, many of which are documented in biblical narrative prose, for example:

World Congress of Jewish Studies, Jerusalem, August 4–12, 1985 (Jerusalem: World Union of Jewish Studies, 1986), pp. *5-*8.

Gen. 32.6 ואשלחה להגיד לאדני

So I sent to inform my lord.

The true short forms had been gradually replaced by the borrowed cohortative, but some examples still remain, as those cited above. The value of the Mesha' examples lies in their ninth-century date. Furthermore, there is no evidence that the borrowing of the first-person cohortative ever took place in Moabite as it did in biblical Hebrew.

Nominal Clause or Extraposition

The story of the conflict with Israel opens with a statement about Omri, the founder of a new dynasty in the ninth century. There is no doubt that Omri himself and not a descendant is intended here. He is designated 'king of Israel', and his overt action against Moab is specified. The question arises as to the clause syntax of that opening statement:

עמר ------------------------------------ (4)

(5) י . מלך . ישראל . ויענו . את . מאב . ימן . רבן

(4)------------------------- Omr-

(5) i (was) king of Israel and he oppressed Moab many days --------- -

One solution here is to recognize the description of Omri as a nominal clause expressing past tense. This is entirely possible, as shown by comparison with a similar statement (in the negative) dealing with contemporary events:

(1 Kgs 22.48) ומלך אין באדום נצב מלך

And there was no king in Edom, a commissioner was king

(24) --- ורב . אנ . בקרב . הקר . בקרחה.-----

(24) ---- But there was no cistern in the midst of the city, in the citadel,

But another solution has been posed by various commentators, viz. to see the noun phrase עמרי . מלך . ישראל as an extraposition (*casus pendens*). The normal construction for extraposition is with the suffix conjugation, but Gibson[15] cited two examples:

Gen. 22.24

ופילגשו ושמה ראומה ותלד גם־הוא את־טבח ואת־גחם ואת־תחש ואת־מעכה

---

15. J.C.L. Gibson, *Textbook of Syrian Semitic Inscriptions*. I. *Hebrew and Moabite Inscriptions* (Oxford: Clarendon Press, 1971), pp. 78, 82.

And his concubine, whose name was Reumah, also bore children: Tebah, Gaham, Tahash and Maacah.

and 2 Kgs 25.22

והעם הנשאר בארץ יהודה אשר השאיר נבוכדנאצר מלך בבל
ויפקד עליהם את־גדליהו בן־אחיקם בן־שפן

Now as for the people who were left in the land of Judah, whom Nebuchadnezzar king of Babylon had left, he appointed Gedaliah the son of Ahikam, the son of Shaphan over them.

Four more examples have been adduced by Niccacci:[16]

2 Sam. 19.41

ויעבר המלך הגלגלה וכמהן עבר עמו וכל־עם יהודה ויעברו
[העבירו] את־המלך וגם חצי עם ישראל

And the king went on to Gilgal, and Chimham went on with him; and all the people of Judah and also half the people of Israel accompanied the king.

Note that it is the kᵉṯîḇ that has a narrative preterit while the qᵉrê᾿ makes the correction to a suffix form.

1 Kgs 12.17

ובני ישראל הישבים בערי יהודה וימלך עליהם רחבעם

But as for the sons of Israel who lived in the cities of Judah, Rehoboam reigned over them.

1 Kgs 15.13

את־מעכה אמו ויסרה מגבירה

And also, as for Maacah his mother, he removed her from [being] queen mother.

The parallel passage in 2 Chron. 15.16 has the suffix form instead of the narrative preterit:

וגם־מעכה אם אסא המלך הסירה מגבירה

And also as for Maacah, the mother of Asa, the King removed her from the [position of] queen mother.

---

16. A. Niccacci, 'The Stele of Mesha and the Bible: Verbal System and Narrativity', *Or* 63 (1994), pp. 226-48 (235); cf. also *idem*, *The Syntax of the Verb in Classical Hebrew Prose* (JSOTSup, 86; Sheffield: Sheffield Academic Press, 1990), pp. 136-37.

And finally 2 Kgs 16.14:

ואת המזבח הנחשת אשר לפני יהוה ויקרב מאת פני הבית מבין
המזבח ומבין בית יהוה ויתן אתו על־ירך המזבח צפונה

And the bronze altar, which was before Yahweh, he brought from the front of the house, from between [his] altar and the house of Yahweh, and he put it on the north side of [his] altar.

There is another example of this construction in the Mesha' inscription that has also been noted by the commentators:[17]

(30)---ובת . דבלתן| ובת . בעלמען . ואשא . שמ . את . נקן[
(31)]די . לרעת . את . [צאנ . הארצ|------

And as for Bêt-Diblatên and Bêt Ba'al-ma'ôn, then I transferred [my] sh[epherds to shepherd the] flocks of the land...

Extraposition with a verb in the suffix conjugation is also used by Mesha'. Note the example in which Lemaire[18] has successfully identified a reference to 'the House of David' (= the Kingdom of Judah).[19] My own reconstruction of the context is as follows:

(31)---- וחורנג . ישב . בה .בתן[ד]וד] . כ]אשן[ר]
(32)]הלתחם . בי . [

(31)- - -And as for Ḥawronen, the [Ho]use of [Da]vid dwelt in it [wh]ile
(32) [it fought with me - - -]

This syntagma is well represented in biblical Hebrew. One example will suffice:

2 Chron. 15.1

ועזריהו בן־עודד היתה עליו רוח אלהים

And as for 'Azaryahu son of 'Oded, the spirit of God was upon him.

---

17. Gibson, *Textbook of Syrian Semitic Inscriptions*, p. 82; Niccacci, 'The Stele of Mesha' and the Bible', p. 235.

18. A. Lemaire, '"House of David" Restored in Moabite Inscription', *BARev* 20 (May/June, 1994), pp. 30-37.

19. Cf. A.F. Rainey, 'Syntax, Hermeneutics and History', *IEJ* 48 (1998), pp. 239-51 (249-51).

However, it may also be noted that extraposition of this type is a natural component in ancient Hebrew correspondence from the pre-exilic period:

Lachish Letter No. 4

(06) - - - וסמכיהו לקחה . שמעיהו ו
(07) יעלהו העירה - - -

And as for Semachyahu, Shema'yahu took him and brought him up to the city

QTL Verbs with Nominal Subject

When a nominal subject is fronted, the verb is in the suffix conjugation. Clauses of this nature can best be classified as a 'complex nominal clause'.[20] The nominal element is fronted, because it is really the 'comment' (logical predicate) of the clause rather than the verb. The following complex nominal clause introduces a new section in the Mesha' narrative:[21]

(10) ואש . גד . ישב . בארץ . עטרת . מעלם . ויבנ . לה . מלכ.י
(11) שראל . את . עטרת| -

(10) Now the man of Gad had dwelt in Ataroth from of old and the king of Israel (11) built 'Aṭarot (Ataroth) for him - - - - - - - - - - - - - - - - - -

This is a good example of the use of nominal subject and suffix verb to express an anterior situation.[22] Such a construction and usage is common in biblical Hebrew (e.g. Gen. 6.8; 31.34). The switch to the complex nominal clause is also employed for rhetorical contrast,[23] especially with a change of subject.

---

20. Niccacci, *The Syntax of the Verb*, pp. 23-29; E. Talstra, 'Text Grammar and Hebrew Bible. I. Elements of a Theory', *BO* 35 (1978), pp. 169-74 (169-70); W. Schneider, *Grammatik des biblischen Hebräisch: Ein Lehrbuch* (München: Claudius, 5th edn, 1982), §44.1.2.

21. Niccacci, 'The Stele of Mesha' and the Bible', p. 228.

22. Cf. Z. Zevit, *The Anterior Construction in Classical Hebrew* (SBLMS, 50; Atlanta: Scholars Press, 1998); E.Y. Kutscher, *A History of the Hebrew Language* (ed. R. Kutscher; Jerusalem: Magnes Press, 1982), p. 18.

23. R.J. Williams, *Hebrew Syntax: An Outline* (Toronto: University of Toronto Press, 2nd edn, 1976), pp. 96-97.

Gen. 13.12

אברם ישב בארץ־כנען ולוט ישב בערי הככר ויאהל עד־סדם

Abram dwelt in the land of Canaan, while Lot dwelt among the cities of
the Plain and moved his tent as far as Sodom.

Gen. 13.13

ואנשי סדם רעים וחטאים ליהוה מאד

Now the men of Sodom were wicked exceedingly and sinners against
Yahweh.

Niccacci[24] has noted that the contemporary Hebrew narrative in
2 Kings 3 uses the same syntactical device to introduce new stages in
the narrative:

2 Kgs 3.1

ויהורם בן־אחאב מלך על־ישראל בשמרון בשנת שמנה
עשרה ליהושפט מלך יהורה וימלך שתים־עשרה שנה:

Now Jehoram the son of Ahab became king over Israel in Samaria in the
eighteenth year of Jehoshaphat king of Judah, and he reigned twelve
years.

As with this biblical passage, the Mesha' narrative, which began with
the 'Man of God' in a complex nominal clause, is continued by a clause
with the narrative preterit:

(10)---ויבנ . לה . מלכ . י(11)שראל . את . עטרת|

And the king of Israel built Ataroth for him...

There is no reason to accept Lemaire's translation, 'The king of Israel
built Ataroth for *himself*.'[25] The same sequence occurs in the next stage
of the narrative in 2 Kings 3:

2 Kgs 3.4-5

ומישע מלך־מואב היה נקד והשיב למלך־ישראל מאה־אלף
כרים ומאה אלף אילים צמר
ויהי כמות אחאב ויפשע מלך־מואב במלך ישראל

Now King Mesha' of Moab was a sheep breeder, who used to deliver to
the king of Israel one hundred thousand lambs, and the wool of one
hundred thousand rams. But it happened that at Ahab's death, then the
king of Moab rebelled against the king of Israel.

24. Niccacci, 'The Stele of Mesha' and the Bible', p. 246.
25. Lemaire, '"House of David" Restored in Moabite Inscription', p. 33.

Another new section in the Mesha' narrative is introduced by the same syntagma:

(18) --------------- ‏ומלכ . ישראל . בנה [.את]‏ .

(19) ‏יהצ . וישב . בה . בהלתחמה . בי |‏ ---------------

(18)-------------- And the king of Israel had built
(19) Yahaz and he dwelt in it while he was fighting with me, but Chemosh drove him out from before me, --------------- -

This construction also denotes an important achievement in the reign of Uzziah:

2 Kgs 14.22

‏הוא בנה את־אילת וישבה ליהודה אחרי שכב־המלך עם־אבתיו‏

He built Elath and restored it to Judah after the king slept with his fathers

Contrast Between Prefix Preterit and QTL

When he wrote his seminal article[26] on the structure of the Mesha' inscription, Niccacci was not aware of Lemaire's major correction of a troublesome *hapax* in line 12.[27] The otherwise unknown ‏רית‏ proves to be ‏הית‏, the 3rd f.s. form of the verb 'to be'.

(11)---- ‏ואלתחמ . בקר . ואחזה|ואהרג . את . כל . העמ[ו]‏

(12) ‏הקר . הית . לכמש . ולמאב|ואשב . משמ . את . אראל . דודה . וא]ס[‏

(13) ‏חבה . לפני . כמש . בקרית|‏

(11)---- But I fought against the city and I took it and I slew *all the people*, [But] (12) *the city* became the property of Chemosh and of Moab and I captured (confiscated?) from there its Davidic altar hearth and I (13) dragged it before Chemosh in Kerioth.

The context is clear: the king of Israel fortified the town of Ataroth for the 'man of Gad' (i.e. 'the Gadite') who lived in the territory of Ataroth. Lemaire was undoubtedly influenced by his discovery of the correct reading, *hyt*. However, he failed to understand the syntactical and rhetorical construction here. First Mesha' says, 'And I killed *all the people*', and then he makes a contrast by saying, '[But][28] *the city*

---

26. Niccacci, 'The Stele of Mesha' and the Bible'.
27. Lemaire, '"House of David" Restored in Moabite Inscription', p. 33.
28. Rainey, 'Syntax, Hermeneutics and History', p. 24.

became the property of Chemosh and of Moab.' The contrast between the fate of the people, who were all slain, and the city itself, which was taken over by the Moabite forces, is expressed by fronting the word הקר 'the city'. This fronting, on the rhetorical level, is tantamount to extraposition: '[But] as for the city, it became the property of Chemosh and of Moab.' With this fronting, the narrative preterit cannot be used as it was in the preceding clause. Instead, a form of the suffix conjugation must be used. The formation of the verb 'to be' plus the *lamed* preposition is normal for expressing possession in the past tense. Actually, however, the construction is a complex nominal clause that is often used in order to stress contrast.[29] A good example is the following:

Gen. 4.2-5

ויהי־הבל רעה צאן
וקין היה עבד אדמה

Now Abel was a *shepherd of flocks*,
but *Cain* was a tiller of the ground.

ויהי מקץ ימים ויבא קין מפרי האדמה מנחה ליהוה
והבל הביא גם־הוא מבכרות צאנו ומחלבהן

So it came about in the course of time that Cain brought an offering to Yahweh *of the fruit of the ground*.
And *Abel*, on his part, brought of the firstlings of his flock and of their fat portions.

וישע יהוה אל־הבל ואל־מנחתו
ואל־קין ואל־מנחתו לא שעה

And Yahweh had regard for *Abel and for his offering*;
but for *Cain and for his offering* He had no regard.

Coming back to the Mesha' passage above, our rendering is the most appropriate and logical. The city became the property of Chemosh and Moab. The switch to the fronting of the subject is a normal means of rhetorical contrast. It refers to what happened after the conquest of 'Ataroth by Mesha'. Formerly, the city had been in territory occupied from of old by the Israelite tribe of Gad. Now it became Moabite. The construction of [*waw*] + NOUN (*haqqîr*) + SUFFIX CONJUGATION VERB (*hayāt*) is perfect for expressing this contrast.

29. Niccacci, 'The Stele of Mesha' and the Bible', pp. 29-33.

QTL Verbs with Pronominal Subject

A whole set of complex nominal clauses characterize Mesha''s boasting about his building projects. In these instances the fronted personal pronoun is, as Niccacci has noted,[30] the 'comment' or logical predicate of the clauses. Thus, he renders, 'It is *I* that...'

(21) ‏אנכ . בנתי . קרחה‏ - - -

(22) ‏ואנכ . בנתי . שעריה . אנכ . בנתי . מגדלתהן וא‏ - - -

(23) ‏נכ . בנתי . בת . מלכ . ואנכ . עשתי . כלאי . האשו\ח . ל]מין‏

(25) ‏ואנכ . כרתי . המכרתת . לקרחה‏ - - .

(26) ‏אנכ . בנתי . ערער . ואנכ . עשתי . המסלת . בארננ|‏ - - -

(27) ‏אנכ . בנתי . בת . במת . כי . הסד . הא|אנכ . בנתי . בצר .‏

(28) ‏כי . ע\ .]ה[א|‏ - - -

(21) - - - (It is) I (that) built for the citadel - - -

(22) - - - and (it is) I (that) built its gates and I built its towers and

(23) I built a royal palace and I made the channels for the reservo[ir for] water

(25) - - - And I hewed the shafts for the citadel - - -

(26) - - - I built 'Aro'er and I made the highway in the Arnon.

(27) I built Beth-bamoth because it was in ruins. I built Bezer because {it was}

(28) a ruin - - -

Note a similar emphasis on the subject of the following biblical passage:

Ezek. 36.36

כי אני יהוה בניתי

הנהרסות נטעתי הנשמה אני יהוה דברתי ועשיתי

that *I, Yahweh*, have rebuilt the ruined places, and replanted that which was desolate; *I, Yahweh*, have spoken, and I will do it.

However, in the following passage the emphasis is surely on the act of building, so the verb is reinforced by the absolute infinitive, which is the true comment or logical predicate:

1 Kgs 8.13

בנה בניתי בית זבל לך מכון לשבתך

Verily have I built you an exalted house, an abode for you to dwell in

---

30. Niccacci, 'The Stele of Mesha' and the Bible', p. 24.

But the Chronicler has evidently altered the text, substituting the short form of the 1st c.s. pronoun in accordance with Late Biblical Hebrew. At that stage of the language, the fronted personal pronoun is not necessarily the comment: it is just the subject, and the emphasis is either on the verb or on the nature of the house that was built:

2 Chron. 6.2

ואני בניתי בית־זבל לך ומכון לשבתך עולמים

I have built you an exalted house, an abode for you to dwell in

In pre-exilic Hebrew the fronted pronoun (note the more conservative long form) stresses the identity of the subject:

Gen. 16.5

אנכי נתתי שפחתי בחיקך

I *(myself)* gave my slave-girl to your embrace

This is especially dramatic in the following passage:

Jer. 27.5-6

אנכי עשיתי את־הארץ את־האדם ואת־הבהמה־ - -
ועתה אנכי נתתי את־כל־הארצות האלה ביד נבוכדנאצר מלך־בבל
עבדי

It *is I* who have made the earth, with the people and animals - - - Now *I* have given all these lands into the hand of King Nebuchadnezzar of Babylon, my servant,

Now, when we compare the above examples with some from the Late Biblical Hebrew book of Qoheleth, we see a marked diachronic change in the syntactical strategy. The suffix conjugation now can take first position in a clause, followed by the 1st c.s. independent pronoun. The pronoun is in a sense in apposition to the personal suffix marker on the verb, 'I myself'.

Eccl. 1.16–2.20

דברתי אני עם־לבי - - - -
אמרתי אני בלבי - - - -
ופניתי אני בכל־מעשי שעשו ידי - - - -
ופניתי אני לראות חכמה - - - -
וראיתי אני שיש יתרון לחכמה - - - -
ואמרתי אני בלבי - - - -
ושנאתי אני את־כל־עמלי - - - -
וסבותי אני ליאש את־לבי - - - -

(Eccl. 1.16) I spoke to myself, - - -
(Eccl. 2.1) I said to myself, - - -
(Eccl. 2.11) Then I considered all that my hands had done - - -
(Eccl. 2.12) So I turned to consider wisdom - - -
(Eccl. 2.13) Then I saw that wisdom has an advantage - - -
(Eccl. 2.15) Then I said to myself, - - -
(Eccl. 2.18) I hated all my toil - - -
(Eccl. 2.20) So I turned and gave my heart up to despair - - -

Genitive Suffix on Genitive Phrase

Although this passage and its syntax have recently been discussed in print,[31] it will be repeated here for completeness. The conclusion that there was an altar hearth of David at Ataroth will not be well received in many circles. But I am confident that the following syntactical analysis of the passage is correct.

(12) - - - וָאֶשְׁב . מִשָׁם . אֵת . אֲרִאֵל . דּוֹדֹה . וָאֶ[סֹ]
(13) חֲנֹה . לִפְנֵי . כְּמֹשׁ . בִּקְרִית - - -

(12) - - - and I captured (confiscated?) from there its Davidic altar hearth and I
(13) dragged it before Chemosh in Kerioth, - - -

The form דּוֹדֹה may legitimately be taken as the bound form of the proper noun, David. Albright[32] proposed to take the form *dwd* as a term for 'chieftain', based on a presumed word, **dawīdûm* ('chieftain') in the Mari documents.[33] In the meantime, I.J. Gelb,[34] following Landsberger,[35] gave the final proof that the Mari forms in question were to be read *dawdûm* and the like; they are a dialectical variant of the well

31. Rainey, 'Syntax, Hermeneutics and History', pp. 244-49.
32. W.F. Albright, *Archaeology and the Religion of Israel: The Ayer Lectures of the Congate–Rochester Divinity School, 1941* (Baltimore: The Johns Hopkins University Press, 1953), p. 218 n. 86.
33. G. Dossin, 'Benjaminites dans les textes de Mari', in *Mélanges syriens offerts à monsieur René Dussaud, secrétaire perpétuel de l'Académie des inscriptions et belles-lettres* (Bibliothèque archéologique et historique, 30; Paris: P. Geuthner, 1939), II, pp. 981-96 (988-89).
34. 'WA = *aw, iw, uw* in Cuneiform Writing', *JNES* 20 (1961), pp. 194-96.
35. H. Tadmor, 'Historical Implications of the Correct Rendering of Akkadian *dâku*', *JNES* 17 (1958), pp. 129-41; cf. also J.-R. Kupper, *Les nomades en Mésopotamie au temps des rois de Mari* (Bibliothèque de la Faculté de Philosophie et Lettres de l'Université Liège, 142; Paris: Les Belles Lettres, 1957), pp. 60-62.

known *dabdûm* 'defeat, downfall'. Albright should have retracted his 'chieftain' interpretation in a later edition of *ANET*, but he evidently overlooked it. Consequently, it continues to appear in handbooks and commentaries on the Mesha' inscription.

However, the problem of a personal name with possessive suffix is not directly pertinent to the Mesha' passage in question. Actually, the present Mesha' passage only places the personal possessive pronoun on the name David (דודה) *incidentally*. The suffix is really intended for the אראל 'altar hearth' as we will now demonstrate. It is necessary to explain the entire syntagma. The closest examples presently at hand are from Ugaritic and Hebrew, but they demonstrate the possibilities in the North West Semitic language family. The expression found in Ugaritic is in a poetic text. A declaration is addressed to Baal:

> *tqḥ . mlk 'lmk drkt . dt . drdrk* = **tiqqaḥu mulka 'âlamika darkata dâta dârdârika.*

You will take your eternal kingdom, your everlasting rule.[36]

Two genitival phrases appear as direct objects of the verb. One of them is a simple construct, *mlk 'lm* 'eternal kingdom', while the second is a circumlocution employing the relative pronoun, *drkt dt drdr* 'the rule of generation after generation'. In both cases the genitive phrase is treated as a unit and the possessive pronoun is added at the end! We would have expected the scribe to write **mlkk d'lm* and *drktk dt drdr* but this is not the case. Still, it is obvious that the intended meaning is '*your* kingdom', and '*your* rule'. Another expression, ** 'bd d'lmk*, evidently stands behind the declaration of Baal, when he submits to the threats of Môt, the god of death:

> *'bdk . 'an . wd'lmk* = ** 'abduka 'anâ wadû 'âlamika.*
> Your slave am I, even your eternal (slave).[37]

It is possible, though not necessary for our argument, to include such expressions as *'att . ṣdqh* = *'a 'aṭtata ṣidqihu* 'the wife of his right-eousness' = 'his rightful wife' and *mtrḫt .yšrh* = *matrûḫta yušrihu* 'the bride of his right' = 'his legal bride'.[38] To these Ugaritic phrases have

---

36. *KTU²* 1.2 IV, 10; cited according to M. Dietrich, O. Loretz and J. Sanmartín, *The Cuneiform Alphabetic Texts from Ugarit, Ras Ibn Hani and Other Places: KTU* (Münster: Ugarit-Verlag, 2nd edn, 1995).

37. *KTU²* 1.5 II, 10, also 19-20.

38. *KTU²* 1.14 I, 12-13; cf. C.H. Gordon, *Ugaritic Textbook* (AnOr, 38; Rome: Pontifical Biblical Institute, 1965), p. 113.

been compared biblical expressions as 'the mountain of his holiness' = 'his holy mountain' (Ps. 3.5 *et al.*), הר קדשי 'the mountain of my holiness' = 'my holy mountain', הר קדשׁך 'the mountain of your holiness' = 'your holy mountain'.

The same construction is attested in Hebrew. Note a late context but in a book that has affinities with both Canaanite and Aramaic:

Eccl. 12.5

כי־הלך האדם אל־בית עולמו

For man goes to his eternal home

There can be no doubt here that בית עולמו refers to a man's permanent grave. It is a construct construction with the genitive suffix added to the *nomen rectum*. One must compare the following circumlocution:

Ps. 49.12

בתימו ו לעולם.[LXX οἱ τάφοι αὐτῶν = קברם]
משׁכנתם לדר ודר

Their graves are their homes forever, their dwelling places to all generations.

Obviously, בית עולמו is the equivalent of בתימו לעולם. Incidentally, the parallel between לעולם and לדר ודר immediately brings to mind the same parallelism in the Ugaritic text cited above. But the main point here is that the construction with a posessive suffix attached to a genitive phrase (a construct) is exactly the same as that in the Moabite passage. The first Ugaritic example above, *mlk 'lmk* 'your eternal kingdom', and the exactly comparable Hebrew בית עולמו demonstrate the addition of a pronominal suffix to the *nomen rectum* of a construct phrase, a pronoun that logically belongs with the *nomen regens*. Further Hebrew examples show that this syntagma is not uncommon. It just has not received the attention it deserves (the Ezekiel passages were furnished by John Huehnergard):

Num 4.2

נשׂא את־ראשׁ בני קהת מתוך בני לוי למשׁפחתם לבית אבתם

'Take a census of the sons of Kohath from among the sons of Levi, by their families, by *their house-holds* (*bâttê 'āb*; LXX οἴκους πατριῶν αὐτῶν)

Micah 2.9   בית תענגוכ

'*her (collective) houses of pleasure* (LXX τῶν οἰκιῶν τρυφῆς αὐτῶν).'

Ezek. 16.18   בגדי רקמתך

= τὸν ἱματισμὸν τὸν ποικίλον σου = '*you embroidered garments*'

Ezek. 20.39   שֵׁם קדשׁי

= τὸ ὄνομά μου τὸ ἅγιον = '*my holy name*'.

Ezek. 23.3 (also v. 8)   דדי בתוליהן

= οἱ μαστοὶ αὐτῶν = '*their virgin bosoms*'.

Ezek. 26.11   מצבות עזך

= τὴν ὑπόστασίν σου τῆς ἰσχύος = '*your strong pillars*'.

Ezek. 27.10   אנשי מלחמתך

= ἄνδρες πολεμισταί σου = '*your men of war*'.

Ezek. 32.27   כלי־מלחמתם

= ὅπλοις πολεμικοῖς = '*their weapons of war*'.

This is what has happened in the Moabite phrase אראל . דודה, which under normal circumstances would have been 'better' rendered אראלה . אשר לדוד or אראל לדוד . דוד אשר לה. This is an obvious example of a genitive phrase (*nomen regens* plus *nomen rectum*) to which a possessive suffix has been added! There is no reason why it should not occur here in the Mesha' inscription. The possessive suffix *-h* may be feminine referring to the town of Ataroth but, more likely, it is masculine referring to גד . אש 'the Gadite' (collective).

This syntactic analysis makes it possible to reach a common-sense meaning of the context in question. Mesha' states that the Gadite had dwelt in Ataroth from of old, that is from long before his own time. When Omri or his successor gained a new foothold in the Moabite plain at Madeba, he also fortified Ataroth for the Gadite (collective). The Gadite had long since possessed an altar hearth ostensibly dating back to the time of David (at least in the local tradition; but there is no reason why David could not have sponsored a cult center at Ataroth). Mesha' conquered Ataroth, slew all the inhabitants, and the city then became a Moabite possession. Mesha' then repopulated the city with his own

people. The very fact that Mesha' transported the altar hearth to a shrine
of Chemosh at an originally Moabite site, Qirioth, on the northwestern
border of the Dibonite territory facing Ataroth, shows that the altar
hearth was a trophy of conquest, an enemy cult object 'captured' (cf.
discussion of ואשב from the root *ŠBY*, above) brought to the
'presence' of the victorious god of Moab. The same thing was done
with the אר[א]ל י . יהוה 'the altar hearths of Yahweh' from Nebo (lines
17-18). The verbal phrase ואקח . משם 'and I took from there' (line 17)
is parallel to ואשב . משם 'and I captured from there' (line 12) and
proves that the latter means 'I captured', not 'I retrieved (something
formerly ours).' In both cases war booty is being discussed: trophies
presented to the conquering Chemosh. The altar hearths of Nebo were
'of Yahweh', but this is no argument that the altar hearth of *dwd* from
Ataroth has to include a deity name. Would-be historians lacking the
proper linguistic training to comprehend the evidence cited above[39] will
find it difficult to reconcile themselves to the interpretation presented
here.

Concluding Remarks

These few observations should make it clear that the Mesha' inscription
is not only a valuable historical document, which it certainly is, but also
a priceless, synchronic reflex of pre-exilic biblical Hebrew from the
ninth century BCE. The language of the Mesha' inscription is that of
first-person narration, typical of display inscriptions from that age. The
literary formulation is according to a well-thought-out plan, and the
subject matter, albeit tendentious, is presented in an orderly and logical
fashion. The synchronic comparison of its morphology and syntax with
biblical Hebrew is a fundamental tool in establishing the basis for a
diachronic study of the biblical text, viz. the marked differences
between pre- and post-exilic Hebrew.

At this point, it seems appropriate to present the text of the Mesha'
inscription as organized in sections based on the syntactical constructions discussed above. It should be noted that those paragraphs that
begin with a prefix preterit deal with the progress of the narrative in the
previous paragraph. Those sections that begin with a nominal clause or

---

39. N. Na'aman, 'Between Royal Inscription and Prophetic Narrative', *Zion* 66
(2001), pp. 5-40 (Hebrew).

a clause with subject plus suffix verb are meant to introduce a new subject, sometimes with background material first.

Mesha' Stele

Introduction

¹אנכ . משע . בנ . כמשׁ[ית] . מלכ . מאב . הד²יבני |
אבי . מלכ . על . מאב . שׁלשׁנ . שׁת . ואנכ . מלכ³תי ע . אחר . אבי |

[1]I am Mesha' the son of Chemosh[-yat?] king of Moab, the Da[2]ibonite. My father reigned over Moab 30 years and I reign[3]ed after my father;

Altar Dedication

ואעשׂ . הבמת . זאת . לכמשׁ . בקרחהׁ|במׂת . י|⁴שׁעכיהשׁעני
מכל . המלכנ . וכי . הראני . בכל . שׂנאי |

and I built this altar platform for Chemosh in the citadel, an altar platform of [sal][4]vation, because he saved me from all the kings and because he gave me the victory over all my adversaries.

Historical Introduction

עמר⁵י . מלכ . ישׂראל . ויענו . את . מאב . ימנ . רבנ . כי . יאנפ .
כמשׁ . באר⁶צה |
ויחלפה . בנה . ויאמר . גמ . הא . אענו . את . מאב |
בימי . אמר . כ[נ]ת ⁷וארא . בה . ובבתה |
וישׂראל . אבד . אבד . עלמ . |

Omr[5]i was king of Israel and he oppressed Moab many days because Chemosh was angry with his [6]land. And his son replaced him and he also said, 'I will oppress Moab.' In my days he spoke [thus], [7]but I was victorious over him and his house and Israel suffered everlasting destruction.

Medeba and Environs

וירשׁ . עמרי .אר⁸צ .מהדבא|וישׁב . בה . ימה . ימה . וחצי . ימי בנה .
ארבענ . שׁת .וי[שׁ]⁹בה . כמשׁ בימי |
ואבנ . את .בעלמענ . ואעשׂ . בה . האשׁוח . ואבנ . ¹⁰[.]את . קריתנ |

But Omri had conquered the lan[8]d of Madeba and he dwelt there during his reign and half the reign of his son, 40 years, but Chemosh [9]returned it in my days. So I (re)built Baal-maon and I made the reservoir in it and I bu[ilt] [10]Kiriaten.

Ataroth

ואש . גד . ישב . בארצ . עטרת . מעלמ . ויבנ . לה . מלכ . י[11]ישראל .
את . עטרת |
ואלתחמ .בקר . ואחזה|ואהרג . את . כל . העמ . [ו][12]הקר . הית .
לכמש . ולמאב |
ואשב . משמ . את . אראל . דודה.ואנ[ס][13]חבה . לפני . כמש . בקרית |
ואשב . בה . את . אש . שרנ . ואת . א[נש][14]מחרת

The man of Gad had dwelt in 'Aṭarot (Ataroth) from of old and the king of Israel [11]built 'Aṭarot (Ataroth) for him. But I fought against the city and I took it and I slew all the people, [but] [12]the city became the property of Chemosh and of Moab, and I captured (confiscated?) from there its Davidic altar hearth and I [13]dragged it before Chemosh in Kerioth, and I settled in it men of Sharon and m[en] [14]of Maḥaroth.

Nebo

ויאמר . לי . כמש . לכ אחז . את . נבה . על . ישראל | וא[15]הלכ . בללה .
ואלתחמ . בה . חבקע . השחרת . עד . הצהרמ|ואח[16]זה .
ואהרג . כלה . שבעת . אלפנ . גברנ . ודרנ | וגברת וג[נר][17]ת . ורחמת |
כי . לעשתר . כמש . ההרמתה| ואקה . משמ . אר[נ][א][18]לי . יהוה.
ואסחב . המ . לפני . כמש |

And Chemosh said to me, 'Go! Seize Nebo against Israel', so I [15]proceeded by night and I fought with it from the crack of dawn to midday, and I to[16]ok it and I slew all of it, 7000 men and youths and women and maid[17]ens and slave girls, because I had dedicated it to 'Ashtar-Chemosh. And I took [the al][18]tar hearths of Yahweh and I dragged them before Chemosh.

Yahaṣ (Jahaz) and Environs

ומלכ . ישראל . בנה [את] . [19]יהצ . וישב . בה . בהלתחמה . בי |
ויגרשה . כמש . מפני | [.]
ו[20]אקח . ממאב . מאתנ . אש . כל . רשה |
ואשאה . ביהצ . ואחזה . [21]לספת . על . דיבנ |

And the king of Israel had built [19]Yahaz, and he dwelt in it while he was fighting with me, but Chemosh drove him out from before me, so [20]I took from Moab 200 men, all of his best, and I brought them to Yahaz and I seized it [21]in order to add (it) to Daibon.

Construction in Dibon

אנכ . בנתי . קרחה . חמת . היערנ . וחמת|.[22]העפל |
אנכ . בנתי . שעריה . אנכ . בנתי . מגדלתה|
וא[23]נכ . בנתי . בת . מלכ .

ואנכ . עשתי . כלאי . האשוֹנח.ל.מיֹן . בקרנב . .]24הקר |

ובר . אנ . בקרב . הקר . בקרחה.

ואמר . לכל . העמ . עשו .]ל[25כמ . אֹש . בר . בבינה.

ואנכ . כרתי . המברתת . לקרחה . באסר]26י . [.]ישראל |

I (myself) built for the citadel the 'wall of the forests' and 'the wall of
22the rampart' and I built its gates and I built its towers and 23I built a
royal palace and I made the channels for the reservo[ir for] water in the
mid24st of the city. But there was no cistern in the midst of the city, in
the citadel, so I said to all the people, 'Make [for] 25yourselves each man
a cistern in his house.' And I hewed the shafts for the citadel with
prisoner26s of Israel.

Other Building Projects

אנכ . בנתי . ערער . אנכ . עשתי . המסלת . בארנן |

27אנכ . בנתי . בת . במת . כי . הרס . הא |

אנכ . בנתי . בצר . כי . עין . .]28ה[א . ?-[

אֹש . דיבן . חמשֹן . כי . כל . דיבנ . משמעת |

ואנכ . מלכֹ29תֹני . על . ה]מאת . בקתֹנ . אֹשר . יספתי . על . הארצ |

ואנצ . בנתֹ30י]בת . מהד]בא . ובת . דבלֹתנ | ובת . בעלמענ .

ואשא . שמ . את . נ]ןֹ?[31]קֹדֹי . לרעת . את .] צֹאנ . הארצ |

I built 'Aro'er and I made the highway in the Arnon. 27I built Beth-
bamoth because it was in ruins. I built Bezer because {it was} 28a ruin.
The men of Daibon were armed because all of Daibon was under orders
and I rul29ed [over] 100 towns that I had annexed to the land. And I
buil30t [the temple of Made]ba and the temple of Diblaten and the temple
of Baal-maon and I carried there the [...]31[...] the small cattle of the
land.

Southern Campaign

וחורנן . ישב . בה. . בתֹן[ד]ודֹן. כֹ]אֹשֹנֹר[32הֹלתחמ . בֹי . [.

ויאמר . לֹי . כמֹש . רד . הֹלתחמ . בחורֹנֹן | וארד . וֹנֹאֹל]33נֹתחמ . בקר .

ואחֹזה. ויֹש]בֹה . כמֹש . בימֹי . ועלתֹי . משמ . עֹשֹיֹ]ן?

And as for Ḥawronen, the [Ho]use of [Da]vid dwelt in it [wh]ile 32[it
fought with me, and] Chemosh [s]aid to me, 'Go down, fight against
Ḥawronen.' So I went down [and I fo]33[ught with the city and I took it
and] Chemosh [ret]urned it in my days.

Conclusion(?)

34[--------------------------------- לע]שֹת . צדק | ואנֹכֹ-?[

Then I went up from there to ma[ke] 34 [...to]do justice and {I} [...]

INDEXES

INDEX OF REFERENCES

BIBLE

OTHER ANCIENT REFERENCES

INDEX OF AUTHORS